MIRROR
IMAGES

Teaching Writing in Black and White

ACTION RESEARCH FROM THE WEBSTER GROVES WRITING PROJECT

Joan Krater
Webster Groves School District

Jane Zeni
Gateway Writing Project, University of Missouri, St. Louis

Nancy Devlin Cason
Webster Groves School District

with

Cathy Beck, Minnie Phillips, Sandra Tabscott
and

Gail Taylor, Mary Ann Kelly, Stephanie Gavin,
Theresa Wojak, Carolyn Henly, Agnes Gregg,
Beth Ann Brady, JoAnne Williams, Chestra Peaslee

HEINEMANN
Portsmouth, New Hampshire

Offices and agents throughout the world

Every effort has been made to contact the copyright holders for permission to reprint borrowed material where necessary. We regret any oversights that may have occurred and would be happy to rectify them in future printings of this work.

Acknowledgments for borrowed material can be found on page 515.

Library of Congress Cataloging-in-Publication Data

Webster Groves Action Research Project.
   Mirror images: teaching writing in black and white / Webster Groves Action Research Project; Joan Krater . . . [et al.].
     p.   cm.
   Includes bibliographical references (p.   ).
   ISBN 0-435-08821-1 (alk. paper)
   1. English language—Composition and exercises—Study and teaching (Secondary)—Missouri—Webster Groves. 2. Afro-Americans— Education—Language arts. 3. Action research in education— Missouri—Webster Groves. I. Title.
   LB1631.W353 1994
   808′.042′0712—dc20   94–22330
                                                              CIP

Editor: Dawn Boyer
Production: Vicki Kasabian
Text and cover design: Jenny Jensen Greenleaf

Printed in the United States of America on acid-free paper
99 98 97 96 95 94   EB   1 2 3 4 5 6

CONTENTS

CHANGING IMAGES

FOREWORD

One of my major goals as president of Harris-Stowe State College has been to recruit African American students for our Urban Education Specialist Degree Program and by way of this program to prepare them to become teachers in our public schools. I am personally committed to this work and to the development of African American role models for youth. With a fully integrated student body, we are equally committed to developing culturally sensitive White teachers who can build personal relationships with African American youth, who believe in their capabilities, and who can educate them effectively and successfully.

When I began my career as a teacher at the all-Black Douglass Elementary School in the Webster Groves school district, I stressed the importance of literacy, of reading and writing, and of high aspirations. Later, when I was asked to serve as principal of a new integrated Douglass Demonstration School, I recruited the best teachers I could find, White as well as Black. I was gratified and reassured to see firsthand that White teachers could also communicate with Black students and could inspire them to excellence.

There are those who believe that only an African American teacher can really understand and motivate an African American student. I believe that school districts must vigorously recruit, employ, and retain African American teachers. But the reality is that many of our young people are being taught—successfully and otherwise—by White teachers.

I am impressed that this interracial group of teachers has been willing to face what so many people in our country sweep under the rug: the underachievement of too many African American students in their schools. These teachers are unwilling to cop out. They systematically examine this challenge, assume responsibility, and persist in making a difference, not just for the students in their own classrooms, but for students in the classrooms of other teachers with whom they have worked extensively. *They persist because of their unwavering conviction that all children can learn and succeed.*

What's more, they don't assume the kids have the problem. They have turned to African American scholars and educators for help in changing their curriculum, their classroom environment, and their own attitudes. They have made their mistakes and taken some knocks, but they've learned. They've come to see that if they really hope to reach African American students they need to locate the problem in the only people anyone has the power to change—themselves.

At Harris-Stowe, I've enjoyed working with faculty and teachers in the Gateway Writing Project, which we cosponsor with the University of Missouri, St. Louis. Some of these teachers are engaged in reflective action research to improve their own teaching in the St. Louis public schools. I am eager to follow their work because I recognize the power of an action research experience.

This book makes a much-needed contribution to the literature that assists future and practicing teachers who want to build positive environments for cultural diversity.

Henry Givens, Jr.
President
Harris-Stowe State College

PREFACE

What happens when dedicated teachers with a passion for the teaching of writing and a sincere desire for student success begin to work collaboratively on their mutual goals? What happens when these teachers discover strategies that not only help African American underachievers but are highly effective for all student writers?

What happens is this impressive team of teachers has a positive impact on their students' success in writing; they make great leaps in their own skills in teaching and in their understanding of the power of the strategies they develop; and they significantly influence teachers across the district in other disciplines and at all grade levels.

This has all come about through the Webster Groves Writing Project—an action research project. Begun in the mid-1980s with a strong district commitment and support through some lean years of diminishing resources for staff development, a strong writing project has emerged and paved the way for action research as a basis for our district's staff development program. These teachers are committed to building classroom environments where cultural differences will be affirmed and high achievement will be fostered among all students, both Black and White. They are committed to learning whatever is necessary to make that dream a reality. They have turned to African American educators for advice, tried new strategies in the classroom, kept journals, and then shared successes and failures with each other in monthly study sessions. Although they have not labeled it as such, they have embarked upon a very effective staff development program.

In my work with the National Staff Development Council (NSDC) over the last decade, I have seen collaborative action research as a staff development model emerge and receive a great deal of attention from researchers and practitioners. Our teachers have found that they can and do change their own behavior through reflective inquiry and mutual trust and support!

Sarah DeJarnette Caldwell
Assistant Superintendent of Curriculum
   and Instruction
Webster Groves School District
Past President, NSDC

ACKNOWLEDGMENTS

A project of this duration and scope could not continue without the help of many people. Max Wolfrum, superintendent of Webster Groves School District when we began, spurred us on to investigate a politically risky issue. Sally Caldwell, assistant superintendent, has done everything in her power to ensure our research continues to receive the financial support it needs. Both have been strong advocates of our work, continually lending their personal and emotional support. Bill Gussner, our new superintendent, endorses our efforts in the face of financial cutbacks. And we thank the members of all the boards of education for their interest and backing.

We thank Paul Fredstrom, Lee Holtgrewe, and Don Morrison, principals at Hixson Middle School, and Dan Edwards and Yvonne Kauffman, principals at the high school, for their enthusiasm and reassurance. As one of them once put it, "The most important thing we can do is to clear the way for you and let you go for it!"

The middle school project members thank their teammates, particularly Anna Belveal, for their flexibility and patience.

At University of Missouri, St. Louis, department chairs Chuck Larson and Jim Walter believed that our research efforts were significant enough to merit faculty involvement and university credit.

Several persons outside the project have responded to our manuscript at various stages in the last five years. Lee Drake, Sally Reagan, and Wayne Thomas made many helpful comments. Lou Smith's perceptions helped us to understand the biographical and historical nature of our project. Geneva Smitherman has kept in touch since her visit early in the project and her work has influenced us tremendously.

ACKNOWLEDGMENTS

Jon Marshall and Steve Spaner helped us better understand the relationship of our descriptive data and our assessment statistics. Terry Moore worked overtime double-checking our calculations on the attitude surveys.

Pat Pingel's energy and efficiency have saved us a great deal of time and confusion. Her unwavering optimism always uplifts our spirits.

Our undying gratitude goes to our families—our greatest cheerleaders.

A Note on the Language in This Book

In a book about cultural diversity, whatever language we use will inevitably be loaded. It will offend some readers and reassure others that we know the score.

The terms we use today for ourselves and for our students are not those we used at the start of our project seven years ago. Our language has changed as we continue to learn and grow. It's tempting to tell this story from the vantage point of our current understanding, however much we still have to learn. But this is a story of action research, of teachers struggling and risking and soul-searching over a period of time. Today we look back at the documents from the first years of our project and wince at our own language and at our unrecognized assumptions.

Amid all the good intentions are numerous signs that we implicitly accepted a "deficit model," locating the problem in the "low-achieving Black students." Soon we referred to "at risk" writers, and at first we saw the term as straightforward and not at all problematical. Gradually, though, we began to suspect that giving kids labels was actually part of the problem. Now when we are forced to identify the students who are the focus of our project, we prefer the term "underachieving" with its implication of untapped potential. But most important, as our research progressed, we began to talk less about "improving the writing of Black students" and more about "increasing the cultural sensitivity and multicultural literacy of White teachers."

So which language do we use to tell our story? In most cases the terminology used reflects its historical context. In the specific instance of racial designation, however, we use our current language throughout the book. The earliest reports from our project referred to "black students";

during the middle years we got more and more comfortable with "African American" (using "black" as a short form); during the last couple of years, we have preferred to capitalize "Black" and "White" when using the shortcut terms.

We know that those capital letters—especially the *W*—will look odd to some readers. Today we believe this language recognizes the diversity of culture rather than simply a diversity of color in our classrooms. Five years from now, we may find this choice embarrassing or wrongheaded, as new language becomes standard. (Twenty years ago, "Each student will do *his* homework" was standard; today most of us find it offensive and sexist.)

These are not trivial issues of political correctness. Language is inherently political, and correctness changes with the times, with the audience, and with the context. Language reflects our view of the world. We hope that our readers will see this book as a history of our changing perspectives, not simply a record of our conclusions.

BLACK
AND
WHITE
IMAGES

Adjusting the Mirrors

hear you, hear me—we two—you, me, talk on this page.

. . . .

So will my page be colored that I write?
Being me, it will not be white.
But it will be
a part of you, instructor.
You are white—
yet a part of me, as I am a part of you.
That's American.

LANGSTON HUGHES,
"Theme for English B"

O ur students talked. We listened. We taught. We all learned. As we changed, our students changed as writers and learners.

Our story began when a few teachers refused to stand by and watch a group of their students slide into semiliteracy. It is a story of changing perspectives. As in a house of mirrors at a carnival, our images of each other had been distorted. During the past six years, teachers and students alike have adjusted our mirrors so we could see clearly, reflect, and bring about change.

Starting with a focus on low-achieving African Americans, our lens has widened into a way of looking at students in general and a way of looking at ourselves.

Perhaps it is typical of White teachers working in integrated classrooms that our first perspective was a limited one: something was wrong with our students' writing; we would ferret out the problem and find a cure. Only after months of meeting and talking about "Black writing" and "Black students" did we look more critically at our own roles in the problem. In fact, the most profound and liberating changes for us emerged from questioning our own behavior, our own classrooms, and the unconscious cultural biases of the educational system. We had to look not only at how we teach writing, but also at how we work with students who might not conform to the academic and cultural mold of our school. An image from *The Bluest Eye* captured our growing discomfort. "This soil is bad for certain kinds of flowers. Certain seeds it will not nurture, certain fruit it will not bear, and when the land kills of its own volition, we acquiesce and say the victim had no right to live" (Morrison 1970, 160).

We painfully realized that what we had been doing in our classrooms did not fertilize the soil for some students and in reality was killing some seeds. What could we as teachers do to improve the writing of our African American students? With this driving question, we six embarked on a continuing journey of collaborative research. That journey changed us, changed our perspectives on our classrooms, and ultimately changed our students' attitudes toward learning with us.

One of our teachers, Minnie Phillips, brought Toni Morrison's lines to a team meeting in 1991 and shared her journal response to the previous quote.

> I'm moving from a teacher who just "teaches" to one intent on helping students grow. That subtle difference lies in the nurturing relationship I work to establish with each of them. And nowhere does that relationship seem more crucial than with "certain kinds of flowers."

Before the soil could be cultivated, we had to know what had grown there in the past; before relationships between student and teacher could grow, we had to understand how our own pasts had been cultivated. The original team of teachers who formed the Webster Groves Writing Project approached this task with an enthusiasm mixed with reticence. Would White teachers be able to reach underachieving Black students? At best the subject was touchy.

Two of the six teachers seemed to have an edge on understanding the community and our African American students because of their backgrounds— Nancy had been raised and educated in Webster Groves and Minnie was our one African American group member. They might inwardly have felt a bit ahead of the game since they knew the cultural and racial community and were part of it. However, they would come to realize that awareness and change were a necessity for them, too. Their stories are important.

A child of the 1960s, Nancy grew up in Webster Groves. She spent grade school, junior high school, and high school in what she perceived to be a comfortably integrated community, one that had achieved integration on its own without legal mandates. This was a town with a rich, historically significant African American community.

Throughout her early years, kids were kids. She does not remember the issue of color ever being raised until eighth grade, when she and a Black male classmate danced together to "Shake-a-Tail-Feather" at a school dance. As she recalls,

> A hand grabbed me firmly on my arm, pulling me aside, away from my friends and my partner, leaving David alone on the dance floor. A parent I did not recognize reprimanded me for dancing with a Black boy. That was my first awareness of a subtle, forked-tongue message that seeped through my community.

During high school, Nancy had lots of White girlfriends and one Black girlfriend, Christine.

> With the White friends, I went on shopping sprees, to Tri Hi Y, and to slumber parties, dancing in front of mirrors, trying to get the moves just right as Motown blared from the hi-fi. My memories of Christine are of

just the two of us, no one else asking to join us. We talked about our futures, shared chatter about boys, and enjoyed music on the radio.

Upon graduation, Nancy planned to attend the University of Missouri, Columbia, while Christine "got married and within a year was a mom."

College was a norm for Nancy, a never-discussed-and-always-assumed expectation. She "got over," studying just as much as she had to. There were, of course, other things to be learned in college and most of them were more fun! She remembers an integrated living community the first year of college in 1969, but after the semester break only one of the Black women returned to school. She wondered why.

Nancy finished college, got married, and began teaching at an up-and-coming rural White community west of the St. Louis area. While mandated integration was on the move within the city and county of St. Louis, the words "White flight" echoed at her high school across the river. Enrollment tripled in one year.

She took time off from teaching to raise a family, yet always remained involved in education through her children. She moved to a rural community in the Missouri Ozarks where few, if any, Black families resided year-round. There, she helped establish a cooperative preschool for the surrounding area.

These two episodes of her life shut out cultural diversity. Nancy rationalized during this period that no community was as strong and as supportive of diversity as Webster Groves. She returned home to teach in 1981, soon realizing that growing up and being a teacher in a community were two different experiences. She believed she held no biases, no stereotypes, no preconceived notions of racial differences. Then, at the start of our action research, Nancy was asked to read student papers and to guess the race of each writer. She discovered that despite her "culturally diverse" upbringing, she did indeed have underlying biases.

> I guessed the paper dealing with basketball to be the African American student's paper. I was wrong. More than that, I felt deceived. I had envisioned my upbringing as one that prepared me for my place in a world filled with people different from myself. One thing was missing—I

did not really know very much about that world, especially the world of African American males.

Not until she took on the challenge of personal change by learning as much as she could about a culture unlike hers could she teach writing to kids from that background. Not until she understood the rich oral history of African American families could she tap into it with her kids. Not until she recognized that talking, laughing, and sharing help generate ideas could she encourage (and stand) those activities in class. Not until she realized that the whole picture was more than the sum of its parts, and that many kids need to see the whole before they can break it down into pieces could she teach to those kids. And not until she saw and understood the individuality of her students could she reach the ones who most needed her.

Looking back, Nancy identifies the theme of her story as "deception"—and gradual change toward a more realistic image of her world. Minnie, on the other hand, tells a story of

> repression. That's what my participation in the writing project brought to the surface. My preoccupation with passing the litmus test of teaching standard English and traditional literature resulted in stifling or ignoring the richness of the culture I shared with many of my students. My "double-consciousness"—the constant awareness of being classified as "other" yet expected to measure up in a mostly White world—was not different from many African Americans working in mainstream settings.

As an African American child coming of age like Nancy in the 1960s, Minnie grew up in a small, segregated town in southeast Missouri.

> Language facility meant adeptness in speech and rhetoric—at emotional persuasion and comic jabs (playing the dozens, quick rejoinders, and embellished folktales)—homespun entertainment which offset the "Jim Crow" humiliation and subjugation imposed by the world outside.

Although Minnie had been raised in a world where oral expression was deeply embedded in poetry recitals, oratorical contests, and dramatic interpretations—

where enunciation mattered little and oral delivery was what counted—she brought little of this wealth to her classroom.

The Civil Rights Bill of 1964 meant for Minnie the end of public school segregation and the beginning of her self-consciousness. She was an oddity as an eleventh grader in her "White school." Her only self-defense was academic excellence. Teachers referred to her and her younger Black class-mates as "you girls" and "you boys" to accentuate their differences, "but we were still a 'we,' so grounded in our home culture, community, and adolescent daring that the insults were shrugged off as the system's old-fogeyishness."

Despite her academic excellence, she was denied high school classes like French or algebra. She became aware of how school could manipulate and skew the lives and futures of Black students. But Minnie was headstrong. She entered the University of Missouri, Columbia, at the age of sixteen, feeling unprepared and without any support system. It was there she recognized both her flair for language and her repression of it. Willingly, she trudged into White civilization—its history, government, literature, arts, and sciences—feeling less and less that her African American background was relevant. She called it "refining her Blackness."

> Missouri bootheel malapropisms, tinged with Arkansas flatness, had to go. I resolved to alter my dialect (a kind of self-taught Eliza Doolittle), and since I was minoring in speech and drama, stage speech seemed properly elevated. I suffered the bigotry of teachers like the visiting speech professor from Oklahoma who explained that I, like most "Negroes," had a "lazy tongue."

When Minnie came to Webster Groves in 1968, she speculated that her employment was a response to a mandate from Black students. She learned of the

> polite tradition of assigning Black students to second-class status. Running away from my culture, I had run into it, but this time I had to choose, I thought, between students or the institution. I was, after all, hired to teach standard English, I insisted to myself, and I set about ferreting out "nonstandard" English with a passion (although I'm horrified to think of

the bodies I left behind . . .). I included a few Black writers and social activists in the curriculum but with such traditional standards that Black students often stared in amazement to see if I was "for real." Less charitable ones dismissed me as "Oreo"—Black on the outside and White on the inside. What they didn't know was not only was I Black, but my overgrown cultural roots still lay in the cotton fields. I had the scars to prove it. I didn't want to be White. I wanted them to be educated. I had just come to think the White way was the only road to the prosperity they coveted.

Minnie recognized that she did not know what to do with her cultural heritage. She could teach a few Black courses or Black writers or Black culture but

I had not realized my self-imposed cultural starvation until I began to connect with Black students and my own children as listener, advisor, and interested reader of their writing. The writing project helped me make those connections systematic. I try especially to interweave examples from my personal background into the lessons and works we study, and invite students to share their examples in class discussions and in writing. It's important that we feel connected, freeing ourselves to learn from our cultural pasts as well as each other.

Both Nancy and Minnie had to revisit their pasts before they could understand their roles and their changes. But they were not alone. Cathy had to come to grips with growing up in a segregated southern Missouri town that had two sides of the tracks—her friend lived on the other side. This dividing line caused emotional pain for both girls. Sandy recalled her experiences as a minister's wife, raising young children in a segregated South. She still has visions of the crosses burned in her front yard as she comforted her children. All of us bring to the classroom our personal biases and traumas along with our lesson plans. Minnie explains how this awareness is changing our roles as teachers.

Nurture is the key word. We make a comfortable place for kids to be, not catering, but a place to grow as a person. We offer a hands-on approach. The kids feel our professional commitment. We establish nurturing as the norm. Once you make a commitment to accepting everybody—you give yourself to all of them and they give themselves to you.

As we changed as teachers, the soil in our classrooms became richer and able to support our students' growth as writers and learners.

When we started the Webster Groves Writing Project, the soil in our classroom environment didn't seem particularly harmful. In this racially stable (75 percent White, 25 percent Black) suburban district, teachers received encouragement and support for innovation. Webster Groves School District was, in fact, the original sponsor of the National Writing Project site serving the St. Louis area, the Gateway Writing Project.[1] Yet in this seemingly positive environment, most African American students were underachieving in writing. Let's look at the writing of one such student who had grown up in our community and entered the middle school just as we began doing our research.

When he came to seventh grade, Daniel appeared less than enchanted with school, especially third-hour English class. If asked to write, he took longer to produce less than his classmates. He would fidget and stare into space or retreat by resting his head on the desk. Occasionally he was openly defiant. Daniel, like many African American males, seemed alienated from his White female teacher and from the curriculum and expectations in his middle school. Daniel began working daily with a teacher who used the project's principles to guide his reading and writing experiences.

Here we will illustrate the extent of Daniel's growth by looking at his papers for the annual Webster Groves writing assessment. As we focused on African American writers in our classrooms, we saw their assessment papers as a rough measure of growth, a mirror of progress—theirs and ours.

For his fall assessment paper, Daniel was asked to write a letter to the principal explaining the qualities of a good teacher. He began;

Dear Dr. Fredstrom
If you were going to hire a teacher the qualities you should look
for are He/she . . .

Then he started over on the same page:

Dear Dr. Fredstrom

If you were to hire a new teacher the qualities you should look for in that teacher should be a person with a good sense of humor. Pick someone not to old under 60 or be low, someone that makes the homework and class assignments fun and interisting. A good teacher is someone with a good personality and . . . .

Daniel never finished the task he set out to do. His reasoning lacked development, yet he explicitly identified four characteristics he felt to be most important: someone who has good sense of humor, who is not too old, who makes homework fun, and who has a good personality. This bare-bones listing included no introduction or conclusion. But his teacher saw the potential in a voice that was strong, vital, and reached out to the reader. Perhaps he didn't relate to this year's topic prescribed for the districtwide assessment. Perhaps in the classroom she could involve Daniel in writing that was closer to his own reality. During seventh grade, he had many opportunities to choose his own topics (which ranged from rap music to street culture to adolescent books he had chosen to read). His teacher felt that he was starting to care about his writing. Would it show when he was once again faced with an assigned topic under test conditions? Here is Daniel's posttest written at the end of seventh grade:

Dear Dr. Fredstrom,

The qualities you should look for in a teacher is that she should look you in the eyes and say, "Dr. Fredstrom, I'm the teacher you've been looking for." You need a teacher who is hard working and work for that pay check, and someone who is kind, likes to help people and someone who has patients because you need patients to work with this class. We also need a teacher who went to a well known college and one who stands up for their rights.

By the second writing sample, Daniel was more fluent; his word count increased from fifty-three to eighty-five words. More writing is not necessarily better, but combined with the fact that in the spring he completed the task, this was encouraging. He added more detail and sophistication in his reasons for selecting a teacher. Dialogue was included, demonstrating some aware-ness of conversational style and punctuation rules. The voice grew stronger.

Daniel celebrated summer and his release from the demands of school and his English teacher. With the arrival of September came his introduction to his second project teacher and more writing. For the fall assessment, he was asked to describe an object that held significance for him and tell why it was important. After a summer spent fishing with his grandpa, Daniel wrote,

> My first fishing pole was given to me by my grandfather. My fishing pole and I had some good and bad times together. I remember when I had a 10 pound catfish on my hook. The catfish fought for about two minutes, then I got it up to the bank ready to take the hook out of its mouth. I tended to wiggle off my hook, ploped on the bank into the water and swam away. My fishing day was spoiled.

His teacher shared her excitement with the team. Daniel had written introductory and concluding sentences. A central idea emerged, represented by a clear thesis statement: "My fishing pole and I had some good and bad times together." Vivid verbs and specific details appeared, too: The reader can see a "10 pound catfish" fight, "wiggle off" the hook, and "plop on the bank." The voice remained strong.

Again, he experienced a year with a teacher who consciously used the project's principles, who encouraged students to express their personal strengths in reading and writing, and who measured her own performance by the response of her underachieving African American students. On the assessment at the end of eighth grade, Daniel again met the "significant object" topic and again chose to write about his fishing pole. Evolution had occurred, transforming the reluctant, "low-skilled" student into a confident, involved, and successful writer in control of his narrative.

> Now I guess you're wondering why I pick a fishing pole. On my twelfth birthday, my grandfather gave me my first real fishing pole. When I first

got it I was amazed because he got me one of the best reels you can buy. It was an Ambassador 5000 red open face reel. Now he brought the pole over. I thought he was going to give me one of his old poles but he gave me a brand new one instead.

My pole and I had some good times and some bad times together. The best times I've had with it is when we went to a small lake. Not a lot of people were catching fish but I caught one that everyone dropped their poles and everything to see the 12 pound 3 ounce channel catfish I had just caught. Everyone from around the lake came over to congratulate me on the successful catch.

I recall two other fishermen asking my wonderful grandfather and I, "What secret kind of bait are you fellows using?" We both said, "Worms."

The worst time my fishing pole and I had is when my grandfather and his friend Mr. Thomas and I went fishing. The day before I had stayed up all night oiling my reel, putting new line on it and everything. So finally I went to bed hoping I was goingto catch a lot of fish the next day. Morning comes, my grandfather rings the door. Then I went in my garage to my fishing poles and tackle box and put it in the truck. Finally we were at the lake. My grandfather and Mr. Thomas are catching all the fish. So we were packing up all the stuff, ready to go and I got a bite and guess what. It was a 4-inch blue gill.

In contrast with the fifty-three halting words Daniel wrote at the beginning of seventh grade, he now produced a well-developed, highly detailed personal narrative of 315 words. His introductory sentence had grown into an introductory paragraph. He followed his thesis, organized well, and used paragraphs. His dialogue had a convincing ring and his vocabulary showed a maturity of word choice (*congratulate, recall*). He connected his thoughts with appropriate transitions. He ended with humor—risky even for a professional author. Daniel still had room for improvement, especially in the conventions of writing, but his teachers were thrilled with his progress. Most of all, Daniel's voice grew still stronger.

This dramatic writing development was not a fluke. During the six years of our project, growth such as Daniel's occurred among many of our African American students—in fact, among writers of all backgrounds. To-day Daniel is preparing for his freshman year of college, along with many other students from the first year of our project. How did they do it? How did we do it?

This book tells the story of our six-year journey that we as teachers and students took together. By learning as a research team, we began to view the "problem" from a new angle—the intersection between race, gender, class, and age. More than a linguistic clash, might the problem be the cultural estrangement of Black teenagers, particularly males, from the world of White females reflected in the school? Was our students' alienation in the classroom a mirror image of our own alienation from their world?

Gradually the focus of our research shifted from changing our students to changing ourselves. And, over time, our mirrors gave us a clearer picture of each other.

NOTE

1. The Gateway Writing Project is jointly sponsored by the University of Missouri, St. Louis and Harris Stowe State College, a historically Black institution with an emphasis on teacher education. Co-Directors are Jane Zeni (UMSL), Michael Lowenstein (Professor of English, HSSC) and Rosalynde Scott, elementary Enrichment Lab teacher from the St. Louis Public Schools.

Story of an Action Research Team

I have jokingly stated that when we are ninety, we will still be involved in action research! But seriously, I see the danger in departments where people are "satisfied." I hope we never are.

GAIL TAYLOR

We wanted to believe that we educated Daniel and all our students equally, but each year's writing assessment told a different story. We could not explain and we would not ignore the dismal performance of so many African American students in our integrated suburban schools.

We had begun by assessing our students' performance as writers. But we discovered that to tackle the problem we had to assess our own performance as teachers. We had to look critically at our lesson plans and strategies. Most important, we had to question how our own cultural assumptions might be blocking our relationships with some of our students.

Our journey took us through what we now see as three phases of awareness that transformed how we defined the problem and where we looked for solutions:

- Phase One: Fix the Writing
- Phase Two: Fix the Teaching Methods
- Phase Three: Fix the Teacher-Student Relationships

These phases are roughly chronological, but they were not linear steps. In our experience, action research is a process that is recursive like the process of writing. We began with a rather limited focus on student writing, but we didn't abandon this goal when our focus broadened to our teaching and to our classroom relationships. Each phase contains all that has gone before.

PHASE ONE: FIX THE WRITING

Holistic Assessment

We were proud of our writing assessment. While today we can see its flaws, our assessment was designed by Webster Groves teachers working with our Gateway Writing Project, and it was probably ahead of its time for the mid-1980s. We knew that we couldn't test writing with standardized, multiple-choice tests. We knew that we couldn't expect writers to show their skill in fifteen minutes. We knew that valid assessment should reflect what and how students learn. So we allowed two class periods to plan, write, revise, and edit a paper for holistic scoring (see Chapter 12 for details). But the results were still a shock (see Figures 2-1 and 2-2).

Of course the chronic underachievement of African American students was hardly news. The National Assessment of Educational Progress (1986, 1990) continues to report a gap between Black and White achievement in most subject areas in most schools across the country. The problem lurks in the corners of department meetings and backyard barbecues. Teachers speak of it in whispers or shake their heads and change the subject. Or they resort to the blame game, as Minnie describes it.

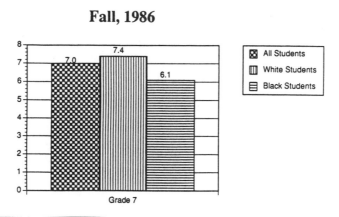

FIG. 2-1 *Mean scores of seventh-grade students at the beginning of the project, fall 1986.*

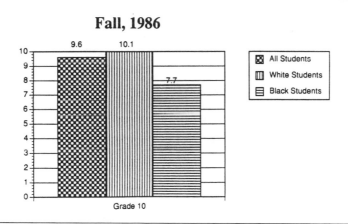

FIG. 2-2 *Mean scores of tenth-grade students at the beginning of the project, fall 1986.*

College professors point to secondary teachers, secondary teachers point to elementary teachers, and elementary teachers to parents. Our hands are tied, we insist, by administrative policies or state and federal mandates. Television, of course, remains the universal culprit, as are on occasion the state of youth, the state of the economy, and the state of the world in general.

For us, these excuses eventually felt hollow. We believed passionately that a good teacher could do something in the classroom to make a difference. The Webster Groves School District had a long history of innovation and a staff of confident, experienced teachers. Yet we too were failing. We couldn't sit back and let our kids continue to slip through the cracks.

Finally a new teacher who hadn't yet mastered the blame game asked the question that sparked our project, as Jane recalls:

> Theresa came bounding into my office that spring day in 1987. "I'm working with Joan! The whole thing started at the department meeting when she showed us the bar graphs from the assessment. And Jane, you won't believe this—I asked why Black writers scored lower than Whites and she'd wondered about the same thing so we're writing a grant. . . ."
>
> Theresa was just a year out of college, a beginning teacher at Webster Groves High School. She'd done her student teaching with me and a writing workshop with Joan. I remembered her enthusiasm, her passion for fairness. But I had to smile at how she'd walked into her first job and voiced the question that her mentor had long been asking.
>
> Joan was an innovator and an organizer who had taught middle school for twenty-five years. As she prepared her annual report on the writing assessment, she'd phoned me about those bar graphs. The gap between Black and White achievement—again this year—gnawed at her. Despite everyone's good intentions, the schools were still failing some of our kids in disproportionate numbers. Why indeed?
>
> Looking at Theresa, Joan saw a reflection of her own commitment.
> "It's time."

Could the assessment papers tell us what was stunting the growth in writing of our African American students? With input from most of the district's secondary English teachers, Joan and Theresa wrote a Missouri Incentive grant.[1] During the summer we would analyze the writing samples, read all we could about African American learners, and develop teaching strategies to address the problem as we understood it. During the school year, we would meet monthly to share concerns, insights, and successes, and we would bring in African American educators for inservice workshops.

Text Analysis

In August 1987, a committee of ten teachers met for an intensive week with Jane as the university consultant. We immersed ourselves in 476 assessment papers from grades seven to twelve. We read papers by all Black students who scored below their grade level means and an equal number of papers by low-scoring White students (see Zeni and Krater-Thomas 1990). We wanted to understand what problems plagued these writers by asking one central question: Do the low-scoring papers by Black writers differ in any consistent way from low-scoring papers by White writers?

Joan had designed a session to prepare for the analysis by exposing our preconceptions. She was suspecting that the low scores of many African American writers might reflect bias on the part of scorers.

First we explained in a freewrite what we thought we might find; we shared aloud our expectations, our questions, and our uncertainties. Joan then handed out ten papers paired by grade level and score, telling her colleagues that each pair included one White and one Black writer. Could we guess which was which? (This was the exercise that jolted Nancy.) "The group correctly classified three pairs of papers, but missed two. We asked readers their cues, in usage as well as style and content. The exercise showed that these cues were misleading; it helped us question all assumptions . . . and focus on the texts at hand (Zeni and Krater-Thomas 1990, 19–20).

So we set to work comparing stacks of papers written by White and by Black writers who had earned the same low scores. We described rhetorical features—fluency, development, organization, voice.[2] We also described control of standard English—common errors in spelling and sentence structure as well as language variations that might be unique to Black or White students. We looked for patterns that might explain why so many African American students were getting low scores.

Our findings would shape the changes we planned to make in our teaching. If our African American writers used many of the forms linguists like Smitherman (1977) call Black English Vernacular (BEV), we might plan some lessons contrasting those features with Edited American English (EAE). But if students were weak in a wide range of rhetorical as well as mechanical areas, we should emphasize writing process lessons tailored to their interests. We were concerned that weaknesses in writing

> might, in the case of African Americans, too quickly be labeled "Black English," causing teachers to focus mainly on surface errors. In a time of areawide desegregation, some teachers have returned to the language attitudes of the past—an obsession with the differentness of Black oral style, and an assumption that if Black students slip into this style on paper we must "fix" their speech habits. . . . Our experience with African American writers in Webster Groves made us doubt that dialect was the key. (Zeni and Krater-Thomas 1990, 16)

In fact, our results showed little that distinguished White and Black low-scoring writers. Looking at surface features, we saw few signs of dialect in either group. Low-scoring African American students sometimes dropped standard word endings—especially the -*s* and -*ed* endings on verbs and the -*s* and -*'s* endings on nouns. Yet these BEV features were not frequent even among the lowest-scoring Black writers, and they were found—though less frequently—among a few White writers, too.[3]

We did, however, find one rhetorical category that clearly distinguished between the two groups: "Black students tended to use a more informal voice and to get personally involved with their subjects. . . . The frequent sound of a convincing personal voice—though not always controlled—was an asset" (Zeni and Krater-Thomas 1990, 22–23). Here was a strength to build on rather than a problem to address! We quickly began talking of more ways to use it in the classroom.

In 1988 we repeated the text analysis with similar results. Low-scoring writers, Black and White, were much alike; low scores were simply more common among Black students. We concluded that only a broad, learner-centered plan would help our African American students develop their potential as writers.

Community Context: What Does It All Mean?

To make sense of our text analysis, we must view it in the context of the Webster Groves School District. Covering five suburban municipalities,[4] the district educates some 4,400 students, roughly 1,100 of whom are African American. Though most families have incomes in the broad middle range, they vary from marginal workers living in subsidized housing to descendants of the wealthy portrayed in the 1966 documentary, "Sixteen in Webster Groves." CBS had sent a team of journalists and sociologists to investigate the generation growing up in an affluent midwestern suburb—ours. When the documentary was televised, residents found the portrait of their town less than flattering.

Several teachers on our team were living or working in the district at the time of the broadcast. "An abomination," says Nancy. "People from Webster Groves resent it even today. The journalists were invited all over town and they used every bad piece of tape they filmed!" The students they interviewed were just one class behind Nancy at the high school. "Oh, yeah, some of my best friends were taped. You know the real somber one at the beginning? Of course she was somber; her class had just returned from a funeral."

Joan interrupted, "Well, I was a beginning teacher in Webster Groves at the time, and I know there were distortions, but as far as I was concerned they got the right thesis." She had been struck by the materialism of some teenagers. "All they wanted in those days was the car, the money, and the big two-story house their parents had."

But "Sixteen in Webster Groves" told just part of the story. Even in the 1960s, there was another Webster. Minnie came to the district as a teacher in 1968, just after the furor over the documentary, in the wake of growing student unrest and pressure from Black parents for Black representation in the curriculum, in school activities, and in staffing. "It was as if a bomb was ready to go off," she recalls. "The school system had been staunchly traditional, and suddenly things were changing. There was a turnover of administrators, an influx of young teachers (both White and Black), and protests from the old faculty."

All three of our teachers agree that African Americans have played a major role in Webster Groves' history. African Americans were living in the area by 1804, and gradually, as free persons of color, they settled in a neighborhood with a strong identity. Even as a child growing up in the other Webster, Nancy knew that early Black settlers had owned large parcels of land in town and that residents spoke with pride of their history. A recent book, *North Webster: A Photographic History of a Black Community,* describes the early community this way:

> Ten miles west of St. Louis in the town of Webster Groves, where two great hills come together and Shady Creek winds down between them, there is an old black community . . . called North Webster. . . . For a long time it looked like much of the rural South: run-down, with dirt roads and privies. But it has always been a wonderful place to live, with tall trees to shade the hottest days, creeks full of "crawdads," homegrown vegetables, a good school, and seven churches. (Morris and Ambrose 1993, 2)

That "good school" was Frederick Douglass. Founded soon after the Civil War, operating for years in a one-room log building, Douglass had added a pioneering "High School Department" by 1928 (20). It was the only accredited Black secondary school outside of St. Louis City. Before the end of legal segregation in the mid-1950s, students from all over the suburbs rode the bus to Frederick Douglass High. It gained a reputation as

> one of the finest schools for blacks in Missouri, attracting black families to the community. The people of North Webster worked together, teaching their children to excel, to aspire, to plan for college. A warm and busy social life was self-contained within the school and the churches. It was only when blacks stepped beyond the hills of North

Webster that a veil of discrimination clouded their dreams and slowed the progress of the dreamers. (2)

Our book is about the people who stepped beyond those old racial boundaries, inheriting both the larger horizons and the dried-up dreams. In 1957, Douglass High School was closed and its nearly 200 students from North Webster enrolled in Webster Groves High School. There they had access to new facilities, course offerings, and relationships, but they lost the close-knit community and its explicit aspirations for Black achievement. Douglass Elementary served North Webster for another decade until it too was integrated and transformed—through quite a different process.

The Board of Education asked Henry Givens, a Douglass sixth-grade teacher, to create "a demonstration school which would be so innovative and so exciting that parents from all over Webster Groves would want to send their children there. . . ." (46). As Givens planned the school, he met with each of the district's principals, their teachers, and their parents, asking for their support and suggestions. He recruited faculty from all over the district. Soon, there were "eighty-five applicants for twenty openings." Douglass became "the prototype for a magnet school," attracting students of both races.

During the summer of 1967, Givens and the faculty of Douglass created a new curriculum and took out walls at the school to create open classrooms. . . . The Douglass PTA became the largest in the district. Eventually there was a two-year wait to get into Douglass. . . . The achievement levels of all the children rose. For Henry Givens, "It was a love affair between a school and a community." (46)

In 1979, amid declining enrollment across the district, Douglass was one of four elementary schools to be closed. Walter Ambrose, then head of the school board, was a Douglass graduate. He worked to save the school, then worked with the community to accept the decision: "Douglass had always been a great cultural center, . . . the nucleus of the community for many years. I'm proud of everything that happened back then. But we can't always be looking back or we will stumble. It's time to hold hands and go forward together" (47).

That "going forward together" is the context of our story. Teachers in the Webster Groves Writing Project still struggle with the cultural legacy encrusted on the brick walls of our schools. Though Nancy and many of her White colleagues once saw the district as "naturally integrated," African American residents saw a different and more problematical history. In so many ways, Webster Groves represents both the successes and the failures of integration in suburban America.

Today, much of our school district is residentially integrated and middle-class; Frederick Douglass School (redeveloped as an attractive, racially mixed apartment complex and community center) remains a landmark for North Webster's lower-middle-income African American residents; a larger area of the district is almost exclusively White and more affluent.

About 25 percent of our students now are African American.[5] About 20 percent of that number are district residents; 5 percent come from the inner city of St. Louis through a voluntary interdistrict desegregation program. The same proportion of residents and transfers is also found among low-scoring writers. So we cannot attribute the poor showing of Black students on the writing assessment to newcomers from the city assumed to be less privileged academically or economically. Even for students who live within district boundaries, race and class are not identical. Some of our Black students have parents in the professions, just as some of our White students have parents on welfare.

The First Study Session

Midway through our week's seminar, reflecting on the text analysis and the community, we were more baffled than ever. If neither dialect nor social class explained why African American students were failing to thrive in our classrooms, where was the problem? Obviously, in that summer of 1987, we could not yet see our own roles with much clarity.

We turned to published research, but the classic 1970s work of J. L. Dillard, William Labov, and Geneva Smitherman had a rather limited focus on Black English Vernacular. Their research was based on samples of speech from the rural South or the urban ghettos. Thinking about our Webster Groves students, we knew our answers must lie elsewhere.

We then explored some newer research that dealt with Black students' learning styles, composing processes, and cultural preferences and with basic writing in general. Each teacher received a copy of Charlotte Brooks' *Tapping Potential: English and Language Arts for the Black Learner* (1985), Farr and Daniels' *Language Diversity and Writing Instruction* (1986), and a stack of articles, especially the 1980s work of Smitherman. We discussed this reading in the light of our own classroom experience. We began with approaches recommended for writing process, and then we noted approaches recommended for African American students—looking for points where they converged. After brainstorming a list of such points, we classified them and selected those that sounded promising. By the end of the week, we had set some global goals that might create a context for writing improvement: self-esteem, role models, teacher expectations, and cultural awareness. We had also agreed upon a tentative action plan of six broad principles[6] to guide us.

> **Provide opportunity for group work.** Many of the African American educators in Brooks' volume (1985) stressed group learning.
>
> **Build on strengths.** Our text analysis showed that many Black writers had strong voices with a flair for conversation. Smitherman (1985) emphasized oral performance.
>
> **Individualize.** Black writers in our study ran the gamut of strengths and weaknesses, so we would need to individualize.
>
> **Increase control of language.** Standard usage was a problem for some of our students and a major concern of Black parents.
>
> **Increase involvement with writing.** Our readings as well as classroom intuition stressed the power of personal interest.

Emphasize process. Farr and Daniels (1986, 45–46) listed fifteen aspects of writing process pedagogy and related them to the needs of students from nonstandard English backgrounds.

PHASE TWO: FIX THE TEACHING METHODS

Years One and Two

These principles led us beyond Phase One, but they spoke in very general terms. They didn't tell us precisely what we were doing wrong—precisely what our African American students needed from us. Our ideas would have to be fleshed out in our own classrooms as we moved into Phase Two. We decided to observe our students on a daily basis to learn more about their writing processes and how they responded to our attempts at using the principles. For this phase of the project, we asked different questions:

- What are the barriers keeping so many of our students from full access to literacy?
- What do African American writers need that we as teachers have not been providing?
- What miscommunication and cultural miscues have been blocking their progress?

In the fall, with strong support from Webster Groves administrators, six teachers[7] volunteered for the "Improving Black Students' Writing Project."

As we reread that title now, our beginning seems quite naive. We started with a simple deficit model: we would track down our students' writing problems and find methods to solve them. On the other hand, it is also true that even from day one we resisted the tendency to look only outside ourselves. We did not, for example, use our grant funds to buy new textbooks or software spelling drills—decisions that would have located the problem and the need for training in our students. Instead, we asked a series of African American educators to help us locate the blind spots in our cultural awareness that could put some of our students "at risk." We were willing to face our own biases. But at first we thought of bias as misinformation or misguided teaching methods; we might, for example, need to learn "the facts" about dialect or about group work. We hoped that outside experts could teach us.

Our consultants included Jacqueline Royster (on the Black learner), Frank Voci (on cultural differences), Walter Wolfram (on language diversity), and Geneva Smitherman (on BEV and assessment). We wanted them to tell us about teaching strategies that would make us more effective with African American learners; we wanted them to help us uncover our own cultural biases. But we soon realized that the outside consultants, like the outside readings, were telling us what we already "knew." We knew—but we didn't understand. We had to ground this knowledge in our own setting, in relationships with our own Black students, before we could change.

Our most practical inservice training dealt with methods closer to our experience, with writing process and with cooperative learning. Joan and some others on the team had long been involved in our National Writing Project site; as we continued working together, we all sought out some formal training in writing process. Cooperative learning was a real catalyst. In 1989 the whole team attended a workshop with Edythe Johnson Holubec (of the Johnson and Johnson program). We found that cooperative learning transformed the effectiveness of group work, so all new members have taken similar training. Chapters 5 and 7 show how we have applied these principles in the classroom.

Our research began by focusing on a small number of students during the first two years. Each of us chose as case studies two or three African American writers who had scored low on the annual holistic assessment. We played it safe, beginning with students we felt we should be able to reach; we didn't choose kids who were rarely in class or who changed schools frequently. Since we tried to "aim" whatever we taught in a way that would best reach these writers, we called our case studies "target students." As we monitored their progress, we fine-tuned our teaching and our principles. As we gained confidence we could target all our students, Black and White, male and female, who were not working to their potential.

27

By contrast with experimental research, we did not offer any treatment or pull anyone out for remedial instruction. We worked with target students in the course of daily classroom teaching, usually in heterogeneous groups. Since we used the team's principles and strategies with all our students, the case study writers were not singled out; in fact, they did not even know they were targeted. We told our classes that *we* were part of a research project to improve our teaching of writing, so we might be jotting notes in class. Throughout this book, we'll be introducing many of our writers. All students we describe and quote will be target students unless otherwise indicated. (Pseudonyms are used.)

Here are a few samples from Joan's field notes jotted in class during the first year of research:

> Alleesha didn't # qts in Jrnl #3. Her ideas, reactions were very jrnl like—just not structured acc to my qts. Maybe I shldn't care—maybe it's best—she needs to talk thru on paper what she understds & doesn't about poem as whole before getting to specifics. . . . I think a lot of kids— [names a highly skilled writer/thinker]—do this—but faster and in their heads.

Note how Joan is struggling to understand her student's perspective and to consider the possibility that Alleesha has reasons for her way of learning not so different from those of more typically successful students. Note also how Joan questions her own assignment and its limits. The next two samples take us behind the scenes of Mark's essay quoted in the thumbprint lesson in Appendix Three:

> 1/15/88
> Mark was in group with 3 White boys; told of physical for football when dr examined near groin: Mark assumes for hernias. Kids reacted with lots of laughter because of topic. Mark didn't know how to phrase the area—I suggested groin. . . . I'm worried that this may not result in a particularly good paper since Mark had few details other than actual exam. Hope we can get a point for it. Hope Mark has draft written by Tues. Will ask today if he did it last night.

28

1/20/88

Mark did his rough draft yesterday in class. I read it in Team Time & talked with him; Asked if could reverse *scared/ cold hands*. He said no. Asked, so *scared* goes with where dr. was pushing? Yes. Then showed R.O. & where period had to go. How that left a sentence with two things together that didn't go. "Could you somehow get the 2 things that go together into one sentence?" He rephrased it—I wrote it. He asked, "Then just have 'His hands were cold'?" I suggested "Besides, his hands were cold." Wish I'd asked What do you think? Damn—too fast again. Then told Mark he had lots of dialog & that quotes wld help rdr be there.

Here Joan works with Mark individually, guiding him through the writing and editing, then assessing herself as she tries to support the writer without taking over his ownership. Some of our field notes reflect more personally on our own work. The next passage shows Joan frustrated, torn between the pressure to drill for standardized tests and the need to get students involved in literature that requires thinking:

3/15/88

I'm so upset I can't get focused on what I'm here to do. Trade who/whom lesson for 2 articles they could read with higher thinking. . . . now do I prostitute my beliefs—wait and see how kids do [by not teaching any grammer]—do bang up job on garbage [like who/whom] or what? Need time to gather more data—have no time! Holistic report—Descriptors—Board report—Grammar Test—this project—CTBS—BEST—Gifted—Team Planning—Proud Statesmen Project—*all* of us have all this! At least Loco [her cat] is okay!

Joan's inner debate here is so typical of this kind of research. Instead of a single variable to examine in an artificial task, we are studying a real-world setting where the variables and the issues emerge in time from the data.

As we planned our lessons, guided class discussions, and organized peer workshops, we kept an extra pair of eyes on the target students in our classes. We judged our own success not by the response of the usual high-achieving students but by the response of our low achievers, especially the African American males. As classroom ethnographers, we tuned in to the students who had been tuning out.

ACTION RESEARCH: WHAT AND HOW

*Classroom action research is owned and operated by teachers.

*It starts with a problem <u>you</u> identify that calls for change.

*It tells the story of what you do & how you interpret what happens.

*It supports collaboration. Groups of teachers can share their
    stories and their perspectives on one another's work.

*Action research is a process.

*Like the writing process, the action research process is recursive.

*Planning/ teaching/ observing/ reflecting are interwoven cycles.

*So what does it "prove?"

*Experimental research finds validity in large numbers, in random
    samples, in control groups.

*Action research finds validity in the human story, in rich detail, in
    multiple perspectives.

Gateway Writing Project

FIG. 2-3 *Action Research: What and How.*

Action Research

In a 1982 article, Nancie Atwell asks, "How can classroom teachers acquire the background in language theory and research procedures to enable them to conduct full, naturalistic investigations of their students' writing processes?" Her answer is simple: "By doing it."

How could we gain insights that were more complete, more focused, more practical than what we learned from the literature and the consultants? Our answer was "by doing action research" (see Figure 2-3). An eclectic mode of inquiry developed to understand and improve social organizations, action research has been adopted by teachers as a powerful way of learning together.[8] Classroom action research is engaged and personal; it doesn't aim to be detached or "objective." It is conducted by those who have a stake in the issues: teachers who ask questions that matter to them, gather the data, share their reflections, and—most importantly—use what they learn to change their own teaching. While experimental research views students as "subjects" or numbers to be measured, action research challenges us to learn from them. And while official views of staff development aim to improve and manage technical skills, classroom action research aims for the "transformation of the professional culture into one which supports collaborative reflection about practice and [involves] the experiences and perceptions" of students, parents, and the community (Elliott 1991, 56).

The key to classroom action research is *triangulation,* which means looking at a problem through several pairs of eyes (students, teachers, outside consultants, others) and through several kinds of data (such as writing samples, interviews, observations). Like a three-way mirror, triangulation shows us the angles we don't normally see.

Over the years, we developed our own model of collaborative classroom action research. Our initial training was minimal. Just a few resources had been published that applied action research to the teaching of writing: Miles Myers' *The Teacher-Researcher: How to Study Writing in the Classroom* (1985), Mohr and MacLean's *Working Together: A Guide for Teacher-Researchers* (1987), and Goswami and Stillman's *Reclaiming the Classroom* (1987). Jane had done graduate work in qualitative research and classroom ethnography, so we asked her to give a brief workshop during our regular two-hour meeting in October. She brought in stacks of field-note logs from her own dissertation so that we could see how our raw data might look. Then she defined some of the tools we would need. Figure 2-4 is a reconstruction of the workshop.

That was the extent of our training. During the first two years, in fact, Jane kept in touch with us by phone but did not usually attend our monthly meetings. Joan led the sessions and we all learned "by doing it."

The initial grant provided released time (one period a week) for each teacher to read over the field-note log and write the reflective entries. This time helped to get us started with our logs, but most of us found that

---

ACTION RESEARCH DATA AND METHODS

Log: An ordinary spiral (or lap-top computer) in which you write your field notes, reflections, interviews, etc.

Field notes: A record of observations and interpretations. Date each entry. Note what you did, what your hopes were, how specific students responded. **Descriptive entries--** Jot in class or during breaks, using abbreviations that you'll be able to decipher. Get the classroom scene down on paper (puzzling details, body language, dialogue, as much as you can). **Reflective entries--**In the evening or in prep time, read over your jotted field notes. Write your questions and speculations on what you think is happening. Reflect, too, on your own feelings and behavior.

Conferences: **With students--**Opportunities for informal interviews as well as for teaching writing. **With team members--**Opportunities for thinking through your data. Keeps notes on conferences in your log.

Writing samples: Copy (with permission) everything written by the students you choose to observe--journal entries, drafts, peer response sheets, final papers.

FIG. 2-4   *Action Research: Data and Methods.*

the work preparing for a weekly substitute was not worth the hour we gained; after the first two years, we chose not to have released time for the project.

From the beginning, our action research team has met in a study session for two hours monthly. A study session is like a response workshop—we read aloud from our field-note logs; describe the progress of specific writers; share our own concerns, insights, and frustrations; and rely on the group for

Tape recordings: It may be useful to get audio or video tape records of peer groups in process, class discussions, student-teacher interaction, etc.

Test data: Keep records in your class. Check on standardized tests, writing assessment scores, etc. Look for patterns and write a reflective entry in your log.

Triangulation: Shed light on your subject from many angles. Have other eyes observe your classroom. Ask a colleague to sit in and take notes on an issue that concerns you; then discuss. Ask your students to write or explain what they see. Collect a variety of data--field notes, reflections, writing samples, interviews, tapes, tests, etc.

Synthesis: Your end-of-year interpretive report with highlights from your field notes, organized by whatever categories your research team decides are important.

FIG. 2-4 *(continued)*

support. These team meetings are a time for pulling together the threads of our own collaborative learning. One of us takes "minutes," which are typed and distributed to all members. These records help us keep track of insights that may seem important only in retrospect. Although the study sessions have met throughout the project, the atmosphere was very different when we began. During the first year, we can recall bringing our field-note logs to the meeting but feeling too threatened to share what we'd written! Gradually, we learned to trust in our colleagues and in ourselves.

Along with our field-note data, we wanted to collect more data on student achievement. Our first grant proposed as an objective that target students would increase their scores on the district writing assessment. Since concern over these scores had sparked our research, we decided to use the fall writing sample as a pretest. The sample would also serve as a means of identifying students we might choose for case studies. We added a spring writing sample as a posttest to provide a rough quantitative measure of progress. The first year we struggled. We spent hours debating the logistics of selecting case studies, planning the posttest, and scoring sample papers. Study sessions were filled with anxiety and self-doubt: "Are we doing the field notes right?" "Will the target students show any improvement?"

In June 1988, we saw the computer printouts of the annual writing assessment scores (see Chapter 12 for details of the assessment). We were thrilled that the nineteen students we had targeted as case studies had averaged a two-point increase on a sixteen-point scale. In fact, teachers stood up and cheered when their target student scored well! Traditionally, our district's students had gained about one point in a year on this assessment; African American students tended to gain less, falling farther behind with each year of schooling. Could our results be just a happy accident? Writing is a complex, developing skill, and we had not expected such dramatic gains in nine months. Encouraged but a bit baffled by our success, we wanted to confirm the results by repeating the case studies. In year two, we had pre- and posttest scores for twenty-three target students. To our delight, we found similar growth on the writing assessment along with a stronger sense that we were getting somewhere in the classroom.

During the first year's study sessions, we had often found ourselves talking about our target students' attitudes toward writing. We suspected that they might differ from the views of more successful writers and might help us understand the kids who failed to learn. Joan designed a forty-statement attitude survey that we piloted during the first spring and used as a pre- and posttest survey in the second year (see Chapter 13).

In June 1989, we saw the encouraging results. Our low-achieving case study writers did not start the year with the same views as other students, but they clearly changed their attitudes during a year of work with the project. In fact, they often moved farther in a positive direction than the rest of the students. One of the most telling items was "I like to write." In the fall of the second year, 64 percent of "all students" agreed; only 32 percent of the low-scoring students we had chosen as case studies agreed. By the spring, these target students responded just as positively as their peers, with 68 percent of both groups reporting "I like to write."

We should explain that while our research was growing and developing, our grant was drying up. The state rejected our proposal for a continuation grant. By this time, however, we were too involved in our work to give up. Fortunately, our central office administrators believed in the project, and the district picked up the funding for year two.

During the second year, we recognized a new angle to our work—one that shed new light on our own attitudes. We were focusing on African American students, and we had lamented the fact that all but one of our district's English teachers were White. But we hadn't thought much about gender. One day at a study session someone remarked that most of our target students seemed to be male. Suddenly, in an unforgettable moment of truth, we looked around the table and saw that *all* of our action research members were female. Meanwhile the media sizzled with warnings that "the Black male" was an "endangered species." We suspected one of the reasons might be a teaching force that was more and more dominated by White females (Kunjufu 1986; Irvine 1988; Ladson-Billings 1990).

We began to realize that schools in the United States were not culturally neutral. We discovered the work of African American anthropologist Janice Hale-Benson on the unconscious biases of schooling (1982). In a study of integrated classrooms, teachers rated each student using a variety of personal descriptors: "White females were highest on *efficient, organized, reserved, industrious,* and *pleasant;* they were lowest on *outspoken* and *outgoing.* Generally, Black males were mirror reflections of the White females—rating lowest" on such descriptors as *industrious* but highest on such descriptors as *outgoing* (8). We realized that if we were committed to teaching all students, we must change how we view our "mirror reflections," the kids who most differ from us in race, class, and gender. We must learn to value the cultural strengths of Black males and to create classroom environments where they, and we, could thrive.

As we learned, we wondered how to share our work with colleagues in our schools and with wider audiences. We hoped to pool the insights from our individual case studies into some sort of team report to multiply our impact on student writing. At the same time, we valued our autonomy as teachers and learners. A team report that homogenized our voices would be false. The solution Jane suggested has become a tradition: the *annual synthesis*.

Every summer, we spend a week pulling together the year's work. Each teacher first rereads her own field-note log, chooses the "telling" examples, summarizes the key insights, and uses the project's principles as an organizing framework. We call this report an "individual synthesis." With copies for each member of the team, we meet in June—teachers and consultant—to share our reports and reflect on our evolving list of principles and strategies. Jane then writes a team synthesis, weaving in quotes from our individual reports and group discussions.[9]

The first synthesis meetings raised our spirits after months of self-doubt. We were proud to see what we had accomplished together—the rich field notes, the gains in writing scores. In 1989 Joan submitted the work of years one and two—data from the writing assessment, the attitude scale, the text analysis, and the synthesis reports—to earn the team a national Classroom Action Research Award.[10]

The annual team synthesis week is still crucial in our growth as action researchers. It is a time to cook and stew and process, a time when we don't have to rush home to read papers and prepare classes, a time when the collective insights seem to leap forth from the daily muddle.

In the tradition of action research, we have continued to clarify and refine what we do in the classroom. The rough six-point action plan we brainstormed that first summer has grown into the eight principles we describe in the coming chapters (see Figure 2-5). Each principle has been fleshed out with practical teaching strategies and concrete examples from our student writers.

WEBSTER GROVES WRITING PROJECT
PRINCIPLES AND STRATEGIES

BUILD ON STRENGTHS
- Affirm strong personal voice
- Build on oral language and oral interpretation
- Create an environment for performance and role-playing
- Bring Black expressive language into the curriculum
- Guide students to investigate and appreciate dialects
- Value African American culture all year
- Value cultural diversity in the daily curriculum

INDIVIDUALIZE AND PERSONALIZE
- Build trusting relationships
- Share of yourself
- Know students' lives outside the classroom
- Orchestrate response to student writing through individual, group, or peer conferences
- Write personalized comments on drafts
- Tailor instruction to learning styles
- Allow flexible deadlines
- Maintain high expectations

ENCOURAGE COOPERATIVE LEARNING
- Develop a sense of community in the classroom
- Establish heterogeneous classrooms and groups
- Build positive interdependence
- Expect group and individual accountability
- Create settings for collaborative composing, revising, editing
- Use peer response, peer tutoring and study buddies

USE PROCESS APPROACHES TO WRITING
- Allow class time for writing
- Model process and product
- Develop papers over time
- Give credit for process
- Emphasize revision and multiple drafts
- Support writing process with word processing

FIG. 2-5 *Webster Groves Writing Project Principles and Strategies.*

INCREASE CONTROL OF LANGUAGE
- Play with language
- Teach editing in the context of writing, not workbooks
- Distinguish between journals, drafts, and published writing
- Provide practice in codeswitching between standard and variant dialects
- Model and use sentence expansion
- Use mini-lessons for instruction in common errors
- Individualize most direct instruction in proofreading
- Focus on a "critical injury" when marking mechanical errors

USE COMPUTERS
- Build on students' positive attitudes toward technology
- Use word processing as an essential writing tool
- Develop a computer-equipped Writing Center--in the school or in the classroom
- Encourage revising and editing, on screen and printout
- Model writing processes with computer projection
- Use desktop publishing for classroom work
- Explore other technology--telecommunications, interactive software, graphics

FOSTER INVOLVEMENT WITH WRITING AND READING
- Immerse students in reading and writing
- Discover and use writers' interests
- Encourage a choice of audience/ purpose/ mode
- Make the writing real
- Affirm personal responses to reading
- Use computers to increase involvement
- Develop a reading/ writing workshop
- Use portfolios to involve students in self-assessment

BUILD BRIDGES, EXPAND HORIZONS
- Build curriculum sequences--
  expressive to analytical,
  oral to written,
  factual to imaginative (and vice versa)
- Build from the familiar to the unknown
- Model a form and "Do it twice" to make new task familiar
- Build cultural bridges linking school, heritage, and the world community

FIG. 2-5   *(continued)*

Years Three and Four

One objection lurked in our minds during those early years. If a teacher chose two or three case study writers, and those writers made dramatic gains in skills and attitudes, were they simply responding to the subtle attention, to her more intense desire to hear them? By the third year we felt enough confidence as teachers and as researchers to cast a wider net. We wrote another Missouri Incentive grant. Like the first grant, this one lasted just one year, but the district again provided funding in year four.

This time we would target all students in our classes—Black and White, male and female—who placed below the mean on the writing assessment. Our experience with case studies had reinforced our belief that a student's writing skills could not be judged on the basis of a single paper. So we added as a second criterion for target student the rating of the previous year's teacher. Students who were below average on both criteria (roughly a third of our classes) would be our concern.

This change complicated our field notes, and again we found our study sessions filled with more anxiety than excitement: "I don't know what to write—there's too much happening!" We soon found that we didn't need extensive field notes on all these target students. Many of our observations simply confirmed what we had found in our earlier case studies; we could make just a brief note of such examples. Also, since our African American male students remained the lowest-scoring race/gender group, our field notes continued to focus on them and on our reactions to them. In June the third year's assessment showed that our target population of almost two-hundred low-achieving students again made substantial gains.

Now we knew that our student achievement data was "soft," as the statisticians would say; our numbers were small, groups were not random, and classroom conditions were not under experimental control (see Chapter 12). Yet the scores were impressive, especially at a time when our confidence in our classroom research was still shaky. Ironically, by the time we had a large enough target population for a proper experiment, we no longer trusted such a limited measure of growth in writing. In retrospect, it seems that the main significance of the writing assessment was to strengthen our commitment as an action research team as well as our credibility with outside audiences.

During these years, we worked with our target students in the classroom, shared that work with teachers in conferences and workshops, and put new energy into our own writing. Nancy led the team in preparing material for publication, with Jane as editorial coach. Papers were submitted to journals and to conferences. A report in *Breadloaf News* summarized the team's research to date (Cason, Tabscott, and Krater-Thomas 1991). Lesson plans based on the eight principles were written for a curriculum guide, *Hear You, Hear Me,* published by the Webster Groves School District (1992). And we started writing, drafting, and redrafting the chapters for this book.

Gradually, as we shared with new audiences, we began to articulate the political and social implications of our work. While our middle school teachers relied more and more on cooperative learning and heterogeneous classrooms, our senior high members struggled. At department meetings, they questioned the high school's continued tracking, which they saw as a policy of low expectations and the legacy of segregation. As team members, we no longer imagined ourselves in a system that educated everyone equally without a shred of bias. We were less naive but no less committed to our kids.

During the third and fourth years, as we began to question the assessment results, we also began to question whether our teaching methods had really "caused" those results. Perhaps the key to our success was not merely in the eight principles, valid though they were. This insight grew as we struggled to answer a challenge that was bound to be heard in any audience where we presented our work: What is there in your project that's specifically designed for African American males? Your eight principles just sound like good writing process instruction. What's really going on?

We knew the answer was not simply increased attention because we were having an impact on individual kids even when a third of our class population was targeted. We also knew the answer was not simply that "good writing process instruction works for everyone." As Lisa Delpit shows (1986, 1988), the methods of progressive White teachers often backfire with African American students who expect a different style of communication.

So at last we tried restating the question. What's happening to *us* that is making "good writing process instruction" work for African American students? Perhaps we were becoming more sensitive to writers who differed from us in color, gender, and cultural expectations. Perhaps we were learning to silence the "rumors of inferiority" said to haunt Black children in integrated schools (Howard and Hammond 1985). Perhaps we were learning to fine-tune the familiar principles of good teaching to create an environment where more kids felt welcome.

We turned to African American educators to tell us more. We read about "Africentric" curricula and "Rites of Passage" programs (Hare and Hare 1985; Kunjufu 1983) involving "an adult role model, skill development, Black culture, and a male socialization process" (Kunjufu 1986, 47). When local counselor Wayne Thomas of the Association of African American Role Models came for a workshop, we were intrigued but baffled. We'd gladly refer our kids to Wayne's program, but how could we—all women, most of us White—use his curriculum? "We're not Black males," thought Nancy. "But we're all they have!"

We were encouraged by the research of Gloria Ladson-Billings (1990) on Black and White teachers who were effective with African American learners: "The real difference between these eight teachers and those who consistently fail with Black students is . . . 'culturally relevant teaching' " (22). Culturally relevant teachers don't necessarily have to be Black teachers. In fact, when Ladson-Billings describes their behavior in the classroom, listeners often object, "But aren't you just talking about good teaching?" "My answer, which sounds like an equivocation, is 'yes and no.' " Her teachers used principles of "good teaching" to help students relate school knowledge and community knowledge (24–25). Perhaps we too could make "good teaching" reflect more diversity than White middle-class culture.

Another question followed: what's happening to us that is making "good writing process instruction" work better for *all* our students? Through action research, we were becoming better teachers. Cathy took part in a study group on teaching literature, began using literature study groups, and brought Doug and Dorothy Barnes to one of our team meetings; soon, personal response to literature was a mainstay of our project (see Appendix One). Nancie Atwell's *In the Middle* (1987) was a guide for Sandy—and then the rest of us—to plan reading/writing workshops. It seemed that the project had set free the power and energy of our own collaborative learning.

Jane went to South Africa on an exchange program between the University of Missouri and the University of the Western Cape (UWC). There she met progressive Black teachers who were using action research (and the ideas of Paulo Freire [1970]) to change their classrooms for a postapartheid South Africa. We read their handbook (Davidoff and van den Berg 1990) and shared materials with the UWC action research project. Back in St. Louis, Minnie and Jane took part in a seminar on qualitative research in history, biography, and ethnography. We began to tell our own stories as well as the stories of our kids. We began to speak of our work in historical terms—as a collective biography of teacher change.

We were outgrowing Phase Two.

PHASE THREE: FIX THE RELATIONSHIPS

Years Five and Six

In Ralph Ellison's *Invisible Man* (1952), the African American male protagonist explains,

> I am an invisible man. No, I am not a spook like those who haunted Edgar Allan Poe; nor am I one of your Hollywood-movie ectoplasms. I am a man of substance, of flesh and bones, fiber and liquids—and I might even be said to possess a mind. I am invisible, understand, simply

because people refuse to see me. Like the bodiless heads you see sometimes in circus sideshows, it is as though I have been surrounded by mirrors of hard, distorting glass. When they approach me they see only my surroundings, themselves, or figments of their imagination—indeed, everything and anything except me. (3)

When we looked at Black male students in our classrooms, what we saw at first was a reflection of our own assumptions, fears, and frustrations—along with the masks the kids themselves put up for protection. Kunjufu (1986) asks teachers, When you see a Black male teenager, do you see "a future Jesse Jackson or a drug addict?" (19). We saw the low test scores, the erratic work habits, and the streetwise teenagers who fidgeted, dozed, or acted out in our classrooms. We didn't always see the strengths in oral language, in personal voice, in a cultural heritage that was not our own. But we were willing to learn. As we learned, Daniel and other student writers experienced a transformation.

Looking back today, we see our own transformation as well. We too had been invisible, and we too have emerged from the shadows. When our research began, we thought we could observe our African American students from a "neutral," "objective" stance, without putting too much of ourselves in the picture. This mask of cultural invisibility kept us no more hidden than an ostrich with its head in the sand. Most of our team might be described as middle-class, middle-western, and (with a few exceptions) middle-aged women. One of us is African American; the rest are European American. Before the project, we had all taught in racially mixed schools, but we varied widely in our political assumptions and in our personal contacts with people of different backgrounds. We soon realized how much our own cultures must color our perceptions. An "invisible" researcher can't see her own role in a problem.

In Phase Three, we still rely on our eight principles. But we now see them as part of a larger picture of good teaching and positive student-teacher relationships in a multicultural context. For the first time, in year six our annual synthesis was organized by two main themes—writing portfolios and writing workshop. But we found that all the principles played a role in how we made these changes in our teaching. Sandy remarked, "I haven't found one of the principles that doesn't hold up under the test of time." The principles have become woven into the fabric of our relationships with students.

Our approach to assessment shows this same change. We still measure our success by the performance of our target students, but we can't limit that performance to gains on a one-shot assessment paper. We look at our gains in building classroom environments where all students, Black and White, male and female, are expected to learn. In year five, our school district abandoned the annual holistic scoring in favor of portfolio assessment. Conferring with peers and teacher, our kids choose samples of their own writing, reflect on their own performance, and measure their own growth. When we view their portfolios, the bar graphs dissolve into human portraits.

Today, we also assess our own performance differently as we reflect on our experience of action research. Under a major federal grant (see note 1), Webster Groves teachers are coaching new teams in two contrasting districts—one mostly White and rural in Washington, Missouri, and one mostly Black and suburban in University City, Missouri. When we first met the new teams, we shared our results, the eight principles, the writing improvement, and the cultural awareness. Teachers were confused. Were they supposed to implement *our* program? Then we saw that what we could "disseminate" was simply the process of action research. The new teachers would find their own principles grounded in their own classrooms. As we watch them struggle and learn, we see a mirror of our own project.

Finally, we have immersed ourselves again in reading. When Nancy took an intensive course in multicultural teaching, she shared with the team the recent research of African American educators such as Shirl Gilbert, Geneva Gay, Claude Steele, and Jeff Howard. Meanwhile, Jane's work with Gateway Writing Project's Urban Sites Writing Network brought us the resources of Evelyn Dandy, Emilie Siddle-Walker, Marilyn Cochran-Smith, and Susan Lytle.

It has been validating to see others drawing conclusions that resonate with ours, conclusions stressing relationships, culture, and self-awareness rather than skills or process in a vacuum.

A TEAM OF ACTION RESEARCHERS

We often refer to the team as if we were a single unit. Of course this is not true. During the past six years, some teachers have left the team, one left and has returned, new teachers have joined, and leadership has changed. It is a sign of the power of collaborative action research that the project continues to change and mature.

After our first year, we survived a major loss. Minnie Phillips, our only African American team member, was taking a leave to teach at a prestigious private day school. Minnie had believed in us, believed that White teachers had the right and the responsibility to do this project. The rest of us, who were White, had relied on Minnie to keep us on track, to protect us from blundering into a fog of cultural miscues. Could we manage without her? Would we make fools of ourselves? Minnie wept through her goodbyes, then the rest of us wept with her. She urged us to carry on, but we were scared.

Two years later, Minnie would return to Webster Groves High School as coordinator of writing across the curriculum—while working on her doctorate in education. She would also return to a stronger, more-confident action research team. (Later she admitted her surprise as well as pleasure to find that we had kept the project going!)

The third year brought more changes to the research team. Joan Krater, who had conceived and led the project, took a year's sabbatical that brought about her reassignment in a very different role, working with middle school students identified as gifted. Again, the team hesitated. Could we maintain our energy, our sense of direction? Another founding member, Nancy Cason, assumed the leadership of the project. A former Spanish teacher who had joined the department just before the project began, Nancy's leadership style was collaborative, nonthreatening, and very supportive of team members' discoveries. The project endured and thrived.

Although Jane Zeni has been the team's university consultant from the beginning, her role has also changed. In that summer and fall of 1987, she was a traditional outside consultant, called in for expert advice on the text analysis, African American learners, and methods of action research. But when the state grant was not renewed for year two, we kept going with minimal support from the district—support which did not include consulting fees. At that point, Jane became a full participant in the action research, a member of the team. She visited some classrooms to triangulate the teachers' data and took part in collaborative writing and reviewing for our curriculum publication. By year four, she was working with Joan on plans for a book based on the annual synthesis reports. Somehow the proposal kept running aground. Was this a story of improvement in writing, of change in teaching methods, or of some sort of personal change among teachers? Jane returned to her old mentor, Lou Smith of Washington University, who helped her see the project's three phases of development. In years five and six, while writing for this book, Jane took on the role of team biographer and historian.

The team is a point of communication between teachers who work in quite different environments. Hixson Middle School is committed to heterogeneous classes and to cross-disciplinary teams. Webster Groves High School has a well-regarded but traditional English department with some ability grouping—basic and college-bound courses—at each grade level. In year six, after much soul-searching, the high school English department voted to phase out the tracked classes with the incoming ninth graders. Instead of the basic groups, Agnes taught three heterogeneous classes and monitored the progress of former target students. This change was based on the success of mixed grouping at the middle school and the conviction of project teachers at the high school that labeling students by putting them in "basic" classes sets them up to remain underachievers.

Now all eight middle school English teachers and five of the senior high teachers are involved in the research; Ted Ibur from the sixth-grade center joined us in 1992. Our active members total fourteen English teachers in grades six through twelve plus Jane. Twelve of us are White females, including Jenny van Breusegen, who joined in 1992; one is a Black female; and two (new in 1992) are White males (along with Ted, we now have Don Eckert).

The distinct voices and viewpoints of individual teachers will be apparent throughout our book—both in the passages from their field notes and in the longer stories of personal change (Facing the Mirror) found between chapters.

What brought us together was our response to the news that the students we were failing most were African American males. We recognized the need for Black male role models in the school, community, and family. But we couldn't meet that job description. Concerned yet undaunted, we believed that good teachers—of any race, class, or gender—could learn to teach all students.

Each of our three phases of awareness helped us see the problem and helped us see how we could change. During Phase One as we tried to "fix the writing," we focused on the text analysis and holistic writing scores. During Phase Two, we tried to "fix the teaching methods" by developing our eight principles and effective lessons to reach our target students. Through the self-reflection of Phase Three, we saw that we must "fix the teacher-student relationships" to effect real change in our classrooms and in our students' writing. Each phase of awareness builds on the others—not rejecting what we learned, but putting it into the big picture.

When presenting our research, we are sometimes asked if we could have saved ourselves a lot of trouble by starting with Phase Three. Did we need to struggle with the text analysis, the writing assessment, or even with the eight principles? We believe that our understanding today, however tentative, could not have come without the whole process of inquiry. Perhaps our story will smooth the journey for other teachers, so they can move more quickly into critical self-reflection. But it was the intensive focus on our kids' writing and their classroom experiences—gained through assessment papers and case studies—that jogged us loose enough from our own cultural assumptions to seek new bonds with our students.

Each of us is striving to create a democratic classroom culture where students of different backgrounds feel safe to grow, where nobody is invisible. The next chapter will show three of our teachers working toward this goal.

NOTES

1. Readers may wonder how much this project costs. Our grant history shows that the annual budget has varied dramatically.

Year One (1987–88): Missouri "Incentives for Excellence"—$14,500

Year Two (1988–89): Missouri continuation grant denied. Project maintained by the Webster Groves School District—$10,500

Year Three (1989–90): Missouri "Incentives for Excellence"—$50,000

Year Four (1990–91): Missouri continuation grant denied. Project maintained by the Webster Groves School District—$11,500

Year Five (1991–92): U. S. Fund for Innovation in Education—$230,000 ($20,000)

Year Six (1992–93): U.S. Fund for Innovation in Education—$216,000 ($20,000)

In 1991, our school district won a large U. S. Department of Education grant aimed at school improvement and dissemination. The Fund for Innovation in Education provided a total of $446,000 to work with two adopting districts for two years; roughly $20,000 per year went to maintain the Webster Groves Action Research Project.

2. For each stack, we made notes in categories we had listed on two record sheets. On one sheet, we described rhetorical features. On the other, we described control of standard English. We looked for patterns rather than scores or statistics.

Our mode of analysis was qualitative. Although we counted specific features (spelling errors, missing standard English verb endings), we also described the many features that could not simply be counted (personal voice, appropriate vocabulary, strong lead).

> *In the tradition of action research, we did not try to eliminate observer bias, but to revise it. The holistic scoring had been blind (scorers did not know race or age), but for this analysis we had to see our variables. At each grade level we compared equal-scoring papers by Black and White writers. . . . Readers built an overall impression of each set of papers. (Zeni and Krater-Thomas 1990, 20)*

3. Most (55 percent) low-scoring African American writers had no more than one such feature of BEV in a page of writing. We also found these BEV features among low-scoring European American writers, though less often (87 percent had no more than one per page). Both groups of writers increased their control of language with each year of school. Since our study excluded all the high-scoring papers, we were convinced that nonstandard usage was not the main problem for our suburban students, Black or White.

4. The five municipalities in this racially and economically diverse school district are Webster Groves, Rock Hill, parts of Shrewsbury, Warson Woods, and Glendale.

5. Almost all the remaining 75 percent of our students are European Americans living within the district. In this part of the Midwest, a "multicultural" classroom usually means Black and White.

6. These principles were derived inductively by discussing the text analysis, teachers' classroom experience, and the literature. The team used the principles as a preliminary plan for the changes they hoped to make in the classroom. Instead of the carefully delineated hypotheses typical of experimental research, the writing project principles were flexible guides to inquiry. In the tradition of cultural anthropology (Malinowski 1961), we entered the field with "foreshadowed problems" rather than "preconceived ideas" (8–9). During the years of the project, the original principles have been expanded, revised, and fleshed out with the insights emerging from the data. The process of inquiry draws on the methods of interpretive ethnography (Hammersley and Atkinson 1983; L. Smith 1979, 1992, 1994), participant observation (McCall and Simmons 1969), and grounded theory building (Glaser and Strauss 1967).

7. Founding members of the team were Webster Groves teachers Nancy Cason, Minnie Phillips, Sandy Tabscott, Gail Taylor, Joan Krater, and Theresa Wojak, with Jane Zeni from the University of Missouri, St. Louis.

8. Action research has become a buzzword in educational circles, but its origins are neither recent nor rooted in the classroom. Sociologist Kurt Lewin coined the term in 1952 to describe a process for improving any social organization through cycles of "planning," "fact finding," and "execution." In the 1970s in England, John Elliott and his associates applied the principles to the work of teachers improving their classroom practices. Still a major voice in the Classroom Action Research Network, Elliott (1991) says that "ethical reflection" rather than "technical rationality" (52) is the heart of action research. See Carr and Kemmis

(1986) for a fuller discussion of classroom action research as a democratic movement for transforming education.

9. At the end of year four, team leader Nancy Cason wrote the synthesis, pulling together the teachers' individual reports, her notes from the week's synthesis meeting, and Jane's notes. Action research is learned by doing, and today several team members would feel confident writing the annual synthesis. However, we still find it useful to have Jane's insider/outsider perspective as we synthesize the year's work.

10. Action Research in Education Award: the 1989 Award of Excellence for the best research in the category of Middle and Junior High School Education. Awarded by the Institute for Educational Research of Glen Ellyn, Illinois.

Close-Up Views

*Treat all of your students as equally as possible
to allow fairness and avoid controversy.*

Advice given to STEPHANIE GAVIN as an undergraduate

A s we began our journey, we tended to look at our target students as a generic group whose individual members were invisible. We focused on their writing scores. We attempted to diagnose writing problems and then prescribe solutions. We didn't realize it at first, but we were in Phases One and Two, Fix the Writing and Fix the Methods.

During the second year, we developed a list of characteristics and behaviors we thought typical of target students—our way then of getting to know more about our students. It was apparent that target students had a variety of stall tactics—sharpening pencils, staring into space, talking with others, tying and retying shoelaces, moving about the room, directing attention to anything except the piece of paper upon which they were to write. We soon came to realize that these could be legitimate stage-setting activities. Professional authors use them; why not inexperienced writers? We watched students who took longer to produce less, who seemed afraid to take risks, and who showed their work to us while asking, "Is this what you wanted?" Our list of characteristics were not all negative. We continued to find rich, colorful, and metaphoric language and a strong voice in the writings of these students, just as the text analyses of the first two summers had found.

We consciously tailored our reactions (our methods) to meet the needs of this target population as we understood them. If a student took longer to produce less, we would adjust our deadlines or conference more often with that student to keep closer tabs on his progress. If a student required praise and teacher encouragement more often than others, we would consciously remember that and perhaps even make a vow to ourselves such as "I will praise Patrice today." When we saw students work diligently on a piece of writing but then lose it, never to take it to its final stage, be absent, or just not turn it in, we arranged storage space and writing folders that remained in the classroom to help these students become organized. And we continued to build on the strengths of the rich language and strong voice by such activities as role playing and devising assignments that would capitalize on those strengths (see Chapter 4).

But even as we generalized these characteristics, we were struck by how dissimilar many of our target students were, an observation that sowed the seeds of Phase Three. Nkwande and Damon are prime examples of two extremes. Nancy wrote,

> Nkwande ambled, no strutted, into the classroom with his jeans barely still on, hanging precariously below the traditional beltline. His left nostril gleamed with a gold ring, which made me wonder how he ever blew his nose. His expensive, new tennis shoes served as a contrast to the low-slung pants and undone belt. He was brand new to the school, yet oozed a huge amount of self-confidence. He bantered with me without disrespect and had a flair for poetry.

Sandy wrote,

> Damon behaved like a displaced person most of the time. He carried his possessions with him in a gym bag and kept them at his side at all times.

He stayed zipped up in his jacket even when the room was warm. He chose a seat as far from me as he could get, was sort of frozen when I came around him. He was only slightly thawed by the end of the year. He had problems with suspensions and absences, so he missed critical instruction, and often didn't make up that work. He never initiated any interaction with me. He interacted only with one person in my class in any significant way, a White punkish person [Sam], also more withdrawn than into the scene.

As the research team talked about Nkwande and Damon, we speculated that the child who strutted into our classrooms rather than the student who resisted interactions and shut the door to others, especially us, would be easier to reach. Sandy wrote,

> But they [Damon and Sam] had an animated exchange when they worked together, so that tells me it was a matter of his [Damon's] trust and comfort level rather than some deep psychological problem. He smiled when I talked to him or teased him or whatever, but seldom verbalized.

Sandy measured initial progress by smiles and occasional eye-to-eye contact—the "slow thaw." Time works against us because rapport between kids like Damon and their teachers develops more slowly if at all. We find that until the "slow thaw" begins, writing improvement goes on hold! Our discussion of Nkwande and Damon marks a major step in our move into Phase Three. We see now that we must first know each child individually and create a safe environment for all children, especially those like Damon. We no longer try to generalize characteristics of target students. Each one has different ways of demonstrating "at riskness."

If we could not depend upon characteristics of target students that applied across the board, then we had to look carefully at the individual student, a unique child. We would like to introduce you to four of these students, and with their introductions you will meet three of the teachers in our project. You will see the dilemmas and mental struggles that both the students and teachers experienced. You will see teacher reflection change from looking at the singular writing to looking at the complete, singular child—home, community, and social life. In order to do this we had to look carefully at our own personal histories in relationship to each of our students.

Gail's story is from the second year of our project. Her persistent efforts to motivate Robert and the rest of her students were rooted in the team's efforts in Phases One and Two. At the same time her reflections foreshadow Phase Three. Minnie's and Stephanie's stories are from later years, when the entire team focused on fixing the relationships.

GAIL AND ROBERT

Gail described Robert in her field notes as "a charming thirteen-year-old." She had been alerted that Robert had difficulties with written expression.

> The tall, slim, African American entered the classroom that September proclaiming, in nonverbal cues, that he had no intention of even attempting the slightest writing project. He studied for tests, but as it became apparent that this was a writing classroom, even those test scores suffered. The little I had seen produced on paper confirmed his difficulty with written expression. More difficult, however, was his defeatist attitude. His mother was a writer, and that didn't help. For this young man whose talk flowed like a turbulent stream, the writing of the simplest sentence seemed almost painful. The words didn't go from the mouth to the paper.

The following is an example of Robert's early writing:

> Yesterday I was in the house sick not real like a pluked nose. I was watching TV Yog bear all of a sutten my mom come in she said come see the snow outside I saw a see from the pocih my brother went in then next then you know my brother seraced and howling it fell in my mother pull him out.

The breakthrough for Robert came serendipitously when Gail was bored and searched for something fresh and different to use with her classes.

Digging through some some books, I had found a "Sketch to Stretch" exercise in *Strategies That Make Sense* [TAWL 1983]. It required the kids to draw what they visualized as they listened to me read a poem. During the ten-minute journal writings, some kids had spent at least five minutes drawing! This would surely appeal to them, but I still had mixed feelings. It sounded terrifying to me, a person who, as I told my giggling seventh graders, "can barely draw a stick person." I made it as nonthreatening as possible and assured them they wouldn't have to share their drawings. I had nearly fainted at a workshop when we (the teachers) were required to put drawings we had done on the wall for all to see. I had feigned an illness and barely escaped with my pride intact. I knew the discomfort this activity could elicit.

Gail wanted no students to experience the panic she had once felt, but she wanted to give them access to a new and perhaps a powerful kind of prewriting.

So she plunged in, watching especially for Robert's reaction. "I read [a Shel Silverstein poem]; he listened . . . I read; he drew." She heard Robert's voice reverberate, "I can do this! I can do this!" while a straight-A student shouted "Wow! Look at Robert's picture!" Gail was relieved and a bit astounded when she heard others saying, "Let's do another one!"

Gail had found an underlying talent in Robert that if used properly might serve as a key to success for him. But then anxiety struck Gail. What would she do with this discovery? How could she use this breakthrough? How could she help Robert use his artistic abilities and his verbal fluency to help him write? These questions foreshadowed the team's later concern with learning styles.

After the drawing exercise, her next step was for her students to choose one of their own sketches and explain, in writing, what they had been "seeing" as she read.

I gave the directions and held my breath. Robert was deep in thought. Then slowly his pencil began forming words under one of the pictures. He was still working when the bell rang. Normally, I would have stopped the class three or four minutes before the bell for that "closure" I so desperately need, but that day I couldn't bring myself to break his concentration.

Gail continued to tap into the power of art for Robert and her other students by showing the face of a woman to spark ideas. This activity (see Gail's lesson in *Hear You, Hear Me!* [Webster Groves Writing Project 1992]) gave Robert an idea for a short story that made both Robert and his teacher proud.

Robert had begun to write. But now came the tedious work of helping him revise. Gail wrote about her conferences with Robert, verbal exchanges that walked him cautiously through the writing process. "Conferencing was something that I had to do constantly. A day didn't pass without him asking me if something was OK . . . I quickly realized that more than one question or direction was overwhelming for Robert. I started suggesting one thing at a time." Gail guided Robert carefully through a process that was broken up into the tiniest steps through a series of conferences. "I felt his trust and desperately tried to keep his ego intact as he made the smallest strides."

The following is Robert's *fourth* draft of a short story. Much revision had already occurred, but he had a lot of work ahead of him.

I was a detective in the 1930 I had run in with a girl name Annabelle an orphan which ,is or was evil , sneaky and a snob ,and she always has a trick up her sleeve. She lived on the outskirts of town.I was on a case when she made a leap in my pocket. I chase her about 5 block I cut her off in a alley suddenly a car pulled up and MACHINE GUN MAC unloaded I dived for her we land on the ground by a wooden fence while medal flow thought the air in to the fence that ended up loking like swell cheese.They left I then turn to her to ask why they were shooting at her and she was going.I decided to go back to the department.when I go there the door was open I knew that I had locked and closed the door.I PULLED MY MAG. out of my holster. And move slowly in to the room . there I found AnnAbelle I asked her how she got in said in a quietly I used a hairpin .There we talked about this why MACHINE GUN MAC wanted to kill her.See she told me she had a top serect form. IT was a key that could open any bank in Brooklyn.Then Ithought they could find her, so we left. When we got tothe street the from a car was shining on us we then made a break.We got seperated,right now I had trouble of my own. MAX THE MALLER was blocking the way.Some how I found myself in an alley.MAX had a chain in his hand which turn to dust.I rusted forward to throw a blow I'd messed him. HE had hit me and knocked me into a trash car I throw it at him and then hand colft him to it. I ran of to save ANNABELLE.I saw Mac pull a gun Ipulled my mag.He shot and then I shot he hit me in the leg I fell he wasn't so lucke he fell into the harbor he was dead when he hit the water,as for MAX he went to jail and as for Annabelle she became my wife & my partern.

Gail and Robert continued their intensive work in recognizing and fixing run-on sentences, spelling errors, and paragraphing. To eliminate run-ons, she asked him to read his paper aloud, to himself and another student with whom he felt comfortable. Orally, he was able to recognize his mistakes. To check spelling, Gail loaded the spell checker into the computer and had a dictionary handy. When those didn't work, Robert called upon his classmates nearby. To instruct in paragraphing (since his paper was without paragraphs), Gail first explained what they were. Then she read the paper aloud and asked Robert to listen carefully. "Can you hear where it needs a break?" He would interrupt the reading with "Oh, that's a new paragraph." He was able to organize similar ideas together—arranging them so that they looked and sounded right. Not error-free, but much improved, the final paper follows:

I was a detective in the 1930's. I had run in with a girl named Annabelle, an orphan. She was evil, sneaky and a snob. She always has a trick up her sleeve. She lived on the outskirts of town. I was on a case when she made a leap in my pocket. I chased her about 5 blocks,. I cut her off in an alley. Suddenly a car pulled up MACHINE GUN MAD unloaded! I dived for her and we landing on the ground by a wooden fence. While medal flew through the air in to the fence that ended looking like swiss cheese. They left I turn to her to ask why they were shooting at her. She was goin. I decided to go back to the department. When I go there the door was open. I knew that I had locked and closed the door.

I PULLED MY MAG, ou of my holster, And moved slowly in to the room. There I found Annabelle. I asked her how she got in said in a quietly way, "I used a hairpin." There we talked about this why MACHINE GUN MAC wanted to kill her. See she told me she had a top secret form. It was a key that could open any bank in Brooklyn. Then I thought they could find her, so we left. When we got to the street the form a car was shining on us we then made a break. We got separated, right now I had trouble of my own.

MAX THE MAULER was blocking the way. Some how I found myself in an alley. MAX had a chain in his hand which turn to dust. I rusted forward to throw a blow. I'd messed him. HE had hit me and knocked me into a trash can I throw it at him and then hand cuffed him to it. I ran of to save ANNABELLE. I saw MAC pull a gun. I pulled my mag. He shot and then I shot he hit me in the leg I fell he wasn't so lucky. He fell into the harbor. He was dead when he hit the water. As for MAX he went to jail and as for Annabelle she became my wife & partner.

Gail recently looked back at this episode, and says it was a breakthrough not only for Robert but for her as well. It showed her the value of understanding the learning style of each student. She knows that not every activity will reach every student and that's why she must have a variety of "tools in her bag of tricks" so she will reach each student. Today she helps students identify their learning styles and their writing processes early in the school year so both they and she will be aware of what works best. She stresses with the students that being "different" is all right; she wants students to be comfortable with their own processes.

Gail's acceptance of Robert's individual learning style (long before the team focused on learning styles) was "the crack in a tightly closed door for Robert."

I realize now that art and drawing are prewriting strategies. Then I thought those kids were wasting their time drawing in their margins. Had I known something about learning styles, my repertoire of prewriting strategies would have included more than clustering and making lists— and Robert probably would have begun writing earlier.

Now as my kids begin a writing assignment, they are comfortable (and so am I) with some kids being in the hall to talk with each other, others drawing, some sitting alone making lists. One student last year drew an entire cartoon strip with talking balloons which led to a two-page paper! I shudder to think that five years ago I would never have allowed him the three days of prewriting it took him to begin that paper.

We look at this case study from early in the project and realize how our collaborative focus has changed. With Gail, we have moved from teachers intent upon looking at students' writing to teachers intent upon getting to know and understand each student, in and out of the classroom. Recognizing and adapting to a student's unique learning style is one aspect of building that all-important relationship. Minnie's story, from year five, reflects this widening of our lens.

MINNIE AND GARY

Working toward her doctorate, Minnie was able to connect a course in qualitative research to what she learned from her target students in the writing project. Minnie exemplifies how we have tried to learn about our students' personal histories, self-perceptions, beliefs, attitudes, influences, and aspirations. For her graduate class Minnie wrote,

> In public schools where cultural and socioeconomic diversity has become the norm, one readily recognizes the categories—"learning disabled," "remedial," "lower track," "low achieving," "culturally deprived," "disruptive," "marginal," and currently "at risk"—denoting a status, condition, or fate rather than an identity. Research data indicate that youths in these categories tend to score below the means on standardized tests, often perform poorly in their classes, and are suspended from school more frequently. The research also reveals that a disproportionate number are poor (whether Black or White), minority, and male.
>
> Often missing from such data is how these youths perceive themselves, who and what they value, where they have been, where they want to go, and where they see themselves going. . . . As their teacher, I wonder how to learn who they are beyond what the school says they are and how to cultivate their individual and intellectual potential.

Minnie saw target students like Gary, a seventeen-year-old sophomore who wanted the American dream. But so often kids like him have been academically defeated in early childhood and they give up on school. According to Gary, he divided his time after school between a sixteen-year-old girlfriend on St. Louis's southside and a few gang friends—the Crips—on the northside. With Minnie, "He talked about going 'down' in the city to get 'down' with his buddies in a maze of adolescent hardness and hipness."

But despite the tough exterior, he revealed his tender, childlike side. "Miz Phillips, I got two babies on the way; what ahm' gon' do?" he asked Minnie in a soft voice while she circled the room, returning papers. That was in February. By the first of April, a miscarriage had solved one of his problems, but the second girlfriend was five months pregnant. Gary sat lost in thought most of that semester. He wrote at the top of a paper, "I worry about my future." He later explained to Minnie that, "I'm kinda down because one of my buddies got popped." As he waited for her reaction, she was torn in her thoughts about how to react. She wrote, "I feel both suckered and befuddled, not knowing how much of Gary's bravado, laced with tenderness, is fact or fiction. Whether real or invented, this welter-weight youth lives two lives."

Gary, like many, struggles to negotiate peers, home, school, and society in general. At best, it is a tedious balancing act. On one hand, "He accepted the conventional place of school and language, yet acted out his lived culture intermittently within the classroom and routinely outside of school." His writing is a balance of "street lingo" and "regular" English.

> His ethnicity remains a subtle yet pervasive strand throughout his texts. . . . Gary's codeshifting (often referred to as a shift of register—the liberal sprinkling of black slang idioms such as "had it going on") brings his cultural identity to the surface. His school writing seems contrived, stiffly presented, and hastily executed, as if to dispense with the extraneous business of school and get back to real, natural living.

Yet Minnie believed that her English classroom could offer Gary the opportunity to make connections personally, culturally, and educationally.

Minnie realized that Gary grasped the here and now. For him, life was what he saw and experienced; it was not what he read or wrote in school. If Minnie could guide him into making connections between reading, writing, and life—between fact and fiction—high school might not be merely a "convenient layover in his rite of passage, but a temporary refuge from the murky outside world."

Gary made connections between his life, *Romeo and Juliet,* and *The Learning Tree* in the following essay.

> William Shakespeare in *Romeo and Juliet* and Gordon Parks in *The Learning Tree* deal with the danger of not controlling one's temper. Marcus and Tybolt both died because they thaught they were tough. Tybolt and Marcus both started a lot of trouble an paid for it in the end.
>
> Tybalt, who always started trouble, learned the hard way that fighting doesn't solve anything. Every time he saw a Montaque he was always ready to fight. The Monteque's really didn't wanna fight but most of them were provoked by Tybolt and therefore started to fight. After Tybolt started the fight and killed Mercutio the person who he least exspected to do something Romeo killed Tybolt.
>
> Marcus in *The Learning Tree* was like Tybolt he also had a temper but Marcus acted more violently than Tybolt did. Marcus also had a family problem. He had no mother; his father was tough and so Marcus also had to act tough. Since Marcus acted tough he ended up in jail for almost killing a man after stealing his apples. After returning from jail Marcus went after New Winger because he belived Newt had him arrested. Chasing Newt with a gun Marcus shot three times at Newt but missed all three times. Then came Sherriff Sweatgland and short Marcus in the back an killed him
>
> As you can see both of these people in my story had a bad problem and because of that problem they both died. The Problem is attitude with a bad attitude you may lead yourself into danger being tough.
> PEACE CUZZ

Gary's form followed the mechanical rules of essays; his connections were apparent; his language seemed to naturally shift from "standard" to "real" language, depending on the context in which it was meant. Most important, he connected with the characters, seeing Marcus, Tybalt, and himself in much the same light—dealing with violence, toughness, and relationships. Minnie had provided the educational opportunity for Gary to cross over and bridge the learning gap. Concluding her case study, Minnie summarized what teachers of writing can do to help students succeed.

> For African American male students, the struggle between acceptance in the white world and affiliation with Black peers in the lived world makes for a frenetic existence. Teachers might help students sort out the confusion by approaching writing as an expression of self and an alternative to speech directed to a variety of audiences. Hence teachers must read, listen, question, and observe closely to understand and help students convey what they want to say.

Minnie felt that for Gary, "the uppermost struggle lies in becoming a man." So, Minnie reassessed her teaching, realizing that

> I'm interested not only in what my students tell me about William Shakespeare, Herman Hesse, Gordon Parks, Maya Angelou, and Langston Hughes, but, ultimately, what they tell me about themselves. . . . I search for who each student is based on who he says he is to discover who I am and what I should be as his teacher.

STEPHANIE, JIMMY, AND MELISSA

Stephanie's case study is three dimensional. It is the story of two African American students, Jimmy and Melissa, and of their White teacher who—like the rest of her teammates—put herself under a microscope to learn how she taught, how she related to kids, and how she might change to be better.

Stephanie came to Hixson Middle School with one-and-a-half-year's experience. She had taught in classrooms with significant numbers of Black students, so she figured she "would teach my Black students as I had before—just as I did the White students. I received some wise advice during my undergraduate days, 'Treat all of your students as equally as possible to allow fairness and avoid controversy.' "

That is the same theory many teachers across the country have sub-scribed to for years. Perhaps a result of the civil rights movement of the 1960s, we once thought it right to see no color difference. Even today many people claim, "I don't see color when I look at a person. I'm color-blind. All people are the same." The research team believes that in theory this works. In reality, it doesn't. People *are* different. As people come in diverse shapes, sizes, interests, and abilities, so do they come in different colors. True respect for the equality of all people comes with the respect and celebration of individual differences. Stephanie changed her theory.

> It sounded good and worked fine until I came to Hixson. Suddenly, I realized that the philosophy of the writing project was different; some students, especially Black males, would need a little individualizing from me to feel comfortable enough to write. And a little (a lot!) of personal-izing along the way could only help.

In her effort to establish rapport with her students, she needed to break down the walls of authoritarianism that she had built in her classroom. Perhaps due to her youth and petite size, her biggest fear was losing control. She wrote, "As Nancie Atwell identified us [new teachers], rather than risk overstimulation, we consciously choose not to stimulate."

Stephanie set out to reach her students by seeking information, training, and the educational tools to help her inspire all kids to learn. She took a major step: the intentional, purposeful incorporation of multicultural litera-ture. Having heard of successes from other teachers, knowing in her heart that kids relate to cultural differences, and having access to over 150 titles with multiple copies of each, Stephanie introduced the literature to herself and her students. (Appendix One describes how many on the team use literature study groups.) And with this literature, we meet Jimmy.

> Jimmy has been difficult for me to personalize with all year, and yet during a conference with his group about *Scorpions,* I learned more about

him than I ever thought I would. Two Black boys and two White boys chose *Scorpions* in Jimmy's class, so an ideal group was created. One conference began with me asking what they thought of Jamal, the main character.

"He's cool!" said Jimmy.

"Do you think he's heading for trouble after joining the gang?" I asked.

"Yep," said a boy.

"I'll bet he'll quit school," said another.

"That would be stupid!" said Jimmy.

I was thrilled with Jimmy's opinion of Jamal quitting school. He's definitely at risk himself, and so it's encouraging that he finds quitting school stupid. It was also super exciting for me to sit with four boys, none of whom are real strong students, and hear them talk so emotionally about a character in a book. They went on to talk about how Jamal was treated unfairly at school just because he was Black (their opinion), and how he was good to his family. Jamal's little sister, Sassy, came up, and they all talked about what a pest she was. I asked if any of them had little sisters, and for about three minutes the focus of the conference turned to Jimmy, who rarely speaks out in class:

"I have three," said Jimmy.

"Three?" said another boy.

"Yeah," said Jimmy, with such a big grin I thought he was going to laugh.

"Are they all your real sisters?" asked Jerry.

Jimmy nodded.

"I have one real sister and one step-sister," said Jerry.

"My sisters all have different dads," said Jimmy.

"I thought you said they were your real sisters," said Jerry.

"They are real . . . to me!"

Those four boys went on to write a skit from a scene in the book and videotape it for the class. It was one of the best projects turned in. Jimmy was especially good as the school bully who beats up Jamal. I showed it to all the classes and he received a lot of positive reinforcement from other students between classes.

Stephanie's field notes reflect the power of personalized learning for students who have perhaps previously been a statistic of low achievement. The power of making connections between literature and the real life that

Minnie described for Gary is repeated here with Jimmy. With one success, one positive moment, the doors were opened for Jimmy to try something more challenging: a script and a videotaped performance.

In order to gather insight into her teaching, Stephanie, like other team members, invited an observer to her classroom. Topics that came to the forefront of Stephanie's reflections were discipline, patience, and tolerance. Later in the year, Stephanie reflected on the change in her tolerance level when she learned Jimmy had lost the book she had loaned him. She contrasts how she might have reacted in the past with her actual response as she recounts the moment when Jimmy told her what had happened.

"Me and some friends was walking home and it started raining so we went to Schnucks [a local supermarket]. When I got there I saw the book was gone and I went back and looked everywere, under the bridge, in the parking lot, but I couldn't find it."

Jimmy was breathless as he spoke, and he looked very scared to me. I thanked him for being honest and told him that the book had cost $2.95, but he only needed to pay $2.50 to replace it. He was noticeably relieved.

I can almost exactly imagine how I would have handled that situation before joining the project. First of all, I'm not sure any student would have had the nerve to be honest with me in a similar situation a couple of years ago. Even if they had, I would have probably lectured the whole class about responsibility and told them how disappointed I was that the first time I let a book out it was lost. As for Jimmy, I would have probably been irritated and cold with him. I would have made a comment like, "Well? What are you going to do about this? I was trying to help you catch up on your reading and look what happened!"

Stephanie's field notes demonstrate the power of self-reflection—not always a pretty picture. However, her honest thought process illustrates the power of a change in teacher attitude and how it affects a relationship both in and out of the classroom.

Melissa was another success story for Stephanie. From Melissa, Stephanie learned the importance of validating and celebrating language variation. After Melissa read Mildred Taylor's *Roll of Thunder, Hear My Cry,* she offered to write a script.

> During study hall one day, she worked all hour writing and leafing through the book, never saying a word to anyone. Her group performed the script for me before school one morning, and Melissa played the main character, Cassie Logan, an eight-year-old girl. The dialect she wrote and used was so strong that the other students had a hard time saying their lines with their faces straight, but Melissa never cracked up.

As Melissa pursued her creation and performance of dialect, Stephanie pursued her understanding of its importance. When she studied *Students' Right to Their Own Language* (Butler 1974), the NCTE position paper, she commented,

> I find it fascinating and true that "educated English" has interfered with honoring a country diverse in heritage and dialects. I've often been guilty of asking students to talk "right"—even in the hallways—if I hear a double negative or an "ain't" here or there. I've quit doing that, aware of the harmlessness involved, as well as the ability of most students to know when and where standard English is necessary.

Melissa continued to employ Black English Vernacular in a number of her pieces, using colorful and realistic dialogue. On an assignment involving childhood memories, Melissa wrote about an argument between her and a close friend in their younger days. Stephanie was excited about the ritual in Melissa's dialogue, a game she had read about called "playing the dozens." Note the contrasting narrative voice in the following excerpt from her story.

> "That's why you can't dress!"
> "Yo mama can't dress, baby! I go to T. J. Max every weekend to get some clothes for yo ugly butt!"
> "Ugly . . . Ugly . . . I'm sorry to disappoint you, but I ain't hardly ugly! My mama told me I was cute just yesterday."
> This conversation went on and on, some of these things neither one of us meant because she liked my mother a lot. I had never met her father and we both sat in the mirror all the time and repeated over and over

how cute we were, so we couldn't have meant any of it. But back to the story.

During a conference, Stephanie asked Melissa what she liked best about her paper. The reply: "The conversation." And why? "Because last time you [Stephanie] said you liked the way I wrote the way people talked, and so I put more in this paper. You said just to let it all out, so I did." Stephanie's encouragement, her recognition of a student's ability and interest, and her method of personalizing provided the groundwork for a bond between them and opened the door to Melissa's creative talents. With all of her case study students, Stephanie was aware of the power of sincere, verbal encouragement.

> I make a daily effort to praise students, especially any at-risk student who appears to lack self-esteem. Gloria Ladson-Billings points out that successful teachers of minority students believe all students can succeed. Even in their scolding, Ladson-Billings observed praise such as, "You're too smart to be doing that." In my last two years of teaching, I have become aware of the power of praise and the results of believing that all students can succeed.

Both Melissa and Jimmy responded positively to praise. However, Stephanie balanced the compliments, guarding against empty praise to students "like Jimmy, who might stop trying if rewarded too easily."

Praise can come in the form of compliments on academics, but while attempting to personalize with students, compliments often move to a more personal nature. For Melissa, an extremely positive response came from Stephanie's admiration of a new hairstyle. Melissa proceeded to tell Stephanie the story of how her aunt had spent hours doing her hair.

Through personalized instruction, Jimmy and Melissa have experienced academic successes that they can build on in the future. Through reflective teaching, Stephanie has learned and grown as a teacher.

> My overall awareness of the needs of Black students and of how, according to Jeff Howard, they lose confidence with every year of school

after fourth grade, has increased my motivation to do everything in my power to help them feel comfortable at school. Until they do, I know I can't improve their writing skills, or any other skills for that matter. I've discovered my power is almost limitless, as long as I'm consistent and sincere. . . . After all, being a nation full of diverse backgrounds is our source of pride, but we don't appear to be meeting everyone's needs. But some of us are sure trying.

In our collaborative attempt to meet the needs of every student, our research team has identified eight principles of education that serve as the basis for our united teaching philosophy. The next eight chapters place each principle under the magnifying glass, looking at the various strategies that we use to implement each principle. We tell how we used to teach and what changes we have made. In the "Looking in the Mirror" sections at the end of each chapter, we reflect on how each principle has affected the way the team members have studied and learned together. The final portion of each chapter offers specific strategies for that principle that all teachers can try in their classrooms.

REFLECTIONS
ON
TEACHING
STRATEGIES

Build on Strengths

I write a lot of things that people today are familiar with. Because 9 out of 10X's if you put a group of "AFRICAN AMERICAN SISTERS" in a tiny little room together and lock the door, they will start to gossip about the latest dirt on EVERYBODY and their family. And "DOG" every "BLACK-MALE" on the face of the earth today. And like I said before, I can relate to the what's going on in todays world, with my form of "BEAUTY-SHOP GOSSIP." . . . I love this kind of writing! It's fun for me to write things that people can laugh at or say "Girl, I know what you mean. (It's people chat.)

KAROL,
tenth-grade portfolio reflection

In conference, most teachers would affirm the energy and vitality that shines through Karol's writing. She still has weaknesses in punctuation and other skills. But if we want to succeed with African American writers—as with any of our writers—we should start by looking at their strengths.

We discovered some of these strengths in the summer of 1987 when we immersed ourselves in reading all the low-scoring papers from the districtwide assessment. We found that Black English Vernacular (BEV), something we identified as a possible cause of the poor performance of our Black writers, rarely appeared on paper. More intriguing, the turned-off attitude we often saw among African American students in our classes was equally rare in these papers. As we read hundreds of writing samples, we were struck by the strong personal voice and frequent sense of audience even on papers with many other weaknesses.

The assessment prompt had asked for a letter advising the principal on the qualities of a good teacher. One African American basic writer ended his letter with "I hope you will agree with me on this if not we can sit down an talk about it." We saw that Black writers often surpassed their White classmates in the ability to set on paper a convincing, informal voice. Here was a strength we could cultivate. Spurred on by this evidence and by our firm belief that all students have something worthwhile to say, we proposed a first principle to guide our teaching: *build on strengths.*

Five years ago, *build on strengths* represented our commitment to grow beyond a deficit model of thinking about African American students. Instead of labeling them "remedial" or "at risk" or "skill deficient," we realized these were writers with a tradition of language power and richness. We would focus on developing in our students the strengths a White middle-class teacher might otherwise miss. As Jawanza Kunjufu (1986) says, "I do not believe you can teach a child you do not understand or respect. Black, Hispanic, and White children are culturally different, but not culturally disadvantaged, unless the definer is culturally arrogant" (14).

In our study sessions, we read the work of African American educators to improve our own knowledge of our students' history, literature, culture, and language—strengths that might be tapped to build competence in English. We quickly identified a variety of oral-language strategies. When we learned that many Black students prefer working with others rather than in isolation, we found a strength to capitalize on through cooperative learning. We saw BEV as a potential strength, as well, a strength giving our students fuller access to the many voices in literature and to the skill of codeshifting between varieties of English when writing for different audiences and purposes (see Chapter 8). Along with cultural strengths, we looked for individual talents. If one of us knew, for example, that Lamont played the saxophone, we had a clue to building a relationship with him and a topic that might engage him in reading and writing.

Over the years, we have learned more ways to draw on the strengths of students who don't identify with the world of school. We realized how school culture typically ignores or devalues the skills African American students bring from their home communities. We recognized that honoring a set of cultural artifacts for a few weeks before getting on with the real business of the curriculum is tokenism. For instance, Black History Month has played an important role in acquainting teachers with the contributions of African Americans, but we believe that this "event" is just a start; our goal must be to open up the culture of the school so that it reflects cultural diversity all year. Today, *build on strengths* means that a sensitivity to our students' varied assets must color our *daily* work in the language classroom.

Our strategies build on oral language, on the multifaceted Black performance culture, and on appreciation for language diversity and African American literature.

BUILD ON ORAL LANGUAGE

How are talking and writing connected? Our strategies are based on the two key premises that (1) oral language is more "basic" than written language and that (2) many low-achieving writers are much more fluent and competent when expressing their ideas orally.

Orality may be viewed as either a limitation or a strength. Walter Ong (1983) calls the written language of urban teenagers "secondary orality," rooted in a literate society but more influenced by media than by books. Orality uses cliche and repetition instead of logic to make a point, which can be a handicap in academic writing. Shirl Gilbert and Geneva Gay (1985) see the same phenomena in a more positive light: "Black students are accomplished verbal performers," skilled in "artistic, dramatic talking, in which nonverbal nuances, the placement of words, and the rhythm of speech are as important to the meaning as the words themselves" (135).

Now consider the oral strengths of African American learners with reference to classic theories of writing. James Britton (1970) sees "good talk" as the foundation and seedbed of "good writing." Moffett (1983) adds that teaching "style, logic, and rhetoric" makes sense only in the "context of somebody-talking-to-somebody-else-about-something" (5), and concludes: "Reading and writing have an oral base," which means "monologue emerges from dialogue" (31). When we build on strengths in oral language, we are actually taking the most natural route to teaching writing for all students.

The Natural Voice

In our classes, we plan lessons highlighting the personal voice. Short stories and personal narratives tend to feature a conversational style. In these forms, our target students produce longer, more-coherent pieces and work harder at revision than in formal exposition. To strengthen imaginative writing, we guide students to become more aware of memories, sensory experiences, and other personal resources. We may ask the class to close their eyes while we talk them through a guided imagery experience to tap a memory. We may have a writer stick a hand in a paper bag containing an apple, a feather, a shell, a cassette tape, and a snapshot, then describe the objects through the sense of touch.

Much as we value the personal voice, we know that *building on strengths* means teaching how to adjust one's voice for different purposes and audiences. Successful writers must be able to shift their voices from personal to public, from spontaneous to edited, and from expressive to informative or persuasive. Good writers also must understand *why* as well as *how* to shift so that the personal is not devalued. Our team has consciously used the personal voice as a bridge to more formal writing (Chapter 11). For example, we use reader-response journals to develop personal reactions to literature before sequencing to a more formal expository essay on the same piece of literature. We also encourage narration, concrete details, and dialogue as techniques within the expository essay—techniques that are transferred from the use of personal voice.

Some teachers question the value of a personal voice in formal exposition. Shouldn't writers learn to handle the traditional academic style, using the third person and exclusively public language? While we agree that students need to master a range of styles, we don't believe that formal exposition must be voiceless. An afternoon's reading of good published essays will show, in most cases, a strong, literate, well-edited but personal voice. As teachers, we need to question our definition of good formal writing. Is our goal the artificial, voiceless style of a bureaucrat?

We believe that the personal voice is *the* strength that is natural to most young writers and must be treasured and developed. The academic world can seize, criticize, and destroy this strength: "Never use *I* in an essay" and "Show your sources, not your opinions." Instead, we try to help writers—both Black and White—stretch their voices to address more formal and public situations.

Interviewing and Oral History

Pairing up students for interviews early in the year builds individual pride as well as community. We may suggest some questions to start the process, such as, What is the most bizarre object you own and why do you own it? Each interviewer takes notes on the partner's responses before they exchange roles. Finally they draft an informal interview and introduce one another to the class with an oral summary. Many target students write longer-than-usual pieces because they have the details for developing the interview at their fingertips. Writing about an interviewee is easier than revealing their own feelings and noteworthy accomplishments, particularly early in the year. At the same time, they get to know a classmate—and inadvertently let us in on the individual strengths through which we may reach a student.

Joan's class first interviews her. To model the problems of interviewing she gives deadpan one-word answers to such questions as "Are you married?" Kids soon learn the skills of asking open-ended and follow-up questions, and they also learn about her stepsons, her newly-finished basement, and her computer conference in Germany. This exchange, early in the school year, helps establish rapport. Next, students pair up to interview each other and write their notes. The final drafts of the interviews are mounted on construction paper silhouettes, matching each paper with the silhouette of the person interviewed. The writer is given credit, but the subject of the interview remains anonymous. Finally the writer reads the paper aloud as other students try to guess the person being described. The "mystery paragraph" builds on oral language, collaboration, and involvement with a real audience. Published on the classroom wall, it becomes a written tribute to each student's uniqueness.

Several of us have built on the experience of interviewing through some form of oral history, sending writers out to collect stories from their home communities. Cathy's students interview older relatives or friends about past holidays and then weave those memories into an original holiday tale. Like Joan, she begins by developing interview questions that call for detailed responses rather than one-word answers. She gives the assignment in early November so that students seeing relatives during Thanksgiving will be able to do their interviews. Cathy was impressed with the work by target students as well as by traditionally successful writers. Students received "wonderful, rich information" and it was "smoothly incorporated into their stories."

Parents have told us of family gatherings where the interview snowballs as everyone chimes in with their memories. Students may receive lengthy handwritten responses from distant relatives, who always express their great pleasure at being asked. The details of a mantel decked with real holly or a gift wrapped in handmade paper find their way into the stories of a new generation. Since the writers have free choice of genre, there are Westerns and science fiction as well as more conventional winter holiday stories. The stories can then be given to those who shared their memories as gifts for Christmas, Hanukkah, or Kwanza. Sandy does a similar project in the spring. Students interview a grandparent and can give the paper as a Mother's Day or Father's Day gift. We consider oral history an invaluable mode of writing. It helps students connect the world of school with the world of family and cultural heritage.

A social studies teammate working with Mary Ann developed a genealogy project that included interviews, oral history, and research at the first-rate St. Louis Library collection. She was very pleased with the project—except for one major flaw. African American students could not find their own family roots beyond a couple of generations since the names were lost in years of slavery and exclusion. Mary Ann made the best of the situation by inviting students to talk about the pain and anger of seeing their people lumped with the livestock in official records. Today we would use a variant for this project with the teacher developing a packet of questions about real families of various backgrounds—those who came over on the early colonial voyages, those who were forced to come, chained in slave ships, and those who came later, bound for Ellis Island, free yet jammed below deck. Students research the names and stories in a library genealogy collection and then write responses, speculating about their own family journey to America. They need not trace their biological roots in order to do genealogy.[1]

Mary Ann chose instead to adapt her project by linking oral history not to genealogy but to literature (see her lesson "Extended Family Interviews" in *Hear You, Hear Me!* [Webster Groves Writing Project 1992]). Her project builds on earlier lessons in short story techniques and "showing" rather than "telling." Students interview a family member and then choose a literary mode for their story, such as a first- or third-person narrative, a diary, a biography, or an autobiography. Some retain the form of the interview.

One student's father spoke about playing as a kid with his older brother and years later losing this brother in Vietnam. The son wrote this into scenes of little brothers wrestling in the living room and talking in bed at night, using typical dialogue. He deftly captured the father as a little boy and also years later as a grown man, poignantly quoting him, describing his face, actions, and mood during the interview as he recalled his brother's death.

Mary Ann has found this a powerfully affirming project.

You keep repeating the family story until the nonessential details drop out and the key points—the literary themes—remain. These are the stories that people are obsessed with. And you know, I think it's Theodore Roethke who says, "You go with your obsession." This is the way families teach their values through oral tradition. Sojourner Truth said it's the strongest kind of teaching.

Speech

Of course, oral language is a legitimate end in itself. Our attitude toward classroom speech has changed as we have become more aware of whole language theory. Literature, speaking, and writing all have intrinsic value and support one another as they develop. Five years ago, we didn't see it that way. Oral language was important as a form of prewriting. Actually, literature often seemed that way too in our early enthusiasm for writing.

Today we validate our students' oral strengths by encouraging "good talk" in such forms as class discussion, debate, book talks, oral sentence combining, daily edits, and other speech activities that don't immediately lead to writing. Oral language is integral to the way we teach writing, literature, and grammar.

Our classroom community is based on language variation. Students talk freely in a style that is comfortable for them, and the teacher widens the repertoire of classroom talk. Sometimes we tell stories from history in informal, adolescent language, and other times we drop polysyllabic words into a class discussion.

CELEBRATE PERFORMANCE
AND LANGUAGE PLAY

African American oral language is rooted in a culture of performance, of verbal playing and displaying. As Gilbert and Gay (1985) explain,

> Conveying messages and meanings is not the only purpose of verbal communication in the context of black culture. Of equal importance is the style of the delivery. . . . In schools, when oral communication is used, its purpose is exclusively utilitarian. As with writing, school culture values directness, precision, and conciseness in speaking over stylistic flair or aesthetic flourish. Thus, there is a dual conflict in communication styles between black culture and school culture: written versus oral and direct versus dramatic. When black students are challenged to demonstrate their achievement in written form, they must first engage in a process of translation from an oral expressive mode to the written form before they can begin the actual task. (135)

In our classrooms, we help students connect their oral creative strengths with the demands of school. We use storytelling, oral interpretation, role playing, improvisation, script reading, memorizing poetry or quotations, "call and response," "lining out," and rap, the tour de force of the African American teenager.

A stress on oral performance fits beautifully with our broad view of curriculum. According to James Moffett (1983), drama should be the foundation of the language arts. His basic skills are "dramatic improvisation, discussion, performing scripts, and monologuing" (89), which lead naturally to writing in the forms of "eyewitness recording and playwriting" (109). We feel confident emphasizing performance with all our students, White and Black.

Storytelling and Oral Interpretation

We build on the power of the story in whole-class sharing and discussion. The electricity generated by telling a story aloud with the attention of a live audience convinces students they don't really have a boring life and can use personal material to write. We encourage them to trust the validity of their own experience and also to draw on their own imagination. Sharing their stories orally before writing often helps later on in the process. After drafting the story, a student will read it aloud and peers will say, "But you left out that really good part—put that in!"

Literature is storytelling. We find that oral language plays a powerful role in appreciating literature. All of us read aloud to our classes, usually from a large collection of multicultural adolescent novels. But we do not limit ourselves to books matched to our students' supposed reading level or maturity; we believe that such literary "tracking" has soured many low achievers on books.

In fact, by listening to a teacher's expressive reading, even middle school students can get a feel for the sound, vocabulary, and sentence structure of adult literature. Mary Ann has read parts of Toni Morrison's *Beloved* to her seventh graders. She comments as she reads, guiding her students through the author's "challenging flashback technique in which she layers the events in time as though in the shifting ground, as one critic suggested, of an archeological dig." Oral interpretation makes quite difficult texts accessible. All of us find that students love to listen to good literature—provided the subject matter grabs their attention.

Carrie, who has taken courses in oral interpretation and storytelling, makes these experiences central to her high school literature classes. Once a week, she begins class by telling a story before inviting students to tell one of their own. Sometimes she models a specific kind of presentation for students to try.

1. Tell a personal experience.

2. Collect a story from a family member.

3. Choose a passage from a novel for oral interpretation.

4. Choose a scene from the *Iliad* or the *Odyssey*. Recast and perform as a script.

5. Memorize a passage of epic poetry and present it dramatically.

Role Playing and Improvisation ·

Improvisation sounded good in theory, but most of us were dubious at the start of our project about using it in our classrooms. Whenever we had tried it, we found that many kids got silly, some had trouble getting into a role, and the whole process seemed very time-consuming relative to what it accomplished.

For us, the key to our change has been learning how to work with groups. Role playing often falls flat if "basic" students are grouped together. We realized that many of our target students had learned to associate real work with dittoes on a desk, so they got silly when asked to describe a character by acting out. This is ironic, because research suggests these are the very students who benefit most from social and cooperative activities and from language that is first generated orally and then written down.

Fortunately, all of our classes at the middle school are heterogeneous, and teachers at the high school deliberately mix their groups to provide some range of skills. In heterogeneous groups, we find that role playing doesn't get out of hand and most students participate fully. They may act out an alternate trial scene for *To Kill a Mockingbird* with judge, jury, and attorneys. When Theresa's class read *Romeo and Juliet,* members of cooperative groups acted out the responses of the characters. Each group was given a situation and asked to brainstorm possible solutions, reach consensus, and present the results of that consensus to the class through improvisation. "To come to consensus, they had to listen to the group members' feelings, which could not be wrong or right. Students became really involved in these scenarios. They argued their points, trying to explain their positions and persuade others to see it their way."

We use role playing to develop specific language and reinforce new vocabulary. Say a teacher asks, "Can you show us 'depressed'?" Natasha then acts out the concept. Others tell how she looks, generating the details she needs for showing rather than telling that a character in her story is depressed. In our high school, district policy requires classes to cover a prescribed list of vocabulary words. Role playing has been a real aid to comprehension. Students in collaborative groups present their assigned word by acting out skits, often using props to create a vivid image.

Theresa has students role-play a teacher while leading the class in review. She has observed more than one target student mimic her style—walking around the room, randomly calling on classmates, praising ("Good answer!"), prompting ("Can you elaborate on that?"), and even confiscating a student's magazine. This imitation happens in an environment where it's safe to try out different roles and voices. Such verbal experiments are fun for all, including kids whose home language is BEV. It's easier to take the risk of "putting on" formal standard English when you already know you can "play" a rapper, a toddler, a grandfather, or a teacher.

Script Reading and Writing

Most of us find that students are attentive audiences for script reading and are patient with peer readers and eager to participate. While some of us began by simply having students read parts from their desks, most of us now invite them to act out the parts, script in hand, at the front of the room. Through readers' theater, Gail gets students involved in dramatic reading without elaborate props or lengthy rehearsals. The lines are not memorized, but they are practiced until the cast can perform them with expression.

When we ask for volunteers, the least-proficient readers often want the biggest roles. Far from being intimidated by reading aloud before their peers, many see the star as the one who gets the long parts. Dale, a very poor reader, volunteered for the role of Tony in *West Side Story*—an experience that had a powerful impact both on his reading fluency and on his self-confidence in class.

For some readers, comprehension seems to improve with reading aloud; for many, reading aloud brings more involvement. Some readers, however, are distracted away from meaning, so we try to observe their individual learning styles. Note that we do not—ever—do "round robin" or "cold" reading. With any oral reading, we follow one rule: don't ask a student to read aloud material that has not already been read silently.

Sandy sometimes writes out a fictional dialogue to introduce the point of her lesson. She assigns parts for students to rehearse. They enjoy such humorous anticipatory sets as this one on "showing" versus "telling"—a skill we stress so often we abbreviate it (SDT).

Milo: What does that poster mean that Mrs. Tab has on the bulletin board: "Don't say the fat lady screamed. Bring her on and let her scream"?

Bruce: Look at the fine print. It says Mark Twain said it. He wrote funny stuff. Maybe it's a joke.

Milo: Yeah, she jokes around a lot. But usually her jokes have a message. This poster probably does, too.

Bruce: I'll bet Barbie-the-bookworm knows what it means. She knows everything. . . . Hey, Barb, I guess you get the message on that poster.

Barb: Certainly. But can I help it if I'm brilliant? You know how Mrs. Tab gets when we write boring words like *nice* and *good* and *walked* and *came?*

Milo: Yeah, she does one of her Godzilla routines—stomps around the room tearing her hair and drooling. . . .

Bruce: Hey, Milo. She loves words like you just used, like *stomped* and *tear* and *drool.* Icky stuff like that.

Milo: So that poster is probably propaganda about stuff like that.

Barb: By Jove, I think he's got it. *Telling* a thing usually only communicates to the left side of the brain . . . well, never mind. You have to *show* it so a reader can experience it with the senses.

Milo: So how would you *show* "The fat lady screamed"?

Barb: Well, think of words that you see, hear, taste, touch, or smell when you think of a fat lady . . . and don't be gross, or I'm ending this conversation!

Milo: I think I'm getting the idea. To show in writing, pick words that appeal to a sense.

Barb: Yes. That way the reader experiences the words with more than just the intellect.

Bruce: Intellect? That word makes me sick. Oh, I mean, it makes me want to barf great gobs of green . . .

Barb: Enough! You got the point!

Our students enjoy script writing as well as script reading. They pair up to write dialogues, sometimes taking turns at a single keyboard in the writing center. They have many options for response to literature, including diaries or letters in the role of a character. One middle school group chose to write and perform a skit placing the characters in their novel on Arsenio Hall's talk show. Another group based their script on scenes from *Flowers for Algernon*.

Performing a script draws on both sides of the brain, using body and hand movements as well as language and intonation to express meaning. For many of our target students, reading parts is a positive way to practice a standard English voice without rejecting the voice of their peer culture.

KNOW THE STYLES
OF BLACK EXPRESSIVE LANGUAGE

Some modes of oral performance are rooted in African American history. During the early years of our project, we focused on the secular tradition of Black oral language—the rapping and rhyming many of our students do whenever they're given a chance. Later, we got to know the strength and potential of the sacred tradition, the language of the Black churches, which our students also love to perform.

Rappin', Woofin', the Dozens, and the African American Male

Most White teachers have at one time or another been handed a list of terms like *the dozens* and admonished to recognize them as games students may use to challenge their authority. If we see African American culture as different rather than deficient, we can choose a more positive response (for a detailed discussion see Smitherman 1977; Kunjufu 1986; Dandy 1991; Lee 1993). Today's verbal games are rooted in very old traditions, rites of passage into Black manhood. *Signifyin'* is a general term for communication filled with metaphor, irony, and artful insult. *Rappin'* is a stylized, flamboyant monologue designed to persuade or impress the listener; it was originally used when a man introduced himself to a woman. *Woofin'* is an aggressive verbal or nonverbal bluff; often misunderstood by White teachers, it is used to avoid a physical fight. *Playin' the dozens* is a verbal dual, and opponents may swap elaborate insults worthy of Cyrano de Bergerac; slurs are often applied to female relatives, especially "yo momma."

We started doing action research about the same time that *rap* became a household word and its tough-sounding lyrics, chanted in rhyme to a strong beat, filled the airwaves. We assigned ourselves time listening to Majic 108, the favorite radio station of St. Louis' Black teenagers. We started noticing in our classrooms that a student who was scribbling with concentration was just as likely to be writing a rap as a note to a classmate or a math assignment. We allowed, even encouraged, rap as an expressive genre for book talks, character sketches, and advertisements. Such projects have become popular with African American males. In fact, when the classroom climate is positive, we find White and Black and male and female rappers whose performances bridge cultural gaps. Our best rappers can spontaneously create intricate rhymes that carry a message, and they can improvise a rapid-fire performance without missing a beat. If a performance goes beyond the bounds of good taste, we stop it, not by punishment or humiliation, but by discussing language appropriate for specific audiences and purposes. We agree with Kunjufu (1986, 41) that we must first show kids that we understand the games and recognize how clever they are before we can set boundaries.

By tapping into these games, we have been able to enjoy the quite remarkable verbal facility of kids who may once have been called language disabled!

> Those African American males who are most adept at rappin', woofin', and playin' the Dozens are least successful in the school setting. Yet, to be successful at these verbal games students must have the same intellectual ability that is needed to become school leaders: quick wit and the ability to capture the attention of an audience with linguistic ingenuity and verbal fluency. (Dandy 1991, 94)

85

We see these verbal games as a potential asset, a cultural strength that can transfer to the classroom. For example, Joan has observed that many of her African American students effortlessly write complicated rhymed verse forms such as limericks. A recent study by Carol Lee (1993), *Signifying as a Scaffold for Literary Interpretation,* found that Black students made rapid progress in understanding such techniques as symbol, metaphor, and irony when their teachers built on their knowledge of their traditional verbal games. Lee argues that "novice African American adolescent readers bring into classrooms a powerful intellectual tool which goes unnoticed, devalued, and untapped" (13). Her "instructional model. . . enabled students who were academically marginal to interpret figuratively dense works of fiction and answer difficult inferential questions of those texts" (135). Our own research has tapped these strengths primarily in students' own imaginative writing rather than in their interpretation of literature by others; we are eager to try some of Carol Lee's strategies.

Memorizing Poetry and Quotations

Early in our research, several of us noticed that Black students tended to do well in performances that required memorization. We didn't know why, but when others on the team shared the same observation, we began to plan lessons using memorized poetry and quotations. Later we learned about the probable roots of this talent.

In traditional African American families, memorizing Bible verses and poetry has long been customary. Minnie explained to her White colleagues that young children are asked to recite and adults praise them ("Look at that baby!") for saying their verses correctly. When they go to school, being asked to memorize and recite feels safe; they know they can succeed. Shirley Brice Heath (1983) found this response among both White and Black children in the rural South.

Several of us have built on this strength. Carrie assigns lists of meaty quotations from literature, history, and the arts—from sources that include many African Americans (see her lesson in *Hear You, Hear Me!* [Webster Groves Writing Project 1992]). She observed that "learning the quotations helped writers improve their papers. . . . Curtis and Tony chose to use the quotations as bases for expository writing whenever they had a chance."

Call and Response

When a Black orator makes a speech, his supporters often interrupt with responses like "You said it, brother," "Yes, that's right," or simply "Amen!" Call and response is a key process in African American expressive style. Originating in Africa, call and response developed into secular work songs as well as the preacher-congregation dialogue of many American churches. Again, this is a pattern we described in our field notes long before we discovered an analysis such as Dandy's (1991), who says, "In call-response, both parties talk and both parties listen. . . . Speakers give one another constant feedback. . . . The only wrong response is no response. There is *no* communication without acknowledgment." She contrasts the middle-class "European world view," which suggests that "one who 'listens' to a speaker does so by sitting quietly, looking at the speaker, and rarely displaying an outward sign or response. It is impolite to talk when someone else is talking" (30). All of us have used call and response in some way in the classroom. Minnie reports,

> After studying a famous sermon in my American Literature class, such as Jonathan Edwards' "Sinners in the Hands of an Angry God" or Martin Luther King's "I Have a Dream," my eleventh graders write and "deliver" a sermon, urging the class "congregation" to respond.

Lining Out

In early American churches, there were no hymn books; few members could even read. People learned the hymns orally from a leader who called out one line at a time and waited for them to repeat it back. "Lining out," a variant of call and response, was used by many communities, including Shaker and African American churches (Hale-Benson 1986, 81–82).

Mary Ann uses lining out to get students involved with short poems, limericks, and puns. She reads a line aloud, like a preacher leading a congregation, and the class repeats the line in chorus. Mary Ann reports that her target students respond especially well, often writing their own words to finish a line in the right rhythm.

New Research on African American Language

We began our action research by analyzing the features of Black student writing in Webster Groves. This analysis, conducted in 1987 and 1988, was published in the *Journal of Basic Writing* (Zeni and Krater-Thomas 1990). A recent study by Geneva Smitherman provides a larger context for what we observed in our text analysis and in our classroom research. After examining 867 samples from the National Assessment of Educational Progress (NAEP), Smitherman's team of teachers found a distinct style of discourse common to many Black writers. Here are the features they identified (1994, 86–87):

Black Expressive Discourse

1. Rhythmic, dramatic, and evocative language.

> EXAMPLE: *"Darkness is like a cage in Black around me, shutting me off from the rest of the world."*

2. References to color/race/ethnicity (that is, when topic does not call for it).

> EXAMPLE: *"I don't get in trouble at school or have any problems with people picking on me. I am nice to every one no matter what color or sex."*

3. The use of proverbs, aphorisms, Biblical verses.

> EXAMPLE: *"People . . . shut me off from the world cause of a mistake, crime, or a sin. . . . Judge not others, for you to will have your day to be judge."*

4. A sermonic tone reminiscent of traditional Black church rhetoric, especially in vocabulary, imagery, metaphor.

EXAMPLE: *"I feel like I'm suffering from being with world. There no lights, food, water, bed and clothes for me to put on. Im fighten, scared of what might happened if no one finds me. But I pray and pray until they do find me."*

5. The use of direct address/conversational tone.

EXAMPLE: *"I think you should use the money for the railroad track. . . . it could fall off the tracks and kill someone on the train And that is very dangerius. Dont you think so. Please change your mind and pick the railroad tracks. For the People safelty O.K." [From letter writing, persuasive task]*

6. Cultural references.

EXAMPLE: *"How about slipping me some chitterlings in tonite."*

7. Ethnolinguistic idioms.

EXAMPLE: *" . . . a fight has broke loose"; "It would run me crazy."*

8. Verbal inventiveness, unique nomenclature.

EXAMPLE: *"[The settlers] were pioneerific";
"[The box] has an eye look-out."*

9. Cultural values/community consciousness.

EXAMPLE: *Expressions of concern for the development of African Americans—for entire community, not just individuals. . . .*

10. Field dependency (personalizing phenomena).

EXAMPLE: *Involvement with and immersion in events and situations and a lack of distance from topics and subjects.*

Smitherman's list echoes other published descriptions of "Black Communications" (Dandy 1991, 12) and of "Africanisms" among Black Americans (Hale-Benson 1986, 16–17). We encountered these studies with an "Ahah!" Outside scholars were explaining what we had seen and heard in our classroom research.

This new work validates our own view as teachers and researchers that a personal voice strengthens writing. Smitherman (1994) says that "Black Expressive discourse *style*" (represented by the ten items listed above) is not the same as "Black English Vernacular *syntax*" (represented by such dialect features as omitted verb endings). BEV syntax ("John work" or "she busy") was penalized on NAEP holistic assessments. On the other hand, writers who used "Black expressive discourse style received higher NAEP scores than those who did not" (94). Clearly some students do master the grammatical forms of Edited American English (EAE) while retaining the strong, expressive voice of their heritage. Smitherman advises teachers to "Capitalize on the strengths of African American cultural discourse: it's a rich reservoir which students can and should tap . . . to produce more powerful, meaningful, and highly rated essays." Then, appropriately, she ends with an African American proverb: "The blacker the berry, the sweeter the juice" (95).

TEACH APPRECIATION OF LANGUAGE DIVERSITY

So how do we bring the sensitive area of dialect into the curriculum? Before the project, we had generally ignored the subject, but as we began working with the principles we had to reconsider. We were eager to use Black literature and oral expressive discourse, but dealing overtly with grammatical inflections was a different matter. We worried about making African American students self-conscious and about the unpredictable response of their White peers.

As teachers, many of us had lived through language battles—from the 1960s, when we were urged to accept all dialects as legitimate, through the 1980s, when accepting any dialect but the prestige standard was considered racist in some circles. Even at the start of our project, we recognized the inherent bond between selfness and language and did not condemn variant forms of English. Most of us held a bidialectal view: there is a "standard" dialect—EAE—which is arbitrary but essential in formal business, education, and social settings. In addition, everyone needs a repertoire of language varieties—registers appropriate to specific audiences and purposes, as well as "nonstandard" dialects like BEV.

We comforted ourselves that most of our African American students, even the least-skilled writers, didn't use a nonstandard dialect in formal papers, and that we could work individually with those who did.

For example, see how Curtis responded to a letter-writing assignment. His audience was his brother in college. He wrote the first draft in BEV—playfully, it seemed. Nancy felt it was quite appropriate to write to his brother in the style of informal speech. But did he have conscious control of his register? She reports,

> In conferencing with Curtis, I asked if he could switch from dialect to standard English. Within five minutes a second draft of his letter was on my desk. Changes made:
>
> | | |
> |---|---|
> | "How's they" | to "How are they?" |
> | "dis" | to "this" |
> | "Yo" | to "Your" |
> | "Nutin" | to "g" ending |
> | "eatin" | to "g" ending |
> | "drinkin" | to "g" ending |
> | "ain't" | to "you're not" |

Nancy concluded that Curtis was bidialectal and wouldn't need special instruction in codeshifting. Because all of us have observed such patterns, our work with language tends to focus on information and appreciation rather than remediation.

Dialect in Literature and Writing

During the first year of the project, about half of us tried at least one lesson dealing directly with regional or social dialects. Today, we all plan classroom experiences to affirm language diversity, but we tend to emphasize variation in register (bank, school dance, basketball court, grocery store) more than variation in dialect (region and culture). Most of this instruction is indirect and in the context of literature and writing. We teach about dialect and register through our familiar concept of voice—dialogue within a narrative, dramatic monologue, point of view, and the verbal trademarks of a literary character. We encourage our writers to use audience and purpose as guides for deciding when they need the more formal, "standard" variety of English.

Nancy designed a whole unit on language variation (see Webster Groves Writing Project 1992) to accompany a play, *The Golden Axe,* in which some characters use Ozark dialect. She approached the subject by presenting some dialects she could model from her own experience (from New York, Hispanic America, and the rural South), and having students demonstrate others they knew, such as Cajun. She felt more comfortable broaching the topic on neutral territory, using dialects that nobody would "own." Students had time to play with language and apply the concepts inductively to their own social groups. Nancy especially wanted to avoid a focus on nonstandard African American usage, which would confirm the stereotypes of some White students that Black people talk funny and everyone else talks right!

Her inductive approach seemed to get across. Both Black and White students spontaneously offered many expressions.

> We heard terms like "He be chillin," laughed at the fact that in St. Louis many of us say "axe" for "ask," "egsactly," "harses," "farty," and "melk." We discussed the fact that I would not say to our principal, if he had made a mistake, "You be chillin." Here entered the idea of standard English and also the awareness of audience. Dialect began to encompass slang as another student cited the language of a Skater [skateboarder]: One does not jump on a board and become "bageesh," which is an odd term for today. I explained correctness in terms of fitting dialect (voice) to audience and purpose. During the lesson, I found that target students responded with strong eye contact with me and chuckling among students. This lesson led into oral practice with irregular and troublesome verbs, including *to be.*

Nancy's goals were language awareness and fluency both in standard English and in the natural voice. Her unit brings together literature, oral interpretation, writing, and language study.

Cathy developed a very successful fairy tale unit that showed the range of the storytelling voice. She expanded her repertoire with folk tales from many cultures, including *Mufaro's Beautiful Daughters,* the *Egyptian Cinderella (Lon Po Po),* and *East of the Sun and West of the Moon.* One White target student wrote his fairy tale in Cajun dialect. Cathy learned that he had family in Louisiana, where he had lived as a young boy. After spending much time revising and reworking his tale (time he had never given before to any piece), Doug brought a copy of his tale to his grandmother as a Christmas present. This project had already been graded when he returned from his winter holiday, but with a new Cajun dictionary in hand, Doug chose to revise some more. Cathy wrote, "The strength of his ability to use the dialect, as well as the wider audience, certainly had a positive effect." The story was published in the team's literary magazine, and Doug made six copies for his relatives in Louisiana.

After this success, an African American student decided to try writing in his conception of pre–Civil War slave dialect. This paper was less success-ful. Cathy thinks he had trouble creating a believable voice because the language of slavery was foreign to a contemporary teenager from the urban midwest. Two students—both Black and female—had better results with their rap fairy tale.

> Gloria [not a target student] and Jan wrote and illustrated the tale as per the regular assignment, but they took it a step further by performing it in front of the class in costume and with other students in key roles. Both Gloria and Jan were beaming with their success with this project. They had worked very hard during class and stayed after school several afternoons to finish the project.

Gloria and Jan sustained the rap for forty-one stanzas, some of which are excerpted here. It began,

> Once upon a time not long ago,
> There lived a little Cinderella who lived life slow.
> She had a nice mother, you know what I mean,
> Until her mother got messed up and left the scene.
> Her father went out and got drunk one night,
> And came home, he had married an ugly sight.

She had three ugly daughters, just like her,
When they came in Cinderella didn't know who they were.

. . . .

She made the dresses and did their hair,
When she ask could she go they did nothing but stare.

They said you're too ugly, they don't want you there,
Check out your clothes and look at your hair.

Later, after the fairy Godmother worked her magic,

They [two evil sisters] scrunched up their noses and were
  ready to fight,
They tucked in their shirts and pulled out a knife.
Cinderella ignored them like a young lady would,
Because she knew they weren't any good.

And after the prince visited with the lost shoe,

The shoe fit without a twitch or slide,
The prince would now have his bride.

The most important way we teach about language variation is by helping students fine-tune their voices when appropriate in their writing. When Sandy asked pairs of students to furnish dialogue for cartoons with cut-off captions, one humorous skit used such expressions as: "Girl, this . . ." and "Yo' mama goin' upside your head. . . ." Joey wrote a detective story with a narrator's hip voice modeled on his own: "A good-looking foxy babe switched in. . . . When she kissed him, he melted like butter on a steamy hot biscuit." Note that the first example uses BEV; in the second, the grammatical forms are standard, but the style is Black expressive discourse. Sometimes writing groups collaborate on a script in which different characters use different registers. Sandy remarked, "It really gets creative when an urban Black writer does Ozark rural and vice versa!" In year six, JoAnne put a stronger emphasis on "dialogue and dialect" as writing skills.

Early in the year, I required all students to use dialogue in a folktale they wrote. Many had to revise to include this. By second semester, dialogue seemed to be a "given" for any fiction written in workshop—and even some nonfiction. African American students usually used dialect in their stories, keeping narrative standard. Leeta commented in her end-of-year portfolio reflection, "I think this is my favorite piece because mainly of the dialect . . . that is what I think hooked my readers." Leeta describes another piece as enjoyable because of the "dialect. Meaning that is the way we talk in our every day language. I tryed very hard to make this my best piece that I have written and I think I accomplished that."

Our students' facility with language is rooted, we believe, in the many voices they hear in the literature we select. Through literature, they see that all groups have members whose usage differs more or less from the standard—including regional, social, and ethnic groups they may not encounter in St. Louis. We point out the language varieties among White characters in such school classics as Steinbeck's *Of Mice and Men*. We also look for variations of register and style among the African American characters in fiction. Minnie, for example, used Gordon Parks' *The Learning Tree* (which is set in a small, racially segregated Kansas town during the 1920s), with kids who had not lived under overt segregation. She observes,

> The realness of setting and family shine through as well as the interweaving of the author's voice, a fourteen-year-old's voice, and the voices of educated and uneducated adults. Several of our class discussions incorporated reading aloud dialogue from the novel—to sustain interest and indicate the character's tone and feelings.

Dialect and Performance

Performing aloud is a great opportunity to show the skillful variation of language. Sandy reports here on a jive version of Cinderella: "Meg, so shy and quiet in class, little bitty voice, blossomed in Fairy Tale Theater. Meg was a *wicked* stepmother, great big voice and uproarious use of dialect. That positive experience transferred. She was noticeably more comfortable in class."

Four African American girls asked Gail if they could write a play and present it in class. "An interesting request," thought Gail, since two of them had not willingly completed an assignment all year. Gail arranged for Aisha, Erika, Sabrina, and Shantel to go to a room in the library with a computer. There they worked every day for two weeks, and according to Gail's drop-in visits and the librarian's assessment, it was a very productive two weeks. All four authors contributed to the dialogue, with the fastest typist trying to keep up. An observer would have thought this was an impromptu play in action. While composing, they moved around the room with sweeping gestures to accentuate the dialogue. The result was a four-page play with three charac-ters and a narrator. Gail reserved the auditorium and gave them two class periods to rehearse. They brought in simple props and blocked their stage movements. When the day finally arrived, the remaining twelve students, all of them White, filed into the auditorium. The show was a hit. The following are two excerpts from their play, *Girl Talk*.

> *Janet:* If she say he is ugly he's ugly.
> *Shont'a:* Baby Demar look better than your man.
> *Janet:* Whatever, my man look ten times better than your man.
> . . . .
> *Candy:* Hey yall look over there. There's a gang of boys.
> *Tayon:* That's all you think about Candy. That's why Demar don't want
>   you now.
> *Shont'a:* I knew he didn't want you in the first place.
> *Candy:* He show don't want you.
> *Tayon:* Don't start that stuff again, yall had enough time to argue last
>   night.

The playwrights had done a good job, and the applause of their classmates validated their use of dialect to create a lifelike scene.

We model and affirm a variety of literary voices. But we generally make performing aloud an option rather than a requirement so that kids do not feel pressured to play a role that makes them uncomfortable. When the climate is supportive, White students can learn from Black peers how to fit their own voices to a role. In year six, when Stephanie was teaching *Raisin in the Sun,* her White students had a hard time reading the dialect aloud and everyone felt awkward. She reports, "Latoya broke the ice by helping out one White boy, Nathan, with his lines. Pretty soon the whole class was relaxed."

Performing aloud in many voices is a powerful learning strategy. But a teacher must be alert and sensitive. There is a fine line between painting a character with dialect and creating an ethnic caricature. Tami, an eighth grader with a beautiful speaking voice, was asked to prepare an Eloise Greenfield poem for oral presentation. Sandy tells here how she affirmed Tami's voice.

> It has music and charm, and one feels soothed and nurtured when she speaks gently to you. When she's angry or upset, she's not at a loss for words to let you know how she feels! One of my strategies was to let her know how much I valued that "voice" when she was able to get it into her writing. She wrote, "Well, let me tell you about my lovely boyfriend, Rodney. He is one sweet person and really built."
>
> Before a minilesson on dialogue-dialect, I brought in "Honey I Love" by Eloise Greenfield, which has the "music" in Tami's voice. In a brief conference, I asked her if she would take it home and work on it to read to the class. She came in after school in a few days to read it to me. Yuck! Very wooden and boring. (Perhaps Tami was attempting to read it as she thought I wanted it read?) But it gave me the chance to explain why I had particularly wanted her to read it, and I modeled my version of her version! Her face beamed when she realized that I truly did value what she could do for the poem. She took it home again, practiced, and read it next day for the class—and two days later for my other three classes. The positive response was another boost to Tami's self-esteem.

One of Sandy's male students prepared a reading of "Stagolee" from Julius Lester's book of African American folktales. The response of students, both Black and White, was so good that word got around the school and several team teachers agreed to dismiss the performer to repeat the telling. There was just one class from which he could not be dismissed. When the English class that met that hour protested that they would miss it, Sandy agreed to try and perform "Stagolee" herself. She reports that students were very appreciative of her attempt at an oral interpretation in a Black expressive style, and there were no negative responses at all. Perhaps this was because they knew that an African American had developed the performance and that Sandy valued it enough to learn it herself; the sequence of events made it impossible to see her oral interpretation as mocking or patronizing.

Of course, not all African American students seize the opportunity to use dialect in their own writing or performing, even when they do passages of dialogue. Perhaps some can't figure out how to transcribe an oral style. Perhaps some have trouble seeing it as legitimate—because past experiences have delegitimized it. But our field notes give many examples of writers spontaneously using African American discourse patterns. Our approach is summed up by Dandy (1991).

> Culturally-sensitive teachers openly teach students to distinguish between dialect renderings and Standard English (SE). Since these teachers are familiar with most of BC's [Black Communications] distinctive features, they can demonstrate to students what they are doing with the language when they speak in their own dialect. These teachers provide ample opportunities for students to communicate in speaking and writing with one another. They set up role-playing situations wherein students have to select the most appropriate language for the situation or audience: formal or informal language, school talk, home talk, or street talk. . . . These teachers provide problem-solving situations in which students must talk through how they would react to peer pressure. . . . They allow students to learn from one another by using cooperative learning. . . . Culturally-sensitive teachers learn to capitalize on cultural strengths. (106)

This is the challenge for teachers: to recognize language variation as a resource for writers rather than as a problem to be fixed. The focus should be on dialects in literature and in oral and written role playing to build bridges to standard usage. First the learner must gain an intuitive feel for the difference between dialect and standard discourse before later analyzing and contrasting their grammatical rules (see Chapter 8).

VALUE AFRICAN AMERICAN CULTURE ALL YEAR

Most of the teachers in our project went to school in an era when "literature," "art," "music," and "history" meant learning the achievements of "dead White males." Few African Americans had been admitted to the literary canon. In retrospect, we feel that the most dangerous thing about our education is that it seemed *normal;* we didn't *see* the bias. Today's teachers have access to textbooks and anthologies that are much more inclusive, yet a recent study of literature in the secondary school (Applebee 1993) concludes that "the changes that have taken place in the curriculum have hardly been sufficient to reflect the multicultural heritage of the United States" (103). The choices are problematical for teachers. When using an anthology, if we don't consciously think about choosing Black literature, we tend to select the pieces we've known and loved since our own school days—and so unconsciously repeat the White-male bias. In fact, the past thirty years have brought little change in the canon actually taught. According to Applebee, "Of the selections teachers reported using, only 21 percent represented works by women, and 16 percent works by nonwhite authors" (193). We monitor our curriculum to be sure that all our students are exposed to African American and other cultural traditions.

When our project began, whole classes were reading a pretty standard range of novels designated for each grade level, which teachers would supplement with their own favorites. A major change came when we began working with literature study groups (see Appendix One and Chapter 10). Today, instead of classics in class sets, the middle school relies on multicultural adolescent novels; we have several copies each of 176 titles. African American literature is not a February crash course. We believe a regular exposure to cultural diversity is imperative in today's classrooms—for White as well as Black students.

Several years ago we discovered Virginia Hamilton's collection of African American folktales, *The People Could Fly,* and the high school purchased one class set to circulate. Teachers have made good use of this anthology. When Chestra decided to try it in a sophomore class with many Black students, she found that White students also enjoyed it. As a final project, groups collaborated to choose, prepare, and present a story. The media specialist

> filmed the groups doing their presentations. Once every group had gone, we watched and critiqued the performances. Students tended to be very positive and also saw areas where they could improve. Jack made the comment that he needed to work on adding emotion to his part. Elizabeth received accolades for giving such an emotional rendition.

Chestra's target students generally experienced much success in this project, which draws on African American heritage, collaborative learning, oral expression, and dramatic performance.

Because our approach is not remedial, we do not limit our selections to easy reading. JoAnne shared with her seventh graders some excerpts from Alice Walker's *In Search of Our Mothers' Gardens*. Normally regarded as adult literature, the text worked well with younger students as a catalyst for writing character sketches with vivid adjectives and figurative language. To make the difficult text accessible, JoAnne read aloud, stopping for questions along the way and clearing up muddles of comprehension. Then students talked about the gifts that earlier generations handed down to them.

> It was no surprise to hear that Matthew's grandfather liked to draw or that Max's was a musician. Vanessa's grandmother helps people. Other grandparents were woodworkers or good cooks. Students who couldn't have bragged about the financial wealth or political power of their ancestors took pride in sharing a different type of wealth and power they had been passed.

An "African American Read-In" sponsored by NCTE is observed throughout metropolitan St. Louis in February. It has proved to be a very popular activity, with ripple effects lasting throughout the year as students continued reading, sharing, and borrowing favorite titles. Cathy checked out from the public library more than thirty titles by Black authors and made them available to her students. She explains, "Even though we have a large number of books written by African Americans, the Read-In allowed a concentration that isn't present in the usual class setting." As Jim wrote in his portfolio, "I really enjoy reading books that have been written by African American authors. I'm not only saying this because I'm African American but I can most of the time relate to what they are writing." Jim's favorite book was *Let the Circle Be Unbroken* because "it was about togetherness of an African American family."

Black poets are also popular, with Langston Hughes a top choice. Various classes study Paul Laurence Dunbar, Nikki Giovanni, Gwendolyn Brooks, and Sterling Brown. We also take seriously such rap poems as "Self Destruction." When given a choice, Black students often (but not always) choose poetry by or about African Americans. Sandy invites students to give a "real, living, breathing" personal response to poetry. She plays tapes of Langston Hughes reading his own work and recordings of other African American authors. Students find the voices motivating. We often discuss *how* the authors read (some with expression, others in monotone).

Discussions of voice in literature also bring to light some negative attitudes toward African American language, perhaps left over from past teaching at home or school. One class of Nancy's didn't relate to Langston Hughes' "Motto," which advises the reader to "Dig and be dug in return"; one student wrote in his journal, "It sounds like the streets." Paul Laurence Dunbar, like Hughes, wrote poetry in standard English and also in the style of Harlem in the 1920s. One eighth grader wrote that he "chose to write in slave's dialect instead of in standard English like we do now." It is interesting that among critics Dunbar's "standard" verse is less widely acclaimed than his dialect poetry. "Sympathy" and "We Wear the Mask" are good examples for discussion of the two styles.

When choosing literature for the classroom, we consider how it will affect students' language attitudes. We look for novels which use Black expressive discourse not as a bit of color in a stereotypical or comic tale but as a technique in serious and skillful literature. Richard Wright is a favorite author among middle school students. Joan has great success with response to "The Kitten," a chapter from *Black Boy* often anthologized in texts for young adolescents. She asks students to assume the role of a minor character and create a new paragraph at a particular point in the story. Writers may choose the mother's, father's, or little brother's point of view.

Before they become the character of their choice, they must fully understand the verbal game Richard played with his father. A few need their peers' comments to understand that Richard baited his father by taking literally his instructions to "kill the damn cat" because its wailing was keeping him awake. After Richard killed the innocent kitten, his father is trapped: he feels he can't punish Richard because he did exactly what he was told to do. But Richard's mother knows he is manipulating and needs to be taught a lesson.

Daniel and his partner captured very effectively the character of the mother, though they had trouble with the verb tense.

I was in the kitchen cooking dinner, standing by the stove stirring a pot of stew with a long wooden spoon. It smelled delicious. I was thinking about Richard and how he killed the cat. I thought about how I was brought up as a Christian and how I brought up Richard the same way. I thought I raised him to obey me and his father and to be respectful to everyone and everything. The way Richard killed that cat made me feel like a failure. Like I hadn't raised him right. I had to show Richard that what he did was wrong. "Quit bothering me, I'm trying to cook dinner," I said to my youngest son. Go in your room." I wanted Richard to know that everything should be respected—alive or not. That everything is God's creatures and they all deserve to live. He had to know that him killing the cat was wrong to do. I know what I'll do. I'll make him bury and have a funeral for the dead cat. Then maybe he'll learn his lesson.

Joan builds on the skills of dialogue, vivid details, and interior monologue in a second assignment following "The Kitten." Students write a
personal narrative dealing with a punishment they themselves have experienced. She suggests topics such as:

A time you got away with something.

A punishment you didn't deserve.

Your most unusual punishment.

Something you chose to do, knowing it was worth the punishment.

Eighth graders get very excited about the topic. Many have written their best
work to this assignment.

When we teach works of fiction, we focus on themes and experiences
first and literary techniques second. Most of us now find ourselves encouraging kids to read strong, issue-oriented books and discuss them critically as
well as personally. Nancy's class had a "megadiscussion on wimpy dads"
after they noticed that many adolescent novels presented family systems
where the mother assumed the power and responsibility as head of the
household. At the high school, too, we have moved toward books that are
mature and realistic in subject matter, books that involve kids in writing about
real issues and problems in their world.

We stress the African American tradition because it has been underrep-
resented in the past. At the same time, we choose our reading lists to involve
all students. Our collection of adolescent literature is intentionally diverse in
mode, gender, age interest, reading level, and ethnicity. Often we group two
or three novels dealing with similar issues from contrasting perspectives—
Black and White, male and female, upper and lower class. Thematic groupings give our kids a mirror of common experiences in which to view more
clearly people who differ from them.

Mary Ann uses thematic pairs when she reads aloud from adult novels.
In her middle school class, she pairs excerpts from Toni Morrison's *Beloved*
(rural Black experience set in slavery times) with selections from Lee Smith's

Fair and Tender Ladies (mountain White experience set in nineteenth-century Virginia). She finds that kids recognize the feelings that transcend differences of culture and language. Sadie, an African American who rides the bus to Webster from the inner city, showed great interest in the dialect used in both novels. She would stop the oral reading to ask the meaning of odd words, and write down unusual phrases such as "fotched on the moon" in *Fair and Tender Ladies*. Sadie identified strongly with Ivy ("Was she a slave, too?") and was stunned to learn that Smith's heroine was White.

African American novels are often selected by White students in literature study groups. JoAnne reports that in one seventh-grade class, a group of five White students chose *Teacup Full of Roses;* in two other classes, the group discussing the book was racially mixed; no group was all-Black. Minnie has observed the same pattern among high school students.

> I've found that culture—as exhibited by style and subject matter in reading and writing—is limited only by the teacher's own vision. We simply need to learn more about other people, especially if language is an extension of culture. For instance, Toni Morrison's *The Bluest Eye* was a favorite of many White students. They understood her tragic character and the rich tapestry of words, images, and sequences Morrison uses to tell Pecola Breedlove's story, and by implication ours, and America's own.

So we work to make our classrooms as well as our curriculum reflect a wider world than that of middle America. One way is to recognize our own cultural baggage and how it can sabotage our efforts to teach students who differ from us in color, class, or gender (or all three). We try to build a classroom community where, for example, a young Black man from an urban housing project doesn't feel like an alien in an integrated suburban school.

We struggle to teach American history and literature accurately, including the African influences that too often seem invisible. Black people have helped to shape American culture since colonial days. We must break the polite silence of the curriculum to say that racism, sexism, and classism have also shaped that culture from the beginning. Claude Steele (1992) explains these omissions as the source of Black "disidentification" with mainstream culture. If we knew only what is taught in our schools, we would not guess that the American tradition has grown from many roots.

> A prime influence of American society on world culture is the music of Black Americans, shaping art forms from rock-and-roll to modern dance. Yet in American schools, from kindergarten through graduate school, these essentially Black influences have barely peripheral status, are largely outside the canon. Thus it is not what is taught but what is not taught . . . [that] keeps Black disidentification on full boil. (77)

It's important for all our students, White and Black, to fill in some cultural gaps and experience a richer, less ethnocentric canon. When Nancy talks about the achievements of Egypt in her social studies class, she shows on the map that Egypt is in Africa, which is a shock to many of our kids. In the same way, she presents the age of exploration through the experiences of the Indians as well as the Europeans. As students see the same events reflected in different mirrors, they gradually become more open to multiple perspectives on their own culture.

LOOKING IN THE MIRROR:
"BUILD ON STRENGTHS" IN THE RESEARCH TEAM

Members of our action research team have learned to build on these same strengths in our own professional community. Our communication is oral and personal and informal in a way that we could hardly have imagined five years ago. We call on one another for feedback to writing, solutions to classroom problems, and the interpretation of stories in our field notes. We talk and we share.

Gradually, we believe our own cultural boundaries have expanded. By learning to see more of the world through the eyes of African Americans—in literature, in the media, and in the classroom—those of us who are White feel less isolated. We feel free to share our own cultures with our students, our roots in Italy or Appalachia, our stories of growing up poor or privileged or female. We also feel free to draw on some features of African American heritage. Perhaps we are beginning to share what W. E. B. Du Bois calls "second sight." He says that Black Americans must of necessity learn to see the world twice—through their home culture and also through the dominant, White culture:

> It is a peculiar sensation, this double-consciousness, this sense of always looking at one's self through the eyes of others, of measuring one's soul by the tape of a world that looks on in amused contempt and pity. One ever feels his twoness—an American, a Negro; two souls, two thoughts, two unreconciled strivings. (Du Bois [1903] 1961, 45)

White teachers are not born with this "double consciousness." But they can choose to acquire some of it, in time, by opening themselves to Black experience. African American teachers are closer to the world of Black adolescents; their choice is to value that world along with the European American tradition of the school. If we want our students to become bicultural, it is our obligation as teachers to make the same attempt.

An episode from our fifth year's synthesis meeting suggests what is happening to the culture of our action research team:

Jane: I think what you're saying gets beyond the secular rapping, into the expressive language of the Black church—like "call and response."
JoAnne: What's that mean?
Sandy: You know how in church you all say "Amen"?
Chorus: Oh, yeah!
[*Sudden recognition followed by collective laughter.*]
Minnie: Come on with it, sister—
Nancy: Hey, who's changing, the kids or us?

The strengths of African American discourse are now familiar to teachers schooled in the literary canon; we have gained access to another culture of reference. In that moment of laughter, we felt a new pride in our personal histories as well as those of our students. Our mirrors were starting to reflect images other than our own. This "second sight" brings us beyond the labels, beyond the "we" versus "them," to our common gift of language.

The change in our cultural perspective shows through the names we have used to represent our project. Compare the title of our first presentation at NCTE with our newest one four years later:

November 1988:

"Suburban Black Student Writing: Text Analysis and Classroom Action Research."

November 1992:

"Deliberation, Collaboration, Celebration, Rejuvenation: A Model of Collaborative Action Research."

From stuffy academic to the expressive mode of African American discourse. "Who's changing?"

WHAT YOU CAN DO

Build on oral language. Remember that speaking is the basic skill of writing. First strengthen the natural voice, then teach editing.

Celebrate performance and language play. Make time for storytelling, oral interpretation, role playing, improvisation, and reading and writing scripts.

Know the styles of Black expressive language. Broaden your own cultural base. Learn the verbal games of Black teenagers and the styles of the traditional Black church.

Teach appreciation of language diversity. Bring regional, ethnic, and social dialects and registers into your curriculum. Most African Americans are more or less bidialectal, needing conscious awareness rather than remediation. Most White students have still less awareness.

Value African American culture in the classroom. Stress African American literature and multicultural experiences all year. Expect growth among White students as well as Black.

Read:

DANDY, EVELYN. 1991. *Black Communications: Breaking Down the Barriers.* Chicago: African American Images.

KUNJUFU, JAWANZA. 1986. *Countering the Conspiracy to Destroy Black Boys.* Vol. 2. Chicago: African American Images.

MOFFETT, JAMES, and B. J. WAGNER. 1992. *Student-Centered Language Arts, K–12.* 4th ed. Portsmouth, NH: Boynton/Cook.

NOTE

1. This genealogy project was developed by Ed Murray, a science teacher, and Ilene Murray, a language arts teacher. Both teach at Brittany Woods Middle School, University City, Missouri, 63130.

Facing the Mirror: Cathy Beck

Katherine Anne Porter once wrote, "I have not much interest in anyone's personal history after the tenth year, not even my own. Whatever one was going to be was all prepared before that." I'm not at all sure that I entirely agree with her sentiment. I have, after all, tried very hard to rid myself of much of my early influence. At the same time, I—like Maya Angelou—recognize that one cannot shake the past entirely. Try as hard as I might, it has lingered to haunt me, though I have been gone from my birthplace for twenty-seven years.

My story is basically one of friendship denied. Like Minnie, I grew up in the rigidly stratified society of a southeast Missouri town proud of roots that extended deeply into the culture of the old South. As eighth and tenth graders annually refought the Civil War in their American history classes, most dinner table conversations mourned the social changes that had occurred since 1865. In the 1960s many residents of my hometown fervently wished that the South would rise again. The old men who sat on the two-foot-high wall surrounding the courthouse and spit their tobacco juice to punctuate their conversations bitterly denounced the advances that African Americans were beginning to make.

As one might expect, race relations were not good. African Americans were governed by a set of rules different from the rest of us—the rules of Jim Crow. They were herded into one section of the town and in no way were they allowed to take full part in society. They were stopped and questioned if they stepped out of the prescribed boundaries. Certain behaviors (like absolute deference to the White folks) were demanded and there was hell to pay for those who didn't comply.

I have vivid memories of incidents and stories revealing racial bigotry: White adults discussing in hushed, heated tones the closing of the Black high school, the integration that would follow, and the resulting destruction of the world as they knew it. The owner of an Arkansas plantation not far down the road who pulled African Americans off trains that were passing through and forced them to work his land; those who tried to leave were shot or beaten to death and buried in mass graves. Four White teenage males with baseball bats—classmates of mine—who circled the drive-in parking lot boasting they were going "nigger bashing" later that night and asking if others wanted in on the fun.

Within this strictly divided social setting, though, I can't remember a time when I wasn't closely connected with African Americans. Although my parents had grown up in areas where prejudice was accepted and even encouraged, they always treated everyone with respect and courtesy. When my brothers and I were young, we had an African American baby-sitter whom I dearly loved. Mary was a rotund woman, and I loved crawling into her lap and getting lost in her folds. No matter what I did, Mary would scoop me up in her arms and let me know that she still thought I was the greatest. My dad picked her up and took her home on the days she stayed with us, and sometimes I'd ride along. Even at that early age, I realized the barriers placed on Blacks. I could see it and feel it on those rides to Mary's.

I attended an all-White elementary school even though *Brown v. the Board of Education* was decided the year I went to first grade. Change came slowly and grudgingly to southeast Missouri. I met Ginny when I went to get my locker assignment in the seventh grade. Neither of us had a partner in mind, so I asked her to share a locker. Ginny agreed and from that moment on we were friends throughout secondary school. Quite a few people had a peculiar attitude toward our relationship, though. You see, Ginny was African American. Whites weren't supposed to share lockers with African Americans. I can't tell you how many times I heard "nigger lover" hurled at me through clenched teeth or curled lips. My parents had always encouraged us to think for ourselves and to set our own course, but I wasn't prepared for the scorn I encountered. Even today I'm amazed at how quickly I became an object of contempt to some because I had crossed over their line of social expectation and acceptability.

My friendship with Ginny taught me a number of things about the society in which I lived. Many of the activities that friends routinely share with one another were denied to us. Ginny couldn't go into the local drugstore for an afterschool soda because Blacks weren't allowed at the soda fountain. On band trips she took sack lunches to eat on the bus because the restaurant owners of smaller Missouri Bootheel towns would certainly not serve her. Ginny and I couldn't go to movies together because Ginny would be required to sit in the balcony. Swimming together was also eliminated; Blacks were allowed to swim at the public pool only on Mondays, after which the pool was thoroughly scrubbed before the Whites resumed their swimming Tuesdays through Sundays. Though we were both of the same denomination, worshipping together in my church was not possible. The deacons refused seating to African Americans and directed them to the Black church of the same denomination. The color of a person's skin decided what one could and could not do. Character didn't seem to matter much.

The local society in which I was reared in the 1960s was the ultimate in hypocrisy. One set of important messages of the 1960s was fairness, doing what's right, and service to others. I took those messages to heart, but they conflicted so much with what I saw and experienced. Where I grew up, these ideals were not to be extended to African Americans. What was fair or right about that and, interestingly, whom was it supposed to serve?

If I was formed, as Katherine Anne Porter said, by the time I was ten, then I know I surely adopted my family's belief in independence and fairness. I know, too, what Maya Angelou means when she says that going back reopens old wounds and brings back old hurts. But today, going back to my hometown hurts most because the social structure that was in place during my youth remains. People *can* change if they wish. They can throw off previous influences, habits, and even societal expectations. Our experience in the writing project has been all about change. Each of us has changed and grown as teachers and as human beings through our participation in the project. Perhaps Katherine Anne Porter should have spent some time with a group like ours!

Use Process Approaches to Writing

I'd have to say that my writing is like a tree.
My writing starts out small, like a seed, and over the years it has grown
to be a very special thing in this world, just for me.

SHERRILL,
grade nine

We began the project feeling secure about one particular principle: we knew how to do *process.*[1] Building on this base, the other principles would change our classroom activities and give our teaching of process a new focus. The process approach would be enhanced but not changed. Little did we know. We used to talk about peer evaluation groups; now we speak of peer response. We used to talk about which assignments were most successful; now we speak of writing workshop. We used to talk about "the" writing process; now we speak of process writing. These distinctions are not mere semantic quibbles. "The" writing process assumes all writers, in all pieces of writing, go through the same stages or steps, albeit recursively at times. Process writing recognizes the uniqueness of each task and each author. "The" writing process typically keeps the class together on a particular writing experience, even if students have much choice as to audience, topic, and purpose. Process writing finds students at different "stages" on any given day.

Many interpretations of process exist; let us describe where we were when the project began. In 1987 we were celebrating our big change from an emphasis on product to an emphasis on process. We were reading Applebee and the NAEP reports and feeling dismayed by their conclusions but good about our own progress. Applebee's 1986 study of secondary schools found

> very few [process-oriented approaches to instruction] in English or any other subject. The typical pattern of instruction was to give an assignment, allow the students to complete it, and then to comment extensively on the students' work. (100)

The NAEP (1980) reported that only 7 percent of the seventeen-year-olds experienced fully process-oriented instruction. By 1986, NAEP found that many students were *talking about* a process approach, but few actually *used* process strategies to work through a paper. The NAEP research team led by Applebee confirmed Applebee's earlier conclusions.

> These findings may suggest that process approaches have been superficial rather than unsuccessful. . . . Simply providing students with exposure to new activities (whether revision exercises, peer response groups, or prewriting sessions) may not be enough to ensure that students learn how to use these skills effectively. Students may need more direct instruction in when and how to use such approaches in their own writing and more practice in actual writing situations. (82)

The distinctions between the ideal process and the extreme product approaches are well known (see Figure 5-1). The product model emphasizes the end result. Teachers dominate the "instruction" by assigning a topic and due date, expecting all writing to occur outside the classroom, collecting a single draft, marking the errors (especially proofreading mistakes), and returning the paper with a final grade. Some product-oriented teachers ask

PRODUCT MODEL	PROCESS MODEL
1. initial task assigned with deadline	1. a number of strategies for getting started
2. a single draft produced	2. numerous drafts
3. models of good writing were literary giants	3. product models include student writing
4. audience was teacher	4. audiences vary: often real
5. evaluation focused on end product	5. evaluation considers growth as well as product
6. mode was typically expository	6. all modes experienced
	7. student receives feedback in process from peers and teacher

FIG. 5-1 *Differences between product and process models.*

students to rewrite the draft that incorporates all the teacher's corrections before assigning a final grade. Comments—brief phrases or a short paragraph at the end of the paper—typically justify that final grade.

The concept of audience is seldom mentioned; everyone knows the teacher is the sole reader. When good writing is modeled, it is through published pieces by professionals whose styles are worthy of imitation. Expository writing is generally the mode (except for the "creative" writing class) with literary analysis and research papers as the most frequent tasks.

The process model, on the other hand, emulates the methods of experienced writers. Students use a number of strategies for getting started (typically called *prewriting*), take it for granted that numerous drafts will be written, communicate with an audience different than the teacher, and practice a number of specific revision techniques. Good writing, both by students and professionals, models the product, and teachers model the process itself as well. Sentence combining and expansion, as well as guided editing, help students gain control of their language. Drafts are tried out on peer groups who practice giving positive and specific feedback. The teacher confers and gives thoughtful responses throughout the process. Students receive credit for the process and typically turn in all their drafts.

Students are encouraged to evaluate their own writing, which may be a literary analysis but may just as likely be a personal narrative, a poem, a piece of fiction, a personal essay, or any other mode.

When our research project began, we felt confident that we had made the change from product to process. We had convinced parents that grammar taught in isolation did not improve writing, introduced the concept of multiple drafts to seventh graders who had been taught to proofread but not to revise, taught prewriting techniques to jaded tenth graders who sometimes resisted right-brain activities such as clustering and drawing, learned that our feedback was more effective on early drafts than on final drafts, and created new lessons focusing on revision techniques.

What we knew of process *teaching* then was rooted in case studies, mostly of White middle-class students (Calkins 1983, 1986; Emig 1971; Graves 1983). A few studies had focused on basic writers (Perl 1979) or Black writers (Fowler 1985), but none that we know have yet examined suburban African American students in grades seven through ten.

When we came together for this project, we confirmed each other's experiences, especially on two concepts: the amount of time needed for the process and the importance of teacher intervention in the process. Later, as we read new research on how African American students learn (Delpit 1986, 1988; Hale-Benson 1988; Ladson-Billings 1990; Siddle-Walker 1992), we realized that these two points were even more crucial for the students we most wanted to reach.

A process approach requires time: time for prewriting (sometimes three and even four class periods on one prewriting activity); time for multiple drafts; and time for peer response. Peer response groups take at least one period, whether they are formally structured for a specific date or occur more spontaneously in the course of a writing workshop. When we began using computers, still more class time was required because most of the actual writing had to be done in the writing center.

But we didn't resent the time. It is part of the process philosophy. Experienced writers don't dash off a piece of writing that is a new or challenging task for them.[2] And every piece of writing is new territory for the inexperienced writer. If experienced writers need the luxury of time, inexperienced writers must have the same "luxury" of letting ideas simmer on the back burner, of attempting a draft only to decide to change topics, of allowing days to pass between drafts so audience problems can be caught more easily.

All of us found that process approaches work best if the teacher intervenes in the process by responding to student drafts prior to the final copies. It seems naive now, but some of us recall taking our students through the "stages" as a class and never looking at a draft prior to the final! Our intervention went beyond responding to students' drafts in process; we were teachers who planned lessons in prewriting, revising, appropriate peer response, and other facets of the process. Hillocks' metanalysis (1986) validated our methods: the "environmental mode" in which teachers play a definite role in structuring classroom activities is more effective for most writers than the "natural process mode," a rather laissez-faire approach of letting students write whatever and whenever, with very little negative feedback from the teacher or peers.

Later in this chapter and in Chapter 8, we show the direct instruction we give on writing skills, the written and verbal response we give to individual students, and the attention to proofreading and mechanics we insist upon for the final draft. The key, however, is to relate the instruction to the writing issues being encountered at the time and to give the feedback during the writing process. Waiting until the final draft for teacher feedback makes it almost meaningless to the student—and especially to the less-confident student.

When we began our study sessions, we weren't surprised to learn that each of us had different strengths in teaching "process." Some of us had a real talent for responding to student writing. Others knew we needed lots of practice before we could ignore spelling errors on a first draft or find qualities worthy of praise in a weak piece of writing. Some of us found it easier than others to learn from our students—to listen rather than talk during conferences, to pull from our students their perceptions of a draft's weaknesses and strengths rather than prescribing solutions to problems we perceived. Some of us used modeling more than others; some emphasized sentence combining more than others. Most of us had problems with peer groups since students didn't always give helpful responses to each other.

We shared our weaknesses in our study sessions and listened to suggestions like "If proofreading errors bug you, go through the paper and note them in what fashion you think best. Then when that's out of your system, read it carefully for its attention to detail or organization or whatever," and "You might want to read this article by Graves that talks about miniconferences and suggests some good specific questions to ask." As we tried out these ideas, we shared the results with the group, getting pats on the back or understanding nods and more ideas.

During the first three or four years, most of us guided our students very carefully through a linear process where the individual student had many options but, in general, the class moved through the process as a class. Many of us used a visual (see Figure 5-2) to introduce or reinforce writing process. Typically the entire class spent a day or two prewriting, a day or two drafting, a day on peer response groups, a couple of days in the writing center to key in and revise a draft, and a day on peer proofreading groups.

As we reflect on our linear approach to process at that time, we realize there were good reasons for it. It was the popular approach assumed in most professional articles on writing process; it fit the constraints of the high school curriculum; and it was easier to schedule the writing center if an entire class used the computers on the same day. We also believe we needed the security of being in control, of directing the class activities. While taking the risks of participating on an action research team and trying new strategies, we needed the structure of teacher-directed activities. Beginning with a linear approach to process seems natural to us.

This teacher-led approach provided structure for our African American students as well as ourselves. We learned in the third year of the project that some researchers assume process teachers have a laissez-faire style. And such

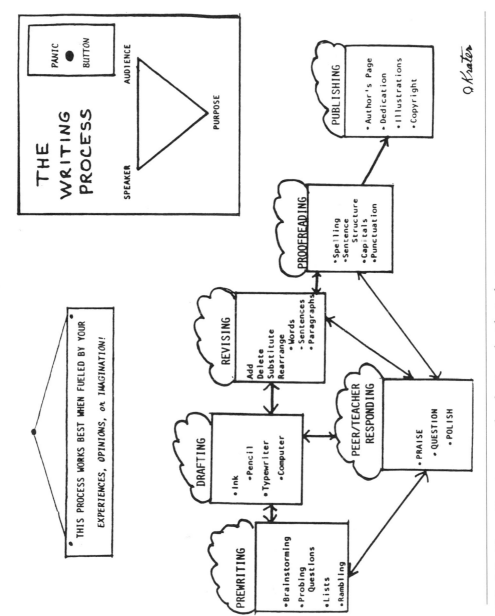

FIG. 5-2   *The writing process—the chart used with students.*

119

a style may not mesh with the expectations of those African American students who value "teachers who are directive and 'in charge' of their classes" (Siddle-Walker 1992, 323). When we moved to the more student-centered writing workshop in year five, we maintained some direct instruction and, probably more important, our attitude. We are still more directive than a sounding board, but we don't dominate the classroom.

We have found five guidelines most critical for our target students in these teacher-guided classrooms. We'll discuss these in turn, then show how they apply to the writing workshop.

- Students should do most of their writing in class, not at home.
- Students must receive credit for the process.
- Students need flexible deadlines.
- Students need process and product models.
- Teachers must give direct instruction in process.

PROVIDE CLASS TIME TO DEVELOP PAPERS

We estimate that our middle school students do 80 percent of their writing in class. At the high school, the amount varies but is typically less than 80 percent because of curriculum requirements and because once the students have internalized the process they are more independent. We believe this first guideline has a different application at the two levels, reflecting the development of the student: students *must* do most of their writing in class in the middle school; students *should* do much writing in class in the high school. This time includes prewriting activities, drafting by hand and at the computer, peer response and conferencing, and guided revision and proof-reading.

When we give assignments, we always begin them in class. It makes sense to allow basic writers to compose mainly in class until they develop confidence. These are the students who often do not do homework. If we expect students to do all their writing at home, they will once more fall between the cracks and fail to learn.

Equally important, students writing in class have access to support from both teacher and peers. Students can clarify ideas by talking and their partner doesn't have to be someone more skilled than they. Talking is particularly important for middle school writers. This support is a central principle of process approaches. Research on cognitive development has shown that learners can perform at a much higher level in a supportive environment with access to help from adults or more skillful peers than they can in isolation. Vygotsky (1978) calls this leap in learning a "zone of proximal development."

Writing in class also allows the teacher to see what sort of composing process each student uses. While we may divide the processes of writing into "stages" for a poster, in the real world the process is continuous and recursive and highly individual. When students write in class, teachers can see who methodically plans a paper and then follows the plan. We can see who dashes off a discovery draft and then revises repeatedly. Then we can reinforce a student's natural composing process, suggest a different approach to a frustrated student, and discourage counterproductive strategies such as premature proofreading.

We often observe seemingly off-task behavior in both Black and White students such as sharpening pencils, stacking paper just so, and arranging erasers and extra pencils on the desktop. Early in Phase Two while we were identifying characteristics of target students so we could fix our methods, we identified these delaying tactics as a form of prewriting—getting the mind in the groove, getting ready to write. We now recognize the likelihood that the stage-setting behaviors of some African American students reflect their performance culture (Gilbert and Gay 1985).

> Stage-setting behaviors may include such activities as looking over the assignment in its entirety; rearranging posture; elaborately checking pencils, paper, and writing space; asking teachers to repeat directions that have just been given; and checking the perceptions of neighboring students. To the Black student, these are necessary maneuvers in preparing

for performance; to the teacher they may appear to be avoidance tactics, inattentiveness, disruptions, or evidence of not being adequately prepared to do the assigned task. (135)

Whether culturally based or not, these actions must be accepted as necessary to the process rather than inhibited by the command to "Get to work!" The students *are* working.

All major writing assignments are done over an extended period of time, some as long as five weeks. Where does this time come from? Cooperative learning, process writing, and reader response journals all take more time than the lecture method. What did we "give up" from our earlier curriculum in order to make time for more writing? The middle school teachers found extra time by eliminating traditional elements of the English classroom (testing, using spelling and grammar texts); both levels gained more time by integrating literature, grammar, and writing.

One traditional element middle school teachers have reduced is formal testing. In the past, every major test over a literature unit, for example, took a minimum of three days: one for review, one for the test itself, one for returning and going over the test. Today we seldom test and opt instead for short quizzes and evaluating students' knowledge and skills through writing in various contexts. For example, personal response journals and group essays on a poem indicate clearly the student's thinking, learning, *and feeling*.

Middle school teachers also eliminated the routine use of spelling texts (see Chapter 8). This freed half a period on Mondays and Wednesdays and the test time on Fridays (high school teachers had not been using a spelling text). Grammar lessons isolated from writing used to claim as much as one-third of our teaching time.

During the first four years of the project, we experienced a temporary loss of emphasis on reading. A more balanced approach evolved through workshop (explained later) wherein students read even more than they did prior to the project. Students at both levels did not read as many literary selections as they had earlier; nor did they spend as long focusing on any one selection. Instead we incorporated more skills (both literary and writing) into a single selection. As Carrie says, we now teach "six skills with one book rather than six books." Content coverage (depth or breadth) is simply not as important to us as it once was. This has not presented a problem at the middle school level, but has led to debates within the department at the high school where course requirements tend to be more restrictive.

Curriculum integration gives us even more time for writing. Much of the teaching of grammar is incorporated in writing activities such as sentence expansion and guided editing; more is accomplished through individual conferences and minilessons (see Chapter 8). Literature and writing become meshed (see Chapter 10); students produce short stories, poems, and essays and have a deeper understanding of them—their structure, their nuances, their limitations—than by passively analyzing other people's work. The emphasis in literature units is no longer on factual recall but on interpreting and making connections. Reader response logs and literature study groups are more effective for these skills than teacher lectures.

GIVE CREDIT FOR PROCESS

It can be a long way from the seed of an idea to a final piece of writing. Student writers are experimenting, thinking, and learning every step of the way. There's a certain fairness that says this work in progress must receive credit. All too often the final product alone doesn't reflect the real effort and learning that were required. Have you ever shared a student's paper with a spouse or a friend, bubbling with excitement about how good it is, only to watch the studied reaction of that person trying to share your enthusiasm? Not knowing where the writer started keeps a reader from appreciating the progress.

Our students learn that the process "counts." We monitor the process carefully: All drafts, editing sheets, brainstorming products, and so on are collected with the final product and credit—whether points, letter grades, or checks—is given for each phase of the process. Mary Ann describes the resulting packet of drafts as a "sandwich," from "first handwritten to last printout. The idea that these stacks are quite thick often encourages the target students that they are really putting out some work!" Now quantity does not equal quality, but collecting all the drafts validates the process. The big sandwich affirms the hours and hours spent on revising more than a two-page final draft does.

Giving credit for process reaffirms the value of working toward a goal, of sticking with a job in order to learn how to do it. Jeff Howard (1990) believes the importance of effort is a crucial message for students: "If you believe in yourself, if you 'think you can,' then you will be able to 'work hard' at what you're trying to learn. And if you really work, if you don't give up, you will learn. You will 'get smart' " (12).

Students typically receive points or an A for completing a prewriting activity, a first draft, a revised draft, and giving peer response. Students often have specific revising activities to complete during the process (for example, finding three places to add concrete, vivid details) and these receive grades on quality as well as for completion.

We also validate all students' efforts—their false starts, unsuccessful drafts, and attempts with new forms. These negative-sounding events are positives. The writer didn't give up after a topic lost its appeal, a draft was going nowhere, or a formal essay didn't flow as smoothly as a personal narrative had. Giving credit for the process encourages the students to take risks and recognizes the value that African American culture places on striving for a goal. "Black students . . . will argue for recognition of their efforts to complete a task, even though they were unsuccessful" (Gilbert and Gay 1985, 134).

KEEP DEADLINES FLEXIBLE

We have noticed that students who score below the mean on the district assessment also typically write fewer words in the same amount of time. We have observed in our classrooms basic writers requiring more time to produce less writing. These patterns may reflect a reluctance to write or a problem getting started, but inexperienced African American writers must sometimes cope with other issues that inhibit their output and production. In some cases codeswitching[3] slows the writer down. "The greater the degree of Black dialect utilized by an individual, the more time is required for that individual to start and complete a writing assignment, generally" (Fowler 1985, 183). Many low-skilled writers also have poor attendance due to absences and suspensions. Stage setting may use up time as well (Gilbert and Gay 1985). Alleesha wrote Joan a note at the bottom of a ten-minute freewrite that produced sixty words: "This took me ten minutes I just culd get the right words for it. I had to think. Sorry [sad face drawn]."

After two full periods of working on their joint book review project, Dwayne and Lawanda had just four sentences written on the computer. Tracy always changed topics two or three times before she found one that sustained her interest; she would not have met deadlines in a traditional classroom. But when target students become involved with an early draft, they are willing to work and work and work on a paper, often sacrificing other activities to get the time they need—staying after school, seeking extra help from the teacher during class time, and working hours at home. Once students are out of sync with the rest of the class, their drafts may not be ready for a scheduled peer response or for a scheduled visit to the computers in the writing center—and target students tend to need more time in the writing center anyway. As Gail observed,

> It takes my target students at least one day longer to produce less than my other students. They have increased the amount they write, which is good. So many times a target student will just sit intently before the computer. When I question him or her, the response is, "I'm thinking." I really feel they are.
>
> On our last assignment in the Writer's Center, my TS [target students] felt they needed to go four times when, in reality, I had signed up for only two times. I was able to send them in three times by doing some creative scheduling. I felt even more time would have improved the clean-up.

125

"Late" is not determined by a date. If a student has been working hard but changing topics, writing a much longer draft than most other students, or making more extensive revisions, then the teacher and student will agree on a new deadline and the paper will be considered "on time."

This willingness to adjust deadlines didn't come easily to all of us. The high school has a policy requiring a penalty for lateness, and Agnes, a ninth-grade teacher, viewed meeting deadlines as an important value to teach students.

> I have difficulty with not believing that the phrase *flexible deadlines* is an oxymoron and I fought this strategy. I believe that the one thing English 9s need is structure and, of course, I provide it. But I learned this year how to bend a bit without compromising me or them. I was up front about my ambiguity on time needed for the first few writing assignments until I could better gauge how much they could work. I set deadlines with a bit of give to them.

Deadlines may also represent a mismatch between a school culture that emphasizes punctuality and the African American culture as described by Gilbert and Gay (1985).

> The learning styles of Black children tend to be relational and field dependent. This means that they tend to function better in cooperative, informal, and loosely structured environments, in which students and teachers work closely together to achieve common goals. . . . The pace of the learning effort is set more by the momentum of the group than by some arbitrarily determined time allocated for the completion of an instructional task. (134)

We have a sense of when deadlines need adjustment because we are involved in the day-to-day progress of our students. When we simply gave an assignment to be completed outside of class, we were unaware of the hurdles involved. Our goal is for students to always experience the process through to an end product.

USE PROCESS AND PRODUCT MODELS
FOR DIRECT INSTRUCTION

Many of the finished products—personal essays, I-Search projects, research papers, nonrhyming poetry, literature response journals—are unfamiliar modes for our students. Pursuing the processes of writing to an acceptable finished product is also an unfamiliar task. Basic and nonbasic writers need to see samples of good papers written on the assignments they attempt; they need to see successful writers in action; they need to see the whole without being overwhelmed. In other words, they need models.

Yet showing a sample essay or even modeling the process by writing with the group is not enough. Direct instruction in prewriting strategies, revising techniques, and editing skills is essential. Inductive teaching has its place, but too much indirection can backfire; one researcher writes, "Teachers turning questions back on students and/or giving suggestions rather than direct instructions could be construed by African American students as efforts to minimize rather than increase their learning" (Siddle-Walker 1992, 323). According to research such as Michelle Foster's, many African American students value teachers who are directive. Teachers who refuse to answer questions completely or fail to explain the material clearly are perceived as keeping secrets, as keeping others from learning. To avoid these negative messages, we use modeling and direct instruction. Models—for both process and product—often are the most helpful for a student. Teacher instruction that focuses on the specifics and the "how to" can be the key for another student. Modeling and direct instruction together are powerful. Modeling without instruction and explanation can be misleading or result in imitation rather than creation. Instruction gives the model a context, emphasizes the significant attributes of the model, and helps the students focus on what the modeling reveals. Instruction without examples is abstract, skeletal, and meaningless to the students. Modeling makes the instruction concrete, fleshed out, and memorable.

Visual aids can help students understand the "steps" in the process. Sandy's eighth graders create class posters, making the process shown on the teacher-developed poster their own (see Figure 5-2).

> Small groups took a process activity and decided how it could be shown in a Polaroid picture. Each group had to present and defend their scene to the whole class before I took the picture. Asking how does it look and how does it sound involved right-brained movement and kinesthetic activity to add other styles to the usual left-brained instruction.
>
> For prewriting, one kid was standing in front of a cluster on the board, another was making a list, and another was staring out the window. For editing, one kid was at the computer and the other was behind her, pointing to a word on the screen.

Students need constant reminding that even skilled adult writers use process approaches, with multiple revisions and drafts. Nancy happened to see her principal toss an old draft of a paper into the waste can. With his permission, she retrieved it immediately and showed her seventh graders Dr. Fredstrom's efforts.

> He was working on the eighth draft of a professional article. [The typed, double-spaced draft] was filled with red, blue, and green marks, arrows, scratchouts, etc. I shared his work with the class. When it was finally done, he shared his finished paper with the class. This demonstrated to all students that no one, not even the principal, writes his best alone, without feedback, without discussion and thought.

These visual aids and modeling of the overall process are helpful. Product models for particular modes help students visualize what they are trying to produce. Using our own writing to serve as a product model can have good results (see Appendix Four). Tenth graders learn they can use an informal tone when they read Beth Ann's response to her own assignment on *To Kill a Mockingbird*. They are to take the point of view of a boy or girl Jem's age visiting a grandparent in Maycomb, Alabama. Writing a letter home, they tell the story of one day in the trial of Tom Robinson and include at least one example of the theme of good versus evil.

The students got a kick out of reading something I had written in an assumed, younger voice. I used nonstandard English and some slang I used as a kid to let them see that such informal English was appropriate in a personal letter. My letter gave them a clear picture of an example of good vs. evil. I think *modeling* the writing was the single most important factor in what proved to be an "aha!" experience. Seeing the example gave students such as Paul permission to free up some juice. The freedom he felt when he was allowed, encouraged, to write with his own language was obvious in his letter.

We often put student writing (from the current or a previous class) on the overhead to model process or product. Usually we call on the whole class to offer feedback; this procedure allows us to model helpful kinds of feedback as well. (Detailed examples of teaching peers to give good responses and feedback arc in Chapter 7.)

The team has discussed the benefits and dangers of modeling. Some writers, especially those with little confidence, may copy a model too closely and fail to make it their own. Cathy and Mary Ann found a solution. When they introduced literature journals with a single model of a response, certain kids saw the model as the "right" answer, following its style, length, and even its content. So teachers now model a whole range of responses and help students examine and discuss the alternatives. With this approach, our target students catch on to the process more fully than with no models or with just one type of model.

When teaching the expository essay, most of us tell students to begin by deciding what they want to say, then develop the body paragraphs with examples, and lastly go back to compose a introduction to "hook" the reader. Often they start drafting with "In this essay I want to write about. . ." This gets the pen (or keys) moving to conquer the blank page (or screen). On a later draft, they cross out the original lead and hunt for something better. Again, we provide specific but varied models. Cathy says, "Think of something personal to connect with your topic," then leads the class to brainstorm examples on the board. Joan asks, "Who is your audience and why should they read this?"—again following with models drawn from the group. We demonstrate effective leads based on questions, quotations, and other models. Carrie offers a handout of six ways to write an introduction with several examples for each way. Once students have a chance to play with writing different leads, they can usually transfer this skill to their own essays. Note too that we avoid giving just a single model. Students need a range of options to help them gain confidence in making their own rhetorical decisions.

Sometimes, however, a single model helps. When an inexperienced writer faces several constraints—distant audience, formal tone, essay mode—reducing the range can be comforting. An essay map provides structure for kids to hold on to as they grapple with the new task. So we do teach the five-paragraph essay. After years of experience with the purely inductive approach advocated by such writing process leaders as Emig (1971), Macrorie (1970), Moffett (1983), and more recently Nancie Atwell (1987), we went back to try the old formula. Sandy did this initially because we had noticed that our higher-skilled writers and readers could usually make the transfer from narration to exposition without explicitly teaching form, but our target students got stuck at this transition. Hoping to improve their performance on the annual writing assessment, Sandy tried teaching her eighth graders the five-paragraph formula. She was so pleased with the results, and with the new confidence of her weakest writers, that most of the middle school teachers followed suit. We have observed that most target students like the security of the formula essay—just as they like formula poetry, from diamonds to raps.

Delpit (1988) argues that students who are not "participants in the culture of power" need skills to help them break the codes.

> Schools must provide [children outside the culture of power] the content that . . . families from a different cultural orientation provided at home. . . . [This means] ensuring that each classroom incorporate strategies appropriate for all the children. . . . (286)
> Teachers do students no service to suggest, even implicitly, that "product" is not important. In this country, students will be judged on their product regardless of the process they utilized to achieve it. And

that product, based as it is on the specific codes of a particular culture, is more readily produced when the directives of how to produce it are made explicit. (287)

Models with structured formulas that help the student understand how those models were produced are essential.

The danger is that students can get hooked on a formula so that they apply it rigidly, without asking whether this is the appropriate form for this paper. Our less-confident students are the most likely to get stuck. At study sessions, we have grappled with the pros and cons of models and formulas. After much discussion, we found that our team was in basic agreement:

1. Models and formulas are helpful to support inexperienced writers as they gain new skills.

2. A formula can easily become a straightjacket, restricting further growth.

3. To minimize this risk, provide options. Discuss *why* a writer might choose a particular form for a particular message.

Once students have a notion of what a final draft will look like, they need help in getting there. Process takes on meaning when students work through a well-sequenced lesson in class. Some teachers begin the year with a paper that incorporates and models the key strategies of the process approach. When working with students who have had no exposure to process, the early activities can be overwhelming. It is only after several different assignments that they can picture the process from start to finish as a total experience. Target students need to be walked step-by-step through the planning, drafting, revising, and editing of actual papers. At each point, they need modeling with direct instruction or one-on-one guidance from teacher or peers. The first time they try a new writing mode or task, they may find it overwhelming to spend much time previewing the whole process. A product model is enough to give them a picture of where the process is going. Then they need to have the process broken down into manageable pieces.

Using *The Simpsons* as a broad topic, JoAnne leads her seventh graders in a prewriting minilesson. The class explores different methods of gathering information, narrowing topics, and organizing ideas.

> Students used brainstorming, freewriting, clustering, analyzing, questioning, outside sources, and lists to make some sense of Bart, Homer, Marge, Lisa, et al. Students had some familiarity with some of these methods, and they seemed to enjoy talking and writing about these characters. They kept the notes in their writing folder to remind them of all the options available as part of prewriting. It was well worth the two class periods used to give everyone this same working information.

Before partners tackle a collaborative book review on a book both have read, Joan's students brainstorm a plan of action. Prior to this planning session, partners have each kept a response journal, reading and responding to each others' journals at four points during their reading. Joan begins the planning session by discussing the assigned audience (other students in the school who will be looking for a book to read in the library) and the assigned purpose (to help students select a book they would enjoy).

As they sit with their notes and response journals on their desks, she urges students to take control of the task by asking, "How would you start right now?" Joan helps them develop a working procedure from their brainstormed list that often includes ideas such as the following:

- Mark with highlighter ideas in our journals that might be used in the review.
- List possible ideas to include.
- Agree with each other which ideas will be included.
- List details/explanation/examples for each idea.
- Start drafting.

After they have used the highlighters and listed their ideas and support but before drafting begins, Joan intervenes again to remind the students of the audience and purpose *and* to model an organizational pattern they find helpful.

Students can learn how to cluster, how to draft, and how to revise by watching us on the overhead do it ourselves or by being part of collaborative clustering, drafting, and revising. Mary Ann describes the impact of her own clustering on her seventh graders.

> Even in November, some target students were still struggling to get a more "global view," but they were willing "to go along" with me. The idea that they would work throughout an extended open-ended time period and work with partners was novel to most of them. And they were also surprised at first when, with an early assignment about a personal experience, I modeled one of my own clusterings on the overhead for them. They soon grew used to the modeling and depended on it to see how the teacher would go about accomplishing the same task. The target students were only briefly silent while I was doing this (compared to the other students), always fascinated and would frequently ask when something unusual appeared on the overhead as I wrote, "Well, what does *that* mean?" or "I know what you're going to say!" getting a kick out of projecting my thoughts.

Whole-class drafting and revising often use an overhead projector linked to a computer via an LCD panel. Nancy uses one to develop "I am . . ." poems. The class comes up with similes first, then deletes the "like" or "as," revising the results into rewarding metaphors (see Nancy's lesson in *Hear You, Hear Me!* [Webster Groves Writing Project 1992]). Nancy also models drafting with the computer and LCD when the class writes collaborative poems and revises them (see Chapter 7).

Many younger students, especially target students, have a knowledge-level understanding of process. Questions such as "Now this is just a draft, right?" suggest a process concept at work. They seem to accept the concept that writing can always be made "better" and will turn in multiple printouts of a paper. But when we closely examine those multiple drafts, we all too often discover their grasp of process writing is superficial. Unfortunately, most of the changes are in mechanics. These students do not effectively plan or revise a paper to work through the process to an edited final copy.

Mark was typical of those knowledge-level students. In the eighth grade he appeared to work through a process. But in an interview after the paper was completed, it was clear he didn't really grasp the reasons behind the various revisions (which Joan had suggested) or the purpose of an ending. He equated revisions with errors and length with quality.

> "What was the most important change in your wrestling paper?" Joan asked.
> "I don't really know."
> "How is your final paper better than your original printout?"
> "It's longer . . . got more details," Mark said.
> "You say you think it will get a C+—why?"
> " 'Cause all the changing I had been doing. . . . I just thought it was going to be not so good 'cause all the changing I had to do . . ., " he said.
> Joan then asked, "Why did you cross out the ending sentence [There are many benefits of wrestling.]?"
> "It just seems like it was small."

Although Mark has obviously heard that "more details" are good and has good instincts about the quality of his original ending sentence, he clearly is not in control of his revision process. His instincts need to be nurtured and his current thinking needs to be built upon so that he can get to the critical thinking level. A first step is to help students distinguish between good and poor writing and to give helpful instruction in those characteristics of good writing.

When we teach writing process, we find direct instruction is needed most in revision techniques. As we read student drafts in progress, we note areas that could benefit from a minilesson. We provide students with the keys of how to make a piece of writing more interesting such as adding dialogue, checking for state-of-being verbs, writing the introduction *after* writing the body, writing two alternate introductions, and considering each of the five senses to come up with more details.

To free students from the bondage of their own first drafts and help them get into the practice of revision, we use Graves' (1979) technique of asking students to write two versions of their introductions and conclusions and then choosing the better one. Julius concluded his first draft of a story about his dog by writing "But I think when he gets older he'll learned how to get around people real well. I still like him because he's our little watch dog."

When Joan asked him to write two more versions of an ending, he came up with these options:

> (1) Benji is now changing out of his visciousness; he's now getting along with our neighbors and I'm proud of him for that.
> (2) Our friends and neighbors is not afraid of Benji anymore soon they found out that he's trying to get along with them; everybody including me is proud of Benji's new attitude without being viscious toward them, but he's still our watchdog, and I'm proud of him.

Julius chose the third version (with some proofreading changes) for his final draft, probably because it combines the ideas of the other two.

Direct instruction in revision is most effective when it focuses on one problem at a time such as specific and concrete details, wordiness, or strong verbs. During a "show, don't tell" lesson, Joan's eighth graders share with each other what they see when they read, "My father was a slob." Five o'clock shadows and stained and mismatched clothes head the list, but there are at times disagreements. "No, no, he's not fat, just sloppy." She then projects the description from Richard Wright's excerpt known as "The Kitten" (see Chapter 4). "His huge body sat clumped at the table. . . . he gulped his beer, . . . sighed, and belched. . . . His bloated stomach lapped over his belt" (Wright 1989, 16–17).

If specific details are the focus of the lesson, the class discusses how Wright's images differ from their own and how his selected details help all readers to see Wright's vision of his father. If word choice is the objective, then Joan asks students to compare Wright's version with her attempt: "He sat at the table. He drank his beer and burped. His tummy stuck out over his belt."

The infantile connotations of *burped* and *tummy* are picked up immediately; the nuances of *lapped* and *stuck out* are not as obvious. Which one suggests more weight? rolls of fat? The two words *clumped* and *bloated* are the most fun (once the students are finished making various burping sounds). Many students aren't familiar with the word *bloated* until they hear it in a more familiar context such as "bloated fish." The connotations of death and swollen to the point of exploding bring new life to their interpretations of Wright's brief description.

The students immediately take the sentence "I'm scared" and write three or four sentences showing details with vivid verbs. They exchange descriptions with their study buddies who underline action verbs and circle their favorite details. The study buddies volunteer to read aloud from their partner's work, not their own. This lesson successfully combines process writing, revising, cooperative learning, and private and public praise.

Students enjoy reading the story and comparing their versions with Wright's.

> I stumbled out into the black night, sobbing, my legs wobbly from fear. . . . What would that kitten do to me when I touched it? Would it claw at my eyes? . . . Shuddering, I fumbled at the rope . . . as I handled the kitten's cold body my skin prickled. (20)

Since the context of Wright's sentences is so specific, students' paragraphs are never similar, so their writing is not put up against a professional's.

Middle school students get involved with such tasks, particularly when the subject matter invites gross details. Knowing involvement is a key principle, Stephanie wrote a story in a "blatantly teenage style"—something she would have hesitated to do prior to the project.

In the story, the girl "opened the door and got sick in the grass." Well—this is where all of my classes went crazy! First, I asked if she would just "open" a car door if she was going to be sick. Immediately, better verbs were shouted out—threw open, fumbled, slammed, flung, etc. Then I asked if we could show the reader the woman getting sick by using vivid verbs. They came up with retched, heaved, choked, spewed, vomited, hurled, gasped, spit, sputtered—the list was endless. As the day progressed, I could tell that students had heard about the activity from earlier classes—always a sign of success, I think, if they leave my class still thinking and talking about whatever we've done. I noticed the boys got into the assignment more than girls. The girls giggled and acted as if it were too gross to contribute.

The direct instruction and modeling are essential, but giving the students time to apply what they've learned must be part and parcel of direct instruction. Teaching vivid verbs will fall flat if students don't immediately revise dull state-of-being verbs in one of their own papers.

As we walk students through the processes of writing, we are developing a classroom writing community with shared experiences and understandings. Nancy makes exaggerated faces when she hears trite words like "nice." Soon her seventh graders are scrunching up their faces in response to bland diction. Within the classroom, process becomes a tradition, something dependable and consistent, like a family ritual or game. More than by abstract knowledge, students come to understand—and command—the process approaches to writing.

USING PROCESS IN WRITING/READING WORKSHOP

This community of writers evolved into a writing/reading workshop at the middle school during the fifth year when we were in Phase Three. The emphasis on fixing the methods and how process was taught changed to a focus on the individual student. As early as 1988, Sandy took what the rest of us perceived as a great risk in giving students control over their reading and writing processes. She devoted a semester to a workshop patterned after Atwell's *In the Middle* (1987). Sandy planned two days each week for reading and three for writing, interspersing ten-minute minilessons as needed. She wrote afterward that "The choices in workshop were powerful for getting kids involved with topics and modes with which they were comfortable." Sandy ended that year exhilarated, exhausted, and ready to start workshop at the beginning of the next year.

But in the process of change, all does not run smoothly. The following year, Sandy began workshop much earlier. She also had surgery that year. As we speculated on why she found workshop less successful and actually moved back temporarily to a more traditional classroom design (she "got back behind the big desk"), we realized that some ingredients were missing, the absence of which undermined workshop's success. Energy, stamina, and knowing students well were a necessity, and they were missing when Sandy began workshop early in that second attempt.

This story reveals two of the greatest benefits we have found in action research: if we were not sure why a strategy we tried did not work, our collaborative team would talk us through a thought process that eventually might show us the way. Just as important, we realized if something did not work, we could change it. As Sandy identified the reasons why the second year of workshop was less successful and as we shared in her speculations, we learned what to do and what not to do. We did not abandon the idea, but we were apprehensive. It was a big step—another total revamping of the curriculum and our approach to process. JoAnne spoke for all of us in her synthesis of year five.

> Having read and reread Atwell's *In the Middle* for about four years, I finally quit "toe-testing" the waters of reading/writing workshop and completely immersed myself and classes throughout second semester this year. At different times we flailed and floundered, treaded water, floated, and on occasion, even swam with ease and grace. After all that, I won't say we were always closer to water ballet than to dog paddling, but at least we stayed afloat and made progress.

We found practical help in Atwell's book, especially on how to begin and organize workshop. We envy Nancie Atwell's access to a daily double period for reading and writing. Our middle school periods average forty-three minutes.

Stephanie started writing workshop with her eighth graders this way with a topic search almost exactly the way Atwell describes it in *In the Middle*.

> I began by telling the students all of the topics I had thought of just by what had happened to me in the last 24 hours. The examples I gave them were: Advice for the parents-to-be; Why I lived in the city; Why I don't think *Their Eyes Were Watching God* is a feminist novel; Comparing/contrasting Bill Clinton to George Bush; My subway ride to Yankee Stadium in New York; A description of my cat, Anastasia; College spring break—getting stranded in Kansas in a snowstorm on the way to Colorado.
>
> Since writing a nonfiction paper was going to be one of their requirements, I tried to focus on nonfiction topics. After I went through my commentary of all the above topics and why I thought of them (driving to school in the snow on Grand made me think of city living and my college spring break; Anastasia had begged for the milk from my cereal that morning; KMOX news listed the results of a presidential primary and talked about spring training for baseball results; I had read *Their Eyes* for my class at UMSL and we had discussed it the night before), I gave them a few minutes to jot down ideas of their own.
>
> A few minutes for jotting down ideas, a few more for sharing with someone nearby, and then volunteers gave topics aloud. By the end of each hour I had an incredible list of topic ideas ranging from the environment to squirrel hunting to how to make people laugh. When the bell rang, I actually heard moans because the students were so eager to begin writing! Like a lot of my so-called minilessons, that one lasted all hour.

Stephanie never heard "I don't have anything to write about" the rest of the year.

All of the teachers using workshop set their own expectations. Cathy, for example, establishes "external criteria" based on Linda Rief's *Seeking Diversity: Language Arts with Adolescents* (1992).

three to five pages of rough-draft writing per week (called *text pages*)

one polished piece per six-week period

writing should be done in different modes

read at least thirty minutes per night

read different genres

maintain a reading response journal

participate in one literature study group

conference with Cathy weekly

establish own goals for reading/writing improvement

maintain an in-class file of all writing

Initiating workshop did not go smoothly for all, however. A new problem emerged when Nancy's eighth graders suddenly turned to her again for all feedback, finding their classmates engrossed in other activities. Nancy was surrounded by impatient students, causing her to describe workshop as Collaborative Classroom Chaos.

> Andrew has tried an essay about how to be a teen radio announcer, a poem, and a letter from a boy who is contemplating suicide; Kelly is writing a short story about a boy and his guardian angel. She's stuck. After conferencing with me, she seems to have found another focus. Julie is writing a modern day *Little Red Riding Hood*. Jill is searching in the library for the "real" version of the "The Princess and the Pea"; John is responding to an essay on pollution by Michelle; and five kids are in the writing center! *Help!* And each one of them wants to talk to me, *now!* Conferences continued all hour; students hovered over me. They didn't want to disturb each other! If I can learn to manage this, we'll be all right. . . . I'm seeing more active learning now than in years.

Nancy installed a new rule: "Mrs. Cason will read no paper unless I see written feedback by at least one other student *and* both responder and writer join me in a conference about the piece."

Establishing routines such as Nancy's helped all of us. We expected the ˜nosphere to be busy and somewhat noisy with students taking time to settle down to work, forming spontaneous response groups, feeling their freedom. Actually, once the rough spots are worked out, workshop is surprisingly quiet. Many students are out of the room in the writing center or the library, and those in the classroom may be working collaboratively but are intently involved. Each teacher uses a checksheet to track the students' use of time. Within three to five minutes, roll is called and each student states his plan for the day: research, drafting, revising, writing center, reading, reading response, peer response, conferring.

We incorporate a workshop approach in our classrooms at different times of the year. In some cases, we might begin workshop on the first day of classes or by November or in other cases by midyear. The choice is up to the teacher. It is imperative that the mood is right—that rapport, trust, and confidence are the focus, and that students understand workshop and teacher expectations. We must each establish our own method of management. Students must understand their role in accountability and that their tasks must be internalized. Perhaps most importantly, the teacher must feel energized and strong.

Students receive more individual attention in workshop than ever before. Delpit (1986, 1988), Siddle-Walker (1992), and others have raised the question of the appropriateness of workshop for African American students, fearing they will slip through the cracks with all the hubbub. It undoubtedly makes a difference that we started workshop *after* four years of intensive efforts to attend to basic writers, particularly African American males. We have never lost that focus, even when we expanded our project to all low-scoring writers. For example, Cathy collects the weekly text pages from all her students during workshop and checks every student's work by skimming but *reads* the text writing of all target students. Every teacher tracks every kid, asking the librarian and writing center aide for their observations, conferring with each student at least weekly and typically two to three times a week. Some target students get daily conferences!

Minilessons provide the direct instruction during workshop. We are learning to explain the difference between active and passive voice, to show the effectiveness of vivid verbs, to contrast two methods of combining kernel sentences, or to read an example of a narrative poem in five or ten minutes. Just eliminating the traditional question-and-answer pattern saves lots of time. A true minilesson delays—not replaces—our interaction with the students until we can talk one-on-one. We have all found, however, that too many minilessons end up taking the entire period. When students have lots of questions on a daily edit or want to share every version of a sentence-expansion task or connect to a poem with personal experiences, then we capitalize on their interest and ignore the breakdown of the "mini" concept!

Ironically, we find in the reading writing workshop that once again students are reading as much or even more than they had been reading in the years preceding process writing. When we break the lockstep of everyone reading the same story or novel for class activities and discussion and students read their own selections at their own pace, they read far more than we had ever required. The reading/writing connection is much more balanced. Before workshop, literature often served as a prompt for writing. Now literature is often its own reward, as it should be.

The biggest plus of workshop is the students' freedom to choose topics (see Chapter 10). The students write about what is important to them and explore areas that they are truly interested in. They enjoy having control over their own learning. They work at their own pace. Some finish long before the deadlines, others finish just in the nick of time, and still others need extensions due to problems encountered in research.

During that fifth year, all seven middle school teachers used reading/writing workshop for at least twelve weeks of the year. The high school teachers listened intently, questioned, and absorbed. Most of their target students were in homogeneous groups and many of our efforts do not work as well in that setting. But year seven will find heterogeneous grouping in most of the high school English classes. This could bring about many changes, perhaps even a reading/writing workshop.

During the synthesis discussion in the summer of 1993, Jane listened "to the diversity of classroom life that was subsumed under the heading 'workshop' [and] got the sense that it was less a 'method' than an approach." Team members had developed quite diverse ways of interpreting and implementing a workshop environment. We found it very helpful to see these differences, to realize that "workshop" was not some monolithic structure that had to be done exactly as Nancie Atwell describes it. As Sandy says, "Workshop is the setting that allows me to work the principles most effectively."

CLASSROOM EVALUATION AND PUBLICATION

Professional writers evaluate their own work (Is this good enough to submit?), receive an editor's evaluation (Is this good enough to publish?), and have the pleasure of seeing their work in print, reaching an audience that sometimes lets the writer know what they think of her ideas.

Student writers need to learn how to evaluate their own writing (Is this as good as I can make it?). Peers give feedback but do not evaluate; teachers give feedback and *must* evaluate. Student writers also must reach audiences outside the classroom—must be "published," at least informally. Chapter 10 describes ways we publish student efforts, from class books read by future classes to book reviews hung in the library to letters to the editors of local newspapers. The wider audience can validate a student writer's efforts in a way that a teacher's evaluation, however supportive, cannot.

We evaluate our students' products developmentally. In other words, we are very much aware of how much they have improved. We compare the final draft—the product—to the first draft rather than to published writing or external standards. We give credit for growth as well as achievement.

During the fifth year, the research team piloted portfolio assessment, with each of us trying a different approach so we could compare procedures and results. We brainstormed some possible criteria to guide students as they select pieces for their portfolios:

> most and least satisfying
>
> example of writing from a class other than English
>
> piece from early in the year that best represents where you began the year
>
> two of best examples of responses to reading
>
> a piece of new writing
>
> revise an earlier piece of writing
>
> a piece you found most challenging
>
> your choice ("wild card")

The power of having this control over the evaluation of one's own writing is described in Chapter 10.

Each student wrote a letter to the teacher, and some also answered specific questions. Suggested topics and required questions included:

> What does one have to do in order to be a good writer?
>
> What is the easiest/hardest part of writing for you to do?
>
> How do you go about choosing books to read?
>
> Are there similarities in your different pieces of writing? Explain.
>
> Explain the reasons for selecting a piece to revise and the specific changes you made.
>
> What does a selected piece reveal about you as a writer? as a person?
>
> How do you come up with ideas for writing?
>
> Did you reach any roadblocks or problems? What did you do?
>
> Were you ever surprised by what you wrote or how you wrote it?
>
> Do you have any writing rituals or routines?
>
> In the past year, how have you changed or grown as a reader? How is this shown in your reading responses?

Tenth graders in Minnie's class chose an earlier piece of writing that was "representative of their writing" to revise again. They then explained in a reflection the reasons for their selection, the changes they made, and what the piece showed about them as writers and as persons.

Ninth graders created portfolios at the end of each semester, selecting four pieces: one they liked, one they didn't like, something from a class other than English, and something that had never been graded. They also wrote a letter "explaining the contents of the portfolio." After the first semester Chestra learned to be more specific about the letter. In May she asked, "Why is each piece included, how did you go about creating the piece, and what did you discover about yourself as a writer and/or a person by writing this piece?"

Most eighth graders selected six pieces of writing and answered a set of questions about themselves as writers and readers such as, "What does one have to do in order to be a good writer? How do you come up with ideas for writing? What is the easiest/hardest part of writing/reading for you?" Their portfolios included the process piece, a response to literature, a "wild card" (student's choice), the most satisfying piece, and the least satisfying piece. Cathy's students wrote reflective pieces about each choice plus a reflection about the portfolio process.

JoAnne helped her seventh graders begin to reflect on themselves as writers by focusing on one piece of writing at a time. Her questions included, "Did you sit down and write all at once or in spurts? Did you have enough help to begin and sustain your writing? Did you reach any roadblocks or problems? Who helped you with revision and how?"

The process of reflection needs instruction, modeling, and practice, just as the process of writing does. At various times during the year students wrote letters to us answering questions such as, "What is the best part of your writing? the hardest part? How would you judge your work? How should I judge your work?"

In May every middle school student and many high school students in project classes were working feverishly on their portfolios, going through their writing folders, vicariously reliving the year through their writings, making some tough decisions, and doing a great deal of thinking about themselves as writers. The response from students was exhilarating! Laetisha, a seventh grader, wrote,

> The piece which I found most challenging is my story called "Kina and the Boys." I found this most challenging because of how long it is, and I didn't think I could write anything so long and what I think is a pretty good story alone.

Students gave us clues as to what helped them be better writers. An eighth grader named Barry wrote,

> My least favorite paper was the poem we wrote in class at the beging of the year. For one thing I hate to write poems. This assigment was so dull and boring. Another thing is I had to write it; we did not have a choice to what we wanted to write. I like to write nice long stories and do revision.

Students also reflected on themselves as readers. Theodore (eighth grade) wrote,

> When a person reads a story or a book you have to have a feel for the book first. If the book takes place in the 1950's then you should think in about the 1950's and try to get a feel for that time. When you start reading, you can really get the feel of the surroundings of the book. You also need to wipe your mind of everything that went on that day. . . . I like to read in a nice quiet room with no commotion goin on. I find it hard to read when there is talking and people walking around. That's why I hate reading in a classroom. I really don't have a hard time reading except when I have to finish a book for a book report. . . . If a book has enticement then that book keeps you entertained. That's why we read books, isn't it?

Martin, also an eighth grader, wrote,

> The best book I ever read was *Teacup Full of Roses*. I liked it because it told you alot about an black family, and truth about what goes on in there neighborhoods. I understand it real good. I even make a picture in my mind of it.

And students looked at themselves as persons who had something to communicate. Amber (grade ten) thought, "The dramatic monologue shows about me my imagination, my sensitivity, compassion, love, anger, and fear."

Woody, a seventh grader in Gail's class, is "a street-wise kid who failed math, science, and social studies all four quarters. He maintained a B for me and a B+ fourth quarter. He worked nonstop on his portfolio and seemed shocked when I told him (a day early) that he had everything he needed." Here is his letter to Gail:

> The portfolio I've done has been fun working on. I felt good about the work I put into it. I think my best piece of Street Knolge. Because it's a totaly non-fiction story. About the streets. And how to survive. When I write stories like The Hood and Street Knolge. It all mostly comes from the heart I don't know how it does that but it does. So if any one who reads my stories knows what I am talking about or has gone through some of the things will agree with me. But if you don't ever have to go through any thing I talk about I'll be glad for you.

All of us responded to our students' portfolios in some manner. Minnie made the response part of their final exam. Chestra wrote a brief affirming comment on the letters and returned them on the last day of class. Sandy promised students a personal letter of response in the mail, anticipating "fifty (uncompensated) hours of reading and being chained to a computer." The students' portfolios are passed on to the next English teacher who will learn much about their new students as writers and their understanding of what good writing should be.

In the sixth year, the entire department (grades seven through twelve) agreed on four criteria that a portfolio should demonstrate:

- beauty and power,
- craft and care,
- variety and versatility, and
- thoughtful reflection.

These four criteria had great appeal to the research team: they summarized what we wanted to assess. We anticipated that beauty and power would be the most difficult for the students and feared we would be rereading sappy love poetry in this category. But this was the most successful criterion.

The criteria became the center of many spirited classroom discussions, as students defined the terms and made them their own. Middle school teachers spent whole class periods helping students brainstorm questions they could ask as they searched their writings for ones that illustrated the terms. High school teachers developed extensive handouts that defined the traits and terms that are useful in discussing one's own writing (genre, mode, point of view, purpose).

Students understood craft and care as a request for their revising, mechanics, and organizational skills. However, all students (and we) found the last two criteria fuzzy. Was the thoughtful reflection to be shown in the letter about their selections or in a particular piece of past writing? Did variety and versatility really apply to the whole portfolio? What were the odds that one piece could illustrate versatility?

The students' selections did indeed illustrate the four criteria, but their reflective letters tended to analyze their own writing process, their strengths, and their weaknesses. For example, Franklin is forming his definition of poetry here: "I prefer writing poems that don't rhyme because poems that don't ryhme you get to express your feelings, poems that ryhme are more of a rap. When a poem is more of a rap you're not expressing your feelings you're just trying to find words that ryhme."

Teachers again responded to the portfolios. Chestra found the letters she wrote to the students (at the end of her semester class with them) to be time-consuming but rewarding, writing that "This is a great exercise in sharing with the students what I had discovered their strengths to be. Vic thanked me once a day for the rest of the year."

We still have questions, many of which center on how uniform the procedures should be and how portfolios can be used as a district assessment (see Chapter 12). Our procedures will continue to change as we and the students continue to grow. But all agree that portfolios as self-evaluation are a rousing success. They have given the students the opportunity to reflect seriously on themselves as writers, to see the growth in their own writing, to verbalize that growth and to celebrate it. It is tangible support for what we had intuitively known: the students think of themselves as writers.

LOOKING IN THE MIRROR: THE RESEARCH TEAM AS PROCESS WRITERS

Process writing, our basis for all seven principles, remains our foundation. We are immersed in it. It is not a classroom strategy, a method, a piece of pedagogy. It is the fiber of our professional lives as English teachers. We live it as well as teach it.

We take the risks of stretching ourselves as writers, just as we ask our students to do the same. Carrie began writing fiction for the first time in her life.

> For a couple of years I have diligently written to every topic that I gave my students so that I would be able to share the writing experience with them, but sometime early this year I realized that I was only pretending to write. It's no challenge for a person with a master's degree to write a three-page essay on a play she has read a dozen times—especially when she has written the paper topic herself! Furthermore, my writing was not being submitted to an authority—or anyone!—for evaluation.
>
> So this fall I enrolled in a fiction writing workshop. I put myself in a much more vulnerable situation, a situation much more akin to that which my students experience every time they write an essay and turn it in to me for a grade.

Our students observe us as we write, whether it is in journals or daily writes that we share, in a modeling activity, or for professional publication. Students staying after school often get to hear a group of us responding to each others' drafts. They hear Joan ask Nancy for help in working in an example—"How can the transition be smoother?" They see drafts on Stephanie's desk of her writing with scribbled comments from Mary Ann. They work in the writing center while two teachers on their plan period also write, get frustrated, confer, and write some more.

In 1988, the team began writing *Hear You, Hear Me!* (Webster Groves Writing Project 1992). We would convene after school in one of the writing centers and work at the computers, meet with a partner, and revise. The first drafts were quite different in approach and a great deal of time was spent collaboratively designing a common format that would incorporate the eight principles and include the basic elements of any lesson.

Mirror Images was started in 1989 (we were still in Phase Two), but didn't receive a contract from Heinemann until 1992. Writing collaboratively added a new dimension. How could three authors write fourteen chapters that incorporated the experiences of the fifteen teachers who had been team members? Our solution was for the three of us to collaborate on the prewriting and responding but to draft independently. We met to launch each chapter, discussing and outlining the main points to be included. One of us then drafted that chapter. We asked three other members of the team to serve as readers, and they along with the other two coauthors responded to each chapter—throughout several draftings. As time went by and the team moved into Phase Three, we constantly updated the chapters to include workshop, portfolio assessment, and new insights.

WHAT YOU CAN DO

Allow class time for process. Use that time to observe and learn your students' own composing styles. Go easy on the stage-setting behaviors. Walk the room as students work—they're more likely to ask for your help if they don't have to come to your desk. Do miniconferences (read Donald Murray [1985] for help in two-minute conferences).

Give credit for process. Make those sandwiches! Give credit along the way and again at the end. False starts, unsuccessful drafts, attempts with new forms are positive events. Validate them.

Keep deadlines flexible. This is easier to do if you're involved in the students' progress as they draft and revise (see above!).

Provide models of product and process. Give direct instruction, especially in revising techniques.

Teach a minilesson. Remember, no inductive teaching, no question and answer format. Short and sweet with individual follow-up. And don't be upset when the minilesson takes more than ten minutes.

Brainstorm several possible audiences and purpose when a topic is known.

Search for real audiences.

Use a computer, overhead, and LCD panel to model composing or revision strategies.

Ask students to evaluate their writing.

Have students keep all *their writing* during the year. Try portfolio techniques.

Form a writing group of your *peers.*

Read:

ATWELL, NANCIE. 1987. *In the Middle: Writing, Reading, and Learning with Adolescents.* Portsmouth, NH: Boynton/Cook.

DELPIT, LISA. 1988. "The Silenced Dialogue: Power and Pedagogy in Educating Other People's Children." *Harvard Educational Review* 58 (3): 280–98.

RIEF, LINDA. 1992. *Seeking Diversity: Language Arts with Adolescents.* Portsmouth, NH: Heinemann.

SIDDLE-WALKER, EMILIE V. 1992. "Falling Asleep and African American Student Failure: Rethinking Assumptions About Process Teaching." *Theory into Practice* 31 (4): 321–27.

NOTES

1. The National Writing Project has been a major force in the spread of process approaches to teaching writing. The Gateway Writing Project, its local affiliate, held its first summer institute in 1978. Jane Zeni led that institute and continues to direct the Gateway Writing Project today. Joan Krater and Agnes Gregg went through Gateway in 1979. Stephanie Gavin, Mary Ann Kelly, Minnie Phillips, Sandy Tabscott, Gail Taylor, and Theresa Wojak have taken Gateway-sponsored classes and institutes through the years. When the district employed new English teachers, experience with process writing was a requisite. In recent years, the University of Missouri, St. Louis, has provided a graduate credit option for our study sessions, and members of the team often serve as teacher-consultants for the Gateway Writing Project.

2. Reporters who have a short deadline use a formula (the five Ws and the inverted pyramid) approach—and even in the short time available do revise and receive editorial feedback.

3. The ability to "translate" from one dialect or register to another in any language (for more information, see Chapter 8).

Facing the Mirror: Sandra Tabscott

My roots are in Appalachia. For my first six years, my mother and dad and I lived with my grandparents. One of my earliest memories is from World War II days, with my dear grandfather trundling me on his knee and teaching me to say, "One Grick [Greek] can whip ten Wops." Don't ask me now what that means because I don't know. The point is that derogatory names for other ethnic groups were part of the normal conversation. The woman who helped my grandmother spring-clean was called Nigger Clara, both behind her back and to her face. She and my grandmother worked side by side all day, but Clara was sent to the basement with her dinner on a tin pie pan with a Mason jar for her tea, while everyone else sat at the kitchen table upstairs. Even as a four-year-old, I knew that wasn't right. After all, I was taken to Sunday school from the time I was two weeks old, and the Key Street Methodist Church of Princeton, West Virginia, told me "Jesus loves the little children, all the children of the world. Red, yellow, black, and white, they are precious in his sight." That's the message that took root in me. I don't know how I came to reject the subtler messages, because most people my age learned early that Jesus really only loves nice, clean white people, that Jesus loves WASPs, and that's who we should love, too.

Family stories often had Black people as a component. They teased me that the first time I ever saw a little Black girl about my size was at the local five-and-dime store. I walked up to her, put my arms around her, and gave her a big wet kiss. Everyone laughed uproariously when one of the adults told that story of Sandra Jane kissing the little nigger gal in G. C. Murphy's, and I burned with embarrassment. It is interesting to me that even though I hated being ridiculed about the incident, I didn't feel even at that young age that I was wrong to hug her. I knew there was something wrong with their attitude toward that little girl.

When I was in second grade, my life changed radically because my mother and father and I moved to a little town in northeastern Pennsylvania. It is significant only in the fact that I hardly saw a Black person, except on summer visits to West Virginia, for the next eleven years. The story told proudly there is that a Black family came there once. The sheriff ordered them not to let the sun set on their Black behinds, and it didn't. But that wasn't the end of my experience with prejudice. There was a swarm of new ethnic groups for my father to be prejudiced against! Italians, Poles, Russians, Czechs, and Hungarians were there. I heard the derogatory terms for all those groups in the first week, both from my new friends and my father. I didn't buy this new prejudice either.

My father forbade me to associate with "garlic snappers," "Wops," "Pollocks," or whatever but I learned defiance early. My special boyfriend all through high school was Joe Dantini. The first time he came to the house, my dad wouldn't let me leave with him. He told me loudly, in Joe's presence, that Wops are just like niggers and no daughter of his was going to go with one. Again I burned with shame at his behavior, and that was probably the moment when I became confirmed in multiculturalism! With my mother as an ally, I managed to see Joe quite regularly, probably more regularly than I would have if my father hadn't been so mean about it.

I returned to West Virginia to live with my grandmother to go to a small, provincial college. There I remained fairly insulated against ethnic diversity. There was literally one Black student at my school of fourteen hundred. He lived in a room over the gymnasium with his wife. I only caught a glimpse of him a couple of times and have no feeling for or memory of what that was all about. My freshman year, I wrote a research paper for English 101 about Aberdine Lucy integrating Little Rock High School, my first awareness of the civil rights movement; my activity during those college years was laughable and solitary, limited to sitting in the back of the bus and drinking out of fountains marked "Colored."

After college, my new husband and I moved to the heart of the South where he studied for ministry in the Presbyterian Church. By the time he graduated in 1962, the civil rights movement was in full bloom and we were swept into it, not because we planned to be crusaders, but because the confrontation was everywhere, especially in the churches, and our convictions and circumstances converged. Our first pastorate—in a sleepy little farm community—evolved from storybook serenity to heat of the night. Because my husband accepted an invitation to preach at a little Black church near our own, political lines were drawn in the board of elders, which escalated to threatening letters from the KKK and a flaming cross in the yard of the manse. That was the first of a long series of struggles in and out of the church over several years. Our third church job, in Mississippi in March of 1967, was roughly akin to taking a swim in a tub full of alligators. The action there was intense because of national attention. When my husband spoke on the floor of synod meeting in favor of accepting Black Presbyterians for membership, our name, address, and phone number were printed in the Jackson *Clarion Ledger* along with the editorial comment that "all outside agitators should be castrated with a dull knife." Harassing and threatening phone calls started that night and never stopped until we left two years later. Callers were forever asking me what nigger I was sleeping with or, worse, telling our seven-year-old "We're gonna kill your daddy. He's a nigger lover, and we're gonna kill him." We couldn't take the threats lightly since others sympathetic to civil justice were regularly bombed. Our friend the rabbi had his home blasted once and his office and synagogue twice. One clergy friend had his car forced off the road and over an embankment by a police car. He went through the windshield and wasn't found until the next morning. He survives but is horribly scarred, physically and emotionally. The climate inside the church was almost as stormy, with regular meetings to try to fire us and an almost equal number of meetings asking us to stay to help them make a stand for justice. In a little less than three years, *they* got their majority and we had to leave. But you can imagine the ways that the experience sensitized and galvanized us to work for justice.

When we moved to St. Louis in 1970, we found a community further along the road to integration. Our four children were among the first in our community to form friendships and learn to work and play with children of a different race; they forged the kinds of relationships that heal the schisms of racism. Mark, our second son, has always been particularly gifted in reaching across barriers of race with his natural warmth and humor. His first year at the junior high was also the first year that students from the largely Black junior high from across town came to Hixson. Mark's principal told me just recently that Mark had made the difference in the peace and stability of that year with his ability to form friendships in both groups. He and the other children in Webster Groves schools learned the lessons that we their parents had only theorized: working and playing together makes it possible to see beyond color. While the children were on the playing fields, on the stage, or putting out a newspaper, parents were in the bleachers together, making costumes together, or at PTO—learning to cross barriers, too. I credit the children for showing us the way out of the tangle of racism. We still have work to do, of course, but that was my background before I came on the scene at Hixson.

After years of volunteering in the schools, I began teaching when I was forty years old. My first assignment was in a program for underachieving students. There was a disproportionate number of Black students in those lower-level classes, and it was with that group that I first began to question my assumptions about Black learners. For all my defiance at stereotyping in the past, I assumed that dialect equaled ignorance! My views didn't jive with how bright, expressive, and language-rich I found these students. Now I know all that good stuff about Black English as a rule-governed and grammar-based language, but it is my involvement in this ongoing study that brought me to some fundamental truths: Standardized tests tell a very short story. We all speak a dialect of some kind. Most humans, including school-aged ones, need to be loved and accepted and nurtured before they can be their best. The principles of the project are based on those truths and that's why they work. I haven't forgotten that attitudes in my own White community, especially with my generation, must change before all children will get a fair shake in our schools. I see my mission there, too, as well as with my sisters in the project.

Individualize and Personalize

*Do you think you could write a letter about me so they'll know
I'm a good writer and won't think I'm dumb just because I'm Black?*

CHARLENE,
grade eight, on moving to another state

Charlene recognizes that some people—some teachers—make assumptions about individuals based on their membership in a group rather than getting to know them as unique persons. Charlene also knows that Stephanie, her English teacher, does not do that. Although Charlene is in fact a skilled writer rather than a target student, she too has been empowered to take control of her education. All of us have grown during the course of the project in this area; while none of us thought we were guilty of racial stereotyping six years ago, we had no idea of the power of personalizing our teaching.

When we began to focus on alienated students, we figured that teaching them would be a one-on-one proposition. Somehow we would find the time to diagnose individual writing problems and coach students through individual processes of drafting and editing until they gained control as writers (Phases One and Two, "Fix the Writing," "Fix the Methods"). Somehow we would find ways to convince the turned-off kid with the hat pulled over his eyes that we believed he could write and cared about what he might have to say (the seed of Phase Three, "Fix the Relationship"). We knew we wanted to treat our case study writers as individuals. What we didn't know and what moved us into Phase Three was that a personal relationship was going to be the *prerequisite* for almost any progress. By the end of the first year, we decided that the principle *of individualizing* had to be expanded to *individualizing and personalizing*. Siddle-Walker (1992, 322), reflecting on the "failure of process theory to provide African American students . . . access to literacy," agrees. She maintains that when African American students fail to respond, the issue may "have more to do with the affective domain of English teaching" than with methods.

> By "affective domain" I mean that subjective relationship which exists between teachers and students and which is influenced by, but not limited to, methods of instruction. This area, little considered in the teaching of writing, is equally operative in explaining the failure of some African American students to respond receptively to "process" methods. (322)

In six years of action research, we have found that the most powerful strategies for reaching hard-to-reach students are based on the principle we call "individualizing and personalizing." This principle affirms a child for who she is, not for what she does. Claude Steele (1992) asserts that "No tactic of instruction, no matter how ingenious, can succeed without" establishing this kind of relationship, particularly with the African American student.

> If what is meaningful and important to a teacher is to become meaningful and important to a student, the student must feel valued by the teacher for his or her potential and as a person. Among the more fortunate in society, this relationship is often taken for granted. But it is precisely the relationship that race can still undermine in American society. As Comer, Escalante, and Treisman have shown, when one's students bear race and class vulnerabilities, building this relationship is the first order of business—at all levels of schooling. (78)

Our sensitivity to all students has grown over the years as we have focused our attention and concern on the ones who most often sit on the sidelines. Beth Ann found this personalizing of the individual a key change for her after she joined the project.

> For me the most palpable change was an inner one. Before I joined the project, I truthfully hadn't given much thought to the fact that my English 10 students needed and deserved special consideration, and that I was responsible for giving it to them, not the next guy. What this realization did for me was force me to look at the students as individuals (how radical!) rather than just a whole mess of kids whose needs were pretty much interchangeable. . . . The angelic student is always right so he/she gets affirmation that way. The whining obnoxious kids get everyone's attention! I realized I was often ignoring some of those very quiet students because they simply didn't demand my time. They were content (I thought) to be there and to sort of slide along, with others getting the strokes and smacks.

We have learned that sincere interest in a student that is doggedly held during trying times enables us to see what works best with each individual: who responds to verbal praise, who needs coaching and encouragement, who warms to physical touching (and who draws back), and who relates to our attempts at humor.

And so today "individualize and personalize" means something quite different from the principle we proposed six years ago. Of course, that's what usually happens with action research. We started by defining our terms, then we redefined them in the course of the project as our own understanding evolved.

As we lived through our first year of research, we grew aware that much more was involved than the management of individual learning tasks. The case study writers with whom we had established a real rapport, who felt comfortable and safe and respected in our classrooms, improved their writing. Oddly enough, those who caused discipline problems, who resisted our efforts to work *with* them instead of *against* them, apparently felt enough of our concern and interaction to form a kind of bond—and their writing improved, too. But those students who were withdrawn and quiet, who came into and left our classrooms with little or no personal interaction, who wouldn't respond to our efforts to build trust or communication, were the ones who did not improve their writing. Because of this pattern of achievement, we added "personalize" to the principle and we came to see this principle as basic to changing the way alienated learners see themselves. Irvine (1988) believes the impact a teacher can have on a student's self-concept is especially strong for African American students. Irvine writes, "The role of the teacher in the lives of minority students is far greater than for middle-class majority children. Minority students' . . . self-concepts are to a large extent determined by how they perceive that their teachers view them" (506).

We are convinced that any committed teacher can become better at helping turned-off students find their power as writers. But learning how *is* a process, especially for a teacher from a different cultural and economic background.

Here too, our understanding has evolved with our research. Initially the White female teachers who are the majority on our team thought of personalizing the curriculum by carefully including African American literature, images, quotes, and other cultural material. We did this, and it certainly has helped to move our teaching away from the dominant European American culture of the schools. But we soon recognized that building a personal rapport goes beyond changes in curriculum. The key is interacting with our students. We interact with our students in ways that at first were very consciously applied. We could not assume that a good relationship would happen simply because "we cared."

We learn from our students through a process of watching, listening, and reflecting, which challenges us at a very personal level. We monitor our messages, reactions, body language, tone of voice, and the responses we get from our kids. We take risks and change old assumptions while standing firm in our own identity. The goal is the intuitive "realness" that empowers a White female teacher to convince a low-achieving Black male teen to trust her.

161

BUILD TRUST

Making contact

So how do we begin to *individualize and personalize?* Sometimes we plan specific trust-building activities for our classes. But personalizing is a daily effort that occurs spontaneously as we learn to focus on the students who might otherwise get lost. A welcoming comment as Paul enters the room, a follow-up question to Brenda on her personal feelings during a class discussion, a pat on the shoulder as we pass the desk of an alienated student, a warm comment written in Robert's journal, a personal reaction to a formal narrative, eye contact, a compliment on Lucinda's running in the track meet—these are sincere even though we make a conscious effort to increase these small signs of interest, concern, and—yes—love.

We try to make our expectations for the classroom atmosphere of trust clear from the first day. Joan uses two posters, one with a turtle that says, "If you don't stick your neck out, you don't make any progress," and another that reminds the class, "Caution! Humans! Handle with Care!" She assures her students in September that nothing shared will be ridiculed or discounted. Theresa establishes two big rules for her classroom: "We will respect one another," and "No one disturbs the learning or teaching in the classroom."

We all try to learn our students' names quickly, to find out what they prefer to be called—and honor that—and to use their names often. We make a point of using a target student's name in conjunction with something positive. This seems to be an empowering gesture, maybe because many are used to putting up a wall when they hear their names, perhaps wondering, "What did I do now?"

Andy's teacher used his name to help him create a new image. His negative attitude and behavior had led to trouble with all authority figures in the first part of the year. When discussing the vocabulary word *amble* in class, Nancy coined the phrase "Amblin' Andy" to describe his swagger.

She then playfully imitated his walk herself—leisurely gait, arms loose, head high. The kids laughed and Andy grinned, "That's right, that's just how I walk!" This phrase, linking a stylish word with his name, was repeated throughout the year by classmates and by Andy himself, always with some pride. This easy exchange between Nancy and Andy may well exemplify the "affective orientation" that Hale-Benson (1986) finds to be a "critical factor."

> Rapport with the teacher . . . seems to be strongly related to academic performance for Black students and not very critical for Whites. . . . Piestrup (1973) identified some factors which created good rapport in the teacher-Black student interaction, including warmth, verbal interplay during instruction, rhythmic style of speech and distinctive intonation in speech patterns. (125)

Even though Piestrup's work dealt with first graders' reading proficiency, we've found the verbal interplay works with adolescents as well.

Jane observed trust building and its effect in Nancy's classroom:

> Nancy's seventh graders are working on their "uglifyin'" papers. They have brainstormed possible topics, things that "uglify" the world [spin-off from play, *The Golden Ax*, set in Ozarks]. Topics include river pollution, Black-on-Black crime, teenage suicide. Today a group, mostly Black males, surrounds Nancy as they enter the room. Scott, who is writing about gang violence, wants to tell her something. Two of his friends encourage him to share. I can't hear the conversation clearly because they stand in a tight circle close to Nancy and speak in low, but excited voices. Afterward she tells me that Scott had just learned his brother was shot in a street episode. He wanted to talk about the tragedy and how the family was handling it—and also to suggest changing his paper to focus on the story of his brother. Nancy nods, "Of course." She and the kids in the group give Scott a spontaneous hug.

In many classrooms, Scott would have sat stony and bitter—or have acted out. But in Nancy's room, he could share his pain and allow Black and White students to comfort him.

Siddle-Walker (1992) cautions that trusting relationships cannot be assumed simply because "we care."

> At the root of the paradigm [of process teaching], particularly its emphasis on narrative and personal writing, is the assumption that trust will be the basis of the relationship between teachers and students. This belief leaves unquestioned the assumption that all teachers will be able to create the relationship between themselves and students and facilitate relationships between students.
>
> For many teachers confronted with cross-cultural teaching circumstances, however, creating these relationships may be difficult. (325)

Nancy shows how concern coupled with close listening and attending to a student's needs creates a trusting relationship.

Our attempts to build these relationships have not always been successful. During the third year, Sandy never really reached Maurice.

> Maurice is from a family with whom I have some personal connections because of the friendship between my children and Maurice's big brother. I talked with the parents on a regular basis, and we plotted and planned ways to get Maurice to "play the school game." I read Dr. Robert Comer's books and his several articles on the importance of family involvement in getting Black males, especially, to buy into school, and I felt free to discuss those ideas with the mother because of the rapport we had. Together we came up with strategies to inspire, bribe, trick, threaten Maurice into producing, but none of them worked.
>
> His pattern was to resist my personal attentions; he did not want me to sit with him in prewriting stages to help him use some technique or other; if he got a few sentences down on a particular day, he would conveniently lose it before the next day. I suspected the syndrome described by William Jenkins in his *Essays on Education*, where many African American males decide at around age 14 to assert their "Black maleness" by rejecting the schools they perceive as sissy and White.
>
> I generally learn to like and enjoy almost every student before the year is over, but those nice warm feelings never came to me from Maurice. Write on my tombstone that I meant well!

We've each experienced the frustration of not establishing that rapport; we literally never give up for the whole year because we know how essential it is.

Affirmation

Most students respond to praise most of the time. We know, of course, that praise given inappropriately can backfire; several of us have learned the hard way about the "perils of praise" described by Haim Ginott in *Teacher and Child* (1972). But praising a student's work or effort in specific, descriptive terms is motivating. Praising in too-general terms ("Nice job!") or in terms of personality ("You're such a good writer!") can be perceived as pressure to continue "measuring up" and leave the writer feeling inadequate. When a student-researcher gets an A but isn't sure what was praiseworthy, she may give up, rest on her laurels, and avoid the risk of failure on her next assignment. When an inexperienced poet doesn't know what warranted his teacher's praise, he cannot know how to repeat his success. So we try hard to focus on a student's behavior or writing rather than on personality when praising, disciplining, or offering suggestions for improvement.

At first Robert was very reluctant to write, as shown in Chapter 3. He was pressured at home to excel but he was aware of his own weaknesses. To counter this, Gail consistently offered specific positive feedback: "Your verbs are strong and active." She also asked leading questions that helped Robert add details. Gradually Gail walked him through the process of writing good papers and finally, near the end of the year, he decided to trust her. When he got a B– on a paper defining *courage,* which had gone through several revisions, he was thrilled. He realized the process could work for him. This time, Gail gave him personal affirmation. "I told Robert 'I loved' his paper. Instead of being embarrassed by that, he went around and told all of his friends, 'She loves my paper!' "

Robert focused, of course, on the summary comment; don't students always look first at the grade at the end of a paper? But in the many conferences leading up to this point, Gail had given him very specific feedback, both in the form of praise and of suggestions for improvement.

Some kids can't seem to handle praise. They discount it ("Oh, it's not much good") or withdraw from the conversation. Unlike Robert some are embarrassed to have a teacher praise them in public, but actually crave affirmation so long as it is given discreetly and in private. When Henry, a withdrawn student, shared with Joan the plaque he had won for saving a rape victim, she responded with honest admiration. But by this time she knew Henry's shyness and his fragile trust, so she knew not to ask him to show his award to the whole class.

Overcoming Negativity

Most of our case study kids have had negative experiences with writing or with school in general. We must work through this backlog of failure before they can become productive writers. Usually we find them emotionally erratic, either aggressive or withdrawn, as they react to academic or personal challenges. As we began to examine our relationships with these students, we wondered, How do we deal with their attitudes? and inevitably, How do we deal with our own attitudes?

We have grown accustomed to taking our own emotional temperature when we think about a chronically negative kid. Before we can deal with their negativity we have to get in touch with ourselves; this may mean settling down to regain perspective or acknowledging our own frustration and putting it to constructive use.

When teachers asked *how* we managed to transform our own attitudes, we were at first baffled. How did we change? As we worked to focus on hard-to-reach students, we gradually found these kids easier to understand and to like. It seems to us that one key to change was our own experience of action research. While we did share and develop some effective teaching strategies, at the center of our work was not a method but a process: the field notes, the case studies, the readings, the informal sharing in the lounge, and most of all the study sessions where we could talk through what was happening with others who were struggling with the same issues.

The perspective of action research helped us to gain some distance from our most difficult students, to objectify their problems. Suddenly their behavior was not simply obnoxious; it was an intellectual puzzle, a challenge for us to solve. In an odd way, making the problem impersonal allowed us to make our relationship with the student more personal. We began by assuming that each of our case study kids was basically OK— bright and likable and able to learn. Somewhere along the way, we assumed, that ability had been thwarted. It was our job to figure out what was blocking their natural desire to communicate on paper. As we shared our field notes with the group, we could get support in times of frustration, applause for every breakthrough, and growing confidence in our collective understanding.

We have changed by becoming less confrontive when dealing with discipline, less afraid of losing control of our classrooms, so that we react more empathetically. We crack a smile on the first day, not waiting until midyear after "discipline" is in place. Sandy recalls that after a derogatory remark under a student's breath, she quietly addressed the student with, "Did you mean that remark to hurt my feelings?" The students looked shocked at her directness and politeness.

When a student has ventured to the edge of staying or being removed from a class, we are more apt to stay calm and ask a face-to-face question such as "Do you want to stay in class today?" It gives the student a chance to save face, think about the behavior, and appreciate the fact that the teacher did not blow her stack. Proximity, eye contact, raised eyebrows, a pause, and other nonverbal cues are usually sufficient discipline procedures. Some of the students who have experienced disciplinary problems in the past respond more positively to gentle cajoling. Our styles have changed from authoritarian and a bit tense to firm but accepting.

Theresa tries to "adjust my behavior to theirs, calm and soothing when they're aggressive, encouraging and affirming when they're withdrawn." Joan finds the aggressive kids easier to reach because "you *must* deal with them. In the process you have some sort of confrontation, and from that you can often develop a relationship."

Nancy tells the story of an encounter that summarizes many such episodes. At the beginning of the year, Wilson had decided not to trust her.

> I told Wilson to remove his hat in the classroom. He took a defensive and rebellious attitude, I tensed up—and we had a stand-off. For at least two weeks, there was no work from Wilson. He sat in class scowling.
>
> Thankfully this happened early in the year, for I had time to undo the damage. After class one day I spoke to Wilson. I apologized for being curt and abrupt with him, adding that I wouldn't expect him to talk to me the way I had talked to him. I dropped that authoritative "teacher" role and approached him on a person-to-person level.
>
> Wilson listened without saying anything, then smiled tentatively. I had offered friendship, and he had accepted. The next day he entered class and took out paper and pen with the air of a dedicated student. From that day he became my champion, scolding others who were talking or not on task.
>
> As the holidays approached, my teammate and I took a group of students to *A Christmas Carol*. My teammate did not want to take Wilson because the scowling, nasty attitude that I had seen from him was ever present in her class. I assumed responsibility for the decision and he went. He enjoyed the play tremendously. He hushed the talking students, held doors open for "little old ladies," and smiled the entire day. The other teacher's faith began to build and Wilson's attitude changed in her class, too.
>
> Across the board, in all four core classes that quarter, we saw more improvement in grades from Wilson than from any of the other one hundred students on team. . . .
>
> Wilson and I had a second confrontation later in the year. He had headphones and a cassette player on as he entered class. I smiled (very important) reassuringly, held my hand out, and requested he give them to me to be returned after school. For a moment, Wilson assumed the same defensive body language and demeanor that he showed in the beginning of the year. His gut reaction was defiance. Suddenly, he returned my smile, his body relaxed, and he handed the prize over to me.

The key to Nancy's breakthrough seems to be a combination of warmth, self-esteem, and nerve. She communicates to Wilson that she likes him, that she isn't afraid, and that she expects certain etiquette in her classroom.

Individual Responsibility

We form bonds and build trust in many ways, and not all of them involve talking directly with the student one-on-one. Building trust is based on trusting. We must take the chance of trusting that our low-skilled writers will come through and then we must overtly recognize their efforts and achievements when they do.

Building this trust is personal and isn't always directly related to their writing efforts. We build cohesion within our classes as well as increasing individuals' self-esteem when we recognize individual contributions to the class. Having responsibility as a member of the class validates the skills of each student and enhances those feelings of acceptance and belonging.

In her second year of the research, Carrie implemented a wholly new management system aimed at achieving discipline through individualizing and personalizing. Since taking a summer workshop conducted by Alan Mendler and Wanda Lincoln, Carrie now involves the students in the running of the classroom. She assigns meaningful jobs such as a notetaker who is responsible for summarizing what happened in class for absentees. Another student is in charge of cleanup—not doing the cleanup but supervising it. Each week one student updates the wall calendar showing due dates of various projects and assignments. Another delivers the mail (notes from student to student and between teacher and students). A teacher monitor—appointed weekly—lets Carrie know when she breaks her own rules, such as putting down a student. Just through this managerial system, Carrie increased the time she spent working individually inside and outside of class with students.

Joan also finds that assigning responsibility to her students helps them feel safe and confident in her class. She asked Daniel to teach the use of quotation marks to students who had been absent for her lesson.

He took his responsibility quite seriously and carried through well. I have to think this boosted his ego—that he has seldom been treated in his school career as an "expert" in any area of English. A couple of days later I asked Daniel to help another group who was having trouble with punctuating dialogue. Again, he handled it well—didn't give the answer, but thought of a clue for that group.

Joan's students have never refused such a request, but typically swagger with pride to the group they are asked to help (for more examples of individual responsibility see Chapter 10).

Personal Sharing

We ask our students to take responsibilities and risks which then are rewarded by better feelings about themselves and overt praise from us. But personal relationships are also built on sharing: sharing experiences and sharing ourselves. And they cannot be one-sided. Kids are often reluctant to reveal their inner thoughts and feelings to someone who is not as open. We validate our students' humanity by sharing our own feelings, needs, fears, and weaknesses. Several of us share feelings by sharing our writing. Sandy makes her classroom a safe, nurturing place by reading aloud from her own journal. She admits her nervousness, her neck gets red, and she shares the fears she has of their responses. This models for students the common fear of reading their writing aloud.

Sandy's first assignment is a "bio" poem that she models with a "bragging, playful" verse:

Sandy
Optimistic, caring, giggly, sentimental;
Lover of my family, "live theater," pizza with anchovies;
Who feels her kissing is a "10," fudge should have no calories, and
    every vacation should be just one day longer;
Who fears drunk drivers, senility, and nuclear war;
Who dislikes cooked carrots, put-downs, and clutter;

Who wishes to win the lottery, David liked WIL instead of Magic 108,
   and everyone at Hixson would pass the BEST Test;
Tabscott

The students enjoy her poem. "It seems to set kids free to play around with how they wanted to present their own personalities."

Class discussions and informal private conversations are perfect for spontaneous revelations. Alayna borrowed a library book, *Under 18 and Pregnant* (Richards 1991), and pored through it in fascination. "Ask me any questions you want," invited Mary Ann. Alayna followed through, sometimes calling her out in the hall to discuss some point she had read about in a book that didn't match rumors she had discussed with her friends ("Mrs. Kelly, Mrs. Kelly, I *neeeed* to talk to you!"). Mary Ann adds,

> Some of these hall conferences were hilarious . . . and she and I would both start to giggle at some of the preposterous things she had "heard." I soon saw that Alayna's tough, worldly demeanor was a cover for a need for affection. She consistently responded to trust and gentle talk. . . . On occasion I would say, "I don't talk to you that way, and I don't think you should talk that way to me," and she'd answer softly, "OK, Mrs. Kelly, I won't."

Freewrites and journals allow us to respond on a human level, non-judgmentally, to thoughts and feelings of students. They also provide an outlet for the student who hesitates to share face to face. Journals are an excellent means for getting to know withdrawn students so that individualizing is possible. Rapport comes faster when there is writing back and forth on a regular basis.

When Gail's students become aware that she is actually reading their journals (where do they get the idea that their writing won't be read?), they start adding personal comments. They especially like the feedback she gives and the encouraging lines she adds to the margins. Questions such as, "Have you read my journal this week?" occur regularly. Robert commented in a group discussion at the end of his eighth grade how much he appreciated the freedom to write about anything at all in his journal both years: "It amazed me that teachers wouldn't care what you wrote about, like personal things. Sometimes I wrote poetry in my journal . . . it was pretty good with lots of description."

You'll recall Robert from Chapter 3—the student who had "a defeatist attitude" in seventh grade until Gail had a breakthrough with drawing. Her success in reaching Robert is clear in his confident remark.

Physical Closeness

The stereotyped image of a secondary teacher is that of a distant lecturer. The image of an elementary teacher is a caring adult leaning toward an individual student with a concerned hand on the child's shoulder. We have found that physical proximity and touching can be powerful in establishing a relationship and trust. We are aware that some students need more personal space than others and that a few resist and resent being touched. But most students respond so positively that those of us who maintained a distance in the past have worked hard to break that barrier. Those of us who are not so close in age to our students find it easier to do.

Minnie used to have a hands-off attitude. She has done more hugging in the last few years than in all her years of teaching. "Maybe it's my age or because everyone had an Aunt Minnie. You know instinctively who needs hugging and who's touchy."

Mary Ann often expresses her affection for her students through touching as well as through words. This must be done carefully, with respect for a child's personal boundaries, but it can mean a lot. Mary Ann describes her "whispered encouragements, private conferences, hugs, pats, and greetings in the hall." Her personal warmth helped Sadie feel comfortable in class and willing to contribute and learn. The girl's problems in attitude (stalling, tattling on others) as well as in academics (lack of fluency, mechanics, incoherence) improved.

Several of us adjust our own physical presence to be less threatening to students. The high school teachers picked up on Sandy's use of a grade-school chair that she carries with her as she moves among the working students to conference. Theresa "used a small stool to sit next to groups and individuals so that I was near and on their level. During two-minute conferences over grades, the students sat on a taller stool while I was in my desk chair." Carrie too "sat in a student's desk in the circle rather than lecturing from the podium, and I carried a chair around with me in class and in the lab so I wouldn't have to tower over the writers."

Sandy made a special effort to build a personal relationship with students during discovery period, an alternating class for various activities including advising. This was especially effective with Richard who was a "royal pain the first semester":

> I was the enemy. He was out to get me every day and usually succeeded. Conferences with him, parents, counselors, and the assistant principal made no difference in his behavior or academic performance. He ended the first semester with Fs in four basic subjects.
>
> All year during discovery period, I did small-group discussions about feeling-type topics . . . friendship, fears, needs, etc. Richard's turn in my group came at the beginning of third quarter and two events occurred that I credit for his improvement:
>
> 1. The topic was the basic human need for appreciation and affection, and how we can manage to get those needs met. I shared a newspaper clipping which said that everyone needs a minimum of five hugs a day to keep the backbone from shriveling (figuratively!). I expanded on that to show that there were other kinds of touching that satisfied that need for human contact . . . a squeeze of the arm, a pat on the back, that butt-patting that happens in football and basketball, even the high five. We talked about the reticence of many of us to touch because of the sexual connotations, and that touching *can* be nonsexual (a new idea to 8th graders!). From that day, Richard made it a point to pat me on the back or shoulder at least once a day, make eye contact, and ask me how I was doing and was I getting my prescribed hugs. Sometimes there was

an awkward one-armed hug, sometimes just a grin that said the same thing, and, of course, he was getting his strokes in return. His behavior and performance began to improve (and so did mine!). He ended second semester with an A- in my class and passed three of his four basic classes with a B or above.

2. The second event happened the next discovery period. Richard stumbled into class first hour ten minutes late, looking like death, glared at us, slumped at the desk, and put his head down. Instead of saying, "Why are you tardy?" I said, "Looks like Richard needs some TLC." The kids moved in around him in a circle, Katie started patting his back, Camille held his hand, and Kirk said, "Another fight with your Mom, Richard?" Richard started to tell about how he had screwed up again and gotten grounded for life, and he had a headache besides. Everyone helped him talk it out, and I started a neck and shoulder massage which some kids finished. I assured him that the neck rub would count for one of his hugs for the day. By the time the bell rang for second hour, he was up, animated, and positive (though still grounded for life).

I think Richard's behavior and performance were radically influenced by the bonding that happened with me and the group. He was so highly motivated for spring writing assessment that he went from a 2 to an 11 and one-quarter page in October to one and one-half pages with good introduction, conclusion, pretty good development, and some dynamite vocabulary.

I am uneasy about telling this because I realize the dangers inherent in a slightly trained person treading on the holy ground of kids' psyches! My goal was to raise awareness of some basic human needs and the skills we need to get those needs met. I was ever mindful of the students' rights to privacy, confidentiality, and especially the right *not* to have some teacher messing with their minds! I'll do it again next year, with trepidation.

In the small groups, kids were given a chance to share (also to pass on sharing) things about their personal lives—mundane, like pets and pet peeves—and heard about my ho-hum life, too. Some chose to share deeper things when they were feeling safe. My conclusion is that the small-group discussions built a sense of trust for almost all kids that translated into better performance.

Physical touching and emotional closeness are an integral part of building trust. But in a school setting, trust isn't an end in itself; it is a basis for action. Along with the personal relationship, we must also build high expectations in academics and behavior.

BUILD HIGH ACADEMIC EXPECTATIONS

Students who are accustomed to failure usually have low expectations for themselves. For the most part, these feelings have reflected their teachers' low expectations. Raising our expectations—analyzing our expectations—has been a slow process, but it can be done. We've found the key is in examining the ways we subtly and overtly communicate our expectations.

Most of us had been trained in Teacher Expectation/Student Achievement (TESA) a few years prior to the project and believe strongly in the efficacy of high expectations. This training helped us become aware of the ways in which expectations are communicated. Although we can say outright and convincingly to a student, "You can do it," we know there are other ways that reinforce—or contradict—the same message. These other ways are found in a teacher's behaviors, body language, and tone of voice.

We accord each student considerable wait time during discussions; we respond positively yet honestly to anyone's comment during those discussions. This is typical teacher behavior toward higher-ability students. When the same kinds of behavior are aimed at low-skilled kids, they discover their own higher ability; they are empowered. So often they have become accustomed to not having to answer, not having to think, not having to react—the teacher will call on someone else. When they realize we respect their need for time to think, when they realize they will have the time, they do produce.

Low achievers often begin to believe their teachers' low expectations are appropriate. Jeff Howard, in an address at Missouri's Leadership Academy, explains the effect of these low expectations and "rumors of inferiority." Students subjected to these societal and classroom expectations avoid the work necessary for achievement.

It [low achievement] is the result of a remediable tendency to avoid intellectual engagement and competition. Avoidance is rooted in the fears and self-doubt engendered by a major legacy of American racism and strong negative stereotypes about intellectual capability. (Leadership Academy 1989, 1)

The problem as Howard sees it is not limited intellectual ability but intellectual underdevelopment. The challenge for teachers is to develop the capabilities of all kids, to live a commitment to the idea that all kids can learn.

Conferences

Conferences, even very brief ones, are an ideal time for teachers to focus academic attention on the individual and reshape the alienated student's personal sense of ability and significance. Conferences are the perfect setting for both individualizing and personalizing, for "providing more human interaction in the learning process" that acknowledges a "cultural trait" of Black children (Hale-Benson 1986, 125).

Agnes reflected in her field notes how the conference can blend the academic with the personal, resulting in better writing and deeper relationships.

I thought I knew what *personalize* meant. I thought it meant to get to know the kids personally. To find out that baseball or football or basketball is important. Or to learn that someone lives in a group home or has to go to court with a parent to make a decision about where to live. Or even to listen to endless stories about new contact lenses, Scout camping trips, or boyfriend and rarely, girlfriend, troubles.

But since I have been involved with the project, I have been trying to meet with the students one-on-one about their writing. Personalizing with their writing in front of us is very different. It means getting to know students on a deeper and, yes, more personal level. They will share so much more that way. And having written work as a vehicle helps me guide my questions and gives them something to respond to specifically.

I can read the paper with them, asking for clarification all along the way or where items confuse. I can show my delight or share the feeling I experience immediately.

Our conferences seem much more effective than those usually reported in other research. Susan Florio-Ruane (1986) and Sallyanne Fitzgerald (1988), when they recorded conferences with basic writers, found them teacher-dominated and mainly a time for pointing out errors and doing individual lessons in editing. By contrast, we have gone to great lengths to respect the writer's "author-ity" when conferencing. The student keeps physical possession of the draft; we have found that when the draft is in our hands, we are more likely to make revisions instead of the writer making them. This approach to conferencing is empowering rather than threatening with all students, but especially with those who don't yet believe in their own power as writers.

Joan tailors her conferences to meet students' different styles. Patrice didn't like to think aloud with a teacher, so Joan tended to comment in writing. "Talk-write," based on the work of Zoellner (1969), involves prompting a student to develop a text orally while the teacher takes notes. Later the student realizes she has something to say and writes out the text. This technique worked very successfully with Alleesha. But Dwayne rambled too much, so Joan didn't record literally but would summarize and ask Dwayne, "This is what I've got so far. Is this what you're saying?"

Oral guidance helps students revise too. Joan found that Mark would carry through only those revisions that he had repeated orally in their conference. Joan writes, "My saying it without his repeating it wasn't effective. (Mark didn't make revisions based on written comments from peers and from me either.) But Alleesha and Dwayne could remember and apply what was done in conference, even over a period of several days."

One-on-one conferences are absolutely essential with target students. The class lessons never seem to "take" with them and they need the individual explanation or conference. Teachers who use conferences the most make them very short but very frequent. Sometimes frustrating, sometimes heartwarming, the individual conference often precipitates a breakthrough in writing skill. (For more examples of step-by-step conferences see Chapters 5 and 8.)

Joan had nine conferences with Anikia in the course of her first big paper, and you'll recall Gail conferenced individually with Robert almost every day (Chapter 3). These conferences, though necessarily brief (sometimes thirty seconds), seemed the key to building trust as well as skills with these two students. In December, Joan and her team teachers discussed how much Anikia's attitude had changed, writing, "She comes in with a smile and often makes a comment about my appearance or about having work completed. In the beginning of the year she seemed sullen, withdrawn, and unapproachable."

Anikia's writing also improved. Her first draft of a paper recounting an undeserved punishment showed some poetic flashes, but its meaning was almost indecipherable.

> I walk in class and there was a note on the teacher's desk. With a flash of take back strock me in my head. As the wind thashed throw the window it silently hit me. As the teacher was saying who wrote this note "Well who I want a answer and a answer now. I scared at the top of my head, Not Me.

This excerpt suggests why so many conferences were needed. Joan first asked Anikia to tape record her draft; upon listening (with her draft in hand), Anikia volunteered that she could fix lots of mistakes. The next draft still was not clear; the identity of each speaker was fuzzy; the paper was written as one long (two-page) paragraph; run-ons abounded. One of the biggest obstacles for Joan's understanding of the story was Anikia's role in the personal narrative. Through the conferences, Joan learned the story of how Anikia had been punished unfairly for writing a vengeful note to a teacher, a note she had not written. A friend had been caught cheating during a test, her parents had been called, and the "friend" had written the note to the teacher in what looked to the teacher like Anikia's handwriting.

The same excerpt in her final draft shows the revisions clearly—not just in proofreading but in added clarifying details.

> The teacher came in and said, "Hello, Everybody, how has your day been?" Mr. Stockenberg turned, picked up a note and then he began to read it.
>
> I saw the funny faces he began to make so I turned around and Mr. Stockenberg said, "Who wrote this note? I want a answer, and a answer right now!" I yelled at the top of my head. "Not Me!"

Anikia's final version still had proofreading errors and not all the problems in content were cleared up, but Joan recognized the conferences were at the point of diminishing returns.

Impromptu conferences—short, sweet, and effective—can occur at any time. Often our target students won't begin work until we personally invite them to. They sit at their desks and wait until we come around with an encouraging word or a motivating question.

The teacher must be accessible for spontaneous interchanges while the students are drafting and revising. Individual attention and assistance increases their confidence in themselves as students and as writers. Individual attention has become much easier to accomplish in reading/writing workshop, but we managed in the years before that to schedule conferences, usually after having read a draft in process. The biggest problem with this kind of conferring outside of a workshop atmosphere is figuring out how to work with one writer during a forty-five- or fifty-three-minute class session without neglecting others. We must have time for troubleshooting and encouraging students who have difficulty beginning and completing assignments. We've experimented with various teaching strategies that free us from whole-group instruction. These strategies include cooperative learning, use of the writing center computers, and teaching minilessons. Topics for minilessons are based on a close analysis of students' papers after collecting drafts and noting a single topic that needs attention. The lessons themselves are usually ten minutes or so, which leaves the rest of the period for impromptu or scheduled conferences.

The writing center is an ideal place for quick but productive conferences. We can circulate around the lab, see the text on the screens, and comment briefly without interrupting the writer's process. Theresa uses a nonverbal system to provide individual help. She glues together red and blue paper cups and sets them on the monitors, blue end up. When students need help, they turn the red end up. This method saves the time usually lost as students wait with a hand raised for a teacher's attention. Instead, they mark the trouble spot with an asterisk and go right on with their papers, confident that the red cup will bring Theresa in due time.

Group conferences, recommended by such writing process leaders as Don Graves (1983), seem ideal for classes with many basic writers. They allow for the necessary individual and personal instruction, but they also provide some structure and contact with the whole class.

Cathy uses them during her novel projects when students are in cooperative learning groups. Group conferences are scheduled every other day, and reveal

> which students are reading on schedule, who is having difficulty with comprehension, and what sorts of personal connections with the literature are being made. Most case study students are eager participants and the informal conference setting really contributes to an atmosphere of easy communication.

Students are more likely to stay on task while we are conferring with an individual if they have more than one task pending. Joan often has a two- or three-week period set aside for students to be working on various cumulative projects for a unit. For example, after reading and discussing several short stories with the total class, individual students select several activities to complete, including reading a minimum number of new stories from a master list. Some activities require writing (e.g., write a letter from one of the story's characters to Ann Landers and write Ann's response) and some do not (e.g., illustrate the main kinds of conflicts). With this kind of arrangement, not all the students are writing simultaneously, and if a student needs to meet with Joan while she is with others in class, the student can move on to other activities while waiting. This kind of scheduling, giving the student choices in both reading and writing, foreshadows the basic themes of reading/writing workshop.

One of the biggest advantages of the reading/writing workshop used in the middle school during the fifth year is the time for conferencing. As Sandy described it when she used workshop the very first year of the project,

> The teacher is able to check in on every step of the process. There is a structure to make it easy for a kid to get input from both teacher and peers, so writing isn't the lonely isolated chore (for some) it once was. There was constant interaction with all the target students, and two of them thrived on the process. Joey was always eager for the next step; he didn't consider it a chore to revise and would frequently ask, "Is my paper ready to be fixed on yet?" I found the daily verbal check for student progress helped keep students responsible. Tami was crafty about saying what I wanted to hear in the check, and then not actually doing what she said she was, having lost the drafts or not doing it in the first place. Under this system it was hard to get away with that for long!

The low-skilled students almost always accept our suggestions. Our attitude survey (Chapter 13) found that Black students agree much more often than White students and that they try to follow their teacher's suggestions even when they don't understand or agree with them. Because of this tendency Gail tries not to give specific suggestions but to ask questions.

> In the beginning students would take very few risks, even though it was not a public conversation. After they became comfortable with me, and realized that whatever they said would be "all right," they started searching on their own for answers and ways to improve writing. Eventually, this led to the confidence to read aloud to the class, and make specific suggestions in peer writing groups.

Written Teacher Comments

We have come to view written comments on a draft as a recorded one-sided conference. This means we tend to write in complete sentences ("I can't see your grandfather") rather than just a word ("details"), to focus on one or two problems rather than commenting on every weakness, to ask questions rather than give instructions, to credit the strengths as specifically as we can, and to build the trust and rapport we know is essential to improvement.

We have learned that reading drafts in process is absolutely essential. Waiting until the final draft for our response does not help kids who find writing difficult. When they have turned in a final draft, they have a real feeling of being finished and resist suggestions for further change. We find conferring with the student and writing responses on a draft before the final are two successful ways to "intervene in the process" that Siddle-Walker (1992) recommends.

> It is important to continue to refine methodologies . . . which might be more appropriate for African American students. This might include, for example, considering more specific suggestions on ways to intervene in the process to ensure improved student products, an area which has remained little researched. (326)

Hillocks (1986) also finds an active environmental process more effective than a laissez-faire "natural process" approach. We find that intervention is helpful for all students, particularly for low-skilled, insecure writers.

While writing comments in the margin of a student's draft is a time-honored way to individualize, students often ignore or misinterpret the comments. Average students do this often, but basic students do it even more. Henry had written, "When I called to Sheba she came back to me." Joan wrote in the margin, "Can we hear you say this?" She had given her class minilessons on direct quotations and showing versus telling. In his revision, Henry added quotation marks, " 'I called to Sheba she came back to me.' "

He tried to follow his teacher's instructions mechanically; the result was neither a direct quote nor a correct sentence.

Because of these misinterpretations, Joan's written feedback to low-skilled students often consists simply of pointing out specific strengths. She underlines good details, action verbs, and nuggets from journals that can be expanded into a full paper and reserves her suggestions and questions for direct conferences.

Gail on the other hand often uses written comments with her seventh graders. She makes her comments very specific ("Please read this out loud and see where the periods go"), and she asks just one or two questions per printout, followed if necessary by a face-to-face check. In this way, the written comments do not bleed all over the paper and overwhelm the student with an abundance of unrelated issues.

Because written comments are inherently individualized, they provide an ideal time to encourage as well as to prod toward higher expectations.

Modeling Peer Response

In our experience, African American students often prefer working with others rather than individually. It is important that this cooperative work embody the same warm regard and high expectations that we strive for between student and teacher.

Our early peer groups had typically focused on PQP responses: praise, question, polish (Lyons 1981). While essential, modeling appropriate PQP response with whole class responses to a sample draft was not enough. We used response sheets to provide structure for the peer groups, and the more skilled writers gave helpful feedback. All too often, though, case study students still had difficulty going beyond general comments like "I like your paper" and "It's a good paper."

During this stage of our development, we typically spent our time during peer response days trying to keep groups on task and working with groups of lower-skilled writers to model appropriate responses.

To make peer response effective, we teach students how to give constructive feedback, most often by having a class respond to a student sample on the overhead or monitor or by sitting in on peer groups. We find that modeling gentle, respectful responses to students' writing helps elicit similar feedback when students respond to their peers' writing.

Theresa models by role playing a peer response group. "One member gives only praise ('It's wonderful! I love your paper!'), the other only criticism ('You should get rid of the whole middle section, it's boring.') The audience then journals and discusses why the group was dysfunctional." She then has students (prepped ahead of time) role-play an effective peer response group.

Transfer is very high from these activities. It is now commonplace to see kids sitting and reading to anybody who'll listen. Chapter 7 describes our procedures in detail and gives more examples of classroom activities.

BE FLEXIBLE

Flexibility is the hallmark of any teacher surviving the pressures in the classroom today. Carefully plotted lesson plans and unit schedules never are executed as planned. Having numbers of targeted students in a class simply intensifies the situation.

Flexible Deadlines

Chapter 5 explores the need for flexible deadlines. Giving the student some control over her own deadlines helps her learn time-management skills more than any teacher-imposed deadline.

Joan gives her students a four-week calendar and has them fill in projected deadlines and planned daily activities. Some students cannot handle this unless she sits with them individually and helps them fill out the calendar.

> Target students could seldom complete the same amount of work as other students. But they were less angry and frustrated having set their

own deadlines which were then not met. Also, through this activity they learned the process of planning time, a new experience for most. Sometimes while planning I'd eliminate one activity or project for these students on an individual basis to give them a better chance to succeed.

Carrie also encourages individual goal setting in her tenth-grade fantasy and science fiction course, relying heavily on keeping goal journals and working in cooperative groups. Students work through a sequence of activities with careful monitoring of their progress. At the end of each class, Carrie coaches, "Talk to your group about what you'll have ready for tomorrow." This sort of freedom-with-responsibility works well for basic writers.

Theresa's triad groups also take responsibility successfully, in this case by setting their own deadlines. Cooperative learning offers more opportunities to individualize assignments and expectations. Sometimes groups or partners assign tasks among themselves so that the expectations for each student are reasonable.

Finding the balance between holding to a (third!) deadline and keeping due dates flexible is analogous to balancing the personal regard and the high expectations. It becomes a less-difficult decision to make when we fully understand the writer's point of view. Again, we place great emphasis on student input, on learning from them, while not abandoning our role of guide.

Flexible Assignments and Expectations

Just as we modified our deadlines, usually letting students establish their own deadlines, we also learned quickly that we had to modify tasks. We must start where the child is, offer support, and gradually reduce that support as a student writer learns to take more responsibility.

Conferences often provide the best opportunity to make adjustments in our expectations. Renata was working on an essay that Nancy had clear expectations for. Nancy adjusted quickly when she saw Renata's efforts were different from what Nancy had expected.

Renata was writing her essay on the importance of parents carefully watching their children. Renata's four-year-old cousin had recently been killed by a car when she ran into the street. Renata worried that this would not have happened if her cousin had been watched more carefully. Renata began her essay following Nancy's organizational instructions, which specified the type of content or purpose for each paragraph:

Paragraph 1   Introduction, Show Don't Tell

Paragraph 2   Problem and Example 1

Paragraph 3   Example 2

Paragraph 4   Solution: What can we do about it?

Paragraph 5   Conclusion

As Nancy looked at the computer screen, she saw that Renata had used verse instead of prose for the fifth paragraph, which was to contain the solution to the problem.

Solution
We can watch our children
but don't be too protective
give them some room
but don't set them free

Nancy drew back, stunned by the mixing of genres. Her first instinct was to ask, "Are you sure you want to use poetry there?" At that moment she realized that "the author's purpose was thoroughly accomplished; the poetry brought personalization to the work; the voice was strong; and Renata had used her authority. Renata's creative approach was discussed and validated in a quick conference. Her self-esteem soared."

Nancy was also pleased to see Renata take control, for so often basic writers fail to see anything but the modeled form. Whenever we maintain our role of guide and respect the "author-ity" of our young writers, we empower them—and the results are rewarding.

INDIVIDUALIZING AND PERSONALIZING: BEYOND THE CASE STUDIES

By the third year, most of us felt confident shifting our focus from individuals to small groups to whole classes. We had grown comfortable relating to our most challenging students in a warmer, more personal way. We had internalized a more sophisticated view of writing process—individual, recursive, and conference centered rather than prescribed linear stages. We had internalized the regular use of cooperative learning. Slowly, almost imperceptibly, we expanded our focus using the techniques to individualize and personalize instruction with all our students. These changes in climate were apparent to Jane when she visited our classrooms. As she observed in her field notes during the third year,

> 24 eighth graders are planning essays on current issues in "scientific manipulation of the human condition." It's a spin-off from the novel *Flowers for Algernon*. Cathy presents 8 categories of science (e.g., medicine) and leads the class in brainstorming examples of little categories for each (e.g., fetal tissue experiments, test-tube babies, organ transplants). Class of 24 is diverse, with 7 Black males. Students move into groups of 3 with colored markers and big sheets of newsprint to continue their lists of issues, aiming for 12 examples for each of the 8 major categories. Cathy assigns roles: recorder, reporter, task keeper.
>
> As she floats around to monitor and chat with groups, there is a lot of noise, but most of the talk relates to the topic. Cathy moves close to each table, commenting on their ideas, occasionally resting a hand on a child's shoulder. She's full of energy, somehow keeping up with all that is going on, unruffled. The questions and the classification task are remarkably sophisticated for this age group and for a heterogeneous class.

We've learned to expand our focus—to nurture many students with short comments and quick smiles. Meanwhile—most of the time—we can keep track of the whole class, the lesson, and the interruptions on the P. A. system. The project has become so much a part of the way we work it no longer requires our full concentration on three hard-to-reach kids. Today it is just the way we teach. Agnes vividly describes here the changes she's made since being in the project:

> I've become more attuned to the needs of students and have grown more creative in my approaches. Being in the project has made me more conscious of how I talk to kids, of my attitude toward them and how it changed so often. I pay closer attention to how I comment on papers and what I say in person or in print. I find something to praise in every piece of writing. . . . I was able to chill out a bit this year, laughing, adapting more quickly, sometimes changing right in the middle of a lesson. I feel myself pulling for these kids more, wanting everyone to do well.

Teachers everywhere are struggling to individualize. Our research suggests that teachers who wish to reach the alienated students must learn to personalize, to learn from their students what it is that motivates them, that makes them respond, that makes them grow as writers and as persons. Mary Ann summarizes the power of this principle:

> In the fall many seventh graders feel themselves to be strangers to the school itself, to their teachers, as well as to sharing personal stories and working through the writing process. They're not inclined to take risks. . . . But with all the individualizing and personalizing we do in our classes, most students feel the comfort of writing in a safe atmosphere where everyone, teacher and student, is considered a writer, and writing is just something we *do*.

Teachers who personalize seem to do so more intuitively rather than as a conscious strategy. It can be learned and made purposeful. When Sandy was presenting our project to a group of administrators, she made the point that we had internalized our individualizing and personalizing. As she put it, "All of us were warm, motherly people, but today we're more purposeful and more devious. We know its power."

LOOKING IN THE MIRROR: PERSONALIZING THE RESEARCH TEAM

Individualize and personalize, like each of the principles, has guided the way the members of the research team interact within and outside the study sessions.

Building Trust

It is clear to us that the personal relationship is a powerful basis for learning. We found this true in our own development as teachers, meeting together and sharing ourselves in study sessions. With the support of the group, we were able to overcome our inhibitions—our fears. We were able to analyze more clearly our own strengths and weaknesses as teachers, as persons attempting to reach out to our alienated students.

We've seen much growth over these six years. The first year's study sessions focused on methods: "How do you do sentence combining? When do you use role playing?" The project itself was focusing on the strategies and so were our study sessions. During the first year, Gail recalls, we "clutched our field notes to our chests, fearful that we would be asked to share them." Sharing became easier during the second year and by the third year, it was an accepted routine.

The evolution from *individualize* to *individualize and personalize* matched a growth in our study sessions; as we realized the need to focus more on the personal with our students, we found ourselves forced to reveal our personal selves with each other. We divulged more of our own personalities. If our project was simply taking field notes and analyzing essay scores, many of us would not have continued this long. It is the study sessions—the personal sharing—that provides our motivation. Minnie explained,

> I look forward to coming to the sessions. It's not an "I-*have*-to-go" situation. This group provides the emotional support missing from

professional development, which ignores that teaching is a personal transaction—between teacher and student and between teacher and teacher.

Gail recalls a day when she and Mary Ann coincidentally met in the hall between their two classrooms each with her hands over her ears. Both were implementing cooperative learning strategies just learned at the Johnson and Johnson workshop and they each found the noise unbearable. This spontaneous sharing of common experience, and talking about it at the next study session, creates a bond between researchers.

The high school teachers do not have the same daily support that the middle school teachers enjoy. Their classrooms are distant from each other; they don't share a plan period or lunch period. About the only time they talk about the project is at the study sessions. The middle school teachers sometimes feel as though the project is their life and that they are constantly sharing their students' work and their own ideas and frustrations. Ideas are more likely to make an impression that way. At study sessions, we'll bring up relevant examples from each other's classes because we've talked about them already, which helps us analyze issues more fully. The high school teachers are a strong group, their numbers are growing, and they are looking for ways to resolve their isolation.

Raising Professional Expectations

Just as we build high academic expectations for our students, we find the project has increased our professional expectations for ourselves. Carrie speaks for all of us when she acknowledges, "If something is too difficult and I am tempted to give up, I know I have to report to the group. We aren't allowed to give up because of the expectations of the project, of the group."

Stephanie sees professional development as a by-product of the action research. "I'm sure this early in my career [her second year] I would not have attempted to write an article to submit to the *English Journal* except for the project."

Minnie sees the study sessions as an exciting form of staff development. After one year with the project, Minnie left the district on a leave of absence for two years and then returned.

> I was surprised you all were still doing this. Usually staff development is cyclical: on one topic such as TESA for a couple years and then on to another topic such as cooperative learning. But here you guys were not only still doing it, but doing it even better.
>
> The research team became a community of teachers who have become learners and therefore better teachers. We've created a little hub that gives us purpose and makes us human. Our sessions don't talk about purchasing equipment or writing objectives as so many staff development meetings do. Instead each of us has a chance to be a person, to be someone with expertise. Our problems will at least get addressed if not fixed by the group. This is nurturing to us. We give nurturing and we get nurturing. We know this is a core group of caring people who will problem-solve with us.

Flexibility

We knew our students would demand flexibility in our assignments and expectations. We found out that we required every bit as much for ourselves. Action research requires fluidity; its strength is that objectives and methods can adjust as the research carries on. We modified the number and wording of the eight principles that guided our project. We changed our focal students from African Americans to all low-achieving students after the first two years. Our research team grew from six teachers to fourteen by year five. Several teachers have left and returned without interrupting the flow of the project or disrupting the bonding.

Our agendas for study sessions are constantly modified. Teaching strategies change, but our goals stay the same. More tasks have been added, such as disseminating our project's results at a particular conference or writing an article or informing our board. (And every time we share with "outsiders," we find ourselves clarifying—for ourselves—what we're doing and why it's working.) The payoff from this project is twofold: not only do the student writers increase their skills but the teachers enhance themselves personally and professionally.

WHAT YOU CAN DO

Build trust. Use appropriate praising comments. Give individual responsibility. Share your personal life. Don't tower over kids. Try touching if you and the student are comfortable with it.

Build high academic expectations through individual conferences, written comments, and cooperative learning groups.

Build flexibility into your deadlines, assignments, and expectations.

Facing the Mirror: JoAnne Williams

I grew up during the 1960s and 1970s in a small, rural town of predominantly German heritage near St. Louis. Most Whites in town prided themselves on the good relationships they felt existed between themselves and the small Black population that lived on the steep slopes of Olive Street. The gospel singers from the A. M. E. church were always included in community Thanksgiving services or school variety shows. The high school coaches made sure that the team bus would only make stops at restaurants where the one Black player would be served without incident, as some neighboring towns weren't as friendly. Yes, the town seemed to take care of its Blacks.

When I went to college in another small town in a part of Missouri known as Little Dixie, I encountered open racial hostility for the first time. The campus and even local social clubs were integrated, but townspeople recalled matter-of-factly the last lynching which occurred in the town square in the 1950s. The counter at the drugstore on that town square reluctantly served the few, mostly younger, Blacks who had the presumption to sit there, and the local tavern was even more segregated in its seating arrangement. When I held open the door at the bank for an elderly, arthritic Black woman, we both received hate stares from onlookers. I was thankful I had been raised in a town that would never have treated its Black citizens so poorly.

I taught in a number of communities after college, rural and suburban, each with a very small African American population that was integrated in the school and communities in the familiar way my hometown had been.

When I was hired at Webster and became part of the writing project with its focus on the African American male, I realized that this was one area of American life about which I knew little. Teachers already a part of the research project provided excellent models for ways in which I could educate myself in a new culture. One thing that happened early on was an awareness that my hometown's benevolence toward its African American residents was not so virtuous as I had liked to believe. I began thinking of incidents I'd heard of as a child. Yes, a few Black families attended the Methodist church in the 1960s—after the White congregation voted to give them the privilege. It wasn't until the mid-1970s that all of the homes along Olive Street were hooked into a water and sewer district that the rest of town had used for decades. There may be a myriad of reasons why the one Black in my high school class of thirty-seven students has never come to a reunion, but one reason might be the memories of a comment he probably heard from almost everyone of us, his White classmates—"You're just like us." His own cultural experience was unique and none of us ever validated that.

I've learned to listen to my African American students when they're discussing subject matter or talking about weekend activities. We talk openly about their bilingual ability to use standard English or dialect and why and how they choose. I'm not too shy to ask what a new (to me) expression means. I've found students are very astute at picking up on when a teacher is honest and when she's not. I work hard at letting them know my interest is sincere. Then they do share, in person and in writing. A seventh-grade target student, Eddie, taught me the internal rhyme scheme used in rap. One day after a near-physical confrontation he'd had at school, he put his arm around my shoulders and said, "Mrs. Williams, you just don't understand. It's like this. . . ." He proceeded very patiently to explain to his student, the teacher, why the rules of his inner-city neighborhood dictated that he would have to fight the other student. He didn't sway my opinion on violence, but I appreciated his effort to help me understand his perspective. The following year, he visited my classroom on occasion to perform the latest rap he'd written.

My aunt, a veteran teacher, told me during my first year of teaching to be a friend but not a buddy. I think I concentrated so hard on the latter not happening that I didn't spend enough time on being a friend to the students. I take the time now. One of the highest compliments I've received as a teacher came this last year. Two of my African American target students were overheard discussing teachers. As Charlotte spoke, Justin nodded in agreement, "Mrs. Williams, she really cares."

Encourage Cooperative Learning

Students are the ones you mostly want to get the opinions by 'cause
they're the ones that read it over and over. They're the ones you really
want to get their point of view—how they feel about your writing.

SADIE,
grade eight

By the mid-1980s, all of us had incorporated peer editing groups into our classrooms. We had to. They were an integral part of the writing process instruction—the core of our philosophy. During the first year of the project, Nancy listened to the other teachers on the research team say proudly, "My students have drafted their personal narratives and are now working in peer editing groups." Another teacher mentioned the poetry revision occurring in pairs or triads. Although the rest of the collaborative team seemed to experience success with their student peer groups, Nancy felt like the exception. Her groups were consistently ineffective, off task, and accomplished very little. But she didn't admit it, at least not for a while.

By spring, the collaborative spirit of the research team had grown significantly. Even this early in the project's growth, Phase Three was popping out its head as teachers' relationships with their kids began changing. An atmosphere of trust surfaced. We were freed to take risks, question failures, and seek answers from our peers. During a study session, Nancy finally confessed, "My peer editing groups are a disaster!" She waited, a bit shamefully. Soon another member timidly echoed her feelings, then another, and then another. Some students were doing all the work; an equal number were doing none of the work; and all students could have accomplished more. All of us had worked with peer editing groups from our writing process training; all of us were disappointed in the results.

We could not, however, throw out this principle. We believed that, successfully used, cooperative learning held the key to teaching low-achieving students in heterogeneous classrooms.

> Researchers in the area, led by David and Roger Johnson, have demonstrated that there are tremendous cognitive, emotional, and social gains when children of different achievement levels work together, with common learning objectives and incentives structured to reward the entire group when everyone does well. Low-achieving students thrive in cooperative groups. They are strongly motivated to learn, since their learning is important to their entire group, and their efforts are encouraged and win them acceptance by other group members. The self-esteem of these students rises as their achievement does, and their attitudes toward academic work improve. High achievers benefit as greatly as low achievers; they develop leadership skills, greater self-esteem, and their achievement levels rise too—probably because of the beneficial effects of having to organize their knowledge and teach it to students who are less developed. (Howard 1990, 9)

Our readings and studies indicated the importance of the "community" atmosphere in African American homes, families, and churches. We wanted to build from this community and transfer it to school. Our students thrived on social interactions in the hallways and on the buses, bringing with them the message that they preferred to collaborate rather than to compete with others; they preferred to work together rather than in isolation.

Yet American education has leaned toward competition for the best grades, the highest test scores, or the "top" reading group. As Jeff Howard (1990) recently wrote,

> Why hasn't cooperative learning spread to all American classrooms? Why is it not taught as a standard course requirement in all schools of education? This approach, and a rich menu of other effective techniques are ignored. . . . Competitive or individualistic classroom structures, where students fight it out to "prove" who is smarter, are far more consistent with the prevailing ideas about the distribution of ability. (9)

We were convinced that all students could bring valuable contributions to groups and wanted to downplay the ethic of competition. We recognized the power of effective collaboration but had to find a way to make it successful in our classrooms.

Immersed in Phase Two, our research team gathered during the fall of the second year for intensive training in cooperative learning. The workshop was designed by David W. Johnson and Roger T. Johnson and conducted by Edythe (Edie) Johnson Holubec. It enabled participants to practice skills of cooperative learning by designing group activities and by performing as a cooperative group. We received released time for the first two days of the training rather than tagging it on to the end of a long work day. Taking what we had learned back to the classrooms, we modified it to suit our purposes. We met after school in two later sessions to process our findings. Our training was basic yet comprehensive; it was not aimed specifically at teachers of writing, but was open to teachers (and administrators) of all disciplines at all levels. The procedures we learned in that workshop proved immensely valuable.

The changes in our teaching because of this workshop were a focal point of the second year's study sessions. We talked of ways we used study buddies, how we built individual accountability and positive interdependence, and what we learned from our students. This was different from the first year when we spoke of peer groups and peer editing, debated the value of structured response sheets, and eventually shared our disappointments in the way the groups functioned. The difference in our approach and understanding is evident in our wording change for this principle: from "Opportunity for Group Work" to "Encourage Cooperative Learning." Before the project began we had known intuitively the potential of students working together, but the workshop empowered us to develop strategies that capitalized on that potential.

The research on cooperative learning is extensive and many books are available on both its theory and practice. We will not attempt to duplicate the Johnsons' workshop in this chapter but will focus on how we implemented its five basic components. We recommend this training to all teachers in all disciplines.

FIVE ESSENTIAL COMPONENTS OF COOPERATIVE LEARNING

In a nutshell, successful cooperative learning in the classroom depends on five basic elements: positive interdependence, individual accountability, face-to-face interaction, interpersonal and small-group skills, and group processing.

Positive Interdependence

Positive interdependence is the attitude of group members that we all sink or swim together. There are ways to structure activities so that the members of the group feel this dependence on each other as well as take on responsibility for each other. We found three methods successful for our purposes: positive goal interdependence, positive role interdependence, and positive reward interdependence.

Positive *goal* interdependence can mean the group produces a single piece of writing such as a book review, a literature study project, or a poem.

Positive *role* interdependence involves assigning specific tasks for each member of the group, all of which are necessary for the group to function effectively. Some of the roles we use include reader, recorder, checker, task keeper, encourager (of participation), and praiser. We also use positive *reward* interdependence: either everyone is rewarded for successful group work or no one is rewarded. For some writing assignments, teachers give a single grade to the whole group. Such group grades get a mixed reaction from students. Most teachers work up to them gradually via tasks with relatively little personal investment, such as writing a new ending for a story. High achievers are the most resentful; it is hard on their egos at first. But in time, most students accept group grades for group work. Teachers may select one paper at random to grade from the three papers each group member has produced. All three members receive that grade, making each member truly responsible for the work of the whole team.

While some people might consider this unfair, a survey of adult professional writing by Steve Bernhardt and Bruce Appleby (1985) shows that collaboration is the norm on projects and reports, even on publications—and all members of a group do take the consequences of their joint productivity. Training in this concept gives students an edge in the ability to be productive group members.

Individual Accountability

Individual accountability is the key to distinguishing traditional group work from cooperative learning. We've all faced the frustration of one or two persons in the group doing all the work while the others "take a vacation." Teacher monitoring is essential. While groups are working on a task, the teacher is actively involved, checking that each person in a group is able to explain the work at hand, conferencing with the group and its individual members. The assigning and monitoring of roles helps in individual accountability as well as positive interdependence. Most of us wander the room, some with a clipboard, listening for appropriate comments from the students in particular roles and questioning individual students on the progress of the group and the current task. If the students are not able to respond appropriately, the teacher presents that as a problem for the group to tackle. The teacher is a facilitator, not a problem solver.

Students earn "points" during their group work. Target students like the monitoring and the prompt recognition for their efforts. Mary Ann describes here her system, based on a "point chart" she carries on a clipboard:

> They receive points for everything—having their materials, being on task, not complaining, the number of concrete details they used, sentences combined after peer response, anything that was related to performance in class. Target students like the immediate acknowledgment. . . . "Did you give me my points?"

Face-to-Face Interaction

Face-to-face (and knee-to-knee) interaction means just that. Group members of any age work together best if they are close physically and can look at each other in the eyes. In a classroom of rows, this means moving desks. When Theresa found that students took inordinately long to move the desks to the proper design for triads, fours, or other configurations, she practiced "desk drills" in her ninth-grade class. Her whistle started the drill and students moved their desks to form their groups, keeping a record of the time it took for the entire class to accomplish this task and praising the group that finished first. They figured out the best way to grasp the top of the desk, avoid pinched fingers, get on their marks, and move quickly and quietly. The teacher got out of the way. The class record: three seconds! Theresa found that "cooperative learning has worked out better this year than it did last year. Most of these freshmen have better social skills than the students in previous years' classes; therefore training took less preparation. I no longer need desk drills!" Others of us, especially seventh-grade teachers, have used desk drills quite successfully.

Many groups find the carpeted floor, a bean-bag chair, an out-of-the-way corner, or under the teacher's desk a favorite setting for their work. Some prefer to gather around a table.

Interpersonal Skills

Group members must be taught interpersonal skills, the fourth element needed for cooperative learning success. Small groups must have a chance to evaluate their performance through debriefing. Johnson and Johnson gave us a helpful hierarchy of small-group skills that aided in identifying the level of social skills in our classes. Now we know which skills should be practiced next.

Theresa's desk drills addressed the basic "formation" skills, which include moving without noise, staying with the group, and using quiet voices. All of us teach the need for "twelve-inch voices" in groups, meaning the individual voice cannot be heard past twelve inches. Also in this "forming" stage are the skills of encouraging participation by all members, keeping eye contact with the one speaking, and avoiding put-downs. When designing any activity for a small group, we include objectives for social skills as well as for the task. These social or people skills must be taught and we use the Johnson and Johnson T-chart often. The T-chart is simply a big *T* separating what a particular skill (such as quiet voices) looks and sounds like. The students brainstorm characteristics that can go on each side of the T, such as the following:

Using Quiet Voices

Looks Like	Sounds Like
Leaning Forward	A quiet mutter
Only 1 person talking	Not able to hear individuals at another group
Eye contact	

After brainstorming and discussing the characteristics, the students practice the skill while the teacher monitors the groups, giving points to those members who exhibit that skill.

The social skill of no put-downs is crucial for our students, especially in the middle school. Even though each of us stresses the feeling of community in the whole classroom, works at establishing an atmosphere of trust, and overtly forbids put-downs, they still occur—most often in the small-group settings, when students feel less constrained. It is exciting to hear peer pressure at work in a positive way with students reminding each other (sometimes forgetting their twelve-inch voices) with "No put-downs!"

We also ask students to practice giving praise. This is not easy for some students, but with close teacher monitoring we find the students approach it as a game. As we roam the classroom, a student will glance at us and exaggerate saying, "Good job, Joe," obviously more for our benefit than for Joe's. Students often imitate the tone and delivery with which the teacher offers praise. But Edie had warned us of this developmental stage and we agree that such overt comments have to occur before they are internalized— and that the recipient of this kind of praise still experiences the positive feelings that accompany such a comment, even though it is obviously a performance. Joan experienced the good feelings when she complimented a group on how well it was performing and then heard two students say, "That was nice of you to say, Mrs. Thomas." The praising comments are the perfect way to fight the put-downs.

The ladder of interpersonal skills builds on these *forming skills* with twenty-one other skills categorized developmentally as *functioning, formulating,* and *fermenting*. These skills include the abilities to paraphrase others' comments, seek elaboration, criticize ideas and not people, and ask for justification.

Socialization is a major benefit of collaborative work. Kids learn to relate in a positive way, to care about one another as people. Students are more willing to take risks in this safe environment where their ideas and feelings will be validated. Cathy noticed among her eighth graders "quite a lot of hostility and rivalry" at the beginning of one school year. By the end of the year "they had far more cooperative spirits. They genuinely wanted to help one another! 'I'll read it for you' and 'I'll help you with it' were frequently heard."

Group Processing

The fifth principle, group processing, allows students reflective time. This time is not on the task necessarily but on the quality and accomplishments of their group work. It takes class time and all too often we find time has run out. It is best done immediately following the activity rather than the next day and involves getting feedback from each other or the teacher. Our three most popular feedback methods are a quick written response by students to questions, problems, and what they learned; a teacher summary emphasizing strengths and successes, with specific examples; or a brief oral report by the designated reporter or each group member highlighting what was accomplished, solved, resolved, or discovered during the day's activities. Typical questions are: Name three things the group did well. What would you do differently next time? What did you learn today? What will you do tomorrow? Johnson and Johnson also recommend using student observers to give feedback on how the group relates, but most of us do not use this method because it relegates students to the role of observer rather than participant.

EMPOWERING GROUPS

Heterogeneous Groups

Tracking is still practiced in many schools with such designations as upper-, middle-, and lower-achieving classes. Too often students in the "lower" classes pour over worksheets, while "upper"-level students work on projects requiring creativity, critical thinking, and other higher-level thinking skills.

Even within classes that are heterogeneously grouped, tracking may exist. Reading groups within a class may have value-laden labels such as Bluebirds, Sparrows, and Crows. The students in the lower groups respond to questions that require simple restatements of what they have read, while students in the upper groups hypothesize or compare and contrast concepts.

Six years ago, Carrie lamented the high school's homogeneous low-achieving classes where all the academic leaders had been removed. She summed up the feelings of all the high school teachers in the writing project when she wrote,

> I have every faith in cooperative learning. I used it a great deal in my college prep classes, and intend to use it a great deal more next year. The problem I found with it in my target student classes was again one of homogeneity. Since much of the success in collaborative learning depends on the better students leading the poorer ones, it necessitates having better students. When there are none, or one or two in a class, cooperative learning becomes very difficult.

One of the tragic side effects of tracking is that teachers are forced to label students as "better" or "poorer." These words fade in truly collaborative, heterogeneous classes. Today, the high school continues to remove the remnants of tracking. As we gather further proof that homogeneous classes are injurious to student success, we see enlightened school leaders eliminating "basic" English classes.

In part because of greater flexibility in curriculum, the middle school has experienced greater success in cooperative learning. Jeff Howard (1990) echoed our thoughts when he wrote,

> Ability group placements represent powerful expectancies; when we group kids according to our assessments of their intelligence, we communicate clearly what we think of them, and we shape their conceptions about their places in the world. . . . Children have confidence in their capacities to learn that are enhanced or diminished by which reading group they are placed in, or how well they did on this year's standardized test. (6)

The Johnson and Johnson theory of cooperative learning believes in the concept of "limited range" for groups within heterogeneous classes. In other words, classes should never be homogeneous, but neither should the cooperative group mixture include the highest-ability students with the lowest-ability students. We agree, in part. Heterogeneous classes are imperative. However, after implementing cooperative learning for five years and experimenting with grouping dilemmas, we do not necessarily build groups with limited range in mind. Grouping arrangements such as the *random* method and *choice* method have proven more beneficial than teacher-determined groups. Using the random method, students may count off and arrange themselves by number. The choice method allows students the freedom to work with students they select—or with students who select the same task.

We find that occasionally students complain at first about working with students they perceive to be as academically less savvy than themselves. Nancy had to enforce group responsibility when, on the first collaborative assignment, Isaac had read just one-and-one-half pages of a four-page story.

> Isaac, a Black student, was in a group with a strong White female and an academically achieved Black female. . . . First, students were urged to accept the responsibility of seeing that each group member finished reading the story. Isaac took longer; he had only read 1 1/2 of the four pages. I suggested the group read aloud the part that Isaac had not completed. He seemed embarrassed that he did not read as fast as the others, or possibly insecure as the only male in the group.
>
> Isaac's second experience was better, although in the same group. Each student had different poems to examine, point out personifications, and share findings with the group. . . . One grade would be given to the group, the final paper selected at random. Through random selection (by drawing one of the three papers) it was Isaac's turn to point out the personifications. He recited the poem from memory, rather than reading it from his notes, remembered each of the personifications, and was able to explain all. He dazzled me, impressed the other students, and with this success, his apprehension of group work disappeared.

Many students (especially high achievers) and some parents question group grades at first, but in time, as groups work more effectively together, group grades are accepted as routine. Edie recommends not using group grades as a strategy for positive interdependence until the groups have mastered some basic interpersonal skills.

One parent complained that it was unfair for her very bright son to be in a group with a student who had the reputation of having unfocused behavior and of being a class clown. Perhaps fearing the behavior would rub off on her son, she protested and challenged the theory of cooperative learning. For students and parents who still object to combinations that don't place the "high ability" students together, we point out research that indicates that all students learn a great deal by explaining to others what they already know. So often higher-ability students have intuitive knowledge yet cannot identify the thinking process through which they travel. They also increase their repertoire of thinking strategies as they learn from others the various problem-solving strategies they use. Better yet, these students often process and learn more by teaching, walking another student through the process.

Group Formation

In our classes, we give thoughtful consideration to many facets beyond ability, including social skills, cultural background, friendships, race, sex, and interests, when forming groups that will work on a prolonged activity. Random grouping usually works well, but letting students form their own groups can lead to certain types of homogeneity: kids tend to pick people like themselves in race and sex. Carrie, a ninth-grade teacher, asked students to write down with whom they might like to work. Some students said, "any White girl" or "any Black boy." Cathy noticed that Aisha nearly always chose to work with two other Black girls; when she worked with White females she didn't really trust them and checked all their suggestions with her teacher. When Sandy piloted the writing workshop á la Nancie Atwell, she too found Black students chose other Black students, usually from among the same three or four kids.

Many teachers counter this tendency by specifying for some tasks to pick a partner of the opposite sex or to pick a partner of another race. This has presented no problem, perhaps because the students are used to similar directions for forming random partners such as find a person you've not worked with before or work with someone who is two inches or more shorter or taller than you. Other teachers have students count off or draw colored strips of paper from a hat, placing those with the same numbers or colors in a group. Gail asks students to count off by twos, threes, fours, or fives. At first, we hesitated to arrange groups so "haphazardly." But as we have grown in our understanding and methods of cooperative learning accountability, we employ these faster grouping methods and they work just as well!

Carrie organized groups on her poetry unit by having kids pick

words (nouns) out of a bag. They had to pair up with someone else who had a noun from a different category. (Colored cards differentiated the categories: foods, animals, and other.) This gave them limited free choice of partner. Then the two of them had to write a poem about the new object they created. Initially there was considerable groaning, but everyone turned a finished poem in, and I thought they were quite clever. Additionally, when I posted them all on the chalkboard in the classroom, a number of kids read each other's poems.

Groups formed on the basis of interest (rather than friendship, ability, race, or sex) are especially successful. Literature study groups are built on this premise. After a brief introduction by the teacher or another student, kids select the novels that interest them most, ranking their first, second, and third choices. Cooperative groups are arranged by interest and book availability, working with students who are reading the same book (see complete lesson in Appendix One). Cathy uses literature study groups based on students' reading selections and finds none of the usual personality complaints: "No one requested a group change, and everyone cooperated fully. . . . I saw a genuine concern for the success of *the group*."

Some of the most powerful learning, discussing, and writing that we have seen comes from groups based on literary interest. One of Cathy's naturally integrated groups exemplified this power.

> White students learned powerful lessons from African American students. One group containing three White females and one Black female discussed *Edgar Allen*. The Black female was very open about mistreatment and name-calling that she had experienced at different points of her life. Her sharing of these painful experiences gave the White students a greater understanding of the society portrayed in the book and of Hixson's current racial climate. . . . The three White girls listened with rapt attention to every word that Erika said during the conference. Erika was able to open new perspectives to the other girls in the group.

Cooperative learning opened new perspectives for us. But how did we actually use these cooperative groups once we understood the components and how the groups should be formed? The primary activities were peer response groups, study buddies, collaborative composing, jigsawing, and literature study groups.

GROUPS IN ACTION

Peer Response Groups

Training in cooperative learning enhances the effectiveness of peer editing groups. It aids during prewriting, drafting, and revision. Students bounce ideas off of one another; they share perceptions about their writing; they speculate and hypothesize on the meaning of what they read. Once etiquette, manners, and goals become second nature to students, active responding seems to follow through all stages of reading and writing. Students somehow internalize the process.

Teachers encourage ad hoc responses to reading and writing in progress. We find that students get accustomed to reading their drafts aloud to another person, trying out ideas on each other, and responding naturally and spontaneously, even outside of class. Gail writes, "I heard of aunt's remarks, uncle's encouragements, and the wary parents who thought their child had copied from a book."

Informal settings provide the kind of give and take from peers that can keep a student writing. Gail tells about Quincy's need for this kind of atmosphere:

> He and three others sat outside of my classroom and "talked" as they wrote. They didn't help each other necessarily or work cooperatively, they just talked as they wrote. They would listen occasionally and comment, but the freedom to talk freed them up and got the mind working. Quincy was in this group. He seemed to need the noise.

Her field notes support Vygotsky's (1962) theory that inner speech, usually silent, resurfaces as "talking to yourself" when puzzling over a new or different task.

Quincy's poem won third place in a schoolwide writing contest (see Figure 7-1). Gail watched Quincy's peer group "whistle and shout when I announced that he won. It was as if they had won, too." Gail went on to reflect that the cooperative spirit seemed much stronger among the Black kids than the White kids.

Throughout the year, students work with partners when revising and proofreading. When it is time for editing, the term "editing experts" is frequently heard in our classrooms. Each student selects an area in which to be an "expert editor," such as choppy sentences, intros and endings, or dialogue. The expert reads papers from his peer response group, writing responses according to specific directions. Each student's paper is typically read by four or five peers within a class period. We construct this activity in a variety of ways. Some teachers create rows that represent experts in certain areas. Stephanie distributes colored pencils—red for punctuation, blue for spelling, and green for sentence structure. She demonstrates how to build in

Pollution

Pollution Pollution Pollution.

There's got to be a solution.

It's killing our life forms away,

Pollution is a predator and life forms are the prey.

I know people don't like pollution but they just sit and let it flow,

They say it's not affecting them so they continue to go

On and on and on about how they don't care,

But they don't realize pollution is polluting the air.

Somebody can make a difference if they had the right stuff.

People are making a difference, but it's still not enough.

I'm not talking about the society even though it is reckless.

I'm talking about pollution because that's what's affecting us.

To every loose chain there's got to be link.

Pollution is causing animals to become extinct.

If we stop pollution, the animals can life without our help

And we won't have to give them a lot of medicine for their disease.

Stop pollution so they can run free in the breeze.

If we stop pollution there will be a treat.

Life form and air, isn't that sweet!?

I know I can't make a difference because I'm too little to,

But this is something the whole world has got to do.

Help me drive pollution away,

FOREVER!

FIG. 7-1 *Quincy's winning poem.*

success for those students whose judgment may not be trusted by peers in this excerpt from her field notes:

> I strategically passed out the pencils to students so I could give good spellers a blue one, etc. Knowing that Craig's spelling and punctuation skills are especially weak, I gave Craig a green pencil. I caught the other two students look at one another in an "Oh no" way when I read off the groups. I kept a close eye on Craig's group. When the groups finished, Bill, one of Craig's editing partners, came up to me. In a low voice he pointed to a sentence that Craig had put *RO* [run-on] in the margin.
>
> "Is this really a run-on?" he asked.
>
> I read the sentence and sure enough it needed a comma and a conjunction, not just a comma. I noticed Craig was watching us; obviously he knew that Bill, not a target student, was questioning his work. Loud enough for Craig to hear, I told Bill that he needed to separate the sentence or add a conjunction. I sneaked a look at Craig and he was smiling.

When groups peer edit, Theresa finds two helpful techniques: peer group checksheets and peer editing cups.

> The checksheets are a quick and easy way to set up the groups and to monitor them. The daily objective is placed at the top, along with the job assignments for the various members. The checksheet is displayed on the overhead and I carry it on my clipboard as I monitor the groups. A quick check shows that the individual and the group has met the objective.
>
> The peer editing cups [the same blue and red cups used in the writing center to let the teacher know her help was needed as discussed in Chapter 6] help keep the room quieter while students work in groups. When a group has trouble, they turn the cups so the red one is on top. I get to that group as soon as I can.

Sometimes a peer partner or group gives bad advice, trying to impose another agenda on the writer. Sometimes the writer uncritically accepts such feedback. Other times they are saved by different feedback from teacher or other peers, or by their own growing "author-ity." We stress the importance of ownership in their writing.

Peer Tutoring and Study Buddies

Activities peripheral to collaborative composing or peer response are often well suited to cooperative learning. Most of us initially used "study buddies" to review for tests and practice such skillwork as spelling and vocabulary. This paired tutoring was very successful. Grades on tests shot up. Soon we were using study buddies for a greater variety of work: poetry techniques, free reading, sentence combining, and notetaking for absent partners.

Early in our study, Sandy and Mary Ann developed a point system to encourage interdependence. If both study buddies received more than 75 percent on a test, each earned an extra five points. The points could be "saved" for other occasions by having the teacher sign their own list of extra points.

Gail also used "reading buddies"—not exactly tutoring but a collaborative version of independent reading. Students

> could read silently or aloud. It didn't matter to me, as long as they read. Robert always read aloud with someone else. I found that the other person did most of the reading with Robert listening. He was able to grasp the content of the materials we read in class much more than with S. S. R. [sustained silent reading] or selected readers. Maybe it became more personal for him.

Theresa uses groups of three to study the three hundred required vocabulary words that have been categorized according to related works of literature. After a lesson on how to put the words and definitions into long-term memory, she assigns groups with specific roles.

> The researcher, who looks up the definition.
> The reader, who reads the definition.
> The recorder, who writes the definition.
>
> The group then devises a way to teach the 4 to 7 words to the class. They may split the words up, teaching them in pairs, or in a triad to the class. The students really became involved in presenting "their" words to the class. They incorporated drama and humor to help move the words into long-term memory.

All members of the group are involved and participate in the presentation. Presenting the groups' lessons takes a full period. On Wednesday, the groups re-present their words as a review, which takes about 20 minutes. The students take the test on Friday.

I am trying to teach the value of studying a little at a time rather than cramming the night before. In the beginning of the year, test results showed that either the students studied or they did not: the majority of the grades were either As or Fs. With the help of a spreadsheet which displays weekly a student's average by student number, students soon realized the benefits of studying the words a few at a time. Test scores gradually improved.

Study buddies are easily incorporated into all academic disciplines. From math to science to home economics, we can all learn and "get by with a little help from our friends."

Collaborative Composing

It is relatively easy to apply cooperative learning techniques to the study of vocabulary, spelling, literature analysis, sentence combining, and grammar activities since these tasks are short in duration. True joint authorship of a text is more challenging.

Joan designed a collaborative character analysis based on Richard Wright's "The Kitten" from *Black Boy*. Triads concentrate on three characters: Richard, his mother, and his father. Each student writes three words to describe each character. The group pools its information and determines the three best words for each characteristic. Then as a group they find evidence from the story to support their selection. Each individual takes on the task of drafting an analysis of one characteristic. The group chooses the best paragraph to revise and proofread collaboratively. This activity uses individual drafting but cooperative learning at every point through the process—for brainstorming, analyzing, organizing, evaluating, revising, and editing.

Much of the group work used in our classes begins with individual authorship and individual voices, then moves toward interweaving the work.

Nancy's eighth-grade class collaboratively composed a poem. While taking a "sensory" walk around the school grounds on a springlike afternoon in March, students wrote descriptive words, phrases, sentences, or paragraphs about four things: a blooming crabapple tree, the trash dumpster after lunch, the traffic, and a tree that still looked winter-dead but had a ring of crocus blooming beneath it. After composing individually, students worked in pairs, highlighting the most appealing words or phrases in each paper. Nancy read each paper and highlighted (in a different color) the strongest parts (teacher and student most often agreed). Each student then chose the word, sentence, or phrase they wanted to include in the poem. Nancy passed around a paper upon which students recorded their selections. Of the students below, one was a target student. Which one, do you think?

> *Don:* Flowers blossom below a tree with blowing, brown leaves, drawing attention to something that would otherwise pass right by you.
>
> *Tim:* The dead tree looking so dead it uses the life it has in it not on itself, but on the beauty of the flowers.
>
> *Carolyn:* … older and wiser
>
> *Alison:* With tiny flowers surrounding its feet, it reminds me of a grandparent that is slowly saying good-bye to its children and grandchildren trying to guard them.
>
> *Sonny:* It has had a bigger and better lesson in life, and maybe now its time has come.
>
> *Rachel:* … a million dying, wrinkled faces drooping in despair.
>
> *Bonnie:* … limp leaves that have already served their time.
>
> *Ava:* … fingers shivering as the cool breeze comes about. The tree acts as a mother holding on to her children, not letting one fall to the ground.[1]

A number of students saw the tree as an old woman, caring for her children, so that became the extended metaphor. Papers in hand, the class composed the first draft together on the chalkboard while Nancy frantically wrote their suggestions for composing and reviewing. Twelve-inch voices flew out the window as suggestions boomed. Students wanted assurance that their ideas would be heard in the room and in the poem. Nancy photocopied the first draft for each student, and students set out to revise independently and then in triads. The next day kids came to class with their own ideas about the poem. They rearranged, deleted, added detail, substituted words, and looked for strong images. Revision continued throughout the week at various times. After editing and proofreading, the final product became:

The Non-Blooming Tree
Rainbow Team's Collaborative Poem
3/10/92

A grandmother with tired limbs
Whose frail arms wave
Under heavy, gray skies
Leaves not dull but awakening beige,
Her fingers shiver in the breeze
Having a bigger and better lesson in life,
But one whose time may have come.
Dying, wrinkled faces, drooping in despair,
Hanging lifeless, having already served her time.
Perhaps a mother holding her children,
Not letting one fall to the ground.
The wilted leaves rustle softly,
Using the life left in her, not on herself,
But on the birth of spring's children.
Protecting and surrounding her feet,
Like a violet mist,
Drawing attention to something that
Might otherwise pass by you,
Slowly saying good-bye to her children,
Yet trying to guard them.

Collaborative Research and Jigsawing

A sophisticated use of cooperative learning allows student interdependence during research. The "jigsaw method" of collaborative research is an excellent organizational technique by which students assume separate investigative tasks, share their findings, and pool their resources as a whole group. Joan has students use four "keys" to unlock a poem's meaning:

- figures of speech
- sound effects (alliteration, rhyme, onomatopoeia)
- contrast and repetition
- the title and ending

She makes use of the theory of jigsawing—"Whoever explains and elaborates, learns." After Joan has helped the class discover several poems' meanings by using the four keys, the students apply what they've learned to a new poem. Four or five students work together using one key to understand a particular poem. Other groups work on the other three keys. Each group prepares a lesson they will teach to different small groups. New groups of four are then formed, with each person ready to talk about a different key. This is where the "jigsaw pieces" are reshuffled. During the jigsaw activity each student as a well-prepared expert contributes to the understanding of the poem. Next, students are grouped into triads that select a single poem to unlock. Each student writes an essay analyzing that poem and then helps to revise the other two essays.

> This jigsaw activity contributed a great deal in preparing the students to analyze their poems in the triad that eventually produced three essays. The essays were personal in tone, but analytical and personal in content. This is the first literary analysis many of the target students had experienced and the results were surprisingly impressive. Furthermore, the target students enjoyed the process, and felt confident as they approached the analysis and drafted/revised their ideas. I am sure that the cooperative strategies used throughout the poetry unit and specifically on the poetry essay deserve the credit for these good results.

In an interdisciplinary social studies and English class, Nancy uses jigsawing as an investigative method for the study of World War II. Each pair of students investigates the role of a particular country. Then each pair must report and act out what happened in the country they represent, explain why it happened, and show how other countries were affected. As a whole group, students and teacher then synthesize what they have learned, putting the pieces of the puzzle together.

DEMOCRATIC CLASSROOM CULTURE

Student Empowerment

Student ownership and involvement thrive in the cooperative classroom. All students have strengths, talents, and skills that they bring to their group. However, students who have been told through tracking, ability grouping, or other more subtle, bureaucratic ratings that they are less able than others may not attempt to participate. How many of us have received messages in our academic careers such as, "You're a great writer, but give up science," or "Stick to computing numbers, but give up on art"? Cooperative learning employs positive peer pressure, drawing on the abilities of all students and leading to success for all.

With positive peer pressure to achieve, kids assume responsibility not only for their learning but the learning of the group. When a group member is absent, the others take notes, and if necessary reteach what the absent member missed upon his return. Teaching the lesson reinforces it for those who were not absent.

The positive peer pressure is paramount for our targeted group of students who often receive only negative peer pressure—to fail. Wayne Thomas, founder of the Association of African American Role Models in St. Louis, notes that among many Black teenagers, it's "in" to be good in sports or music but "out" to study. Collaborative learning helps to diffuse that negative peer pressure so that it no longer sabotages academic achievement.

All of us were concerned at first about how to wean students from depending on others to depending on themselves. This is a slow process and isn't accomplished within a single year. We are convinced that Vygotsky's principle is correct: What kids can do with help today, they can do alone tomorrow. Certainly if they are not able to do it alone today, we must provide the scaffolding that is necessary rather than leave them to fail on their own. The scaffolding that maximizes language includes a context of support, encouragement, and assistance from peers.

The most important benefit of cooperative learning is the empowerment of all students. "Low achievers" gradually gain confidence by adapting group tasks to meet their needs and staying with a task to completion. This sense of control over their environment, their objectives, and their progress enables the students to enjoy newfound success.

Classroom Management

Certain problems of management arise, but we have found solutions and positive trade-offs for most of these problems. While there is less time for whole-class instruction and interaction, there is also less need to repeat instructions and much more time to facilitate. In general, we like the trade-off. Most tasks take longer in groups, but retention is better. Group minilessons serve the needs of all students as a group as well as the needs of individuals.

Management procedures need to be taught. Some teachers post a few rules on the wall; others manage in immature classes by limiting group work to highly structured tasks. As more teachers incorporate cooperative learning in their classrooms, these rules require less time. Students internalize expectations. They understand the importance of forming groups quickly, forbidding put-downs, and assuming equal responsibility for group success.

The benefits of cooperative learning far outweigh the disadvantages. For target students, working in structured groups tends to bring more motivation and more on-task time. We estimate that the at-risk student in effective small groups spends about 50 percent of the time on task, compared with perhaps 25 percent otherwise.

The power of the cooperative, diverse classroom is the respect given to the work of those who may differ from ourselves. Students in a democratic classroom thrive, grow, and learn, sharing their successes with others.

LOOKING IN THE MIRROR:
THE RESEARCH TEAM COLLABORATES

Once upon a time, a community of writers and lifetime learners was established. It grew from the power of collaboration. It began in 1987 when a group of teachers who had been working in isolation united to address a mutual concern: how to improve the writing of African American students. That concern grew to include improving the writing of all students.

This community began timidly, with insecurity and some doubt. Would one teacher be as successful as others? As we forced ourselves to move from "my" classroom to "our" classrooms, trust grew. With trust came the freedom to take risks. From taking risks and trying new ways to reach students, another community of writers and lifetime learners was established. This community included our students.

We model the collaboration for our students and peers. We write together, as in the case of writing, producing, and creating this book. We study together as we have for years, keeping field notes, journals, and logs. We share what works, and what does not! We are as different in strengths, talents, and lifestyles as are our students, but we have experienced the power of successful cooperative learning and know it can be successful.

WHAT YOU CAN DO

Teachers of all disciplines should take the Johnson and Johnson training. It is offered nationwide.

Draw on the strength of the community in which students learn (home, school, peers).

Establish the atmosphere of positive interdependence—we sink or swim together.

Use goal setting by the group as a way to channel energy and focus activities.

Provide a safe environment where students feel free among their peers to take risks.

Provide structure and monitor for individual accountability through conferencing, face-to-face interaction, and through short and simple reporting methods.

Instruct students in the etiquette and behavior that allows cooperative learning to work so well, such as twelve-inch voices, praise, and a ban on put-downs.

Assure that the diversity of talents in the heterogeneous classroom has an opportunity to shine. Form groups in a variety of ways, such as random counting, matching certain colored strips of paper, allowing students to choose, or arranging by the teacher.

Provide opportunities for collaborative composing, research, and response to literature.

Create a structured and democratic classroom that will, in the long run, empower students.

Read:

BRUFFEE, KENNETH. 1983. "Writing and Reading as Collaborative Acts." In *The Writer's Mind: Writing as a Mode of Thinking,* edited by J. N. Hays, P. A. Roth, J. R. Ramsey, and R. D. Foulke. Urbana, IL: National Council of Teachers of English.

JOHNSON, DAVID, RICHARD JOHNSON, and EDYTHE JOHNSON HOLUBEC. 1988. *Cooperation in the Classroom.* Rev. ed. Edina, MN: Interaction Books.

NOTE

1. Ava was a target student.

Facing the Mirror: Joan Krater

I didn't really know an African American person until I taught in Webster Groves, which thirty years ago had a Black enrollment of about 11 percent. My parochial schooling, from kindergarten through college, had sheltered me to a great extent from the real world but engendered strong ideals. A St. Louisan all my life, I was shocked as an adult to be identified as living in a racist city. I was born just a week before Pearl Harbor and I definitely belong to the generation before the baby boomers. My friends and I, on the cusp of the baby boom and in college in the early 1960s, were talkers with strong feelings but not doers. Even after graduation, my college friends and I would sit for hours discussing the civil rights movement and always ended by asking ourselves why we were just sitting there instead of doing something. Then someone would offer that we were contributing after all in our helping roles of social workers and teachers. We all felt the emptiness in our words, though. As I reflect now, it seems we were immobilized, just as the country was, by . . . what? fear of the unknown?

I worked during my high school summers at my father's motel, part of a prestigious chain. Very few Black travelers stopped at our place, but we honored all their reservations even though the law did not require us to do so at the time. My mother, who headed housekeeping, had to convince the cleaning ladies (who were all White) to clean the rooms that had been occupied by Blacks. Our customers came mostly from the deep South, and we lived with a very real and visceral fear that Whites would not stay with us if we "catered to" Blacks.

One time Dad hired a Black painter who couldn't get into the segregated union and was told by the union representatives that he was risking picket lines that could close down the business. He and the painter worked out an agreement where he would paint only in the back areas and on weekends and in evenings, hoping he would attract no further attention. My parents' decisions and actions helped foster my own empathy and social concern—but my personality still wanted to avoid the possible confrontations that could have occurred if I had taken an active part in the civil rights movement.

After teaching ten years or so, I directed a title program aimed at reducing the effects of past segregation. This was my first academic introduction to the study of African American culture. I attended every workshop I could find on cultural characteristics and the theories of teaching language ("Should we accept the language so as to respect the person or insist on standard English so as to enable the child to enter the mainstream society with the good jobs?").

In 1977, I moved outside St. Louis County to an area with low taxes and low services—no library or fire department—and no Blacks. It was then I realized how segregated our society really was, regardless of the progress made by the civil rights movement. Having "lived" in an integrated school setting for fourteen years, I suddenly grew antennae that immediately searched social groups for African Americans. It was an eerie feeling to find myself in all-White groups where racist jokes were shared loudly and openly enjoyed. In a paradoxical way, I had been sheltered in my integrated educational world in a much stronger way than in my childhood.

The biggest change in my teaching came in the summer of 1979 when I participated in the Gateway Writing Project. I knew nothing about teaching writing. I didn't even fit in the old way of teaching writing by assigning topics and correcting errors with a red pen. I just didn't teach writing. Literature genres and grammar with a heavy emphasis on diagramming filled all my teaching time. We'd do "creative writing" once in a great while! That intensive summer institute taught me how to teach process, helped me clarify my attitudes toward dialect, and introduced me to holistic assessment.

I spearheaded the holistic assessment in Webster Groves, leading it from its second year through its last. We initially collected all kinds of data not because we had any hypotheses but because we were curious. It was appalling to see the differences between White and Black students' scores. After the second year of distressing bar graphs, I knew we had to do something about it.

It seems to me that education and integrated schools are the key. When I first taught poetry by African Americans—back in the 1970s when the vogue wasn't multicultural teaching but separate units on Black literature, history, and issues—discussion in the classroom was strained. Typically I had one, two, or three Black students in a class and, typically, they were silent—as were the White students. White students would surreptitiously look around to see how the Black kids were reacting; the Black students kept their heads down. Today, the same poems, part of the total poetry experience, elicit heated discussion. Black students, with pride in their voices, love to explain why "They [KKK members] don't come by ones" in Sterling Brown's "Old Lem." White students share their distress and anger. Typically, all students are eager to tell their personal stories. I listen to the animated discussion, sensing that progress is being made in the only way it can be made—through two-way communication and shared experiences.

The writing project has helped me both professionally and personally. I am a better teacher for all my students and I'm part of a group of doers, not just talkers.

Increase Control of Language

I learned how to use the English language as clay, molding it over and over until it became the masterpiece that produces the effect I wanted. I have also learned to make my essays and stories interesting by using creative similies, new and descriptive verbs which I found in the Theasaurus along with the needed adjectives I could not think of.

DAVID,
grade nine

What is "good writing"? Writing that communicates clearly, convincingly, with a vitality that maintains reader interest; writing that is developed, organized, and has appropriate voice, vocabulary, and diction; writing that achieves its purpose with its intended audience. Such writing by definition must have few errors in usage and mechanics as those errors detract from its content and send unintended messages to the reader.

The students we teach have been using their language for twelve to seventeen years, usually with great success as they communicate with family, each other, and strangers. They use complex syntax and sentence structure. While few can identify an introductory adverbial clause and fewer still can create one on demand, they all use such a structure. On the other hand, while most can identify a run-on and can state that run-ons should be avoided in writing, almost all use them with discouraging frequency. We believe there is little correlation between the ability to define a term or identify its application and the ability to use it correctly.

Our teaching is more concerned with improving writing than with learning terminology or rules. Certainly any high school graduate should have a working familiarity with the terminology of her native language. It's just that this knowledge does not necessarily result in good writing and in fact can inhibit the writing if taught at inappropriate times.

Yet control of language can be taught. "Control of language" is a broader concept than "grammar" or "mechanics" or "standard English." It includes choices of style (subjective decisions) as well as corrections of mechanics such as spelling, punctuation, and capitalization, which are more or less "objective" decisions. We want our students to have the control that frees them, that gives them the power to break free of their first draft. We want our students to see the options available and to select judiciously among them. We want our students to play with language, to be fully aware of the myriad ways in which an idea can be expressed, to see the nuances brought by each phrasing, and to have the control over those options to select the one that is most appropriate. And we want our students to be free of those mechanical errors that will keep readers from paying attention to their ideas. David, who is not a target student, understands what it means to "play" with language; he refers to molding language as one molds clay. David describes the process poetically; all students are able to do it.

Control of language goes beyond correct and incorrect. Even "incorrect" can be appropriate in certain instances such as using a deliberate fragment for conversational tone, or incorporating a humorously casual anecdote in a formal paper. Knowing that "have gone" is standard and "have went" is nonstandard does not necessarily give a writer control. Always using standard forms does not give a writer control. A writer who grabs a word from a thesaurus without considering how that word affects the tone of a piece has no control. A writer in control will select a word, a phrase, or a structure after considering possibilities and their impacts on the sound of the piece, on its tone, and on the reader.

Some readers may be getting impatient: when are we going to deal with Black Communications (Dandy 1991), Black English Vernacular (Smitherman 1977, 1985, 1994), nonstandard English (Labov 1970), and Black dialect—and what are we going to call it? Whatever it's called, *it* is an integral part of the control of language. Nonstandard English was *not* a distinguishing feature of the low-scoring papers written by African American students in our schools (Zeni and Krater-Thomas 1990). That doesn't mean it isn't used in our students' writing by both African American students and White students. White students use rural White nonstandard language, such as "he don't" and "she has went." Nonstandard language is at times appropriate, particularly in dialogue, and sometimes even in narrative depending on the audience and the purpose. Our goal is to help students expand their linguistic repertoire and be able to determine when certain usages are necessary and when they are interfering—in other words, to gain control over their options.

A writer who has control over his language can come up with optional wording, phrasing, and structure, *and* select the most appropriate choice. Students are not aware of their choices when they are frozen into a right/wrong way of thinking about writing. They don't gain control of language in an authoritarian school culture that rejects their language. They do learn control if the teacher's attitude is, "You're smart, you have choices. Look why a writer might want to do this or that." The system is not in control of the student, rejecting or accepting him on the basis of language; the student is in control. Students with a history of underachievement seemed energized by this approach. Listen to Patrick, a White student in Gail's seventh-grade class identified as both gifted and learning disabled in written expression. "In all the english class before this year I had workbook and text books and we just learned about stuff like nouns, verbs, and articles. This year we got to use the nouns, verbs, and articles in our writings and thats better."

How do we help our students gain this control? During Phases One and Two, we fixed some of our methods so as to fix the writing. Spelling workbooks have disappeared. We have moved away from large-group instruction and toward more individualized help on language control. The large-group instruction that is still used tends to be more concentrated in the form of daily edits and minilessons. Sentence combining, sentence expansion, and modeling the revision process reveal the options at the sentence level. They don't help much, however, with misspellings or usage errors. We deal with those in minilessons and daily edits, but especially during individual conferences when we look for patterns of errors, give the student specific clues for conquering the problem, and set goals for the next draft. A short list on the back of a final draft helps students and teacher focus on specific areas during the next piece. Calling this a target list rather than a list of errors sets the positive stage. Minnie finds that the most common proofreading "targets" in tenth grade are spelling, fragments, and run-ons. The discouraging aspect is that seventh- and eighth-grade teachers would have the same list!

Much of what we do to help students gain control we refer to as "playing with language." We use that phrase a great deal with our students: "Play with that sentence. See if you can say the same idea three other ways." "Let's play with how your language would change if the audience were the school board instead of your best friends." It's not only a gamelike approach, it's an emphasis on manipulating language, the first step in gaining control. Our strategies for this language play are codeswitching and sentence combining. We tackle proofreading skills with direct instruction in minilessons and individual conferences. Finally, we teach terminology, spelling, and vocabulary within a context, not with rules and lectures; in other words, we use indirect instruction.

PLAY WITH LANGUAGE

Codeswitching

It is imperative for African Americans to sit at the American language table as members in good and high standing and with strong and positive self-concepts. . . . This will require the development of a kind of bilingual, bidialectal and, in some ways, a bicultural competence. In other words, African Americans, like many other groups, must acquire a language system which often differs in several significant ways from their community language systems, while preserving their community language system for use as needed. (Orlando Taylor in Preface to *Black Communications: Breaking Down the Barriers.*)

Although Dandy's *Black Communications: Breaking Down the Barriers* wasn't published until 1991, the above statement from Orlando Taylor's preface to that book summarizes our views: dialects are different, not inferior or superior; standard English is an admission ticket to certain jobs; the language our students speak deserves our understanding and our respect.

At various times we have referred to the language common to African American students as Black dialect, Black English, and nonstandard English. We have never been satisfied with any of those terms, as each carries an implied negativity. Dandy's title (with credit given to Hoover and Abrahams) appeals to us for the same reason it does to her: It encompasses verbal *behavior,* not just syntax. *Black Communications* is positive—or at least neutral—in connotation. The term itself brings to mind testifying, signifying, call and response, nonverbal stances, and wise sayings that the African American community throughout America uses.

Black Communications (BC) has verve, style, and life that White students obviously admire in their attempts to imitate it. Indeed, the mainstream culture incorporates aspects of BC in its advertising, music, comedy, and television. Ironically, while the American mainstream culture insists that subcultures assimilate, it is discovering that "Blacks are not outside the

American mainstream but, in Ellison's words, have always been 'one of its major tributaries'" (Steele 1992, 77).

We discuss dialect openly and directly in the classroom (Chapter 4). We read literature that uses BC and celebrate the appropriate use of BC in our students' writing. Skilled writers such as Tamara (not a target student) explored vehicles that demanded codeswitching. In her fairy tale that cleverly reverses the expected reality and fantasy, she places a princess in old Africa. The fairy godmother, usually the fantasy element of a fairy tale, presents contemporary reality.

> Once there was a princess named Shari who lived in a kingdom in Africa. Shari's father, the king, was adored by all of the people because he was so caring and wise. Her mother, the queen, was also loved by the people. Shari also had four brothers, Osi, Ganni, Dobi, and Zee. Her brothers were all very handsome, and all the kings from other kingdoms in other lands wanted their daughters to marry one of them. Kings in neighboring kingdoms were jealous of the entire family, and threatened to take Shari away. So Shari was never allowed to leave the palace; she spent most of her time gazing out the window.
>
> One day while Shari was looking out her window, she noticed that the sky was a golden color.

Tamara's control of her language is obvious: the use of the semicolon and of appositives is not typical of eighth graders. An African American, she demonstrates a facility with codeswitching observed among more advanced writers. Tamara's princess speaks in standard English and somewhat formally as befits royalty. On the other hand, Yolanda, the fairy godmother, sounds like this: "Well, I'm somethin' like a fairy godmother, but as you can see I ain't hardly old enough to be nobody's godmother. I'm only 15! But a lot of my hommies have had kids at ages younger than that! It's a trip ain't it? They went and messed up their whole life!" Melissa, whom you met in Chapter 3, was not as skilled a writer as Tamara, but she too could codeswitch within a single piece of writing.

We celebrate the power of BC in our classrooms while at the same time giving direct instruction in formal English. In other words, we strive to be culturally sensitive, "to build communicative competence in the standard dialect without degrading the dialect of the students" (Dandy 1991, 106).

When our African American students use Black dialect in the classroom, we show our respect for them and for their ideas by not interrupting with a correction. (Would you correct a colleague who made a subject/verb agreement error during a committee meeting? In front of the other members of the committee? Why not?) If teachers permit only standard English to be spoken, they will have a silent classroom. Such an exertion of power by the teacher results in a loss of power for the students.

Yet we do assume that standard English is the norm for classroom discourse. We must give students—Black and White—a context for practice or play with a style of language they may not use much outside school. There are times we will playfully tease a student *after* responding to what he had to say. We may repeat his words or ask him to "Say that again?" Standard English usually results. Control of language means knowing not only how but when to codeshift. We always use the rhetorical triangle—speaker/audience/purpose—when helping students decide on the appropriateness of their written language.

Many of our African American students don't codeshift when writing a rough draft. This is to be expected; in fact, we would discourage a student from making codeswitching changes just as we discourage students from using a dictionary to check spelling when writing first drafts. Concentration should be on content and keeping up with the flow of ideas, not on mechanics. Revision comes later and includes switching to standard English forms when appropriate.

Some Black students need only to gain distance, to grow "editors' eyes." They indeed write the nonstandard dialect through carelessness. If we collect their papers, hold them for a few days, then return them for another round of proofreading, they make more changes on their own, as do all writers. In conference we emphasize developing the habit of proofreading, sometimes assisted by reading aloud. Jimmy met with Stephanie on his newspaper article for the invention unit.

> I was reading the article out loud, looking for things to praise and revision suggestions and Jimmy interrupted me several times. First he wanted to correct the spelling of business—he had it *busunes* and I mispronounced it while reading. I didn't say a thing, choosing to come back to it later, but Jimmy said, "It's *b-u-s-i-n-e-s-s*. I know how to spell it. I was in a hurry." I went on and read, "He didn't want to answer none of his phone calls," and Jimmy said, "It's *any*—any phone calls." Jimmy uses a real strong dialect in the halls and with his peers in class, so I was surprised when he caught this error. When we finished, I asked him if he ever read his papers to himself out loud and he said no. "See how it helps?" I asked, and he nodded. I gave his paper back to him and during class the next day he worked on it, and turned in a much improved copy at the end of the hour.

Other African American students don't notice nonstandard usage until we call attention to them in conference. We've discovered that it makes a difference who does the reading. Joey didn't hear the nonstandard English in his own voice, but if Sandy read aloud an excerpt from his own text, he would often hear the dialect features and could easily translate them to standard English. Joey and others like him are jarred when the teacher's voice says, "The kid know the answer; he just don't say it." The same is true for any nonstandard English with any student, Black or White. We wonder if students view dialect not so much as "nonstandard," but as "kid talk"—as an alternate means of communication for them.

Joey's mechanical problems, besides run-ons, included leaving off verb endings: "After they finish drinking, the lady told Adam she want him to find her lucky dime." In her first year's field notes, Sandy was perplexed and concerned by Joey's seeming inconsistencies: "When he read it aloud to me, that's exactly what he said. He got the past tense of 'tell' right, but not the regular verbs. After it was pointed out, he could correct it, but there was no carry over to the next writing. Help!"

Others of us had similar experiences, but as we shared those experiences and discussed readings on codeswitching and dialect, we gained some insight. Target students like Joey have access to both standard and variant forms but not complete control. They are aware that different situations require different language, but they do not have conscious control over which form to use in which case.

The two most common difficulties for our few target students who do not codeshift easily are a final -*ed* and a final -*s*—resulting in nonstandard tense or subject/verb agreement. For Joey, *tell* and *told sound* different; *finish* and *finished* do not have different sounds. Irregular verbs are easier than regular verbs because they signal their tense blatantly, not just with a "silent" -*s* or -*ed* ending. Most Black students have the concepts of singular and plural and of present and past, but their oral language doesn't pronounce most final consonants, much like the French who don't pronounce the *t* in *rapport,* for example. It is interesting that Warriners (1982) and other handbooks stress the irregular verbs; the African American student often needs practice with the regular verbs more than the irregular verbs. We can teach the rule for adding -*ed* to form the past in conference and the student can apply it immediately to the rest of a draft, sometimes with hypercorrection. Daniel, for instance, put -*ed* on the end of every verb (*tolded, singed*) and even some other parts of speech after a conference on this signal for past tense. However, that rule will not automatically be part of the student's language habits—any more than any new grammar rule becomes part of an adolescent's subconscious with one instruction and application.

We've also keyed in on clues to help the student proofread for standard English. For example, if the subject ends in *s*, the verb won't. This rule, like most rules, fails at times—"The dress fits"—but it's great for quick checking. What we know does not work is going through an involved process of teaching the identification of subject and verb, the rules for agreement of subject and verb, and the rules for making nouns and verbs plural. What does help some students is asking, "What happens if I add *s* to a word?" They say, "Makes it plural," and we take the opportunity to clarify that this response is true of nouns but not verbs. This is often a revelation for all our students, not just those writing in nonstandard English.

This kind of direct instruction in an individual conference can be supplemented by a minilesson with a small group or an entire class, with the emphasis on playing with language and manipulating forms and on oral drill. Shaughnessy (1977) and our own experience say oral drill of a word in context helps more than rules. This can be done with group reciting of conjugations, script reading, and role playing (see Chapter 4). Nancy, a former Spanish teacher, teaches verb conjugation. The oral repetition is crucial: standard usage must reach the point of "sounding" right. And context for that sound must exist. Students can't memorize the principal parts of a verb—*go, went, gone*—and hope to use them correctly. The simple context— "Today I go; yesterday I went; I have gone many times"—helps develop that sense of when to use each part.

Nancy begins the minilesson by telling her seventh graders how a student of hers in Spanish class once tried to say, "I am embarrassed," but actually said what could be interpreted, "I am pregnant." The student knew that adding *-ado* at the end of a root word would create a past participle, so she said, "Estoy embarazado." Nancy uses that humorous incident to introduce her point that just a little difference in form can change a word's meaning and using a word improperly can be troublesome.

She draws a chart on the board and fills in the boxes with pronouns, as below, using green chalk for the left column and pink for the right.

I	we
you	you
he, she, it	they

"What do the green words have in common?" she asks. Students eventually will generalize that the green words are singular and the pink are plural. Nancy then says, "All verbs can come with a *to* in front of them, called an infinitive: to play, to see, to dance, etc. Let's fill in the chart with the forms of *to be*."

Nancy jokingly fills in with the word *be* in all six slots; the kids laugh and then they fill in the standard forms together, noticing the great changes. She then shows some Spanish conjugations.

> If you think *to be* is bad, notice how the endings change on all Spanish verbs (shows *andar,* to walk) and how the entire word often changes for some Spanish conjugations (*tengo,* to have)
>
> | | | | |
> |---|---|---|---|
> | ando | andamos | tengo | tenemos |
> | andas | andais | tienes | teneis |
> | anda | andan | tiene | tienen |

She then does a chart with a regular verb in English, pointing out that most verbs don't change so much:

I walk	we walk
you walk	you walk
he walks	they walk

For most verbs, *-s* on the third person singular is only a relic of endings that English, like Spanish, used to have on *all* regular verbs.

Nancy finds this minilesson is useful for all students, whether they consistently use standard English or not. Students who use standard forms intuitively don't really have "control" over this concept if they don't know why.

> I do this lesson only if some in the class need the conjugation to help in their subject/verb agreement. But when some of the students need it, all the students need it. After all, they will be working together in peer

groups. Further, students who have control over their verbs need to know that those who don't aren't dumb. The verbs are just tricky.

Sentence Combining and Expanding

Control of language involves much more than codeswitching. Manipulating full sentences, playing with ways of relating several ideas in one sentence, exploring new syntactical features: these give an adolescent a real sense of power over *thinking,* not just words.

In the first couple of years, our focus was on sentence combining: giving students short, choppy sentences; urging them to combine them in as many ways as possible; and discussing the different emphases of the various results. This method is based heavily on William Strong's (1973, 1976, 1981) "free" combining. Students learn to look not only for short sentences but to note other signals for combining. Anikia let Joan use her sentences in a book review draft as a sample in a minilesson.

Sample One

This book is about a boy named Tom. Tom was a city boy who moved with his family to the country to help his grandpa.

Sample Two

The thing that got me interested in this fiction book is the cover. The cover looked very interesting.

Using the overhead, Joan gave the students the clue by boxing the repetitious words. The direct instruction didn't result in a "rule"—whenever the first word of a sentence repeats the last word of the previous sentence, try combining!—but relied on the visual and oral repetition and a big red *X* eliminating one of them. Then the class played with ways of getting the information into one sentence.

We borrow from Frank O'Hare's (1975) more structured "cued" approach when we notice students need a sentence structure added to their repertoire. For example, our eighth graders are typical of those in Hunt's (1978) study who did not naturally use appositives or introductory participles to combine sentences (98–100). We may challenge a student, in the spirit of a game, with "Could you write this sentence beginning with *running?*" This kind of suggestion usually results in not only restructuring but in adding information. For example, if the original sentence is "He ran down the block and he saw a cop and he came to a quick stop," the new sentence might be, "Running down the block, he was watching for the cops. When he suddenly saw one, he made a quick turn and dashed through the bushes."

We use Strong's exercises, break sentences from our literature into kernel sentences, and write our own using our students' names and school activities in them. We emphasize the oral—the sound—in our whole-class and partner activities. Only a few options are written (usually on an overhead) so we can analyze their varying impacts. When the kernel sentences come from literature, the students compare their sentences with those of the published author; students sometimes hold tenaciously to their version as "better" than the author's.

After practice with a combining exercise, students apply the skill to their own writing. This is most efficiently accomplished if we have marked *S. C.* near a series of sentences on a current draft that can be "played with." Often working with a partner, students push for many oral versions, writing down one they like. We usually insist on three or four written versions and then ask the students to star the one that fits best their own intention and the flow of the draft around it.

Rube Goldbergs (see Figures 8-1 and 8-2) are fun to create and for practice in particular sentence patterns. Students begin by designing a fantastic machine to accomplish a relatively simple task. They list the steps their invention goes through to work, telling each step in one short sentence. Then they combine these seven or ten sentences, aiming for a total of three good sentences. Joan models combining words on the overhead: *which/that, to,* and *-ing* are three patterns that will prove most helpful and give some

Automatic Fly Eater-Upper

Fly attracted by meat flies through open window (a) and lands on piece of
meat (b) on string (c) The force of fly landing on string with meat on it
causes string to break; (d) then meat and fly fall through tunnel (e) equipped with rubber bouncing mechanism.(f) which sends fly and meat to mini-
trampoline (g) that rchochets it to the ceiling. (h) The fly and meat fall
into metal chute (i) causing them to drop on arm lever (j) which flips (l)
hand on far side of lever to balloon which, of course, pops. (m) From
deflating balloon, a high-pitched, screech is produced which calls dog (n)
to din-din; (o) dog eats fly and meat.

1. Dog is potty-trained so dog goes out-side.

Buffy Eades - Wendy Brigham

Fig. 8-1 *Student Rube Goldberg: Automatic Fly Eater-Upper.*

variety to their combinations. Students enjoy the drawing (which is the
prewriting) as well as explaining their Rube Goldbergs to the class.

Joan monitors sentence structure on the next essays, looking for signs
of transfer. She has found it is important to use sentence-combining or
expansion activities that are in the same mode as the upcoming draft.
Narratives and personal writing will likely use embedding through adjectives
and prepositional phrases. Expository writing will use embedding plus
subordinate conjunctions such as *because* and *even though*. This shows how
tricky transfer is. Not only must we model and coach and conference, but

239

Automatic Door Opener for Dog

A lazy old man wants to let out his dog without leaving his bed by
pulling rope (A) attached to board (B) by a pulley, causing marble (C)
to roll down track (D) and tip over glass of water (E) into dog dish
for dog to eat. When dog is finished the dish will spring up and
jiggle bird cage (F) causing bird (G) to fly to perch (H) that lowers
by rubber band so that bird can eat food. When bird is finished he
will fly off perch causing rubberband to snap with piece of wood (I)
hooked on that tilts brick(J) which falls down onto seasaw (K) causing
baseball (L) with string tied on to it to fly upward opening door (M),
so that dog can go out.

Allen Waters
Keith King

FIG. 8-2 *Student Rube Goldberg: Automatic Door Opener for Dog.*

there must be a close connection between the kind of material we use for
language exercises and the kind of original writing students will do.

We learn from our students when they are ready for certain language
options, as Joan did when conferencing with Sidney. He volunteered that he
didn't like a sentence he'd written in his book review.

"When Gilly finds some money she plans to run away to see her real
mother out of town."

> I was at a loss. He was really concentrating and then said, "The *when*
> . . . it sounds . . ." He couldn't articulate it. I suggested substituting *after*
> and he brightened. . . . "Yeah—*after*—that's better." I confirmed his
> choice by commenting, "*After* shows more clearly when things happened
> whereas *when* sounds like everything happened at the same time."

Sidney's previous papers had showed no transfer from sentence-combining lessons, but at this point he was ready to deal with the nuances of expository transitions.

It was during our second year that we had an "aha!" experience. Asking target students to combine short choppy sentences often created awkward results. Try combining any of these three sentences, also from Anikia's book review draft: "This book is about a foster child that moves from one place to another. The book has its ups and downs in it. Third graders would like the bad words." The three sentences are not related in content enough to be related syntactically. One idea can't be subordinated to another as cause and effect or a time sequence or any other way. The *real* problem is not the length of the sentences but the lack of development of each idea. This is the most common problem with sentences among our target students. Sentence *expansion,* not combining, proves more helpful.

Again, we have fun with language. Students enjoy Cathy's alliterative sentence-expansion exercise. She suggests they decide on the base first (such as, "Ollie ordered omelets") and then expand. Aisha wrote, "Outstanding old Ollie Odette once ordered one onion omelet at Opie's Opera House."

Joan challenges her classes to create lengthy sentences through two very structured sentence-expansion activities:

Simple Expansion by Position

Joan writes "The baby cried" on the board and students suggest words to add in each of the four possible different positions to increase information. The first position (before *the*) is the most difficult but can produce a quantum leap in number of words added: "*When* the . . ." Henry worked with his partner Danzel whose writing skills were high average. They inserted an appositive in order to add words between the subject and verb: "Late last night the stinky, nasty baby, Budda, cried loud when it's dirty, empty bottle fell upon the unwashed floor in the bedroom." She then asks students to do expansions with progressively less teacher guidance—in pairs, individually, and for homework.

Expansion by Five Ws

Starting with a sentence kernel, students add details to answer where, when, who, why, how, how much, what kind, and other similar questions. Joan offers "The women were baking a cake." Here's what three students wrote:

> *Daniel:* On July 26 the five obeast {obese} ugly women with no teeth were making 300 pineapple upside down cakes for the same man that they all loved.
> *Henry:* The young sexy women tonight are baking a yellow cake for their five nice boyfriends in the hot and dirty, smelley kitchen for their Birthday.
> *Jeremiah:* Last night at my house down the street from seven-eleven, around eight o'clock the two skiny women from the backery were very quickly with experianced hands making a big Lemon cake with chocolate icing and nuts on the top because it was my sister's birthday. (45 words)

Because our goal was to expand a sentence, we made a game of creating lengthy sentences. Students were able to write sentences (not run-ons) with as many as seventy words! Seventy-word sentences are not usually great models of good writing—and the students know this as they breathlessly read one aloud! But writing must "grow rank before it can be pruned" by selecting the appropriate details (Moffett 1983, 171).

Combining and expanding sentences often produces run-ons or oddly structured sentences. We have no cures for run-ons but know that reading aloud helps many students recognize them. William Strong (1976) emphasizes the importance of doing sentence-combining exercises aloud so students can appreciate the rhythm and flow of the various options. This habit is extremely helpful to writers not only in exercise activities but in evaluating their own writing by its sound. These aural exercises also play into the speaking and listening style of African American culture (Gilbert and Gay 1985).

DIRECT INSTRUCTION

Playing with language—codeswitching and sentence combining—helps students gain control by increasing their options. They select the best option for their writing's context, purpose, and audience. Audience expectations play the same role in helping students select the form that follows conventions of standard English. Students must be taught usage, capitalization, and punctuation. Direct instruction that spells out the conventions of standard English is essential—and only fair.

Delpit (1986) and others fear that White teachers of process writing may ignore the direct teaching of formal English, considering it to be restrictive or even politically repressive. But we have always resisted placing ourselves in "skills" or "process" boxes as if they are mutually exclusive. We believe we "understand the need for both approaches, the need to help students to establish their own voices, but to coach those voices to produce notes that will be heard clearly in the larger society" (296). When several students are having the same problem, we use minilessons. Otherwise we handle proofreading issues in individual conferences.

Minilessons: Common Errors and Usage

Daily edits (Suid 1989) introduce many of our classes. Several sentences or a paragraph containing specific errors are on the board or overhead for students to write correctly as soon as class begins. The errors are taken from the students' current drafts, remaining anonymous unless a student claims, "That's mine." When a problem is common among students, Stephanie writes her own sentences with those errors.

I took notes of punctuation and grammatical errors while reading their journals, and from those notes I developed daily edits. I gave quizzes over daily edits about every three weeks to check progress. Quiz grades were very high from all students.

The daily edits were a wonderful tool for teaching editing skills, as well as grammar and spelling, this year. Target students remained attentive, especially once they realized that I wasn't going to spend a lot of time on them. I feel I really made some progress with distinguishing among *their, they're,* and *there.* This was a common error I noticed in the writing of many students, not just target students.

Daily edits, minilessons, and journal writing are commonly used as beginning-of-class activities. They settle the class, establish a routine, and give the teacher time to take attendance, check with an individual student, or write herself. Target students enjoy safe routines and short tasks and success. These class openers meet those criteria and can be done with the spirit of playing a game, counting the number of words or errors in friendly competition.

We must give direct instruction—whether in minilessons or in individual conferences—about when *not* to proofread as well as when and how to do it. A good revised text is appropriate for proofreading—not a rough draft where concentration is focused on the flow of ideas. There is an appropriate time for the teaching of a proofreading skill as well. We often require dialogue in an assigned narrative. Experience tells us that students will need a review of punctuating that dialogue. However, teaching it before students have written a draft inhibits their flow; they'll be worrying about how to punctuate instead of what to say. After they have a draft, they can see the need for the review and can immediately apply what they've learned to their own writing.

Minilesson: Punctuating Dialogue

When Nancy's students have shown they have difficulty punctuating a conversation, she asks for complete silence for the next few minutes and writes on the board,

"Toni, when is our team going to Texas?" asked Mrs. Cason.

She then hands the chalk to Toni and motions for her to go to the board. Toni might respond with

"We are going to Texas in April" said Toni.

This continues for a few more lines of dialogue before Nancy writes,

Mrs. Cason asked, "Class, does anyone see a possible error?"

The class then discusses and corrects any errors in punctuation such as the comma needed in Toni's response. Nancy then asks,

How many of you have dialogue in your stories? Look at the board, look at your dialogue, get into peer groups, and check it out. Bring your revised pages up and I'll check them.

Minilesson: Homonyms

Joan reviews what homonyms are and shows how students in the past have come up with a visual image and phrase that will help them distinguish between a pair of homonyms. She emphasizes the importance of being outlandish and creating one's own phrase rather than using someone else's. Sidney's example for his confusion of *tail* and *tale:* "Tie the *pail* to the dog's *tail.*" This phrase, along with a side view of a spotted dog dragging a pail behind him, worked for Sidney because he didn't confuse *pail* and *pale.*

Kent (not a target student) helped himself remember when to use *lead* and not *led* by drawing a boy in obvious pain from a puncture wound and the caption, "I stuck *lead* in my *head* (see Figure 8-3).

From then on, whenever a homonym problem appears in a proofread draft, Joan asks the student to come up with an image and caption. If it's on paper, it's displayed in the room for others to enjoy and use as a reference.

I STUCK LE_AD_ IN MY H_EAD_

FIG. 8-3 *Student's visual mnemonic for* lead/led.

Minilesson: Possession

Showing possession has long been a challenge for our students. We clue them in to ask two questions, then add an apostrophe unless the sound tells us to add -'s.

    What is it? a book

    Who owns it? Carl

    Carl's book

    What is it? books

    Who owns them? Carlos

    Carlos's books

This lesson avoids the complex rule about singular possession and plural possession and their exceptions. The real issue is simply sound and whether or not the "who owns it" ends with an *s*.

Individual Proofreading

Minilessons are an effective method of teaching standard usage and mechanics. Siddle-Walker's research as reported by Delpit (1988) found that

> [i]ntervention that produced the most positive changes in the students' writing was a "minilesson" consisting of direct instruction about some standard writing convention. But what produced the *second* highest number of positive changes was a subsequent student-centered conference with the teacher. (288)

We have found, however, that our students are more likely to apply what they learn in a conference, part of which is direct instruction, than they are from a minilesson geared at the whole class with no individual follow-up.

When working with a student who has many proofreading issues on a particular draft, we draw from Shaughnessy's (1977) approach: identify a pattern of errors, learn from a student the conscious or unconscious reason for those errors, and help the student to understand the requirements of formal language. We try to identify the real problem and not the symptom: Why does the student confuse *there, they're,* and *their?* Is the apostrophe understood? Is it really an *ie/ei* confusion? Then we come up with—or guide the student to come up with—a clue or way of coping: Read the draft aloud and listen for the voice to drop. Is there a period at that point? Should there be? Finally we work with the student to set a goal. No more than two fragments per page on the next draft. Many students will aim for perfection, but we usually caution against that. The student needs a fighting chance and can take pride in surpassing the goal when that happens.

Yet it is hard to teach students to recognize surface errors. They get caught up in the meaning—as do we all. A guided process of oral reading and editing one thing at a time seems most effective. We look for what Donald Murray (1968) calls the "critical injury" in a paper—a problem that, if fixed, will make a major improvement. If a student uses fragments that can easily be added to the sentences in front of them, then we focus on that with a lesson and immediate application. Such fragments often occur in a rough draft when a period is placed before the writer knows the next thought. It turns out that thought was actually an extension of the previous one. Helping the student to see the cause of the problem makes it easier to spot the same kind of situation in the next paper.

During these proofreading conferences, we often find ourselves debunking usage myths. Many of our students come to us with one rule ingrained in their grammatical consciousness: never start a sentence with *And.* While their previous teachers may have found that advice an effective method of eliminating a type of fragment so common to younger writers, it is confusing to our students who find sentences starting with *And* in the literature they read. It is always a relief to them to learn that no respected usage manual considers such practice incorrect. Only by listening to our students do we learn of their reasoning.

Robert needed Gail's daily reassurance and support to develop his real strengths—his ideas and voice—into readable words on paper, focusing on one issue at a time and only on the major issues.

> I wrote on his paper, "Please read this out loud so you can tell where to put the periods." He understood why this worked, because I had, on several occasions, read his paper aloud for him. He was able to listen to his actual words that way, instead of what he thought he had on paper. Robert then read aloud to another student and inserted some periods.
>
> Our next task was spelling. Robert used the spell checker, and with the aid of the dictionary and those around him, managed to spell almost all of the words correctly.
>
> The final thing we worked on was paragraphing since his whole paper was one long paragraph. I asked Robert to interrupt my reading of his paper when he saw the need for a new paragraph. After Robert identified good places to start the first few paragraphs, he went back to the computer and divided the entire paper into appropriate paragraphs.

Gail was pleased with the writing Robert produced with this approach, especially since his obsession with spelling had paralyzed him at the beginning of the year. Robert needed the freedom to write *without control* so he could develop fluency and have a draft over which he could gain control (see Robert's first and last drafts of his 1930s detective story in Chapter 3). What Robert had learned was more important than the errors that remained. And notice the variety of support: teacher praise and coaching, peer proofreading, computer revision, a spelling checker, and the dictionary.

INDIRECT INSTRUCTION

Spelling

Fitzsimmons and Loomer (1977) surveyed sixty years of research in spelling and concluded, among other things, that "Most attempts to teach spelling by phonic rules are questionable" (81) and that "The child correcting his own spelling test, under the direction of the teacher, is the single most important factor in learning to spell" (80). We don't have spelling tests for students to correct, but we do ask students to correct their own spelling errors.

Some of us used spelling books into the second year of the project. Joan had dropped spelling texts in 1980 but wasn't yet convinced that spelling couldn't be taught in some way. The second year, Joan again felt the pull of "having to do something" about the spelling mistakes on her students' paper. She tried an experiment teaching explicit spelling rules. She used three slightly different approaches in three eighth-grade classes: individualized worksheets, cooperative learning triads, and teacher-directed exercises. She drilled students orally by asking them to state, for example, the silent *e* rule. She found that Julius didn't know what *except* meant when she stated the rule, "*i* before *e* except after *c*." Many students (not just target students) could rattle off the rule verbatim but couldn't apply it to a single word! They had no concept of the rule's meaning.

> Henry got so flustered in trying to memorize a rule; he confused suffix/root word; vowel/consonant; drop/keep; beginning/end. He kept at it for about seven tries while class was laughing good-naturedly. . . . but he didn't learn a thing!

Joan found that the whole notion of spelling rules was foreign to basic writers. They had trouble phrasing the rules accurately and still more trouble applying them. By the end of the year, she lamented, "They still can't verbalize why one spelling is correct and another isn't." It was no surprise that their scores on spelling tests did not improve and there was no sign of transfer to their own writing. Joan concluded that "teaching spelling rules is a waste of time for eighth graders who can't spell." Her colleagues at the middle school breathed a collective sigh of relief.

It's been a struggle for some of us to "give up" the formal teaching of spelling, whether through individualized charts, workbooks, or rules. It is difficult to get over a nagging sense of abdicating responsibility. A spelling workbook, by its very presence, suggests we are doing *something* about the problem. We are convinced, however, that the workbooks and the rules don't work for our students. The slow methods of conferencing, peer proofing, daily edits, and (less frustrating) the use of the computer spelling checker seem more constructive. (Note that the spelling checker does have its limitations—see Chapter 9.)

Dictionaries and references such as *How to Spell It* (Wittels and Greisman 1973) (wherein you can look up the word as you spelled it and find out if it's correct or not) are used in our rooms; those listing words by their misspellings have proved very popular with our students. Final proofreading for most of our students means checking for spelling, run-ons, and fragments. After receiving a final draft, we often require that spelling errors, or a certain number of them, be corrected before recording a grade. Certainly when student writings are to be published in a class book, for example, we place special emphasis on this "cleaning up." If correcting all the misspellings would overwhelm a particular student, we will correct the remaining ones.

Vocabulary and Grammatical Terminology

Literature was the basis for vocabulary study in the middle school during the first three years of the project, with anticipatory lessons not only hooking the students for the assigned reading but also introducing the words that we knew from experience caused difficulty for most of the readers. Some of us used vocabulary workbooks the first two years. Now vocabulary develops more naturally as students note unknown words in their literature response journals, use the thesaurus while writing, and hear the teacher purposefully sprinkle "adult vocabulary" in her conversations with them.

In the high school, vocabulary has been prescribed for *all* English classes. Carrie wryly reports here how successful this has been:

> One thing we do at the high school is vocabulary. In fact, we do it to death. Every class has a weekly lesson of 10 words, from which we are supposed to teach parts of speech, roots and affixes, multimeanings, and usage. If we did all that we'd spend half the week on vocabulary. . . . Students lost their workbooks, found them boring and wouldn't do them, did the lessons and lost them. . . . It was much more successful with target students when I provided all the class time necessary to complete the lesson as well as the test, but I found no carry over to using the words in their writing.

Middle school teachers use word banks just as elementary teachers of the program Success in Reading and Writing do. If several students will be writing about the industrial revolution, they list or cluster related words. This sharing usually results in each student learning new words that may trigger more development or more specific detail in a paper.

Nancy asks students to brainstorm a list of sensory appeal words before beginning a narrative. As the word bank grows, discussion centers on the connotations of various synonyms. The class comes up with many adjectives and verbs that appeal to each of the five senses, such as *titillating*.

Just knowing a word is not enough. We spend more time helping students learn the nuances of words and helping writers come up with the best word for the situation. This is quite informal, with students asking those around them, "What's another word for _____?" This often leads to an impromptu discussion of the context and how well various synonyms fit the meaning and tone of the piece. It's not easy to grasp the connotation of new words such as *conflagration* or *plunder*. Kids will write, "I roasted my hot dog over the conflagration," or "The burglar plundered the bank." We start with familiar words. Sandy's minilesson begins with an overhead asking, "What's the difference?" and showing a list of twelve words: *woman, dame, gal, babe, lady, chick, main squeeze, girl, sweetie pie, broad, wench, _itch*. Sandy purposely leaves blank the first letter of the last word because of the discussion it will create. Most students will assume she is being coy about writing the word *bitch*. She points out that it could have been *witch* and then leads a discussion on when it is appropriate to avoid words that some find offensive and when they are absolutely necessary.

Literature discussions also provide opportunities to discuss word connotations. For example, our students—both Black and White—are bothered by the use of the word *nigger* in literature such as *Roll of Thunder, Hear My Cry*. We discuss historical context as another consideration in addition to audience, purpose, and tone.

We follow up on words mentioned in the literature response journals either individually or in a short discussion with the class or group reading that piece of literature. Words need to be "played with," not just defined. Students need to test out words in tentative sentences. Our African American students have particular difficulty choosing the correct form of a word they are adding to their working vocabulary. This makes sense because English words usually show grammatical form by a change in the *ending* and speakers of BEV often do not pronounce word endings. They miss the oral clue to syntax. So we show all forms of the word and relate it to other words with the same root.

Joan often reinforces understanding of parts of speech by reminding students that they already know all the prepositions, conjunctions, interjections, and pronouns that exist in the English language. Any new word must be one of the "big four" of nouns, verbs, adjectives, and adverbs. She deals with all derivatives of any vocabulary word, sometimes reviewing the suffix signals to parts of speech that are clues to usage in a sentence (*-ment* means noun; *-ous* means adjective).

Grammatical terms, such as labels for parts of speech, are handled indirectly just as any other vocabulary word. We tend to use such terms the way writers would use them rather than the way linguists would. For example, when a student responds to another's writing with "I love your verbs," it is clear the students have been introduced to parts of speech and think of them as writers' tools rather than as things to underline. Using terms such as *clause* and *appositive* in their natural habitat is meaningful; direct instruction of terminology for the sake of terminology isn't.

We want our students to have a working understanding of terminology, not knowledge based on rote memorization. When students change a passive construction to active voice, we are excited about their revision even if they don't remember the word *passive*. If a student could define active voice but never used it, we would be distressed. In revising, we ask students to substitute "vitamin verbs" for state-of-being verbs. If we require a step-by-step process, asking students to circle the state of being verbs that will be replaced, we don't quibble when they don't include the helping verbs with *been*.

New words often present themselves when we read to our students. While reading a story, Mary Ann defined *seediest* by explaining that the house was in shambles in a run-down area; she noted that the word gave her an image of "things going to seed." Colleen corrected her: "You mean *city-est,* Mrs. Kelly." Students will make meaning out of the unfamiliar.

Another student wrote about his father's favorite piece of music, "Rap City in Blue." These interpretations are a natural attempt to make sense of the unknown, to fit the new into the current frame of reference.

Part of our job is to acquaint kids with new vocabulary, but more than that our job is to make the words *theirs*—to give them control over new words so they are viable options to be used judiciously, not grabbed from a thesaurus and plunked into a sentence that betrays their unfamiliarity. Students need a full, experiential acquaintance with new words more than a galloping tour through a college word list. Asking students to write sentences based on a word list and a definition is setting them up for unnatural, inappropriate usage. First they need a sense of the word's natural habitat in syntax and in connotation. Later they can try using the word in their own writing.

This indirect instruction of vocabulary, spelling, and terminology depends a great deal on the teacher's ability to capitalize on teachable moments, to see relationships, and to follow profitable tangents.

HOW DIRECTIVE?

Whether we are playing with language, giving direct instruction in a mini-lesson or individual conference, or weaving concepts in indirect instruction, we have expectations for our students. And the importance of teacher expectations cannot be overstated. Since students come to believe they can (or cannot) do what the teacher expects (or does not expect) them to do, teacher expectations become self-fulfilling prophecies. We set our expectations high for all students; we believe all students *are* writers, not *becoming* writers. We believe all students can learn the skills needed to "sit at the American language table as members in good and high standing."

We sometimes surprise ourselves with the amount of authority we use in making these expectations clear. During the third year, Carrie lost her temper after having found up to twenty-seven spelling mistakes in one two-page typed paper that had supposedly been run through the spelling checker *and* had been peer reviewed and edited.

> I proclaimed that for the optional take-home final no paper could get an A if it had more than one mistake per page, a B if it had more than two mistakes per page, or a C if it had more than three mistakes per page. Students took my evil threats seriously. That set of papers was the cleanest, easiest to read set of papers that I got all year—or maybe ever! I don't know whether my brutal standards scared them into getting help proofreading or whether they were just getting better, but I saw almost

no grammatical or spelling errors in that entire set of papers, including papers by several target students.

At first Carrie's demands concerned some of us. Was she overstressing mechanics? Would such rigid standards discourage her target students? But we heard the warmth, the banter, in her voice as Carrie talked about her kids. When Jane visited her class what impressed her was the banter along with the toughness—the upbeat humor that teased her students into meeting her expectations. We understood better why this approach worked after reading that African American students value teachers who push students, demanding that they do their best while making learning interesting (Siddle-Walker 1992).

> The authoritative teacher can control the class through exhibition of personal power; establishes meaningful interpersonal relationships that garner student respect; exhibits a strong belief that all students can learn; establishes a standard of achievement and "pushes" the students to achieve that standard; and holds the attention of the students by incorporating interactional features of Black communicative style in his or her teaching. (Delpit 1988, 290)

We all insist that a paper be clean of errors before being published—whether that means being sent through the mail or becoming part of a class book that will be placed in the library. The "final step" of process, proofreading, is as important as the other "steps" in our classrooms.

HOW EFFECTIVE?

Does our approach to teaching control of language work? It is more successful with some target students than others. The students hardest to empower with control of language are the same ones who are hardest to reach on a personal level (see Chapter 6). These passive students tend to have flat voiceless writing *and* use Black dialect inappropriately. The combination of the three characteristics in one student has been our biggest failure. It's difficult enough to walk the tightrope between validating a student's dialect and opening the door to another dialect. We find that delicate balance even more difficult to achieve with a student who gives no feedback—facial expressions, body language, verbal responses—to guide us. It is easy to be misunderstood when discussing changing a language, and a misunderstanding that we don't even know exists can cancel any impact we might have had. Thank goodness we have had few (perhaps two a year?) of these students.

Study buddies can help reluctant writers gain control. Henry, a passive, hard-to-reach student in Joan's eighth-grade class, showed more emotion about a book he disliked than anything else all year. He and his partner Danzel, who is also African American, had chosen *Dear Mr. Henshaw* as the book that they disliked strongly. Henry's response journal is appropriately intense, informal, and unpolished:

> I really don't like the way the author wrote this book. I hate the way she wrote this book every page Leigh is writing a letter to Mr. Henshaw.
>
> Beverly Cleary dose write good storys but I just do not know what happend here. Like her story *Run away Ralph* My little brothes and sister away want me to read that story and *Ramona the Pest* and *Ramona the Brave.* . . .
>
> One idea that struck was when the father said he saw a old shoe smashed on the road. I see smashed shoes, dogs, cats, and pants on the road all the time but I just never though of it or made a song out of eather. I think that was the funnies part, when the were singing there songs.

Danzel, whose writing skills were above average, had the ability to switch from the informal tone of their journals to the formal tone of the book review. Danzel's skill helped Henry as they developed their introductory paragraph: "Beverly Cleary has written many exciting books that most young kids enjoy. This is not one of them. This was written as a diary or a journal.

This book is about a young boy who writes letters to an author, whom he never has seen, but deeply admires his books."

The control of language isn't perfect, particularly in the last two clauses. But the formal tone, the subordination in the first sentence, the effective use of a short sentence following a longer one, and the attempt in the last sentence to incorporate four different ideas all evidence increasing control.

Some target students need more than one year to internalize conventions. Recall Robert who needed Gail's constant reassurance and took his paper through many revisions, focusing on one problem at a time. Robert did not become an independent proofreader by the end of the year. When required to work alone under pressure for an assessment, his score did not improve.

Minnie finds that tenth graders now come to her basic English class with a more positive attitude toward writing, "recognizing a need to revise and willing to work on a piece of writing. They make corrections more naturally as they work through several drafts rather than just slapping a few spelling corrections in a quick once-over on their first draft and calling it finished." This change in attitude is the first step toward gaining greater control.

LOOKING IN THE MIRROR: THE RESEARCH TEAM LEARNS BETTER CONTROL OF LANGUAGE

Writing for publication in articles and then in this book has challenged us to increase our own control of language. Some language options are the same whether writing in the classroom or for publication: how will we get the reader's attention at the beginning of the book? at the beginning of each chapter?

Writing articles and a book *collaboratively* bring new challenges: how can we achieve a consistent tone throughout chapters that have different authors?

Our level of concern over the fine points of editing has been raised because of publishing: Should *Black* and *White* be capitalized? Both? Neither? Only *Black?* Will we use contractions? Should we use the word *kids?* If not, how many synonyms are there for *students?* How do we weave the conversational style of the field notes and the scholarly style of our printed sources into our own narrative style? By grappling with these issues and reaching a consensus, we've gained professional confidence.

WHAT YOU CAN DO

Develop and maintain high expectations. Don't underestimate the potential of *any* student!

Provide opportunities for appropriate use of BC.

Involve students in assessing their own areas of weakness and strengths.

Focus on sentence expansion first, build toward the combining exercises, and fine-tune by reducing. The problems of basic writers are usually addressed better by expanding ideas rather than combining ideas. But check the needs of your students.

Give students a repertoire of approaches to sentence expansion.

Emphasize the oral with sentence combining.

Anticipate the kind of sentence combining that will be most helpful in a particular mode of writing.

Teach control of language in the context of writing, not through a workbook that has no context or whose context does not relate to what the student is doing. Direct instruction in grammar, vocabulary, and spelling is useless without the context that makes language meaningful.

Try daily edits to introduce a minilesson on a problem seen in many students' papers. Use daily edits to reinforce the understanding; use sentences from students' drafts for a reality base.

Devise clues to help students conquer their individual problems.
> Read aloud to hear run-ons.
> Practice *oral* conjugation of problem verbs.
> Read aloud backwards (by "sentences") to hear fragments.

Identify and work on the critical proofreading injury of a paper and ignore the rest (for now). Involve the student in this process and together set a specific goal for the next draft.

You ***read the sentence with nonstandard English aloud for the student.***

Be prepared for hypercorrections (*tolded*); view this stage in learning as "happy errors"—a sign of effort and of readiness to see new distinctions.

Do not publish error-filled writing; edit yourself if necessary.

Let the students draft before teaching a convention they will need in that mode. Better yet, teach a skill individually when a student has a need to know that skill.

Don't waste any time trying to teach spelling by teaching rules once students are twelve years of age or older. Teach the word, not the rule.

Avoid word lists for teaching vocabulary. Use rich context, a discussion of connotations, and lots of familiarity with various forms.

Read:

DANDY, EVELYN. 1991. *Black Communications: Breaking Down the Barriers.* Chicago: African American Images. This short book gives a detailed description of distinctive features of BC, the African origins of BC, and specific suggestions for classroom teachers of standard English.

FARR, MARCIA, and HARVEY DANIELS. 1986. *Language Diversity and Writing Instruction.* Urbana, IL: National Council of Teachers of English.

SHAUGHNESSY, MINA. 1977. *Errors and Expectations: A Guide for the Teacher of Basic Writing.* New York: Oxford.

Facing the Mirror:
Stephanie Gavin

I grew up in Grandview, Missouri, a suburban city of approximately seven thousand people just south of Kansas City, Missouri. Out of 360 students in my graduating class of 1983, a little less than 10 percent were African American. Those 10 percent were Grandview residents; there was no bussing in from the city. And in this typical middle-class community, few of those African Americans came from homes less privileged than my own. However, as I entered my junior year in high school, White flight was beginning to occur in Grandview. It happened quickly; by the time my sister graduated from high school six years after my graduation, her class was more than 30 percent African American. The class of 1993 was almost 50 percent. My parents conformed and moved five years ago to Lee's Summit, another suburban community on the east side of Kansas City.

Recently I returned to Grandview for my ten-year class reunion. It was an enlightening experience. The only Black person who showed up came with his White wife, and very few people remembered who he was. The Sunday picnic was held at a public lake just outside of Grandview. We were the largest group of Whites there. The whole experience made me wonder about the other Blacks from my class. I had to get out a yearbook to remember any names.

Still, I was raised in a more diverse community than my parents. There was only one Black person in their Arkansas high school class of seventy or so. And my grandmother, the sweetest lady you could ever meet, didn't see Black people on a daily (or even weekly) basis until she was well in her thirties and working at a factory job in Fort Smith. I remember one of the first things she asked my husband upon meeting him was, "Since you have a government job, do you have to work with very many colored people?" My husband, all of whose relatives were from Chicago and not small-town Arkansas, was shocked. He was even more shocked when we took Grandma shopping with us in Kansas City once. As we were walking down the crowded mall, Grandma suddenly disappeared into a lingerie store. Now we both knew she wasn't dashing in for a purchase; under normal circumstances she was embarrassed to even go in "underwear" shops. But this was not a normal circumstance. Apparently two Black male teenagers had been behind her, too close for her comfort, and she wanted to get them off her trail.

I realize more and more each year as I become increasingly knowledgeable and experienced that I must surpass several generations of racism to catch up with my liberal, diverse friends, who have liberal, diverse parents and—occasionally—grandparents. My own parents have come a little way from their parents in accepting others. I hope I am coming a long way. If I can keep growing socially and understanding others who are different from me, I will pass my attitudes along to my children who in turn will be even more accepting than I am. Being a part of the Webster Groves Writing Project has given me an understanding far beyond the surface of those with lifestyles different from my own. I feel like I'm acting my beliefs out daily; I'm practicing what I preach, so to speak.

I'm already uncomfortable when my one-year-old hears great-grandma or great-grandpa talking about those "coloreds" in town, or those "good-for-nothing half-breeds" moving in from across the Oklahoma border. But I'm anticipating the day Claire asks me why they use terms we don't allow in our home. That will prove I'm making progress.

Use the Computer

*The only way a person is writing a good story is if they want to. If they
don't have the heart to write then they will not write a good story. I think
that the person should have the right tools too. Personally, I can write better
with a computer then I can write on a piece of paper. I can make
corrections easier and the teacher usually wants your drafts on a computer anyway. I have had teachers in the past who have made me write
my drafts on a piece of paper. I hated that because my paper was filled
with scratch marks and corrections, which made it hard to read.*

THEODORE,
eighth-grade portfolio reflection

U sing the computer emerged as a principle through our experience
of action research. Our readings on African American learners did
not mention technology, nor did our original set of six principles.
But during our first-year's synthesis meeting, we discovered that every
teacher had used the writing center for major papers. All of us agreed that
word processing made it easier for writers—especially for our target students—to succeed.

By then, we were in Phase Two of our research, exploring key principles and methods of teaching writing. We first talked about using computers as a strategy under the heading of *Involvement*, but in our discussions that proved too limited a role. We came to see the computer as a powerful learning tool that reinforced many of our other principles:

Process: The computer supports ongoing revision and informal publishing. Our students regard a pass to the writing center as a phase in the process.

Individualize and personalize: A writing center with competent staff helps us individualize. Writers who are ready can go to the center while others keep working with us in the classroom. A computer environment also facilitates on-the-spot writing conferences.

Cooperative learning: A computer is an ideal place for collaboration. A partner can assist with editing on screen, and groups can pool information for projects.

Control of language: Only at the computer (preferably one with a spelling checker) is it realistic to push a very low-skilled writer through repeated editing to a clean copy.

Involvement: The computer is a hands-on writing tool. Target students noted for short attention span will concentrate at the keyboard, and they value the printouts more than handwritten drafts.

Convinced of its importance, we added the computer to our list of principles in 1988. Today it seems obvious that access to computers can help almost any writer work through the process. But this chapter will describe our low-tech approach in some detail because we have realized that our approach is not the norm, either in the literature or in the schools.

Jane's job brings her to classrooms throughout the St. Louis area. Even in districts known for a sophisticated use of technology, she sees many students given access to computers only for typing a final copy. All their drafting and revising (which tend to be minimal) are done by hand. These same schools may spend large sums on the newest hardware and software for synthesizing, hypermedia, or simulations—but not for actual writing. Our experience makes us challenge these priorities.

The roots of our approach to computers can be traced back to 1984 when Joan and Agnes took part in a Gateway Writing Project technology institute. For the next three years, the project sponsored an action research team that worked with Jane to integrate computers in the curriculum without losing a focus on the writing process and on writing communities.[1] Team members contributed to a book, *WritingLands* (Zeni 1990).

This chapter discusses computer-supported writing from the perspective of students who have been marginalized in the schools. How can computers build on what we know about our target students, their attitudes, and their writing processes and products? How can a writing center support the environment we want to create in our classrooms? On the other hand, how might computers put our students "at risk"?

BUILD ON STUDENT ATTITUDES TOWARD TECHNOLOGY

Fascination

Most of our target students prefer writing on the computers to writing by hand. As others have reported (Wright 1988), we find that students work more intensely in computer-equipped writing centers. Freed of the frustration of recopying, they are more willing to revise. In 1989 Carrie described the response of her ninth graders in the low-tracked classes we have since rejected, which challenged our best efforts at management.

> I have the highest regard for the power of the computer to build motivation and concentration. Students who could not be counted on to remain seated for ten minutes at a stretch in the regular classroom would sit at the computer and work, often ignoring other students' attempts to distract them, for virtually an entire 55-minute class period. Sam is

probably the shining star of computer efficiency. In class, Sam and I engaged in a battle of wills which consisted of him saying he couldn't do the assignment, and me coaxing it out of him one sentence at a time. In the computer lab Sam was suddenly able to turn out quantities of writing with very little interference from me.

When our school writing centers opened we wondered if our students' fascination was due to novelty. But the spell has not faded during the past eight years. Despite the few who insist they hate computers, most kids retain their enthusiasm as the technology progresses. Students who once were thrilled by the "delete" key in word processing now find the same magic in telecommunications and desktop publishing. In 1992 Cathy reported,

> The Macintoshes totally enamored my students. *Everyone* wanted to use this new equipment. They wanted to experiment with *every* function that it was capable of performing to see how the look of the final piece can be manipulated by changing the font and the type size. Their biggest joy, however, was playing with the painting program. I would like to see how this can be used with students who want to draw first and write second.

Sandy added, "I'm dreaming about lap tops for everyone, especially *moi!*" There seems to be no danger that our students—or their teachers—will outgrow their fascination with technology.

We haven't found our African American students to be any more fascinated with computers than their White classmates. But the very active kinesthetic learning that takes place at the computer is ideal for many of our target students who thrive on the hands-on involvement.

Pride and Empowerment but Also Lack of Power

Many target students express pride and competence when they discover the computer. Here is a powerful machine, one reputed to be intelligent—and it obeys their commands. It creates text that looks professional, more like a book than like a school assignment, especially with laser printers.

The computer-printed text is a great equalizer. For students with poor handwriting, it sends a message unencumbered by scrawl. A printout is anonymous; it doesn't identify the writer by race, sex, previous academic record, or behavior.

Even when typing hunt-and-peck, most students produce more words on the computer than with pen and paper (Zeni 1990). They are proud of this new fluency. Kids love the continuous paper rolling out of the printer in thick stacks. The printouts motivate writers who have trouble getting started and trouble keeping going.

When we assist with computers, as with pen and paper, we try to affirm the power of our writers. Cathy describes a hectic day in the writing center when a student

> called me over to ask how to change the location of a particular phrase in his draft. Instead of explaining how he could accomplish this task, I reached over him and made the movement myself. As soon as I touched the keyboard, I realized that like a draft, which is kept in the possession of the writer, the keyboard should be too. After this instance, I became very aware of not touching the keyboard.

The computer gives many students an exhilarating new sense of competence. But sometimes the power fails. Agnes has worked with tracked classes of basic students in the high school. Although most of her students enjoy the computers, each year she finds that a significant minority despise and fear them. In 1991 she wrote,

> Most kids are familiar with word processing. But many are dead-set against the computer and have had enough exposure to know what they like and don't like. I was surprised at the number. Many of them did not know how to type and thus, the computer was part of one long laborious process. This is unfortunate that they are hampered by the one piece of technology that could make a reluctant writer's life so much easier.

Other teachers have seen these negative attitudes but much less often than Agnes, probably due to her largely homogeneous classes. A complicating factor may also be the change from Bank Street Writer to AppleWorks in grade nine.

A more common problem is the loss of power when a writer is suddenly deprived of technological allies. Stephanie tells what happened when a few of her students ran out of time and could not finish their papers on the computer.

> I suggested they handwrite the final copy. Well—you would have thought I had suggested cutting off their hands! It's amazing to me how much the kids rely on the computers. They go through the steps of the process with such ease now. I know that handwriting drafts would not get this kind of polished work.

Stephanie later taught a major unit with a variety of short assignments, too many to complete in the writing center:

> I asked students to handwrite their rough drafts *and* their final copies. They thought that was awful of me. I caught myself telling my classes how I had to write complete research papers by hand, do all revision by hand, and then type a final copy. They were not impressed. I got the same reaction—rolled eyes, no sympathy—as I did when I told them I wasn't allowed to see an R-rated movie until I was 17!

Like Stephanie, we feel some ambivalence about our students' responses to computers. We celebrate their improvement in attitude, process, and product. But we worry about their dependence on expensive technology that may not always be available at their fingertips. One comfort is that kids in a lab depend as much on each other as they do on the technology itself. The power of collaborative learning is one they *can* carry with them beyond the school.

Student Experts

Along with helping one another find keys and commands, students in the writing center respond informally to work in progress. "Often it is a target student helping another," noted Chestra. "They are receiving reinforcement that they *do* know something—that often comes into question at other times."

In most classes, certain writers take on the role of computer "expert." These are the kids who hurry to print their own texts so they can preside over the printer. They reach across the aisle or jump up from a keyboard to show others a sequence of commands. Volunteer experts help others make the most of a printout by widening margins, enlarging fonts, and triple-spacing; they also know how to squeeze a classmate's three-page text to fit a two-page limit.

As we continue to upgrade our equipment, the need for student experts also continues. The Macintosh lab and telecommunications are now inspiring another generation of technical experts.

DEVELOP A WRITING CENTER

Since computers are an integral part of the process for our students, we try to give them a supportive environment, a "WritingLand:" a "context that supports the learner through relationships with peers and teacher and through electronic as well as conventional writing tools" (Zeni 1990, xii).

Our middle school and the senior high each contain a computer-equipped writing center with a staff to help writers. Neither facility could be called state-of-the-art, but English teachers took part in the decisions on equipment, design, and schedule. For the most part, the centers meet our needs and those of our target students.

In our experience, the key to a WritingLand is competent support for writers. We have seen too many schools where a lab is left unsupervised or staffed only by a technician who can help with plugs and disks but not with writing. Both of our facilities began in the mid-1980s with released time for the equivalent of a full-time English teacher (six teachers, each in the center one period per day) to assist with writing at a few computers.

At the high school we developed a tutorial facility, a small room now containing a dozen computers. Students are sent out from classes with a slip telling the writing center staff where they need help—organization, development, proofreading. Later we added a lab of twenty-five computers in the library to accommodate a whole class with their regular teacher.

Today our high school center still has a rotating staff of English teachers while the middle school center is run by an aide trained in writing process. Somewhat to our surprise, both arrangements work well. While the rotation system is best for getting a whole English department involved with computers, the middle school's aide can maintain an established program. To avoid misleading our readers, we must explain the qualifications of our current aide and what happened when we tried to work with less-qualified staff.

As we got involved in action research, struggled with grants, and begged for funding from our administrators, we saw that the middle school would not also keep releasing a teacher to run the writing center. When the principal suggested an aide, we were dubious. The first candidate had training in computers but none in teaching writing. One teacher summarized her role in this way:

> She would sit there during lunch and never engage with the kids. She was useless. Well, worse than useless. One day she removed all the carriage returns from a poem my student wrote. The lines of poetry printed out like a paragraph. The kid came back to me with a puzzled look and said, "I got some help, but. . ."

In 1986 Robin Conerly arrived. Although not a certified English teacher, she is a college graduate trained in writing process. After accepting her new job, Robin enrolled in a Gateway Writing Project course. Today we rely on her as a member of the English department. "Robin is wonderful! She works closely with the kids. She knows the equipment and she knows how to support the writing process. She runs between the new Mac lab and the IIe center. It's hard to keep on top of it all, but she does it." We've asked Robin to lead a guided tour of her middle school WritingLand.

A Walk Through Our Center

As you enter the doors of Room 212, it's hard to believe that what is now the Hixson writing center was once a community daycare. No longer to be heard are the sounds of giggling tots, only the harmonious clicking of computer keys.

The large square room houses twenty-six Apple IIe computers with two equipped with dual-disk drives, five dot-matrix printers, five Macintosh Classics, one Macintosh IIvx, one laser printer, and one ink-jet printer. All equipment is set up on long tables. Four of the IIe computers are connected to a dot-matrix printer by a control switch box. Another dot-matrix printer is connected to one computer that is often kept open for those needing just a printout.

For our Apple IIes, we use Bank Street Writer III software; however, we have AppleWorks available for those students who prefer it (in the absence of dual disk drives, AppleWorks is something of a pain). Both software programs include dictionary and thesaurus disks for checking spelling. Our Macintoshes store Microsoft Works, ClarisWorks, Aldus Pagemaker, clip art, and drawing software.

The walls of the writing center are covered with bulletin boards and blackboards decked with posters, instructional aids, and contest information. Scattered about the long computer tables are dictionaries, thesauruses, printer cables, and miscellaneous lost papers.

Bank Street Writer is loaded into the computers each morning. English classes are held all seven periods, so the writing center is used all day long. A sign-up book and a separate sign-up sheet for the Macintoshes are logged daily. Each team has color-coded floppy disks and each student has a personal disk. The disks are kept in boxes labeled by teacher name and hour residing on the shelves just along the wall near the classroom door. Each student is responsible for his own disk and is never to tamper with another's disk. Students are sent down to the lab with individual passes printed on paper that is the color of their team. With over 650 students at Hixson and only one of me, this helps to avoid some of the confusion of a somewhat unstructured setting.

Due to the popularity of the lab, an English teacher is permitted to send only six to ten students from the team each hour to allow equal time for all. If it seems there is still available space and equipment, teachers will send extra students on a standby basis. *"Standby"* is noted on their pass and if the room becomes too full, these students know that they are the first ones to return to class. A crunch occurs when students are pressed to meet a deadline for an assignment, causing an overflow in the center. In this instance, we make special arrangements within the English department to give one class access to the whole lab.

Today, twenty-five assorted seventh and eighth graders are working. Some of them proofread a persuasive letter for mailing, some tinker with the dialogue in a "modern" fairy tale, some struggle to incorporate feedback on a childhood memory paper, some develop a chronicle for social studies. Writers work individually, but they often pause as they type, leaning over to a peer before turning back to the keyboard. Each computer station has enough legroom so that two students can sit together for collaborative writing or editing when needed. I float around and answer occasional requests for help. The atmosphere is one of relaxed concentration.

Our experience suggests that there is no single environment or formula for learning to write with computers but that certain ingredients are essential: competent help with writing and with technology, ample working space, and access to computers—in a classroom, lab, or center—with social support for writers in process. Our findings resonate with studies that emphasize context (Selfe 1989; Marcus 1992; Greenleaf 1992) and instruction (Wright 1988; Selfe 1992), not just technology.

Slowly and cautiously, we enhance our low-tech, writing-intensive environment with Macintoshes, telecommunications, and desktop publishing. In our field notes and study sessions, we reflect on our progress toward creating a WritingLand. We thought our focus was clear from the start. In our second year, Cathy remarked that kids "seemed to view the writing center as another step in the writing process," and the team adopted her metaphor. Yet it's so easy to get the priorities backwards. In year six, Mary Ann wryly cited a comment from one student's portfolio: "I like to write because it improves my typing skills!"

Routines

Each year, more students come to us who are computer literate and able to type. In the past our district taught keyboarding to seventh and eighth graders. In 1990 the elementary schools began introducing computers in kindergarten with LogoWriter. Today our children learn Bank Street Writer and some touch typing as early as grade three, and we introduce databases in middle school. Still, there is a real contrast between the typing speed of students who have computers at home and the majority who do not. Nancy observed her seventh graders on their first day in the writing center in fall of 1990: "Keyboarding skills are much better this year—familiarity with the location of keys on the keyboard and the speed of typing. The method is still hunt-and-peck, though, using anywhere from two to six fingers. Students keep eye contact with the monitor." Then Nancy took·an informal survey. Despite their fluency, just seven of her twenty-three students reported having a computer with word-processing software at home. In the fall of 1993, she asked the same question in two classes. Twenty-seven of her forty-two students had a computer for writing at home.

As the deadline for a major paper approaches, the writing centers face a crush of students. Stephanie tells of staying in the middle school center to help struggling writers until 5 P.M. every day of the week before a big assignment. Now of course we've learned to stagger our due dates. At the high school, the lab in the library stays open before and after school, though the technical aide doesn't work with the writing.

As access to computers has grown, our routines for giving students access have also changed. At first, computers were available only in the writing center, and we would sign up a whole class. By the third year, all middle school English teachers had an Apple IIe in the classroom. By the fifth year, the Innovations in Education grant added a Macintosh, and the sixth year's grant purchased five more. Although one or two computers might seem irrelevant to a class of twenty-five, we've discovered new ways to be flexible. After a brief conference, we send a student to the computer to revise while he still clearly remembers what we discussed. Mary Ann reports that her two classroom computers are monopolized by her target students. Often two or three kids are writing "fillers"—song lyrics, notes, and jokes—but they choose to communicate by writing and reading.

USE COMPUTERS TO SUPPORT WRITING PROCESSES

From our project's beginning, we found the computer to be an ally in teaching writing as a process. "More than just a stimulus," explained Nancy in year two, "the computers became a carrot to dangle. Students knew ahead of time that if all prewriting, handwritten drafts, peer editing, and responses were not with them, they would not be allowed to go to the writing center." We drew on their fascination with technology to build dedication to writing.

From Drafting by Hand to Composing by Computer

By year two, all major papers in the middle school and about half in the senior high were finished on the computer. We follow a typical sequence for writing process instruction:

Prewriting, journal entry, or first draft by hand in class

Peer response

Revised draft typed on the computer

Peer and/or teacher response in pen on printout

More revision and response until paper is ready

Proofread using spelling checker, dictionary, peers

Publish in some form

Over the years, this sequence has changed as more of the process takes place on the computer. Some students have always asked to compose directly at the keyboard. Although we once required a handwritten draft as an "admission ticket," most of us have gradually softened that policy. First, computers are no longer such a scarce commodity. Second, students who touch-type are free to think rather than hunt while at the keyboard. Finally, we have started composing at the keyboard. Says Sandy, "I've now gotten into composing fresh at the computer so I like to give my students the same opportunity."

Today, most students still have something handwritten before going to the computers, but it may be just a planning sheet or some notes. During workshop, kids go to the center with papers at all stages of development.

Guided Revision and Development

Some writers revise more effectively when working on a fluid computer text than on hard copy. They seem to *see* the process better on screen. As one student explained, "My first draft gets in the way of my paper."

The most striking advantages of word processing are for target students who struggle to develop their thoughts on paper. JoAnne describes a student diagnosed as learning disabled and language impaired. Eddie's handwriting was barely legible, and he often missed words and phrases in his writing. JoAnne showed him that missing text could easily be inserted with the word processor, and Eddie threw himself into revising on screen.

> Eddie's prize piece was the Setting the Moods assignment. I allowed him to do rough drafting on the computer, rather than by hand. What appeared was a very rough, underdeveloped romantic beach scene. I asked him key questions about parts so he could begin to fill out the scene. What did this feel like? What sounds did you hear? What happened next?
>
> Before the period's end, Eddie had created a romantic evening on the beach, complete with sounds of the sea, the rough feel of sand on bare feet, checkered tablecloth with wine, and music for dancing in the moonlight. Female classmates sitting nearby and teacher agreed it sounded like an evening we'd enjoy.

Here is a passage from Eddie's description:

> It is a light blue clear sky. You are on the beach with your friend. Both of them are strolling inbetween the tide and the sand. The water softly touches your toes. It feels so good. The wind blows so softly it goes inbetween your clothes. . . . You feel as cool as a Coca Cola commercial. . . .

In many schools, Eddie would be assigned to a remedial setting where, if he had access to computers at all, it would be to work on drill and practice. National studies (Gomez 1991) confirm that workbook models of curriculum shown to be ineffective with pen and paper are still being replicated in computer software. Gomez deplores "the heavy emphasis on skill-and-drill computer programs for those students (often non-White students, students with low socioeconomic status, or students of limited English proficiency) enrolled in lower-ability classes" (324). We find that most so-called lower-ability students make progress when allowed to do real writing at the computer.

Word processing provides just enough support in handwriting, spelling, and mechanics to free students for higher-order composing issues such as word choice, mood, and voice. What JoAnne did with Eddie we often model for the entire class—with a computer and a projection screen. Carrie typed, "The room was messy" and projected it for a whole-class lesson in revision from "telling" to "showing." The computer helps kids see the writing process in action.

Conferencing

When we do bring a whole class to the center, we often hold miniconferences. Because students tend to be on task, we can confer without the usual distractions of the classroom. As Wright (1988) explains, in a lab the whole environment is more social.

> When the writing is on a computer screen, the students seem to be much less reluctant to let others see what they are doing. In the normal classroom, I have found most students reluctant to let other students or

the teacher see what they are writing until they are finished. . . . At the computer, this proprietary attitude seems to relax, perhaps because once the writing is on the screen it is harder to hide. The class truly becomes a writing workshop. (37–38)

Peer Collaboration

Today, the computer is part of the landscape of our writing workshop. Since each middle school teacher has at least one computer in her room, this setting has become a magnet for collaboration by pairs and triads. Sandy tells how "Brett's group wrote a take-off on Robin Hood, with their classmates as prominent characters. It got pretty playful, with changing typists and everyone composing, reading aloud to each other." Sandy compares the image of kids sitting around the computer to sitting around the hearth or the piano or the cracker barrel in earlier days.

> Chester was new to our school and my English class at the beginning of May. We had just called a break from workshop so that we could read *Diary of Anne Frank* together. That was followed by a plunge into portfolios. Since Chester didn't have any writing to analyze, I gave him a short course in process, explaining that we had strategies for getting ideas for writing, we wrote the first draft without worrying about the niceties, and that we worked with peers through several drafts to make it a polished piece. Then I helped him come up with a topic, and he started on a first draft. The next day in class he worked on it for a few minutes, then boomed out in this fairly quiet classroom, where everyone else was involved in choosing the pieces they would use in their portfolios, "All right, who's gonna help me fix on this story?"
>
> This is the great-looking new boy in school, so naturally, there were volunteers. Tamika was first in line, but Greg and Morgan wanted to help, too. They decided they would go to the back of the room to the computer, and get his story up on the screen so they could all read it. Same kind of scene, gathered around the piano, or hearth, or cracker barrel. Greg read the story aloud, everyone asking questions, laughing, teasing. (The new boy is extremely confident, and could take this scrutiny, indeed, relished the attention.)

Tamika, ready to fix on his story, chortled, "What's this, 'Everybody be clappin'?" Greg and Morgan started slapping their knees and laughing.

Morgan said, "He talk Black, he type Black. Don't worry, Mrs. Tab, we gonna get him straightened out!"

This vignette shows the principles of collaboration and control of language, as well as the use of computers. A reader might be troubled by the notion of laughing at a writer's dialect. But listen to the naturalness of the scene. Students are comfortable with writing, with their own voices, and with their own authority as editors. And they understand language variation, knowing that Black English Vernacular forms may be effective in dialogue but less so in an essay or narrative. Sandy's kids regard "fixing" their language with playfulness and confidence. Access to the computer makes codeshifting a minor task rather than an ordeal.

USE COMPUTERS TO IMPROVE THE FINISHED PRODUCTS

Writing as a process cannot be broken into neat stages (see Chapter 5). Yet the final activities we use to "fix" a text dramatize the support a computer can give inexperienced writers. After drafting and revising a satisfactory piece, a writer shifts the focus from process to product.

Ease of Editing

A legible printout makes editing easier for many target students. Peer group members can see through the penmanship to spot mechanical errors. We hold editing conferences at the computer in the classroom or in the center, often sitting with the writer at the keyboard.

The best way to point out errors is usually to have a student read a text orally, pausing for punctuation marks and focusing on capitalization, spelling, and other mechanics. Reading off the monitor, we may say, "You paused there. Do you have any punctuation to indicate that pause?" Kids don't mind spending extra time on editing as long as they're at the keyboard.

The computer helps us *show* students the effects of line endings (in poetry) or paragraph breaks (in essays). Cathy describes an editing mini-conference with an eighth grader:

> Duke wrote his fairy tale as one long paragraph. He recognized that it didn't look right and asked how he could fix it. He had some idea of what constituted a paragraph. It didn't take long for Duke to break his entire story into paragraphs. He would never have done this had it not been so simple with the computer.

Electronic Spelling

An inexpensive spelling checker is a boon. One ninth-grade target student was astonished to discover seventy-three misspellings on a three-page paper. Even when errors are rampant, writers don't feel overwhelmed when they have a checker. It frees them from worrying about proofreading when trying to compose: "Oh, well, I'll just run the spelling checker later." We have used two different kinds of software.

1. Simple search-and-find programs flag words not in the spelling checker's list and ask writers to correct, ignore, or add them to the list. Faced with these choices, our students typically ask for help from a neighbor or a "good speller." Or they consult a conventional dictionary.

2. More directive programs offer the three options plus a list of possible spellings. These are words differing by one or two letters from the student's version. Since the computer doesn't know syntax or meaning, most words it suggests will not make sense.

Which software is best for inexperienced writers? Members of our team differ on this point.

Those of us preferring the simple kind of spelling checker want kids to learn to use a regular dictionary. We also fear they may simply guess at a word from a suggested list and write nonsense.

Those of us preferring software with a list of words feel that the weakest spellers are least able to use a regular dictionary. They can make an educated guess from the list, and then check the word in a dictionary to confirm meaning. True, some students don't check. But usually this system is more accurate and less frustrating.

One unexpected problem with both systems is that some kids never use them. Nancy explains, "The Bank Street Writer spelling checker is so inconvenient and limited in vocabulary that many students just don't bother to run it." One day Carrie lamented, "There seemed to be a community allergy to the spelling checker."

At the opposite extreme, we find students with an unrealistic faith in the spelling checker. The machine holds more clout than the teacher. Stephanie reports that Fred

> relied on the spellcheck so much that I received a final paper from him with words like *security* and *accessibility* spelled correctly and *to, too, two, their, there,* and *they're* all out of context. He is very stubborn, and although I edited his drafts, the spellcheck had much more clout for him than my editing marks.

One day he ran out of time after editing about half his paper, and tried to manage by just running spellcheck. "He got defensive when I pointed out where it was obvious that he had stopped editing; he believed that since he had done spellcheck, that he shouldn't have gotten a lower grade due to the remaining mechanical errors. We went round and round."

To show students the limits of the software, Nancy put one of her own drafts on a big monitor. She modeled what a spelling checker would catch and what it would miss: homonyms, suffixes, proper names. Of course, even after a minilesson, some kids still want to believe that the computer is magic, but we think it's crucial to make the point—especially with target students—that their own intelligence must be the power behind the machine.

Pride in Publishing

The computer makes it easy to publish student writing with forms ranging from neatly printed papers on the bulletin board to bound and illustrated class anthologies. Chapters 5 and 10 describe the value of informal publication for writers with a history of underachievement. Here we simply add that a computer can support more elaborate publishing enterprises.

"Landmarks" is an annual collaborative research project[2] for the St. Louis area. Topics such as the Depression years or the 1904 World's Fair lend themselves to interviewing and observing as well as to library investigation. Carrie's class researched the environment for Landmarks. Students worked in groups of four to study an environmental hazard; then they forecast its impact on the world a century from now. Finally, each group wrote a collaborative story set in the future to demonstrate that impact. It was an ambitious task. Carrie stresses that it "could not have been completed effectively without the computer."

> To be sure that the work was shared and that students had to rely on each other, I had the kids divide their story-plans into fourths and each student wrote one section of the story. After each section had been individually "completed," they were combined into one file and revised further for consistency and tone. This was an extremely successful assignment—100 percent of my students completed at least a solid draft of the assigned segment of the story, an unprecedented occurrence.

Kids seemed impressed with the results. One target student, admiring his copy, said, "Gosh! It looks just like a little novel!"

During the past two years, we've discovered desktop publishing. Now our publications are even more impressive with charts, fancy fonts, and laser printers.

TRY THE COMPUTER AS A TEACHING TOOL

The most effective way we use computers as teaching tools is to model what writers do. We display work in progress either with a projector for the whole class or in a tutorial conference for an individual writer.

We have occasionally tried commercial software for teaching writing, with mixed results. We avoid the usual drill-and-practice software just as we avoid the workbook grammar exercises on which it is based. The graphics and the novelty might hold kids' attention for a time, but they won't learn most editing skills out of context no matter how long they drill. We focus on the essential writing tool—word processing—with just a few secondary tools.

Lessons on Disk

Several of us have written our own interactive lessons on disk using regular word-processing software. Such lessons are modeled by Franklin and Madian (1988) and by Rodrigues and Rodrigues (1986). We liked the idea of getting beyond the commercial drills, tailoring the lessons to what our own students were learning in class. Franklin and Madian, for example, suggest typing a simple review of a story and then typing some open-ended questions. The frozen text feature of Bank Street Writer can protect certain parts of the file—the teacher's instructions or a passage from literature—so they can't be modified. Since the writing space on the lesson can always expand, students answer in as much detail as they wish. During 1990, Joan organized and led a group of writing teachers from other districts in designing such lesson files.

We found, however, that it took an inordinate amount of time to write these apparently simple lessons. Many students had trouble reading the text and still more trouble managing the way the text scrolled on screen. Target students—so excited about most activities with the computer—often balked or fumbled through our lessons on disk. We also found it awkward to copy each lesson onto two dozen computers during the first minutes of class; once

Sandy copied her new lesson onto one hundred student disks during her plan period.

Reflecting on this experiment, we find that the most successful lessons on disk are short: writing pattern poems, transforming similes into metaphors, rearranging words in a caption or alliterative verse. We now store disks with such lessons in the writing center so that students who finish their work early can help themselves. As a sponge activity, they work well.

Today we don't put much energy into writing special lessons for the computer. Instead, we focus on original composing by student authors—whether they work at a desk or at a keyboard.

New Software and Hardware

We don't dismiss the "higher" technology, but we do look critically at the costs and the benefits of technology to writers. For example, some clever interactive software lets writers choose a situation, then respond to prompts for characters, setting, and plot. Cathy's students were fascinated by Super Story Tree. They tried out all the options for graphics and sound, but they also worked hard writing their stories. Unfortunately, the software allowed just a tiny screen space for writing, which limited its value with our classes.

During our third year (1989–90), Joan took a sabbatical that included an internship at the Regional Consortium for Education and Technology (RCET). She reviewed the latest software and worked with teachers of writing at all levels from many school districts. Joan's internship made her a valuable resource to the writing project, more competent with technology, and more confident in evaluating new products. She was intrigued by the diagnostic software that gave readability scores and analyzed possible errors. She saw potential in lessons on disk, in telecommunications, and in interactive planners. But most new "writing" software still emphasized skill and drill. At the end of her year at RCET, Joan had found nothing that she would urge the team at Hixson to adopt. She returned still more convinced that the computer should remain primarily a writing tool.

Our position here may seem rather bizarre, especially since members of the team have gone considerably beyond dabbling with computers. But we have seen what Steve Marcus (1992) calls the "productivity paradox" in the schools, and felt the "crises of confidence regarding the value and efficacy of money spent on" much new educational hardware and software (13). We prefer to spend our limited budget to increase access to computers, so that students can work through the whole process on the keyboard if they wish.

One of our most successful new applications for word processing is a telecommunications program giving middle school students access to international pen pals. Their letters and newspaper copy are composed off-line, then transferred to the bulletin board via modem and submitted to an international newspaper. Stephanie reports that when Greta wrote two letters to England, she took great pains to edit for mechanical errors. "I teasingly asked why she was working so much harder on the letters than she had on her last paper. Greta, in complete seriousness, replied, 'I don't want whoever gets it to think I'm stupid!'" Several target students threw themselves into describing urban African American life to a foreign audience that found it exotic. We expect to use this sort of program more in the future.

AVOID CREATING A TECHNOLOGICAL UNDERCLASS

Despite our enthusiasm for computers, we are wary of the dangers that may lead new technology to reinforce old patterns. Research over the past decade has shown chronic inequities in equipment, technical support, supervision, and curricular applications. The September 1992 *MacWorld* contains a major report, "Separate Realities," on the distribution of computers in American schools. The conclusion? Despite huge expenditures for equipment, "In most cases, computers simply perpetuate a two-tier system of education for rich and poor" (Piller 1992, 219). The difference between rich and poor school districts can be seen not only in computer purchases but also in computer use. "There is a widespread tendency to use computers only to teach basic skills in poor schools but to provide rich discovery environments in affluent schools" (228).

Within the same school, there may be still more insidious haves and have-nots. The technological haves tend to be White, male, high achievers, and middle or upper class. The have-nots, like our target students, get less access to computers or access only to less-challenging applications such as grammar games. Paul LeBlanc ends a bleak case study by warning of the risk that "technology will only serve to widen the gap between the privileged and the disenfranchised" (1994, 36).

We are angry to see the computer used to reinforce low expectations. At a recent statewide writing conference, teachers proudly demonstrated a grant-funded program for at-risk students. They used the computers—stocked with drill-and-practice games—to reward basic students who finished their grammar workbooks! We resist such misapplications. Technology must support the real "basics" of meaningful expression.

Therefore we do *only* writing (word processing, publishing, telecommunications) on the computer. We refuse to buy or use the gamelike software that clutters the curriculum in "remedial" labs. We expect that all our students, regardless of their tested or assumed ability, can express their own ideas in their own language. Any technology our students use in English classes is available to all and not just to an elite.

While we know the computer to be a tool for empowering writers, it can also be a source of disempowerment. New technology may present some kids with new skills in which to fail, new barriers excluding them from the mainstream. Socioeconomic differences add to these barriers. Middle-class students more often have home computers to supplement lab time and computer-using parents to coach them; lower-class students can gain these skills only in school.

So we deliberately encourage students to try different roles. We keep track of the "computer experts" in our classes so that the new status doesn't fall mainly to males or to high achievers or to kids with computers at home.

We also realize that in the consumer society of the 1990s, owning a computer may not indicate either affluence or academic achievement.

The computer seems most valuable for the least fluent, least successful writers. It's impractical to expect struggling writers to produce four or five drafts by hand, yet we know they must work through extensive revision if they are to develop skills. So we continue to respect the power of the computer to support the growth of our target students. At the end of year six, Minnie wrote,

> I shudder to remember that I once disparaged computers. Now I don't know how we could have been as successful in teaching writing without them. I especially relish the fact that no matter what a kid's socioeconomic status, he or she feels at home using a computer at Webster Groves HS. I honestly think they feel a sense of power or control observing the printer sputtering out their drafts. If only I could convince them to read the text after they tear it off the printer!

Cathy Beck's case study illustrates one eighth grader's encounter with technology.

> Theodore was a reluctant writer at best. Succinctness was his forte. Once we started workshop and he could go to the writing center to compose directly at the computer (always a luxury in the past), Theodore began to produce great quantities of writing. Throughout the 12 weeks of Workshop, Theodore produced 44 ¾ pages of text. All pages were done on the Macintoshes. Theodore has an IBM and previously had done all composing at home. Unfortunately, like most target students, his time management at home was a problem and he missed deadlines, hurried through pieces, and didn't have time for revision. On the major pieces, Scott James [resource teacher/technical whiz] worked with him extensively during resource period, allowing him extra time on the computer. Handwritten assignments in the room would normally result in very short, one- or two-paragraph pieces.
>
> The availability of a computer on a daily basis opened up new horizons for Theodore. His text pages became almost a dialogue between the two of us. He would address me directly ("I got your letter in the mail yesterday. My mom was very proud of me. I wanted to thank you

for the nice letter. We both appreciated it."). He shared his views of the world ("Well I think that the biggest problem of today is drugs and police. The drugs are winning and the police can't stop them."). He shared his thoughts about his peers in a detailed story of how people treated one of his classmates, a heavy White girl. In looking back, I think how awful it would have been if Theodore had not shared this personal part of himself with me. Had he not had access to the equipment on a daily basis, I never would have found out who Theodore was as a person. How glad I am that he had the opportunity!

LOOKING IN THE MIRROR: THE RESEARCH TEAM USES COMPUTERS

We too have been changed by working with computers. When we joined the writing project, our team had a full range of experiences and attitudes. Joan and Cathy represent the two extremes. Joan had done action research with computers and writing for three years and eventually left the team for a technology internship. Joan started the project at a time when she was beyond the fear, the strangeness, and the fascination with computers. She assumed that computers could support a process curriculum in writing but did not expect any technological magic to transform reluctant writers. For Joan, using the computer has meant exploring new software, new hardware, and new links to the curriculum.

Cathy came to Webster Groves in 1988 from a rural district that as yet had no instructional computers. She had never tried word processing herself, and at first she was afraid to touch the keys. Cathy immersed herself in technology with the same energy she applied to the rest of the project. A key asset was her teammate from math—an enthusiastic technical expert. Today, Cathy herself is an expert who calmly exports files from the Apple IIe to the Macintosh and tries out the latest publishing software. Others on the team look to her for help with the computers, knowing that what she can't do herself she will find out from her mentors.

WHAT YOU CAN DO

Buy, beg, or borrow a computer and play. It's great to learn with your students, and it's democratic for them to see you struggle. But if your computer access is limited to school, you'll quit trying in frustration.

Focus on revising and editing. The benefit of a computer for basic writers is working through a piece without recopying. Give credit for the process.

Publish. Students, like most of us, are impressed by results. They love to see their names in print.

Encourage collaboration. Mixed-ability groups can do research that draws on each person's knowledge. Publishing such writing bonds the classroom community.

Avoid creating a technological underclass. Resist any proposals that computers be reserved for advanced classes or that software for basic students be limited to grammar and spelling drills.

Read:

The Writer's Notebook: Creative Word Processing in the Classroom. Eugene, OR. A quarterly journal. Edited by S. Franklin and J. Madian.

Computers and Composition. Houghton: Michigan Technological University. A quarterly journal. Edited by C. Selfe and G. Hawisher.

ZENI, JANE. 1990. *WritingLands: Composing with Old and New Writing Tools.* Urbana, IL: National Council of Teachers of English.

NOTES

1. The action research was supported by a grant (1984–87) from the Fund for Improvement of Postsecondary Education (FIPSE). At the time, Webster Groves had no computers for student writers. In 1984–85 the middle school placed a dozen Commodores and one printer in Joan's classroom as an experiment. She was to integrate technology into her curriculum and monitor the results. It was a learning experience if not a spectacular success. The early Bank Street Writer was excruciatingly slow to load, to edit, and to print. Faced with poor typing skills and a daily crush at the printer, many students chose to handwrite their major papers! The best results came when two or three claimed a corner of the computer table and goaded one another through drafts to a finished paper. Yet Joan's colleagues were sufficiently impressed to found a writing center. District funds (since 1985) and the Federal Innovation in Education grant (since 1990) have continued to expand the centers.

2. Landmarks is led by Dr. Rosemary Thomas of St. Louis Community College, Meramec, and funded through a grant from the Danforth Foundation.

Facing the Mirror:
Jane Zeni

We didn't have segregation or racism or sheriffs with bullwhips in my suburban New Jersey childhood. Our world was integrated, or so I thought. Though most African American families lived in the northeast section of town, their homes were much like ours. My father, an import-export agent, loved to show foreign clients around town, stopping at the fine house owned by the Black man who headed the garbage collection service. I recall my horror as we watched the televised clashes between Arkansas police and little children going to school. "Those southerners," grumbled my mother. "We should have let 'em secede!" I nodded smugly.

I became a bookish loner at a Catholic grade school, an only child taunted by better-socialized classmates ("My sister'll get you!"). Entering the 1960s and public high school, I found a peer group where I belonged—girls who scorned makeup and the top forty in favor of poetry, politics, and folk music. Nearly all of my crowd was Jewish. At Teaneck High, if you were Black or Catholic you got married after graduation; if you were Jewish, you went to college. I suppose school showed me the difference between ancestry and culture. Ancestry is a given, but culture can be adopted.

My one Black friend was, like me, a cultural anomaly. Vice president of our class and a top student, she won a full scholarship to an Ivy League college, then turned it down to attend a historically Black college in the South. Her decision was the scandal of our senior year. In 1963, several classmates rode a bus to Washington to hear Dr. Martin Luther King. Why, when the country was tearing down segregation, would Cheryl want to go back? I couldn't see her dilemma, coming of age as an African American at a mostly White school.

I too won an Ivy League scholarship. As the first in my family to attend college, I went with some apprehension (would they all wear white gloves?) but stayed and blossomed. I lost my shyness, discovered men, and as a junior headed a student organization that placed tutors in the inner city. College was a heady time of idealism, crisis, and assassination. I moved on the fringes of the civil rights and antiwar movements. As in grade school, I stayed clear of confrontation. I'd march, carrying candles and singing "We shall overcome," but I wasn't about to occupy buildings or get thrown in jail.

I married while still in college and embarked on a twelve-year migration for jobs and graduate schools to St. Louis via Germany, Philadelphia, Santa Fe, and Toronto. In 1969, I taught Black and White students at a Philadelphia alternative school, then Pueblo, Hispanic, and Anglo students in New Mexico. (When I heard the term *Anglo* applied to me—with my Austro-Italian and French-Canadian ancestry—I was stunned. Then I learned that New Mexico's few African Americans were also considered Anglo!)

My sons were adopted as babies in Santa Fe. Though my husband and I had talked of choosing an interracial family, the growing racial polarization of the 1970s made us hesitate. Would we be taking on more than we could handle? Would our children be rejected? After much soul-searching, and with more bravado than confidence, we filled out the adoption forms stating "no preference" under "race or ethnic group." Adam Pablo is Hispanic; Mark Hosteen is Navajo and African. Going for adoption—regardless of what "people" might say—was the best crazy decision I've ever made.

An interracial family is a personal rather than a political choice. Still, it becomes second nature when buying a home, joining a church, or choosing a school to check out the racial climate. I was fortunate to find my neighborhood in University City, with a comfortable, fifty-fifty mix of Black and White residents. For about a dozen years I dropped out of social activism to raise my family and teach my classes. I'd quit trying to save the world and accepted the fact that the mood of the 1980s was not the one that had brought me into teaching. Anyhow, I doubted that White people could speak effectively about racism.

Mark entered his teens amid peer pressure to be cool and athletic. His grades fell. When I learned of a young Black male counselor with a support group for African American teens, I enrolled Mark despite some misgivings. Would the stress on African heritage undermine my family? Would this counselor diagnose my unconscious racism or naive liberalism or some other pernicious "ism" as the cause of Mark's low achievement? After two weeks, the counselor told me bluntly that my son was spoiled! With his support, I pushed chores, checked homework, and studied tapes by Dr. Jawanza Kunjufu. I also looked more critically at our consciously progressive public school. The district prides itself on a long history of welcoming diversity and a rich multicultural curriculum, yet too many African American students wound up in developmental classes. Mark transferred for two years to Cardinal Ritter College Prep, an all-Black urban Catholic school that stresses African American experience, academics, and leadership.

My teenagers have grown up with the Webster Groves project. Though I was hired as a consultant in writing, my experience as a parent turned out to be useful to the team. And working with the action research—reading, sharing, reflecting—has been immensely valuable to me as a parent.

Sitting at Mark's graduation (back at our mostly Black public high), I counted the Honor Society members: twenty-four females and four males. Two of the males were foreign students and two were White! The negative images we've fought to change are still blighting the futures of young African American men. (Teachers at the middle school have now started their own action research project to address some of these issues.)

Today both my sons are in college. Mark plans to major in music, Adam in special education. I'm proud and I'm relieved. My children have both developed a multicultural identity. They learned "Black Communication" style with neighborhood kids, codeshift fluently, and date across racial lines. Adam joined a Black fraternity and now prefers his middle name, Pablo.

Perhaps it is my own cultural past—my tentative belonging in Catholic, Jewish, and Anglo circles—that tells me it's OK. I've learned that integration is no magic solution to racism and that White people can't drop out because we're all in this together. My children give me hope that we may get beyond racism, not by becoming colorless or color-blind, but by sharing who we are and who we choose to be.

Foster Involvement with Writing and Reading

The portfolio I did was difficult and I had fun writing it. I liked my storie My Best Baseball game. My new storie is Black Power its 28 pages long I couldn't finish my story on time because I was only on page 8. I've been working on it for 5 days straight I started last Frioday, Saturday, Sunday, Mon, Tue. I like the work I do in English it cools me down. It helps me talk about my feelings.

WALTER,
seventh-grade portfolio reflection

Involvement—the burning interest and the fun—makes students jump to the task. Both the process and the product change when writers are motivated. We've seen dramatic growth, especially among Black male students dulled by low expectations from others and from themselves. No, we do not reach all our kids—at least not in one year. In fact, we often check with our teammates to see if the next teacher has gotten across to one who left our classrooms still uninvolved. In the first years of our project, we noticed that giving students *choice* was linked to involvement. Today, while we see the issue more broadly, the most powerful ingredient for our target students is still choice.

There is a delicate balance between free choice and expanding the range of choice. Imagine a child whose only experience with ice cream is vanilla. Offered the choice of thirty-nine flavors, she'll probably choose vanilla. We start where the kids are but we don't stop there; we build on choice and involvement to expand horizons (see Chapter 11).

LISTEN FOR WRITERS' INTERESTS

All of us work to ferret out the signs of a burning interest hidden in an otherwise unmotivated student. Finding such a hot topic is often a break-through, so we can build a sequence of related but more challenging tasks. Sandy tells of the "hockey crowd in second hour" who read a biography of Gretsky and then wrote their own personal narratives, fiction stories, and letters to the pros. Sandy fed their involvement by bringing in hockey books for her classroom library; one eighth grader, a low-achieving White male, immediately

> started looking at me in a different way. He engaged me in conversation every day about something he was reading, went out of his way to thank me two or three times a day for whatever. My interpretation is that he was grateful that he was having such a good time, especially when he had never suspected that books were so interesting.

When our students choose their own topics, they usually write better, produce more, and revise more willingly. Journals and other unedited writing succeed in part because of choice. Sometimes a journal topic is entirely open; other times we give a prompt, perhaps from literature or current events and students respond in any way they choose. Such writing process leaders as Donald Graves (1983) and Nancie Atwell (1987) confirm the value of topics chosen by students for authentic purposes rather than imposed by the teacher.

At times, however, such freedom is inhibiting. When given free rein, most students (regardless of race, gender, or level of skill) tend toward personal narrative and fiction. Our target students have certain problems with "open" topics. Some clamor for structure—to be told concretely what to do and what is expected. If the freedom to choose scares them, they may resist starting at all. We have more success in getting students involved when we take an active role in helping them find their own burning interests.

So we model topic selection, using such idea-generating techniques as clustering (Rico 1983) and memory chains (Moffett and Wagner 1992). We may provide a broad topic for writers to connect with their own personal stories. Joan gives each student a miniature poster with a slogan like "There are those who make things happen and those who watch." Poster captions tend to generate expository essays, but students can choose their own focus and audience. Such an approach offers the structure and the personal energy that get more of our target students involved. To the prompt, "The biggest problem in the world today," Henry wrote,

> I think the biggest problem in the world today is drugs. Drug are everywere. I see it everyday guys standing on corner in cold are hot weather. You know that they have to be saling something standing out in the cold when the temp is something like 5 or 10 outside. . . . One time I even saw a man take some rocked cocine, put it in a bag, and hide it by crub in some leaves. So when the cops come by the can't get busted. . . . [To stop the drug problem we can] start helping these young people and older people get a job because for one reason they can get killed over drug locked up shot at and many other bad things.

Note the strong details that Henry used when he connected the bland assignment with a topic of his own choice. This unedited journal had potential as a seed or a "zero draft," to use Donald Murray's term (1985).

Involvement in honest, personal writing can have a powerful impact. Sandy tells of a student for whom writing about her traumatic past became an unexpected source of pride and confidence:

Mary, who is at [a residential treatment center] because of abuse in her original family and also in her foster family, cranked out many personal papers. There was one other student she felt comfortable sharing her stories with. Explaining her experiences to her peer partner and to me helped her sort out some important events in her life. (She needed assurance on a regular basis that only Judy and I would see the personal writing.) In nine months, Mary went from writing two or three sentences of ENGFISH[1] to sending an interesting article on life at [the center] to our sister school in England. She was thrilled to discover a subject on which she was one of the very few experts.

Early in our project, most of us saw personal experience as the main source of writing topics. Today, the imaginative experience of literature is also important as a catalyst for writing and as a place for students to exercise choice. What topics do kids select for free reading? Cathy noticed that "White target students tend to choose the gruesome Stephen King variety while Black target students tend to choose books written by Black authors." In the case of the former, Sandy faced a dilemma of quality control that led her to reflect, loosen up, and change some of her own attitudes. Here is an excerpt from her fifth-year synthesis report:

I didn't get on my high horse about some of the trash they were reading and writing. I rationalized that position to myself by thinking that we develop taste by reading a range of things, so Stephen King and his gore probably isn't going to set their pattern for life. I sometimes read escapist junk (and watch "Unsolved Mysteries"). Tonyelle wrote a pretty steamy short story with the hero groping at her blouse, then ripping it off. Her writing group convinced her to tone it down, and I'm not sure how I would have handled it if she hadn't. Somebody has to write that stuff. It would be just like Tonyelle to get on a talk show when she's rich and famous and tell how her prudish English teacher thwarted her talent. The mafia books that were hot in second hour—*Good Fellas, The Godfather*—were plenty violent and sexy. I can't imagine myself allowing them before this. And again, maybe I'm wrong. Kids are exposed to more now. I'm thinking of a Holocaust film I show some years. There is a scene where prisoners are lined up, naked, headed for the gas chambers. In earlier years, many kids giggled, commented in ways that showed their inability to handle it. In the last two or three years, kids never giggle, but instead, react to the indignity and humiliation that those people were experiencing. Maybe it's one of the few benefits of the overcharged society they are facing.

Sandy's comment shows the thoughtful process of action research and how it leads to change in the classroom. When we foster involvement, we become more accepting of our students as teenagers, not literary critics.

When the high school added *The Bluest Eye* to the tenth- and eleventh-grade American literature course, Carrie was concerned about possible objections from parents. After preparing her students for the format, warning them about the graphic nature of the book, and offering an alternative for any who found the book too offensive, she "turned the . . . novel over to the students." They were to write response logs for sharing each day in general class discussions. "In the end, my early worries seemed silly. I had no phone calls or visits from irate parents." The reader response logs and discussions helped students clarify their own feelings and learn "some good old-fashioned literary technique by examining symbols and metaphors." Carrie's article, including some of her students' responses, was published in *English Journal* (Henly 1993).

Sometimes we've wondered if our African American students are limiting themselves to racially matched literature. On the other hand, we've learned not to assume that all Black readers will, in fact, prefer Black authors. Cathy tells about Sadie, "who commented that she got tired of teachers pushing Black experiences down her throat. However, when I suggested such books to Sadie, she would eagerly read them (she especially liked Mildred Taylor's *The Friendship* and *The Gold Cadillac*)." So many kids arrive in middle school with very little experience reading African American writers of adolescent fiction. We feel that the exposure in our classrooms is long overdue for White as well as Black students.

Once we learn about our readers' tastes, we can gradually work to vary them. Yet today we feel that variety is less important than enthusiastic involvement. A steady diet of their favorite literary dish—whether science fiction, romance, or Black experience—may nourish a lifelong taste for books of all kinds.

As teachers, we need sharp eyes to recognize, follow, and build on our students' interests. Sandy describes three African American males who were "bright, easygoing, responsive"—but usually off task. Her attempts to entice them (a story on Roberto Clemente and a passage from Maya Angelou) fell flat. Then they moved into literature study groups where kids heard a variety of book talks: "They had a chance to choose *The Legend of Tarik,* a fantasy with an African as the hero. Come to find out, Greg had read quite a bit of fantasy and mythology, so he was galvanized and took leadership in getting his friends as hooked as he was." The group went on to read several fantasies, to seek out books from the public libraries, and to suggest new titles to purchase for their classroom collection. Maybe when students tune out, their teacher doesn't know enough about their world to guess their interests. If we listen, offer choice, and let them lead us, we won't need ESP to involve them in reading!

Even when forced to work under time constraints on the districtwide assessment, our students write better if they can get involved with the topic. One year's assessment question, both spring and fall, was "Write about an object that is special to you." Sandy credits the growth in Tanya's pretest and posttest scores to her choice of an object she could really get excited about: her scrap book. In the fall, Tanya had written briefly about three objects trying to show how she had matured from being attached to her Superwoman underwear, through a Cabbage Patch doll, to a bracelet from her uncle. On a sixteen-point scale, her score went from a four to a fourteen; her writing samples (Figures 10-1 and 10-2) show this growth vividly. Sandy was thrilled: "Tanya's paper had voice—which is another way of saying 'involvement'—pride, audience awareness, transitions, full intro and conclusion, sensory and concrete details. It was two pages long and almost error-free."

When I was about 3 or 4 I had a Super Women underware and I always wanted to wear them. It was a tank top that had the Super Women wings on the front & little pants. When I was 7 or 8 I got a Cabbage Patch Kid her name is Fannie Carol I took her everywhere with me. I took her to Target, Dairy Queen & Restaurants. I got her from my Grams for my birthday. For show and tell in 2nd grade I brought her & when I went to North Carolina I brought her with me she was with me the whole drive that was 2 days. I also took her to see Ghostbusters when it first came out. I also took Fannie to slumber parties and Sunday school. My mom bought me many clothes for Fannie Carol. Two years ago my Granny who lives in California bought me another Cabbage Patch Kid. Now I am out of that stage, now the object that I love most is the braclet my uncle gave to me. I wear it everyday. It reminds me of when I went to California this summer. It was when I got a new object that I love most. I told my uncle that I would wear it everyday. It will always remind me of when I went to L.A. the summer of '88.

FIG. 10-1 *Tanya's pretest narrative.*

Self-selection helps students get involved in their topics, but it's not a sure cure for writing that goes through the motions without a real purpose, serving what James Britton et al. (1975) call *pseudofunctions*. When Joan assigned an explanatory or persuasive essay with a free choice of topic, Mark browsed through his journal and chose an entry on wrestling as a starter. We might expect this process would lead him to a topic of some interest. But his draft had no focus. Joan asked, "When you started to write, what were you trying to do with this paper?" Mark replied,

> Write about wrestling . . . I wasn't really worried about the benefits or nothing. I was just writing about wrestling. You gave us this assignment and I just—and see my title was plain old wrestling. I wasn't really worried about the benefits or anything. I was just writing about wrestling.

My Scrapbook

My scrapbook is very important to me because it has every picture of Jackee Joyner Kersee that I could get my hands on. Jackee Joyner is my favorite athlete in the whole world, and I want to be just like her. These pictures mean a lot to me, because I might not be able to ever meet her.

Also in my scrapbook I have pictures of Carl Lewis, Edwin Moses, Ben Johnson & Florence Griffith Joyner. These are people I idolize, except for Ben Johnson; he gives runners a bad name because he took steroids. I still have that in my scrapbook to remember that to win you don't have to cheat.

Edwin Moses a man to remember! He jumped those hurdles with sunglasses on! In the heats he beat everyone. This man juimps so graceful and high as he strides over those hurdles. To remember him I also placed him in my scrapbook.

Carl Lewis! The man is so fast he could outrun a bike! In the one hundred meter race he runs like the speed of light! He reminds me of Jesse Owens by how fast he runs. I think children should look up to him rather than a dopeman. He is in my scrapbook to remind me that blacks can be in the Olympics & succeed.

Florence Griffith Joyner made history in her own time by having the longest nails in the Olympics! But really the muscles in her legs & arms astound me. She is very good in the 400 meters (1 lap). She is in my scrapbook too! Flojo is the last person in my scrapbook.

I hope you understand why it is important to me now but if you don't let me sum it up. I only have black runners in there for 2 reasons one I want to be just like them and two although blacks are a minority we can acheive things just the same as white people.

FIG. 10-2 *Tanya's posttest narrative.*

Joan learned from this fiasco and began actively teaching students how to make rhetorical choices.

TEACH STUDENTS HOW TO MAKE CHOICES

Too often, students who fall behind in school get stuck in one of two inappropriate environments: the rigid skill-and-drill basics class where writers have few choices, or the laissez-faire "progressive" classroom that offers a wealth of choices and assumes that writers already know how to manage them. In the secondary schools, a student may bounce from one environment to the other in the course of a day. We find our target students much more willing to risk getting involved if we walk them through the choices they must make as successful writers and readers.

Choices for Writers — Audience, Purpose, Mode, and Form

Writing for an audience gives a focus for writing ("Which details in your draft will be most convincing to X?") and having a clear purpose usually adds motivation. Mark's lack of involvement with his wrestling paper might have been addressed through guiding his choices.

The next time Joan asked her eighth graders to write a transactional essay, she offered more direction. First her students selected their tentative topics from ten-minute freewrites and then they brainstormed with a partner all the audiences and purposes they could imagine, filling in the blanks of "To write to _____ in order to _____." Joan modeled: "To write to store owners to persuade them not to stereotype kids by the way they dress." She then asked for samples from the class.

Daniel wrote to the National Collegiate Athletic Association to per-suade them to keep Proposition 48 (much in the news at the time). Sidney needed help in refining his initial audience: "To write to kids to tell them what to look for in a friend." Joan asked, "Do you know what girls should look for? Do you have any experience with this?" At this point, Sidney decided to focus on boys looking for a male friend. The audience and purpose chosen for each paper determined the form. Joan required only that it be public, transactional writing. Daniel wrote a persuasive letter; Sidney wrote an explanatory essay.

Audiences are most important for explanatory and persuasive writings; personal narratives, fiction, and poetry usually need only be appropriate for a general age group. Although we work hard to provide real audiences (such as letters that are actually mailed), we often simply ask students to write with an audience in mind, then arrange for feedback from someone who fits that audience. For example, a writer who supports capital punishment will get reactions to his draft of a persuasive essay from a reader who opposes capital punishment.

We give kids the freedom to choose what they will write, but we guide their choices through individual or group conferences. Sometimes we offer a list of possible projects. Beware if your list includes choices (such as posters, collages, dioramas) that require no writing! We've learned to set some criteria, such as a minimum of choices calling for a written product. Instead of leaving them to flounder, we confer with students as they plan how to handle their choices.

Each year, we introduce a wide range of imaginative and expository writing. We teach traditional forms—even the five-paragraph essay—as useful options, not as mindless formulas (see Chapter 5). We want to expand our students' repertoires. Often we start with a dictatorial requirement just to try out something new; as Nancie Atwell says, "Taste the vegetables." After all, a writer isn't free to choose a particular form if she's had no experience with that form. Some of us require certain forms in certain papers: "Write a narrative introduction to your essay." After students have tried such an option, they can choose whether or not to use it in future writings.

Our aim is to empower students, to give the historically low achievers an experience of making their own choices and setting their own goals. We search for a balance between freedom and structure.

Choices for Readers —
Response Logs and Literature Study Groups

Personal response is the root of our kids' involvement in literature. Reader-response theorists such as Rosenblatt (1978) and Bleich (1975) have argued that all readers, at all levels of skill and sophistication, should have a chance to experience real engagement in a work. What we know about reading comprehension suggests that personal response doesn't just get readers emotionally involved; it gets them cognitively involved. Skilled readers are active—reading between the lines, marking up margins, talking back in letters to the editor. Most target students have never known this kind of reading. Response logs are an effective way to give them choices, ownership, and power in their reading and in their writing. These journals may provide the raw material for more formal papers.

Personal response can take many forms. Some of us have made a double-entry log by drawing a vertical line down the middle of each notebook page. On the left side, students take notes about their reading; on the right, they jot questions, comments, and connections with their own lives, with social issues, or with other works they have read. We find the double-entry log works wonders for informational reading but can get in the way of reading literature. Stephanie prefers a "bookmark" made by slicing a sheet of notebook paper vertically in half. Students jot page numbers on the bookmark and freewrite their responses as they go along.

At first, many students have trouble responding personally and wind up with plot summaries. Cathy models by showing both personal and bland entries on the overhead, then inviting students to tell their own stories, which often show great sensitivity and involvement. Here is Aisha's response to John Updike's "August":

> The poem was about the things that happens in the summer. It reminds me when the summer is here I always eat a popsicle and it stains on my clothes. I usually go down to the park and go into the playground. I play on the merry-go-round and on the swings and you can feel the dust hitting you as you go around or up and down.

Mary Ann designed a lesson on "The Highwayman" for her seventh graders. Stan loved the poem's romance and rhythm, but balked at writing about a time he himself had done something for another person that might have changed a life. Mary Ann reflected that perhaps he resisted seeing himself in such a positive light and having such power.

During the first few years, our field notes show as many failures as successes with the reading log. Theresa observed, "The good readers do it, though they say they hate to interrupt their reading. The weak readers don't do it until it is time for a notebook check." Sandy lamented,

> Reader response journals weren't effective for me with target students, though they were with more able writers. I used modeling, but it must have been inadequate. I'm sure I didn't do it enough through the year. Entries for target students were usually so short as not to be "responsive." This is a weakness in my repertoire which I plan to address in year 4!

Cathy, who had joined the team a year before, introduced a new and powerful context for the reading logs: literature study groups. Based on an idea from Ralph Peterson (1987, 21–23), literature study groups offer a structure for collaborative learning along with personal response to reading and writing. Cathy gives students a great deal of freedom, beginning with the freedom to choose one of a dozen or more paperback novels she introduces with enthusiastic book talks. Students are grouped according to the books they select. Each group designs a major project—creating a commercial to sell the book to adolescents or scripting portions for reader's theater. The teacher carefully monitors the work, meets each group every other day as they share their response logs and interpretations of the text, and confers on their projects.

Literature study groups have become a mainstay of our teaching (see Appendix One). Just a year after the lament quoted above, Sandy got it right: "It gave me goose flesh to see how most students grooved on choosing a novel from the seven I offered. The sight of a whole class reading avidly and whispering about their books was a treat. I think that the *choice* was a strong factor." The same excitement showed in Stephanie's vignette:

> Through literature study groups, I was able to read and listen during conferences to some wonderful responses to African American literature. A group of four girls, two of them target students, became almost obsessed with *Roll of Thunder, Hear My Cry.* Jessica was especially vocal about her feelings. She openly expressed absolute disgust at the way the Black family, the Logans, were treated by Whites in their community. The girls were so engrossed in their own comments that I was able to just sit back and listen without any probing for over ten minutes.

We've found that response logs, often dull in the past, are a great success when shared in literature study groups. Perhaps the social support and the oral language help kids who have been uninvolved to make a connection with literature. Cathy was "amazed at their insight and powerful emotion." Here are two journal responses to poetry from her eighth-grade target students. Doug wrote,

> The title of the poem that I read was "An Actual Individual" by Arthur Jones. It tells about how ordinary adolescents are real people, and that the river of thought runs deep. I can relate to every word that is written in this poem. Especially my "temper simmering" as mine does so many times throughout the day. I like this poem because it tells everything that I feel that I have never been able to express in words to myself or others at this time.

Abe wrote,

> I read a poem in a book called "Beginnings" by Robert Hayden. This poem is about a man who I think is Black. This man is going to join Lincoln's army. I can really relate to this poem in the last stanza when the author was talking about an old woman who is still as active as ever. You see my great great aunt Letha was ninety six and still going strong. Even though she couldn't tote and drop firewood she could do almost everything else. Every night she cooked an entire meal for herself her sisters Grace and Carol and her brother. She would do almost all the work in the house even though she was the oldest. I was about nine when she

died. And I remember not even crying because she was so strong in her soul I thought she was going to wake up and just go back to her regular routine. Now that I look back on it I think it was her soul that kept her going.

In literature study groups, our students listen daily to the responses and feelings of peers from varied backgrounds. A fringe benefit may be empathy. Here's how Chad responded to the young adult novel, *Scorpions:*

> Jamal seems to be resiving [receiving] the unfair treatment that many poor and inercity people do. His father has left them. His brother got involved with a gang called the Scorpions and ended up killing a man. He was sent to jail and has left Jamal, his Mother, and his sister Sassy. They are forced to live on welfare and the money there mother makes doing odd jobs. In school Jamal is treated like he has no hope so he turns to other things for hope and attention. If I were in his situation I don't know if I would go to the extremes he does but there aren't many other things that I would be able to do.

Cathy reflects, "Chad is a typical middle-class suburban student, but he shows a great sensitivity to the living conditions of others. His final sentence shows that he recognizes that Jamal has far fewer options than he does."

Choices in Reading/Writing Workshop

We have struggled to provide a balance of choice and guidance in a workshop environment. As discussed in Chapter 5, the work of Delpit (1986, 1988) and Siddle-Walker (1992) warns that some African American learners misinterpret a teacher who gives them choices. Black communities have traditionally viewed a "good teacher" as strong, upbeat, funny, and charismatic—and always in charge. These cultural norms may jar with the style of the writing workshop. Yet workshop has become an invigorating place for most of our African American students.

Our major adjustment was to move gradually with support to help kids handle the freedom. Success often came in stages. Nancy describes the beginning:

> On the first day, the freedom to write any kind of writing, for any audience, became overwhelming for my students, all of them. We brainstormed writing ideas, some coming up with ideas and a plan right away. Most did not, however. Martin was on a roll responding to "Thank You, Ma'am," by Langston Hughes. I had given students five pieces from the literature book, hoping these would help them generate ideas, as well as get into the reading/writing connection. Aside from Martin, my field notes recorded, "Many are staring, thinking I hope. Alex [not a target student] is seeking perfection and a master plan (that's her M.O.) already worked out in her head before she sets a word on paper." Charlotte concocted a short story of a couple hit by a drunken driver. The father ended up in a coma; the mom told him, while comatose, that she was pregnant; his heart stopped; they revived him; and he miraculously knew his wife was pregnant.

Yet the class soon adjusted, and the mood of workshop grew calm and on task. Nancy reflects on this welcome change:

> Many students will be out of the room, composing in the writing center. Those who remain in the classroom may be working collaboratively, but often are intently involved. The "silence was deafening." In the past, while I was trying to keep everyone together at the same stage of writing, the noise levels were significantly higher.

In January Nancy faced another sort of crisis, "I'm struggling with my workshop. It's a tremendous act of balancing. All my kids, especially target students, want to write. They crank out the material. I must say there is potential." By May the quality of her portfolios convinced her that the struggle was worthwhile.

Given real choices in workshop, students produce a great variety of forms. JoAnne cites "character sketches, 'mood' pieces, friendly and business letters, projects based on books read in workshop, essays for the team newspaper, poetry books, a collaborative story told by letters between characters, etc." Formerly turned-off students get involved in writing because they find the freedom to explore the hot topics they really care about. Stephanie reports that

> Jeffrey decided to write his first paper about gangs and his second paper a letter to the editor of the *Post-Dispatch* about gangs in St. Louis. We had never seen Jeffrey so enthused about writing. It was wonderful. Ted, a very quiet target student, wrote a wonderfully creative (and spooky!) story about a man who sends himself home overseas because he gambled away his plane fare. When we conferenced, I asked him how he had thought of this unique plot. He said he had always wanted to write a *Twilight Zone* type of story but had never done it until we started workshop and he got to choose his own topic.

Our field notes are full of such vignettes, often ending with a comment such as, "I had no idea that this person had such creative talent. Without the workshop and the free choice of topics I might never have known."

The response of target students has surpassed even our own optimism. We knew the warnings that student-centered approaches tended to fail with African American males. We also knew that in our own classes, historically low achievers needed guidance to make choices and stay on task. Chapter 5 explains some of the adjustments we made in Atwell's workshop model to keep our target students from falling through the cracks. A major benefit is that the guidance our kids need doesn't come only from the teacher. Sandy reports,

> Clark was a voracious reader. He had plenty of motivation since his dad . . . had stored the TV in the attic for a year. He was a big Stephen King fan, so I gave him the cash to go to a used paperback place he haunted and get us some books for our classroom. We developed a nice relation-ship, where he would confer with me about titles, speculate on whether we ought to invest up to $2 on such-n-such. He would keep some of my cash in reserve so he could sleuth out some bargains and strike fast when the opportunity arose. He was the King expert on the team, so I sent him "clients" to counsel on what to read next. (*Misery* is the hands-down winner.) He was highly motivated by all that attention from me and

teammates and liked the attention he got from peers for having the longest reading list.

Despite the potentially overwhelming array of choices, our target students showed no more difficulties than their classmates.

GIVE STUDENTS AN ACTIVE ROLE IN LEARNING

Knowing the African American tradition of strong, direct teaching (Delpit 1988), we might hold on to our power and hesitate to bring students into running the classroom. We believe this is a mistake. Our Black students *want* to be involved in their own learning—so long as the teacher also stays involved. They thrive in a democratic classroom culture (see Chapter 7) where both teaching and learning are active processes.

As we grew more confident in our teaching, most of us began sharing with our classes some of the power we once reserved for ourselves. Many of the procedures we have adopted over the years—reading/writing workshop, literature study groups, individual access to computers—serve to decenter the classroom. We give students more responsibility to make decisions about their own learning. Several of us have developed rules for democratic classroom management. All members are to be treated with respect; put-downs are forbidden.

Some of us have our kids write their own study questions and test items. Some students have also written their own progress reports to send home and have found the task enlightening: "I learned that it is harder to grade yourself than to grade someone else." The progress reports were a dramatic sign that they were responsible for their own behavior.

Taking self-evaluation a step further, we have begun asking students to evaluate their writing, their reading, their contribution to groups, and their development as learners. More than a gimmick, this process makes students active participants in their own education, not just bystanders.

One February, Nancy asked seventh graders to look over each piece of writing they had done that year. "What have you learned so far?" Their responses showed serious thought and analysis:

Martin: Writing to me is just like talking something out but you are just writing astead. I like talking so that's probably why I like writing.

Charlie (not a target student): I didn't like my childhood memory because it was written wrong, predictable, and just plain dumb. I really like my short story, thow the title had somewhat to be desired.

Sally: I learned that the characters that are like me are in the books I like to read.

John: I think having a journal is a good idea. I am probably the kind of learner who doesn't understand everything at first. Me, as a writer is hard to believe. I do not think I am an excellent writer. I'm alright thought. I am a better writer know that at the beginning of the year. I am amazed at some of the things I write myself. Also, the literature study groups were cool. I got a book I really wanted which was *Young Man in Viet Nam.*

A new element of choice was provided in the fifth year when we piloted portfolios (see Chapters 5 and 12). The enthusiasm for portfolios was beyond our wildest hopes. As with workshop, we carefully walked our classes through the skills needed to choose and evaluate their own work, so we were confident that our students would *understand* the task. But as Gail says, "What I didn't know and couldn't predict, and actually wasn't prepared for, was the way my students would *feel* about their portfolios. There was a personal, almost passionate feeling about those folders." When Nancy's students got into selecting pieces for portfolio, "an obsession overtook the room. Students did not want to go to other classes. To hell with social studies, science, or math! I have never seen 100 percent of any class so *involved* in what they were doing." Thrilled with her students' portfolio reflections, Cathy concluded, "This is the best, most powerful assignment I've done in years!"

There were differences, of course, between our lower- and higher-skilled students in depth of reflection and control of language. But we found no difference in their involvement with the portfolio process. As our under-achieving Black students take a more active role in learning, we believe they will shake free of that passivity that makes them "at risk" in integrated classrooms.

MAKE THE WRITING REAL

Audiences

Writing means so much more when the audience is real. The impact of sending a letter or giving a poem as a gift motivates students to do their best. So we search for ways to provide real audiences, many of whom write replies. Here are some examples we have used recently:

Letter urging some action by a government official.

Fan letter to famous personality of student's choice.

Letter to a teacher or student in another class.

Letter to eighth graders telling them what high school is like.

Letter to sixth graders telling them what middle school is like.

Letter to a British educator who visited St. Louis.

Thank-you letter to local author who spoke at school.

Thank-you to a career fair presenter, telling own career goal.

Letter interviewing a grandparent.

Business letter to a distant chamber of commerce requesting information.

The Great Mail Race (letters to unknown pen pals).

Noteboard to contact classmates.

Carrie assigns a business letter for which students choose their own audience. She reports that everyone in her classes turned in a letter for mailing. "I had a book of addresses of famous people that fascinated the students—especially target students. They enjoyed reading through it and finding addresses of their favorite sports, music, or film stars."

Nancy is equally pleased with the formal business letters her students have written to chambers of commerce and tourist bureaus. The project is part of an interdisciplinary unit called "Route 66." Isaac had no idea about what part of the country to study. He settled on California, then accepted a suggestion of San Diego which Nancy showed him on a map.

> "Well, I don't know anything about it," he said.
> "Isaac, it's one of the most beautiful cities in the U. S.," I answered. "It is on the ocean, with warm weather almost year round."

Some students wrote stuffy impersonal letters, but not Isaac.

> Dear Sir or Madam:
> Our English class is studying your part of the country. I'm requesting information about the beautiful city of San Diego. Being beautiful is about the only thing I know about your city. That's why I can use any kind of information that you can give. Your cooperation is appreciated.
> > Sincerely,

After proofreading his letter, Nancy handed Isaac an envelope. He was amazed to see that he was actually going to mail his letter, and asked how to address the envelope, sharing that this was the first letter he had ever sent to anyone. She adds, "Isaac took tremendous pride in stamping his letter and eventually receiving an answer from the San Diego Chamber of Commerce. We take so much for granted."

Another faraway audience is accessed by computer. Chapter 9 describes a network connecting our writers with peers in several countries abroad. Sandy's students wrote on "Black adolescent male hairstyles, bussing, in-school suspension. Students felt intoxicated with their unique knowledge!" Cathy has built a sense of audience closer to home by offering her students a noteboard (an idea borrowed from Carolyn Burke at the University of Indiana). On the bulletin board in her room she posts class rosters and headings for each of the periods. She has a stack of ditto forms

313

for the notes. Students write their messages and pin them to the board under the right class period.

Yet real audiences, like self-chosen topics, do not guarantee involvement. Carrie describes a carefully planned sequence of assignments that got lukewarm responses, especially from her target students. Why?

> During the second quarter, students had to read a book they liked and wanted to recommend to their classmates. Later they wrote book reviews, which went into a binder in the classroom. During the third quarter, each student had to read through some of the book reviews to choose a book he or she felt was interesting and read that book. Finally, each student wrote a letter to the author of the original book review to explain whether he or she agreed with that author's evaluation of the book. I duplicated the letters and forwarded them so that the communication between students was real.
>
> Although I thought this project would appeal to students because the task was real and because it involved personal response to literature, neither of these was a popular project among target students; five of the twenty did not complete the book review, and seven of the twenty (including four of the five who did not do the original review) did not complete a response letter. I don't know, though, whether it was the prospect of writing to another student or reading the book which was more intimidating.

In retrospect, we think the idea of writing to a classmate to recommend a book may have seemed contrived. Kids could have easily shared their views over lunch if they were so inclined! Before getting involved in writing for a school audience, they may need more control over topic or purpose—or more ownership of the writing they will share.

As they gain confidence and skill, many students take risks in writing for the audiences that matter the most, in society and in the family. The next episode started with two eighth graders who were not target students. But as they took on the task of writing for a public audience, their involvement spread to hundreds of their peers. Cathy tells the story:

Two students collaboratively wrote a letter to the editor of the *Post-Dispatch* concerning their reaction to the Rodney King verdict. It was an honest and thought-provoking letter [see Figure 10-3]. They shared it with their peers and then began to get signatures of other students who agreed. Within a day, they accumulated over 400 signatures. They discussed the letter with Dr. Morrison [the principal] and he wholeheartedly endorsed their efforts by asking teachers to allow them into their classes to gather signatures. The letter was faxed through the district fax machine to the *Post-Dispatch*. Both students were excited (and surprised) by the support they got for their letter. Even though their letter was not published in the paper, the experience gave both girls a lesson in the power of their own words. This episode shows the power of a burning interest, as well as the power of a real audience with the lure of publication.

Another vignette, from Sandy's class, shows a young woman who became involved in writing to an audience that really counted in her life. Fortunately, her message was heard:

Leslie noodled around with ideas until she decided to write about her dad, who has been out of touch with the family for years. It was a moving piece, and she saw me tear up when I read it. That turned her on like a light bulb. Then she wanted to show it to the counselor; she made copies for her mom. She liked to talk about what a good piece we all thought it was, wanted to know if I had told the other team teachers. One of those days I said, "Leslie, how about sharing it with your dad?"

She doubted that her grandmother would give her his address, but she decided to try. The short of it is, she mailed a copy of her story and a note saying that her English teacher thought she should share it with him, and received a very touching reply, inviting her to come for a visit. Here is an excerpt from Leslie's paper:

My mom and dad got a divorce when I was three. I really don't know why he tries not to see me when he's in town, or why he never writes. I feel like it is something I did, but deep down I know that it has nothing to do with me at all. [She describes how the stepmother sends her birthday cards and Christmas presents and signs his name, but that isn't the same as knowing your dad.]

I really hope when I get married it is to someone so sweet and loving that he will never leave me for as long as I live.

```
                    Hixson Middle School
                    630 South Elm Avenue
                 Webster Groves, Missouri 63119


                       April 30, 1992




Dear Editor,

We were shocked to hear the outcome of the trial concerning the
police officers' beating of Rodney King.   To have found the
officers innocent was an outrage!

Having had a primary source, the videotape, we cannot comprehend
how a roomful of well-educated, fair-minded jurors could let such
an act of hatred and prejudice pass.

If the roles had been switched, the officers black and the victim
white, there is not a doubt in our minds that the officers would
have been found guilty and appropriately punished.

If this world is to become a better place for future generations,
we cannot allow such violence and discrimination to continue.  It
has been said that the children are the future, but how can we be
expected to make any good of the world when this kind of example
has been set?

In the Rodney King case, the word justice has lost its meaning!

                    Sincerely,




                    Colleen Kelly, Natalie Homan

and the Hixson Middle School students, which includes all races,
who have signed the attached sheets.
```

FIG. 10-3 *Letter to editor from students.*

Publishing

Eventually our students present some of their work to a less-intimate audience through informal publication. We're ready to "go public," we tell our writers. The most popular form is the anthology, which includes the work of every student in the class. Papers are edited on the word processor following some agreed-upon format and printed on the laser printer. Students typically design the cover, often using graphics software and adding color. Laminating the cover and adding a spiral binding gives the book a less amateurish appearance. A table of contents listing titles and authors, along with an explanation of how the papers came to be, creates interest when the books are displayed at the educational fair or at open house. Publishing motivates our target students to go back for a final round of proofreading.

The following year, the books are available for students to read at their leisure or to consult as product models of a topic or mode being worked on. Mary Ann adds, "Sometimes they will find an older friend's paper and show it to me." She recalls the reaction of one previously uninvolved student to her stack of laminated interview books: "Reggie asked about his interview, 'Do you mean you're going to show this to the sixth graders?' When I said I was, he asked for more felt tips and more paper, and took more ownership in his project."

Some of us publish individual books for each student to take home at the end of the year. This is not as popular as the class book because of the expense involved, plus the time squeeze of trying to get the last important pieces of writing included and over a hundred books bound before the kids leave.

We also publish simply by posting student work. The work on display is always a clean printout—without teacher grades, corrections, or comments—to validate the author. Joan laminates the book reviews and hangs them with yarn on the outside of the book spines, like big bookmarks, in the school library. The librarian continues to hang these reviews in succeeding years since students enjoy reading them.

Along with class books, anthologies, and bulletin board and library "publications," Gail uses lunch-sack book reports. Hanging above the chalkboard in her room are the small brown bags that typically hold lunches that are decorated to give a feel for a particular book. Inside the bag is a short review written to advise the prospective reader.

Several of our middle school teachers have helped their classes to produce a team newspaper. Students love the features, including record reviews, surveys, student interviews, and cartoons. Editorials comment on school-related issues. News articles are the most difficult since getting out the paper takes so long the news is often no longer news and therefore no longer motivating. Our journalists have to keep in mind their audience: not only other students but also parents. Newspapers are often sold during the lunch hour to help pay for the duplicating costs.

Publishing for a real audience gives status to writing. Todd, a target student, was talking with his math teacher about the team publication, an anthology of everyone's best writing. The teacher observed that the book was a lot of work. His chest puffed out, Todd replied, "Well, it *is* going to the superintendent, you know!"

PROVIDE ROLE MODELS FOR READING AND WRITING

African American Male Authors

Students—of any race or gender—need contact with adults who can challenge their negative stereotypes. They especially need African American male role models who have succeeded in work that demands reading and writing talent. Mary Ann designed some writing activities to build on the visit to Hixson of Eddy Harris, the St. Louis–born author of the true adventure, *Mississippi Solo*.

> He had a quiet soft-spoken presentation that brought out a very positive enthusiastic response, particularly from the target students. I feel they identified with him because of his youth, ease and self-possession,

sophistication and encouragement, and probably even more so because he was Black. The next day they recapped what he'd said, looked at the book, talked to each other about his exploits (wide-eyed), and jotted drafts of a thank-you letter.

Students were thrilled when their class received Eddy's reply from Africa, where he was researching his next book, *Native Stranger*. This experience has many powerful elements: real audience, oral-language base, response to reading. But perhaps the most powerful is the model of a Black male who is a star in a field other than sports or music. Ultimately, the value of this modeling is not so much that it prepares students to become authors (though we rather like that idea) but that it prepares them to be members of an African American community that values literacy and achievement.

Community Involvement

Emilie Siddle-Walker sheds light on the wider implications of role modeling through a case study of a successful Black high school in pre-integration North Carolina. She asked parents, teachers, and graduates, "What made this school 'good'?" Their answers did not dwell on facilities, curriculum, teaching methods, basic skills, or parent control. Instead, what people remembered was an ethic of "interpersonal caring" (1993, 65). Teachers and principal pushed the children academically, believed they could learn, and indeed would be personally offended if they failed to learn. Parents and graduates who were interviewed recalled the "personal encouragement" (70) and "individual help and personal inspiration they had received from teachers" (72).

Reading this slice of history, we nodded "Aha!" at the emphasis on caring teacher-student relationships. But we were chilled by the aftermath. This positive, strict, but nurturing climate tended to vanish with integration, when Black children felt adrift in an unfamiliar and often unfriendly culture. The process echoed our own history in Webster Groves: the victories of the Civil Rights legislation led to the loss of Douglass, the successful Black school with which the community identified. North Webster historians Morris and Ambrose (1993) describe the education of African American students before and after integration:

> All the students at Douglass School learned how to be successful. Douglass students knew all the Negro heroes, such as Crispus Attucks, Frederick Douglass, Harriett Tubman, Sojourner Truth, George Washington Carver, Booker T. Washington, and W. E. B. Du Bois. These heroes made Douglass students realize how much can be accomplished from a modest beginning with hard work.... The faculty...helped students choose colleges and find scholarships. Douglass gave its students a special appreciation for their heritage and their potential that no other school could give them. (42)

When the school closed in 1956, "Only seven of the nineteen teachers from Douglass high were given jobs at" the school that would now serve both Black and White students (42).

> The integration of Webster Groves High School went smoothly except for the fifteen lonely students from Douglass in the class of '57. At Douglass they would have been involved in the choir, the orchestra, the band, football, basketball, or track, and they would have looked forward to dances, concerts, and talent shows. At Webster High School they felt lost and were reluctant to compete. The guidance counselors had never heard of Lincoln University, Fisk University, Howard University, Tuskegee Institute, or Booker T. Washington. It was not until [the sixties, when some former Douglass students made their mark in athletics] that Black students began to feel they had an important place at Webster Groves High School. (43)

Today's African American students are living the effects of their history, even if unconsciously. At the 75-percent-White high school, they have access to the modern facilities, books, science and computer labs—the advantages of a large institution with many courses and programs. But they cannot feel the community ownership that characterized Frederick Douglass High.

Is it possible to recreate this nurturing climate in a large institution with predominantly White teachers and students? This is what we are trying to accomplish, on a small scale, in our own classrooms. We agree with Siddle-Walker that "African American teachers and principals who taught" in good segregated schools can teach today's educators working in today's integraded settings "the importance of building self-esteem, of placing high expectations on their students and of being willing to provide individual attention" (76). She urges "a dialogue on how to create integrated environments where African American children can again be made to feel as if they are 'somebody' " (76).

Parent Involvement

Alumni and parents have many resources to offer—if the schools know how to reach them. It is especially important in integrated schools with few Black teachers to build on the involvement and talents of African American adults. We believe that such community support benefits White as well as Black students.

We mulled over the possibilities during the early years of our project. We knew of college student, parent, and senior citizen role models, as well as tutors and volunteer counselors, serving in other districts. Much more could and should be done to build partnerships in our community, especially in the African American community of Webster Groves. Since we are English teachers and the focus of our project is writing, we chose to begin by inviting parents to share in the writing process.

During our fifth year, middle school teachers scheduled a community meeting on teaching writing. Our goal was to inform parents of how we work through a process of multiple drafts and how we deal with grammar and mechanics in the context of editing. We also hoped to reassure the parents as they found their children doing something in English class quite different from what they themselves remembered.

It was a "show, don't tell" meeting. We invited seventh and eighth graders *and* their parents or significant adults to experience an abbreviated reading/writing workshop. In case student and adult could not both come, teachers arranged a match for the occasion. Close to a hundred people turned out, including school-board members. The mood was energetic and upbeat. Parents were thrilled to have been invited into the process. They seemed to feel the same relief that kids do when they realized they were free to think and create on a first draft without fearing the red pen. When the meeting ended, nobody wanted to stop. One African American teenager commented, "I learned that my Mom is a pretty good writer."

The session was such a success it has become an annual event. It's a small beginning in the large task of re-creating the "care ethic," the involvement North Webster felt in Douglass School. But a small beginning is better than none at all.

TEACH TO A VARIETY OF LEARNING STYLES

At the start of our project, most of us probably taught in ways that favored middle-class students, especially White females. Of course we did not do this out of deliberate bias, but today—looking in the mirror of action research—we can see it. Gradually, we worked to broaden our range and appeal to a more relational, holistic style of learning. Most of us believe these changes in our teaching style have contributed to the growth we observe in many target students.

Awareness of style was an evolutionary process based on reading, discussion, and observation. As we entered Phase Three of our research, we recognized that conflicting styles might be blocking some teacher-student relationships. Today all our project teachers have been trained in learning styles. We've taken the Myers-Briggs inventory and administered it to our students; we've studied with Hanson, Silver, and Strong and used their inventory. We have listed the dominant learning style for each of our students, and we recognize our own dominant teaching style. We find these data help us involve and reach more of our kids.

According to some African American educators, there is a mismatch between the learning environment of most schools and the learning styles of most Black students. Gilbert and Gay (1985) explain, "The learning styles of Black children tend to be relational and field-dependent. . . . The learning style normally expected and rewarded in schools is analytical and field-independent" (134). Hale-Benson (1986) adds pointedly, "One reason for the high failure rates of some cultural minorities is the mismatch between the school culture and the social, cultural, and experiential background of minority children" (103). Similar statements from Cureton (1985, 102–8), Kunjufu (1986, 33), Dandy (1991), and Smitherman (1994) paint a composite picture.

Relational learners—of any culture—need to see the point of a whole lesson before they can tackle isolated steps. They like to make choices rather than simply follow directions. They need to apply abstract concepts in practice, taking an active role in the process. They express ideas through art, music, drama, or other creative activities. They expect a teacher to be active, too—warm, demanding, and humorous. The key to learning is affective; how they feel about a teacher and how they think a teacher feels about them may determine how well they learn in that teacher's class.

When we first encountered theories of learning style and descriptions of African Americans as "right-brained" or "relational" or "field dependent," members on our team were suspicious. Was this just a new way of making our students' culture the problem? Would learning style set the stage for a new kind of tracking or remediation or segregation to confirm—again—our kids' own doubts about their abilities? Later, as we discovered the Black educators cited above, we came to see learning style in cultural perspective. It is not our *students,* of any color, who are narrow or limited intellectually. It is the *school* that, as an institution, has catered to one group—linear, analytical learners who reflect the culture of middle-class adults. So do we abandon analytic teaching? Of course not. But we can reach more students if we expand our teaching repertoire. In previous chapters, we've described such active learning tools as role playing, oral interpretation, collaboration, and writing on the computer.

This chapter discusses other ways we involve the kids who do not readily identify with school. When our project began, most of us taught in quiet classrooms. Today, we often bring talk, music, and art into the curriculum. Black educators like Hale-Benson (1986, 40–44, 165) advocate more creative expression in the classroom. Kunjufu (1986) urges teachers to present every concept through a variety of modes: "readings, oral presentations, pictures, artifacts, and fine arts" (39). He adds, "Black boys often learn a speech or story better through music than a book. A person who chooses to teach Black children without music or art is an instructor, not a teacher. Fine arts and the oral tradition are two cornerstones of Black culture" (40).

In our classrooms, music is often a background for reading/writing workshop. We try out many styles—classical, reggae, R & B, jazz, rap. When disputes arise between Black and White students, some of us choose music we're sure will be outside their experience (Bulgarian women's chorus). Caribbean and African music work well, too—played softly—as does much classical music. Frank Smith (1982, 206) points out that the conditions in most classrooms—sedentary, quiet, orderly—would immobilize many adult writers. This is another case where we have found the advice of Black educators well suited both to process pedagogy and to the multicultural classroom. Music seems to relax and focus most students, not distract them; and we also provide library space for individuals who need silence to think.

Like music, art is hardly a new discovery in the English classroom. We have found it very motivating to some students (see Gail's case study in Chapter 3) who are hesitant to write. In year six, Chestra shared with the team a highly successful activity she adapted from *Notes Plus* (Paprocki 1993), "Poet-Tees." Students cover their shirts with poetry they have found or written themselves. To conclude the project, everyone wrote a short piece explaining why they chose the poetry on their shirt. But even the most powerful strategy isn't magic. All the excitement did not touch Chestra's target student: "Al had no interest in doing the shirt. Even when I offered to give him a shirt, he refused. I also gave him the option of doing the shirt on paper so I would know what it looked like. He still refused. This has bothered me as I'm not sure what it would have taken to get him involved." We don't reach every kid—at least not every time. But we keep trying.

We've observed that students who have been adrift in school, especially African American students, must become personally involved in reading and writing before they produce good work. Kids with a history of success might work hard on a paper simply for the grade or because it is required; our target students will write just a few lines. Involvement energizes them to stick with a paper through drafts and conferences and revisions to a quality product. That involvement is fed by ownership and choice in learning, but it is rooted in a personal relationship with a teacher who matters. We know that we must build caring relationships if we hope to build skills.

START WHERE THE STUDENT IS, THEN STRETCH

A new insight during our fifth year was the link between *foster involvement* and our eighth principle, *build bridges, expand horizons.* As we tried in a team discussion to define *involvement,* we realized that the key was starting with the student's interest *but not ending there.*

The caricature of a sloppy "open" classroom is that students follow their own interests but are rarely challenged to move onward. So much of what we do with target students involves building a bridge from where they are to where they might be, even though most teachers report that they rarely think in any conscious way of bridging. As in the curriculum theory of James Moffett, we plan a developmental sequence of writing or reading activities such as exploring the same topic through a freewrite, letter, dialogue, description, I-Search, and formal essay.

The next chapter shows how we design these sequences and how we help students cross the bridge from personal involvement to academic performance.

LOOKING IN THE MIRROR:
INVOLVEMENT AND ACTION RESEARCH

The action research team has given us a learning space in which we are academically challenged, personally engaged, and professionally empowered. At the end of our fifth-year synthesis meetings, Jane asked each of us to anonymously write a reflection on the experience of action research. A few samples paint a picture that fits what we have called involvement: relational learning, intense interest in the topic, and active empowerment. Longtime members expressed commitment to the project and loyalty to their colleagues. New members were attracted by the team's "sense of shared excitement, trust, and discovery." One said she had never worked with "such caring, upbeat, smart people" in her entire career.

> I can cry or laugh or yell and they will accept, encourage, and advise. The group is a sounding board. They respect both my suggestions and my questions with honest feedback. This group validates me.

Yet another values a sense of empowerment.

> I feel that I have seized control of the work I do and the decisions I make, that I am not a foot soldier, dumbly and sometimes numbly carrying out orders from headquarters.

WHAT YOU CAN DO

Let students choose their own topics for writing.

Guide them through a process of making rhetorical choices including audience, purpose, and mode of writing, as well as kind of response to reading.

Experiment with literature study groups and a reading/writing workshop.

Give students a role in classroom management and assessment. Emphasize self-evaluation and reflection through portfolios.

Find a network of real audiences for writing. Publish student work for the classroom, the school, or a wider audience.

Connect your students with reading/writing role models. Call on parents, alumni, and especially African American male authors.

Encourage relational, holistic learning. Help students connect what they do in school with their personal lives. Show you care about who they are as well as what they learn.

Start with involvement—then stretch to new tasks and experiences.

Read: Your students. Watch and listen to discover their burning interests.

NOTE

1. *ENGFISH* is the term coined by Ken Macrorie (1970, 1) for the fishy, phony, please-the-English-teacher style into which many student writers have been socialized.

Facing the Mirror:
Gail Taylor

The paper was blank. The pencil was sharp. Myriads of thoughts and questions darted through my mind with only a few lingering. It was the beginning of our action research. We had just determined that the low writing assessment scores of our Black students had nothing to do with nonstandard English. We had to answer the question, "If not dialect, then what?" Were we, as teachers, somehow responsible for these low test scores? Did we expect less of our Black students, or were we satisfied with less? Did we push them as hard to achieve? We were faced with the painful task of looking at ourselves to determine if our own biases had anything to do with this dilemma. Biases? Did I have biases? This was only my second year of teaching in an integrated classroom, but I quickly discovered my Black students were far more honest (and vocal) in their assessment of me and my teaching methods than my White students were. They also appeared to bond more completely, and trust was clearly a factor in how well they did in class.

The year before, a teacher had resigned after five weeks and I was given her classes. Those who seemed the most hurt by her leaving and who appeared to actually feel abandoned were the Black kids. I had to prove myself before many would even open a book. It wasn't until they believed that I cared about them as individuals that they began working. Did my perception that the Black students were more vocal, honest, and personally involved in their work constitute a bias?

An image of a well dressed, strikingly attractive young Black woman came to mind and lingered. It was the spring of 1972 and an overflowing crowd packed the large church in a small college town in mid-Missouri. It was "Race Relations Sunday" and her task was to talk about her own personal experiences. She was a dynamic speaker who had grown accustomed to accolades. She was affluent. Surely, those who put the program together thought, she would be a good choice to say something positive, possibly encouraging, to this group of well-meaning academics. Those of us who knew her well waited in silence. Even we were not prepared for her opening. She quoted Countee Cullen's poem "Incident" and then went on to describe how she and her family had had to live in a house they did not want because they were not allowed to purchase a house anywhere else. They were an affluent family, but money could not break through the invisible barriers. Did the previous acceptance of segregation perpetuate its existence? Did acceptance of an unfair act constitute a bias?

Another image lingered. Only a few weeks earlier an African American teacher friend of retirement age and I were talking about the tumultuous 1960s and so-called progress. Her closing comment was, "It doesn't matter where I go. I am still Black." Had we made progress? When people looked at her they didn't see the academic degrees, the children who had been enriched by her guidance, or the knowledge she had gained from traveling. I realized I had never experienced such bias personally. Somehow, my experience of being a woman in a man's world paled in comparison.

I scribbled a few questions, not answers, on my paper and waited. A daring soul ventured the uncharted waters with, "I was surprised to find the person who wrote about basketball wasn't Black." Others murmured, then were quiet. Again I searched for a fragment of truth. When I was a senior in high school we had a Black student teacher. His was the only minority face in our entire school district of over two thousand. He was a star player on his college basketball team. He also didn't come to class much. When he did come, he wasn't prepared. We liked him because he talked to us and even stopped by some of the guys' houses to shoot baskets. Few were surprised when he was asked to leave before the assignment was completed. After all, he hadn't done his job. For the first time I asked myself, "Would I have been more surprised by his behavior had he been White?"

Difficult, painful questions. More comments. Then another thought: Is this about the giving and taking that occurs in relationships? I had given. What had I allowed myself to take? I married while still in college and my husband and I graduated together. From there we traveled to seminary and, after his graduation, to churches in towns ranging from five hundred to seven million. We had lived in an area that was quickly becoming Hispanic and had helped support a Hispanic church. Through our encouragement our church had opened its doors three summers in a row as a school of three hundred children of migrant farm workers. We bought fresh tortillas for our tacos, struggled to communicate, and never made a trip to the local grocery store without wondering what languages we were hearing. We had lived happily in a multicultural community. Why, then, did the question, What have I allowed myself to take? bother me so much? My own children had always attended integrated schools and their friendships crossed racial lines. I had confronted my neighbors when they made comments about my son's friend and when the neighborhood buzzed because a Black family had shared our dinner table the previous Sunday. It had been our yard and our dinner table. A feeling began to push its way into my consciousness. Had I only worried about what I did as a teacher? Did I expect my students to take what I had to give and then spew it back to me in another form? Was I willing to accept their own ideas, thoughts, attitudes? Could they choose their own assignments, reading material, and partners and make the right choices?

Personal choice. Personal involvement. Individualizing. Building on strengths. And, eventually, teacher change. When my White students read *Roll of Thunder, Hear my Cry,* they become angry and see the injustice. My Black students see a family that sticks together, survives, and eventually triumphs. We try to understand each other's perspective. We accept that we will never be able to fully understand each other's viewpoint. One answer is not less or more complete than the other. It is only different. Progress?

330

Build Bridges, Expand Horizons

Dear Reader,

My name is Bob, an African American writer. Writing was not a thing I did too often when I was younger. I didn't really enjoy reading or writing, to be exact. If it wasn't on television or had colorful pictures, I wouldn't look at it. I was just an athlete that placed himself under the stereo-type of a "Jock." . . .

My third grade teacher knew that all I did was play sports. She could tell that I didn't read or write a lot. So what she did was to combine the two together. When I tried it, writing became a whole new thing. I could write about all the baseball, basketball, soccer, and diving I had done up till them. I could read books on how to improve my game and the stars that do these sports for a living. But writing about this couldn't last.

It was in high school that I realized that I had to learn to write something new. I was interested in poetry, but only limericks. I tried a little, and I realized that, since being a percussionist, that rhythmic patterns were fun. But poetry couldn't be written for every paper.

I learned how to use my imagination to write new things that interested me. Since my imagination was unlimited, I could write about anything I liked. Because of an unlimited imagination, my papers from then on always became enjoyable.

The first piece of writing is titled, "If Things Don't Fall My Way." This piece represents beauty and power. This experience happened to me when

I was quite young. It was when the coaches pitched, and second base was the high school pitcher's mound. The beauty was the story itself. The wonderful thing that happened. Something that would probably happen once in a lifetime.

The next piece I have chosen was . . . "Children's Tales." I chose this piece to show craft and care. I wanted to write something that a young audience would comprehend to. This is a piece full of rhythmic poetry. The craft is the rhythmic poetry, and the care is the audience intended. . . .

The final piece in the portfolio shows variety and versatility. This piece shows that limericks are not the only poetry I can write. That's what I classify as the variety. The poetry . . . was constructed by me. The rules, the topic, and the rhythmic pattern was constructed by me. Because of me constructing everything in this piece, gives me that versatility. I really enjoy this piece. Maybe cause I thought of it. . . .

I learned, from this portfolio, that writing is still enjoyable. Writing doesn't have any limits. . . . It's a sport where who ever can write a story or poem, will win.

BOB,
ninth-grade portfolio reflection

We struggled to find a single piece of writing by a target student that could illustrate what we mean by *bridging*. Bob's letter shows how his personal talents and experiences lay the groundwork for his writing, and how his teachers encouraged him to connect with such interests as sports and music even while attempting the usual academic modes of writing. He shows a great deal of self-awareness about his learning. In his portfolio reflection, he builds bridges that link writing, culture, and selfhood. This "African American writer" believes that he can be a Black male with interests valued by his peer group and also "win" at school.

HISTORY OF A CONCEPT

During Phases One and Two, we hoped to "fix" our teaching methods, to plan new lessons that would reach our target students and to "fix" their writing. We found, of course, that hard as we worked to design effective lessons—and much as we succeeded—our successes were based on well-known principles of "good teaching." There is no magical Webster Groves lesson plan to empower a writer. The magic is in learning to communicate and to build relationships with kids who may differ from their teachers in race, class, and gender—as well as in English skills.

But now, as we conclude our eight principles, we must look back and consider how our teaching methods have changed, how we have built bridges for learning. We have, in fact, reached some insights about designing a curriculum that works in heterogeneous classes, using lessons that let kids start with varied skills and bridge from familiar to more challenging tasks with extra support at their own individual points of difficulty. We plan developmental sequences of activities. But as Shirley Brice Heath (1983) explains, a teacher can't build a curriculum that starts where the student is without being sensitive to that student's customary language use. Geneva Smitherman (1977) describes the African American struggle to survive in an alien society ("How I Got Ovuh," 73–100) by mastering enough of the majority culture to "make it" without losing one's roots. It's a feat that requires cunning—and humor—as much as competence. In our project, we try to help our students "get ovuh" to the language and culture of the school while we ourselves "get ovuh" to the edges of the Black adolescent world. This chapter will explain the ideas we find helpful as we continue to puzzle through such a curriculum.

Bridging was not one of our initial principles. It emerged through an inductive process during Phases Two and Three of the action research. In the first years, we'd end our annual synthesis of field notes with a catch-all section called "curricular issues." Here we noted the thorny matters—testing, grouping, required courses—that we couldn't change by ourselves but which had played a part in the dilemma of our target students. Here we also described new ways we were learning to prepare kids for academic requirements outside our classrooms. Gradually, we were learning to analyze the trouble spots in a difficult assignment and to plan short tasks that could teach the necessary skills in a low-risk context. For example, we might build a sequence of writing or reading activities to explore a single topic (a youth club in the neighborhood) through a freewrite, letter, dialogue, description, interview, editorial, and public speech. Or we might prepare students for the academic research paper through such familiar tasks as interviews, reader response logs, and informational reports. We began to talk of *building bridges*.

We recognized that a crucial time for bridging was the transition from middle school to senior high. In fact, many students were drowning for lack of a bridge. There was much more freedom to do personal writing in our district's middle school than in the senior high. Our curriculum tended to break abruptly between grades eight and nine, with a stress on first-person narratives in the younger grades and a stress on third-person expository essays later on. All of us felt the need for curricular bridges to ease the transition. We knew that our African American writers were often strong in voice and involvement; how could we carry these strengths across to the senior high? Gradually, our middle school teachers have learned to bridge outward from personal to more public modes, while senior high teachers bridge inward to the expressive, building the formal essay on an underlying bedrock of personal experience.

During the second year's synthesis meeting when the conversation turned to curriculum sequences and social support for growth in language, Jane mentioned Britton, Moffett, Vygotsky, and others. It was the sort of dialogue that happens quite often in our team meetings: Teachers describe a process in their field notes and recognize a pattern, then Jane tries out labels, concepts, and theorists until we see a "fit." (It's not that others on the team aren't familiar with curriculum theory. But Jane talks theory fluently while for most of us theory is a second dialect.) She'd just gotten James Moffett's new essay, *Bridges: From Personal Writing to the Formal Essay* (1989), and the whole team read it. What Ken Macrorie (1988) calls the I-Search paper had long been a staple for us; suddenly we saw it from another angle. The I-Search could bridge the gap between first-person narrative and the academic research paper.

Bridging was adopted, tentatively, as a new principle in that June 1989 synthesis week. We decided to watch as we wrote our third year's field notes for examples to flesh out the concept. *Bridging* is closely related to the term *scaffolding*. Both structures are based on the idea that learning is social and developmental. As Langer and Applebee (1984) explain,

> We believe that individuals gain access to the store of cultural knowledge through the social process of interaction, and during that process gradu- ally make that knowledge their own. From this perspective, the role of instructional scaffolding is to provide students with appropriate models and strategies for addressing new problems . . . [and] with the resources to eventually undertake similar tasks on their own. (176)

Bruner (1978) defines scaffolding as building on students' prior knowl- edge, guiding them in collaboration, and giving them access to new ideas. Ann Shea Bayer (1990) gives a detailed plan for scaffolding based on Vygotsky's (1978) concept of the zone of proximal development (see Chapter 7). Bayer (1990) shows how students can work in partnership with a teacher and with peers whose skills are higher or lower than their own. In such an environment, the process is collaborative but the finished products may be written by individuals or groups.

Bridging is central to James Moffett's writing curriculum. Journals, diaries, and logs are the base on which higher levels of abstraction are built (see Figure 11-1). The curricular bridge is inductive and sequential, from simple jottings to academic and imaginative writing. The learner draws on sources of ideas inside (left column) and outside (right column) the self.

335

THINKING UP	THINKING OVER/ THINKING THROUGH
(Imagination)	(Cogitation)
Fiction	Editorial
Plays	Review
Poetry	Essay
LOOKING BACK	LOOKING INTO
(Recollection)	(Investigation)
Autobiography	Biography
Memoir	Case
	News article
	Feature article

NOTING DOWN

Journal

Diary

Logs

FIG. 11-1 *Bridges in the writing curriculum.*

Moffett says, "I'm all for the essay, and I think we should do as much of it as we can. However, I believe that if we move into it developmentally we will get better results" (1992, 181). He suggests journalism and memory writing as bridges—intermediate forms carrying the vitality and involvement of personal writing into our students' more public academic essays.

Another view of bridging comes from the reader response theories of David Bleich (1975) and Louise Rosenblatt (1978):

1. What is it about? (literal message of text)
2. What does it remind you of? (connect with self)
3. What does it say about life? (connect with world)

In this sequence, the reader begins with factual summary, then moves inward to personal history and then outward to explore social and universal implications.

Bridging and scaffolding overlap, and good teaching relies on both. In fact, the lessons that work best with our target students often build a variety of support structures:

Instruction (teacher response and support during process)

Environment (cooperative learning, computers)

Curriculum (sequencing of writing)

Culture (African American, European American, and so on)

As we grappled with these concepts, we began to identify the first and second types of structures as scaffolding—the support our writers get from teachers and peers, a safe place for learning. Scaffolding of instruction and of the environment figure prominently in the principles described in earlier chapters: process, individualizing and personalizing, cooperative learning, computers, and control of language.

This chapter looks more closely at the third and fourth types of support—bridging through the curriculum and across cultures. We build sequences of lessons starting with the student; we base an unfamiliar task on the familiar; and we link our students with worlds they may see as alien or irrelevant. After building these bridges, we cross them ourselves.

BUILD CURRICULUM SEQUENCES

Bridging extends what we already do in our writing/reading curriculum:

- Start with student involvement, but *don't stop there*.
- Start with what students know, then stretch.
- Start with prewriting, then continue the process.

We think in terms of skills: Our kids can do this today; what comes next? We plan for transfer from one activity to the next. We analyze a major task to see what skills it requires and where we must offer support. We emphasize collaboration. Gradually, students internalize what they have helped their peers and teachers do. Moffett's *Active Voice* (1992) includes a reprint of his 1989 essay "Bridges" and detailed plans for such a curriculum. Our own lessons form many kinds of bridges:

- Expressive to analytical
- Informal to academic
- Factual to imaginative—or vice versa
- English class to writing across the curriculum
- Personal to public
- Oral to written
- Black English Vernacular to Edited American English

We build many bridges from safe, comfortable modes (journals, letters, improvised scripts) to formal exposition. As theorists warn, if we cut off the "expressive base" of writing, we will be left with bloodless academic prose (Britton et al. 1975).

For example, in Joan's book-review sequence, students first share journals informally with a peer to generate ideas for a familiar audience. Later the partners write a collaborative essay reviewing their novel. Sandy makes a short bridge from improvised oral dialogue to fiction writing. First she gives out two-character cartoons with missing captions. Pairs of students discuss their cartoon, improvise a dialogue between the characters, and then present it orally to the class. Finally, the same pairs flesh out their dialogues into stories that they revise and edit, checking for the correct use of quotations.

Chapter 4 describes two quite different middle school sequences that bridge between oral history and fiction writing. Cathy's class first explores holiday traditions through questions discussed with older family members; each student then creates a holiday story weaving in authentic details from their interviews. Cathy's story is fiction embellished with historical data. Mary Ann's story, on the other hand, is history embellished with fiction. Her students interview an older relative and then choose an episode in that person's life to re-create using such techniques as dialogue, scene shifts, and point of view. Both lessons bridge from imaginative writing, where our target students are often strong, to exposition and research, where they need to gain confidence.

Moffett (1992) goes further, arguing that the dichotomy between creative and expository writing is false.

> We generally think of all fiction writing—poetry, plays, short stories—as being very different from the writing of ideas. I regard all writing as idea writing. To me the difference is not whether the writing has ideas but how buried the ideas are, how implicit or explicit the ideas are. In literature and recollection, the ideas are more implicit. They are there, but they are embodied, incarnated in personages, incidents, and events. If this is not true of literature, why do we have students digging for meaning all the time? Why do we have them chasing symbols and doing vivisections of poems and postmortems on novels, digging, digging, digging, all the time for meaning? (181)

We agree that all writing is creative and all writing exposes the author's meanings and ideas. Most of us teach some form of structured reading response to help students dig for meaning without losing the personal connection (see Chapter 10). Index cards provide one convenient format. Carrie's students jot reading notes on one side of four-inch by six-inch cards and personal responses on the other side. Carrie builds on this experience for the research paper; students use one side of a card for notes on their sources (including books and interviews) and the other side for their own comments and questions. This procedure helps guide them away from straight summary—or patent plagiarism—by drawing on the power of relational learning.

We use the principle of bridging to build units based not simply on a common topic (the Civil War, the short story) but on a developmental sequence. Farr and Daniels (1986) call these writing activities *transitional,* which they define as

> activities that build natural bridges between the narrative-expressive modes of writing appropriately stressed in the lower grades and the more challenging transactional modes increasingly required in high school and on into college. Such activities include reports from personal interviews or written surveys; descriptions of objects, persons, or places; analyses of social behavior, rituals, or values; comparisons of products used by students in their daily lives; and notes and letters related to personal or school issues. The keys to good transitional writing assignments are (1) making the work real and meaningful, (2) leaving plenty of authentic choices and decisions for the writer, and (3) engaging students in writing as a tool of learning, not as an exercise. (57)

Joan's "thumbprint lifeline" sequence (see Appendices Two and Three) has evolved over several years of reflective teaching. It guides her eighth graders from expressive prewriting through an expository essay with a thesis supported by an anecdote. This chapter will analyze the unit as a series of bridges. Students begin by drawing a "lifeline," with ups and downs and hairpin curves to fit the events of their lives. They stamp the lifelines with thumbprint illustrations evoking significant memories, and they tell their stories aloud as they draw. Finally they choose one of the memories to write up, revise, and publish in a classroom display. This is Mark's story:

My First Physical

To play football they have to give you a physical. One of the things they check in a physical, is if you have a hernia. As I was standing there the doctor said, "Drop your pants."

I said, "What for?"

He said, "So I can check for a hernia." It didn't seem right cause he was a stranger to me. I figured he was telling the truth so I dropped my pants.

Then he said, "Drop your underwear."

I asked him, "Do I have to pull down my underwear?"

He said yes, so I did. It scared me when he pushed in the spot right next to my testicles. Besides his hands were cold. When he said I could pull up my underwear and pants and leave, I pulled them up and got out of there. After I got out, I was relieved it was over!

Up to this point, Joan's lesson follows a familiar bridging sequence: it begins with the oral, artistic, and expressive, then guides students to a personal narrative edited for a public audience. But several months later, this narrative in turn becomes a bridge to the expository essay. Joan brings to class some published essays, explaining that many writers use anecdotes to illustrate their points. Students pull the thumbprint papers from their folders and consider what idea their narratives may exemplify. They develop that main point in an introductory paragraph. With some fine-tuning of the original story and a brief conclusion to restate the thesis, each eighth grader produces an expository essay. Mark didn't revise his original story, but see what he added (for his resulting essay, see Appendix Three):

My First Physical

My parents told me to be prepared. I have always tried to be prepared. but one experience showed me that you can't be prepared for every thing. . . .
. . . People try to be prepared for things. But some things you think you're prepared, you're not. Sometimes you can't be prepared for every-thing. So you will just have to be surprised.

Another look at Moffett (1992) reveals the architecture of Joan's bridge. Moffett teaches the essay inductively, from the "concrete particulars of personal experience and narrative" to "generality, which is not 'once upon a time' but *any* time." He notes that this strategy is common among professionals, citing Orwell's "Shooting an Elephant." Moffett asks his students

to choose a personal incident in their life, something interesting, and then to write about it. Then I ask, "Of what is this incident a metaphor?" . . . What does it represent? . . . As soon as you begin writing about types . . .

you are dealing with what essay essentially consists of, which is coordinating an idea with an incident or instance. (181–84)

Carrie used bridging with her ninth graders to develop an essay analyzing a single word in *Romeo and Juliet*. She began with a handout of the most frequent words, such as "love" and "hate," asking students to choose a word, meet in groups, and generate meanings based on their own knowledge. Next she brought her class to a college library where they delved into the *OED (Oxford English Dictionary* 1961*)* to explore the history of their word and its use by authors before and after Shakespeare. After collaborative research and discussion, each student wrote a paper on the significance of the chosen word in the context of *Romeo and Juliet*. Carrie explains her sequence: "By breaking it down into a series of small assignments, any one of which each student could do, I enabled all of them to complete the larger task."

With the support of such bridges, students can cross over to the world of traditional academic expectations. Minnie sees this bridging as especially vital for many African Americans: "You need to walk some kids through the fear, walk them through the writing process, until they see they *can* do it. Teachers need a combination of high standards and empathy."

Nancy now teaches both English and social studies to build bridges across the curriculum: from *Anne Frank* to persecution to World War II or from the Civil War to *Roll of Thunder* to "Eyes on the Prize" to Rodney King. Writing and reading across the curriculum has made both subjects more accessible, more meaningful, more powerful. Bryan, not a target student, wrote in his journal:

> I've been thinking about making up a story inspired by what we've been reading about in Solcial Studies. Mabe about the everyday life of a Greek or Roman guy in the army or something. I realy like writing about historical fiction. I guess it comes from liking Solcial Studies . . . and watching all those WWII movies. I also have been thinking about writing about a sailor on one of Germanies prized U-Boats of WWI or II.

342

The next week, he drafted the story of an attack on a Greek city. Notice that through the process, along with gaining control of mechanics, Bryan strengthens the curricular bridge:

> As the sun rose up over the mountains, a thick fog rose from the river. As we slowly approached the walls of the city, we could tell death was as thick as the fog now engulfing us as we stepped out of the woods. We crept noiselessly through the dew-covered grass slowly picking up speed. We got to the point where I could smell their soup cooking, when suddenly a man from the back of the ranks charged past, then several others, and quickly the whole army was running and cursing up the hill toward the gate to the city. Within seconds of the first shout a rain of arrows cut through the thick fog. I quickly pulled up my shield, covering as much of my body as I could with it, and the gallant charge became a slow crawl towards the gate. . . .

Bryan has learned to connect the vivid particulars of fiction with the factual information of history.

Curricular bridges may be short range (a well-sequenced two-day lesson), middle range (a major unit with a sequence of writing and reading activities) or long range (spanning several years). Because our team includes middle school as well as senior high teachers, we have been able to collaborate during our monthly study sessions. What follows is a multiyear sequence for building research skills.

In seventh grade, Gail introduces an I-Search project. Students ask their own questions and explore them through reading, interviews, and observation. They pull together their data into a report to share—informally and orally—with a classroom audience. Gail teaches a written bibliography, but she doesn't get into the mechanics of quoting and paraphrasing, footnotes and parenthetical references, what is "common knowledge" and what must be credited. In grade nine, Theresa does a similar I-Search project leading to an oral presentation with one new wrinkle: a report is written in an informal voice and organized as a story of the search. Finally, in grade ten, Minnie teaches a more traditional research paper organized as an expository essay with all the academic trimmings. By this time, our students have had two prior experiences that focused on the real basics of research—the questioning, the inquiry, and the search through multiple sources (in person as well as in print). They do not view the research paper as an exercise in bibliographical punctuation to prove they have "done time" in the library. Minnie has noticed a gradual but major change in her students' preparation during the six years of the writing project. Because of the bridging experiences, she believes, most of her tenth graders can now write a formal research paper while retaining some ownership and voice.

BUILD AN UNFAMILIAR TASK ON A FAMILIAR BASE

A new task is made easier if some part of it is familiar, if it draws on knowledge or skills or forms or routines with which students are already confident. When planning to teach something new, we can use the power of repetition as a bridge:

> Link the new task with students' prior knowledge.
>
> Model the task before asking students to do it.
>
> Teach specific forms to choose and apply.
>
> Have the class "do it twicc" and reflect.

Models can help students learn to do a new task independently (see Chapter 5). We often use the overhead to share a piece we have written for our own assignment. In a unit on drama (see Appendix Four), Minnie introduced her tenth graders to such dramatic monologues as Robert Browning's "My Last Duchess" and Langston Hughes' "Mother to Son." First she made the genre more accessible by performing her own monologue as the mother of an urban teenager killed on the streets. Later her students read the professional poems. Finally, they created their own scenarios and wrote dramatic monologues to present orally in an appropriate voice. With this sequence, Minnie felt she had walked her students across a three-part bridge (1) identifying with a dramatic presentation of a story from personal experience; (2) identifying with a dramatic presentation of a story from literature; and (3) creating an original dramatic presentation of a story with which others can identify.

Like models, formulas can support an inexperienced writer. But we are wary that forms can become all-purpose substitutes for rhetorical choice. As Chapter 5 explains, we walk a tightrope on this issue, trying to teach a repertoire of forms.

Beth Ann taught students a formula to develop and organize a summary. She began with a process model. "Using a simple short story, I guided students through the elements of introduction, rising action, climax, falling action, and resolution." (Most tenth graders were familiar with these terms.) Beth Ann put the concepts on a narrative map. She writes,

> We plotted the five elements on a diagram (a highly successful visual aid). We wrote two or three sentences for each element on the overhead. We painstakingly dissected each part, then put the little boxes from the diagram together and voila! A valid, five-paragraph summary appeared.

This lesson provided such a clear structure that students were almost guaranteed success. They next day, Beth Ann asked them to read another short story silently and prepare to summarize it the same way. Cooperative groups talked until members agreed among themselves. "Each person was responsible for recording one or two elements in the boxes on a blank diagram. This activity produced some of the most intellectually challenging dialogue of the entire year." Samples from Beth Ann's field notes:

> — So the climax is when she goes to the orphanage and finds out he doesn't have a mother.
> — No way. The climax is the turning point. The turning point is where he decides to run away. That's where everything changed. That's gotta be the climax. When she goes to the orphanage is falling action, before the resolution.

— Now. The external conflict was between the lady and Jerry, right?

— Yeah, but so what? Where does the conflict go? I mean, is it in the climax, or the rising action, or where? And his internal conflict came before that.

"Aah . . . music to my ears," thought their teacher. Each group then used their diagram as a guide to writing. Beth Ann collected the drafts, "made a few guiding comments and asked questions to help them flesh out bony areas," and returned the summaries for students to revise. Summary was now part of their repertoire.

But Beth Ann didn't stop there. Over a few months, students

> summarized a longer story, a nonfiction adventure selection, several news stories from the daily paper, a magazine article, etc. Their writing was on target and had an identifiable form. They took pride in these pieces, also. I think they relished the feeling of being competent.

Using the same structure repeatedly (while moving from expressive drawing and talking to analytical writing) was the key to success.

One of our favorite mottoes for bridging is "Do it twice" (or, as in the summary pattern, more than twice). We find that after our kids have tackled a new skill, they enjoy a chance to do it again. Even when the assignment has a new twist, kids respond with a flash of recognition and pride: "Hey, we know how to do *that!*" The second experience helps them gain mastery, to move beyond the discomfort of the unfamiliar.

Cathy reinforced her work with the formal essay by having eighth graders do it three times: once to get a feel for academic prose and then twice more to learn how to manage comparison and contrast. She introduced the latter by having the whole class compare two versions of the ballad of John Henry. "With this practice piece, we went over the use of a T-chart to organize their data, reviewed the essay format, and brainstormed the similarities and differences in several teacher-specified categories: character, setting, events, figurative language, etc." Two weeks later, each student wrote another comparison and contrast essay based on two other narrative poems.

"Again, we used T-charts, reviewed the essay form, and brainstormed similarities and differences" in specific categories to prepare for drafting the papers. Cathy concludes, "There was no question that students vastly improved" in their grasp of essay structure through the repetition. "They did not like working within the confines of the essay form, but by the third essay they had achieved a far greater comfort level." Doing it again brought the new skill of analysis into their repertoire.

BUILD CULTURAL BRIDGES

African American students often feel that they belong neither to the White culture (mirrored in the classroom) nor to a culture of their own (consigned to the academic shadows). Lacking a bridge between lived and academic worlds, they fall through the cracks or simply drop out. Our schools must provide bridges

- between African American culture and a wider world;
- between home, school, and career;
- between today's teens, their heritage, and their future goals;
- between middle-class White female teachers and lower-class Black male students.

Minnie, the one African American teacher on our team, often maps out such bridges for her colleagues. At a 1991 study session, she shared a paper she was writing for her graduate program.

School in this suburban world seemingly offers safety without solace. Color circumscribes one's course in the White world, and Black peers demand constant, signal proof of masculinity. Add to this pressure the surrounding, seething urban world, and growing up for these African American male adolescents becomes a turbulent, if not treacherous, undertaking. School, by comparison, seems like child's play, or more cynically an anglicized and feminized ritual dance leading nowhere.

347

One's marginal existence in the school presages one's marginal existence
in the larger society, drawing closer and closer.

The culture of the "public" school reflects images of race, class, and gender
that leave most African American males out of the picture.

Yet our kids often seem to be bicultural in a negative sense. They have
bought into the American Dream and its material expectations—money, car,
cellular phone—while living in a culturally distinct group that has for
generations been excluded from that dream. Perhaps it is a distorted clash
of two styles of materialism: *Sixteen in Webster Groves* and urban cool.

The state of living between two worlds was described by W. E. B. Du
Bois in 1903 (1961) as the "double consciousness" of the Black experience.
Michael, a seventeen-year-old sophomore, tells how it feels today.

> The person on the inside of me is very different then the person outside
> of me. I don't know why & I probbly never will.
>
> The person on the inside want's to have a nice smooth life, the inside
> want's to have a very good education. to have a nice job & intelligent
> wife two kids, two car's. I want to grow up and not have to worry about
> watching my back all the time . . . the inside cares about everybody and
> wants everyone too care about him.
>
> The outside of me cares about a couple of people and very few things.
> The outside of me wants money money and more money. . . cloths. . .
> three or for girl's. . . .
>
> Right now I just want to get out of school and live on the edge.

"Living on the edge" may be the root of the disengagement from school
of many African American students. Minnie sees it as

> a way of life, a way of distancing oneself emotionally from a world where
> one must perform but cannot fully participate nor enjoy the same
> rewards. So what appears [to be] disinterest or alienation might in fact be
> logical deduction or grim resignation. "My life is nothing like Siddhartha's
> and Pu Yi's," write basic tenth graders in response to world literature.

We believe it's our job to connect the cultural experiences of our
students to the privileged cultures of the academic mainstream. And as

teachers, we must cross that bridge ourselves before we expect our kids to travel in our direction. We can't afford to stay "on the edge," shrinking from emotional involvement. We must learn to think from the point of view of a marginalized student. Minnie struggled with her basic English 10 curriculum in her field notes.

> The challenge of planning reading, writing, and language study assignments was how to plug into where they lived, pull them further along, and extend each student's thinking and language skills. For the most part, I adopted a reader-respondent attitude toward student writing rather than my traditional authoritarian approach.

Watch how Stephanie works with Malcolm. Her first impression was that he had "low self-esteem" and an even lower motivation for academic endeavors.

> Nov. 10: Every time I have worked with him on a writing project, I have discovered that he has a tunnel interest in sports. I have tried to use that interest in everything so far. Well, we have begun discussing heroes in America's past. Malcolm was the only person in 5th. hour who had heard of Jessie Owens, and he gave additional comments on Jackie Robinson when I spoke of him. Black athletes seem to be his specialty. He also seems very interested in the *Jeopardy* game we will be playing next week. I know he watches a lot of television at home, and he plays hours of Nintendo (according to his journal), so he may be more familiar with the concept of *Jeopardy* than some of the others.
> Nov. 17: The *Jeopardy* game was successful. Malcolm was more alive than I've seen him all year! He made the final round in 5th. hour and I could really see the excitement on his face. He wrote his hero paper about Tony Dorsett [and] I was impressed with how much he knew.

Action research helped Stephanie listen for Malcolm's interests and concerns, helped her cross over to his perspective.

In an ambitious new study, Carol Lee (1993) shows that African American language can "serve as a bridge to certain literacy skills" (11). Lee's high school students began with the ironic, metaphorical style called "signifying" (a current synonym is *disin*):

> Expert signifiers think analogically, looking for unusual verbal inventions and unapparent similarities between events, objects, and/or people. When teaching students who are good at signifying, but not proficient at interpreting literature, the challenge is to help them become conscious of the sensibilities and strategies they unconsciously apply when signifying. (8)

Lee's curriculum is based on an inquiry model of instruction, small-group oral collaboration, and responsive writing to literature—all principles we have used in our own research. But along with descriptive data from classroom observation, Lee has statistical evidence that her students made greater gains than control groups in using higher-order thinking to discuss literature.

Several of us found that our classroom talk became more thoughtful when we changed our questioning procedures. Instead of teachers who ask factual questions for recitation, we became learners who support and attend to our students' thinking. At the same time, the solution is not simply to be less directive. We have learned from research by sociolinguists (Heath 1983; Delpit 1988) that what seems to our middle-class ears to be a polite request ("What is the rule about hats in my classroom?") may baffle a student accustomed to direct commands. If we want a democratic classroom where teachers and students are free to ask questions and to take initiative, we must build bridges to other modes of discourse. Minnie and Agnes work with "basic" classes at the senior high. They encourage students to generate their own questions—leading to *why* and *how* rather than the *who, what,* and *where* questions often thought more appropriate for "basic" students. Agnes establishes a routine, always beginning a class discussion with a higher-level *why* or *how* question. Student-generated questions thus became a bridge to discussion.

Gradually, some kids start building bridges back to us. Jacob wrote an editorial titled "In the Mind of a Black Man." His eighth-grade teacher affirmed the paper, and Jacob used the freedom of writing workshop to "do it twice." Stephanie notes that "they were both very powerful, well-written essays." In May, Jacob selected one of the editorials for his portfolio, explaining in his journal that

> "In the Mind of a Black Man" was a real big challeng for me because I talk about how I feel about wrong things in the Black communaty, but I've never writen it down befor. I was surprised that I found the courage to write what I wrote and turn it in to my White teacher in a prodamatly White school."

In her classic 1983 study of a small-town elementary school, Shirley Brice Heath found three quite distinct groups of language users among the students: lower-class Whites, lower-class Blacks, and middle-class students (both Black and White). All the teachers were middle class; lower-class students, whether Black or White, tended to perform poorly in school. After observing in this setting, Heath concluded that class-based styles of communication were preventing teachers from reaching all their students. Teachers working with Heath became "ethnographers" doing action research in their own classrooms. They wrote field notes recording their students' language patterns, favorite stories, questioning styles, and preferred work habits. They shared their findings in a study group. Gradually, they built a two-way bridge between community and school, making it possible for lower-class students to feel "at home" in the classroom. Students, too, became ethnographers by investigating the way language was used in their families and neighborhoods. Through this curriculum, students learned to codeshift culturally, to communicate with diverse audiences.

Janice Hale-Benson (1986, 190) explains how certain people inside and outside a minority group can serve as human bridges to help members cross these cultural barriers. She describes the roles of "translators, mediators, and models." *Translators* are the most powerful agents. They are members of the minority group "who have been successful at dual socialization. . . . They share their own experiences . . . and convey ways to meet the society's demands without compromising ethnic values and norms." *Mediators* are "individuals from mainstream culture who can serve as guides for minority persons." Such formal mediators as teachers may not be as powerful as translators because they are less fully bicultural, but they can provide valuable information. *Models* are minority-group people whose successful "behavior can serve as a pattern to emulate," especially when students perceive a similarity between themselves and the model.

We believe that teachers must draw on the resources of cultural translators, mediators, and models. Minnie, as an African American teacher, serves as a cultural translator for her Black students and a cultural mediator for her White students. Notice her attitude when she reads their writing.

> In the role of ethnographer and translator, I examine the personal, internal messages through the eyes, worlds, and words of my students. For my own sake I want to stave off the seeping and creeping detachment where proximity does not equal connectedness and teaching does not equal learning. In this scenario, the teacher learns from the student.

Process writing allows us the time to develop both skills and relationships. We start with writing as an expression of self, as a hard copy version of speech. Then we conference, giving personal support to help students clarify their ideas and revise for specific audiences. Minnie adds, "such a stance, I believe, moves away from the arrogance and ignorance of the past—of researchers and teachers who presume they know more than those whom they're studying while actually understanding very little."

Those of us who are White work especially to build our own skills as cultural mediators—middle-class professionals who have become reasonably bicultural in order to teach more effectively. We listen to our Black students and we learn from Black educators. Our classroom culture feels richer today, less bounded by White middle-class experience.

Bicultural socialization is just as much an asset for our White students. They are preparing for a world that is increasingly diverse, that demands the ability to communicate and to build working relationships across old cultural barriers. A few years from now, they may need to "get ovuh" on a job with a Black supervisor and co-workers of many backgrounds. Consider the impact of African American literature on the sensitivity of a White female eighth grader (not a target student). The excerpts are from the journal she kept for her literature study group:

5/7/90

My book, *Roll of Thunder, Hear My Cry,* by Mildred Taylor, is so far about a bunch of Black kids on their way to school. I'm not even to the second chapter and they have already experienced some predudice feeling toward them. Everytime I read about these situations I always feel sad because as long as this has been going on, it still happens today.

5/9/90

All the White people in this book have a horrible habit of calling the Black families dumb and stupid, but Stacy has just come up with an excellent way to stop the bus from spattering mud and water on them and running them off the road. Even though I don't quite understand what it is (neither do they) I'm very sure it will work & make the bus folks feel stupid.

5/13/90

I've decided that Cassie's family is very modern. I mean, they think like a family of today would. They think everyone should be equal. They're right, but back then, people really didn't look at it that way. Other people in the book think they are kind of off their rockers. I'm sure they won't change.

5/16/90

I'm going to write about something a little different today. It's about how close-minded and ignorant people are. I come from a whole string of people who think Black people are below Whites or, in some cases, just plain worthless. I guess I'm the opposing force, because I've come to believe *they* are the worthless ones. My brother, for instance, somehow got it ingraved in his mind that all Blacks should die. Pretty scary, huh? A sixteen year old! My step-dad has made it clear that he thinks Black/White couples are totally unacceptable. Is it any of his business anyway? I think not. My grandmother, who is now very open-minded, has told stories of when she was a child. She and her friends would sit on her roof and yell nasty comments to Black passers-by. My other grandparents try to cover it up but their predudice can always be reconized by the way they say the words "Black folks" or the "colored". I could go on and on. My question is—will this ever change? Are people

ever going to wake up and realize that Blacks are just the same as everyone else: one brain, two lungs, one heart, etc? When will people look past the outer color of someone and find out what is inside before they judge that someone? This is something I feel very strongly about this, but usually have trouble talking about it. I would just like everyone to be treated equally. Why does it have to be like this?
5/25/90

I finished it and thought it was wonderful. I just can't get over how strong the Logan family was. Getting through their situations would give me ulcers! The end was absolutely perfect! The whole book was, actually. And to think it was mostly true! Unbelievable. I think this goes on my top ten favorites of all time. (I have a copy of the second part reserved at the Library already.) Well, I definitely thought it was excellent and could not have been better!

This reader has crossed a bridge to a richer, more diverse world.

In Chapter 7, Nancy described our ideal of a democratic classroom where people of different backgrounds talk freely. What follows is the full passage from her field notes, a vignette that would never have occurred before the project. Three students were collaborating on a story that appeals to the adolescent fascination with crime and violence.

Martin and Colin began to read John's section of the story on the monitor describing the fight in prison. The dopeman was Black. Martin asked John [Martin and Colin are Black and John is White], "Why's he Black?"

John was stunned, speechless, and a bit embarrassed. I could have stayed out of this, but I'd been observing their work, collaboration, and discussion, and I couldn't keep my mouth shut. I also felt a bit sorry for John. I said to Martin, "Good question!" (Now, he's embarrassed that I heard him.) Since I was already in over my head, I continued, "John, why is the dopeman Black?"

Colin said, "Yeah, he could be White." That opened the discussion, revisiting stereotypes. Martin thought a moment, then asked, "How many White guys have you seen selling drugs on the corner in the city?"

Note: None of the students changed the character roles in their short story.

Nancy saw through the blood and gore to a dialogue. Through action research, she had grown strong enough to confront both Black and White students. She could question the negative stereotypes without pushing kids to see things her way. At the same time, her students had become willing to consider her perspective as well as their own.

As a team, we still grapple with bridging. We use the term to describe a whole range of activities that guide learners to a point that seemed beyond their capacity and ours. If we're committed to helping kids "on the edge" gain access to the mainstream without losing themselves, we must be bridge builders.

LOOKING IN THE MIRROR:
BRIDGES IN SIX YEARS OF COLLABORATIVE RESEARCH

Perhaps more than any other principle, *bridging* describes the work of our research team. What we do today seemed impossible in 1987. It became possible because we kept learning and reflecting, year after year. Our hastily jotted field notes are the basis of sometimes-coherent journal entries. Shared in our monthly study sessions and yearly syntheses, they start to fall into patterns. Over six years, they have become the collective wisdom of the Webster Groves Writing Project. Looking back, we see that we have been putting ourselves through a sequential curriculum.

As writers, we continue to gain skill and confidence. We started with oral presentations (first to local teachers and later to formidable audiences at national conventions). Based on the oral, we wrote—first journal articles, next our curriculum guide *Hear You, Hear Me!* (Webster Groves Writing Project 1992), and now this book of action research.

As teachers, we get better when we "do it twice." We now see our first attempt at a new venture as an experiment, not a final examination. Occasionally we succeed on the first try (as many of us did with portfolios) but we still expect to do better next year! Like all learners, we need to practice.

As an action research team, we have become a human bridge, a staff development project, an informal apprenticeship. Each year, the team adds members—some of them veterans new to the school district, others quite new to the profession. They are asked to read the synthesis reports, articles, and curriculum guide developed by their predecessors. For their first-year's focus, most newcomers choose case studies so they can retrace the steps of the early members. We keep doing action research until it becomes a part of us—the way we think and the way we teach.

But the most important bridges connect us with our kids. At first, our goal was helping our low-achieving African American students cross a bridge from their own experience to the academic world. Today we see more clearly the barriers of race, class, and gender that have alienated them. We need to walk over and meet them halfway. "People who cannot communicate are powerless. People who know nothing of their past are culturally impoverished. People who cannot see beyond the confines of their own lives are ill-equipped to face the future" (Ernest Boyer 1983, 6). These words apply to many Black students, who must expand their horizons to communicate with a wider audience. They apply still more to White middle-class teachers, who must expand their horizons to reach the kids in their own classrooms.

WHAT YOU CAN DO

Build curriculum sequences. Start where the student is, then stretch.

Build an unfamiliar task on a familiar base. Use models, formulas, and prior knowledge to introduce something new. "Do it twice" and reflect.

Build cultural bridges linking your students, yourself, and a wider, multicultural society.

Read:

BAYER, ANN SHEA. 1990. *Collaborative Apprenticeship Learning: Language and Thinking Across the Curriculum, K–12.* Mountain View, CA: Mayfield.

HALE-BENSON, JANICE. 1986. *Black Children: Their Roots, Culture, and Learning Styles.* Rev. ed. Baltimore: Johns Hopkins University Press.

HEATH, SHIRLEY BRICE. 1983. *Ways with Words.* New York: Cambridge University Press.

MOFFETT, JAMES. 1992. *Active Voice: A Writing Program Across the Curriculum.* Rev. ed. Portsmouth, NH: Boynton/Cook.

Facing the Mirror:
Agnes Gregg

My story is one of assimilation. I see myself, in retrospect, as emerging from one isolation to another, with the boundaries expanding at every shift. The concentric circles of this process spill logically into one another, each change expanding my knowledge, scope, and vision.

I'm a baby boomer born in an Italian ghetto—"the Hill"—a small area in the west end of St. Louis with one of the country's largest population of Italian Americans. I was the first in my family to graduate from high school and to have English as a primary language. My mother delights in Grandparents' Day visits to schools when she retells the story of her trek to Ellis Island as a five-year-old.

The Hill community grew from the 1890s through the 1920s as immigrants took jobs as laborers for the developing clay industry. Life centered on the church. The community provided for its inhabitants' every need. It was a place where these non-English-speaking people could work, socialize, and worship. The rest of St. Louis and its prejudices could be ignored.

Although my family was much more Americanized than the early immigrants, venturing outside the safety net of the community caused anxiety. When my brother chose to attend a public rather than Catholic high school, it was disconcerting. And when one of us would mention a new friend, the questions included not only typical "Where does she live?" and "Where does he go to school?" but also "Is she American?" For my grandmother, that was *the* question. She had divided the New World into two groups—Italians and others, who were American.

I left home at thirteen and traded one type of isolation for another. I attended Sacred Heart Academy in Hamden, Connecticut, as an aspirant in training to enter the religious order of the teachers I had known since kindergarten. The Apostles of the Sacred Heart gave me a strong liberal arts education. I especially liked my writing and literature classes and was impressed by the English teachers. Writing was a creative outlet and a therapeutic tool for me.

After high school I entered the novitiate confidently but grew restless and angry. The restrictions and limitations were not healthy for me. I left disillusioned that my dream had not been fulfilled but eager to live in the "real world." The safety and security both on the Hill and in the novitiate had become stifling.

I majored in English at Fontbonne College in St. Louis because I loved language. I wrote poetry in notebook margins during sociology classes and spent hours looking up the etymology of vocabulary words. But it was 1969. J. F. K.'s legacy that we be part of the solution along with the encouragement of a Korean professor to get experience caused me to drop out of the University of Missouri and join V.I.S.T.A.—the stateside version of the Peace Corps.

At the Denver training site, my boundary waters flooded. I anticipated working on a reservation furthering the Native American cause. After a presentation by a member of a tribe in Utah, I realized I was lacking skills and experience. Instead I joined a project in Denver working with high school dropouts who were on probation. On the northside I was exposed to Mexican American customs, food, and people who smiled at my attempts to communicate in high school Spanish. But I was overwhelmed by the outcomes that poverty, drugs, and abuse had set in motion. Patterns that would limit most of them and kill some. These kids had no safety net. After a depressing year and a half I decided that education was after all a more positive approach of helping young people. I returned to the University of Missouri, St. Louis, to finish a degree in sociology with certification in English and Social Studies.

My first teaching job was at a Catholic elementary school in St. Louis City. I taught reading to all fifth through eighth graders as well as religion, art, and music to my eighth-grade homeroom. Every student at the school was African American except for the members of one Mexican American migrant family.

My focus at the school was on the craft of teaching. How to discipline; how to manage five reading groups at a time; how to teach religion, art history, and music appreciation along with preparation for confession and Mass; how to monitor lunchroom and playground behavior. There were no plan periods or aides. Sometimes our checks would be delayed. Over half of the families were not able to pay the tuition.

The students saved me many times—they assured me that singing along with the record was sufficient music appreciation. I didn't consciously wonder about how to reach the African American child. I was immersed in a segregated situation where I thought about pedagogy and practice, grading systems, record keeping, bulletin boards, and the theme of the month.

After three years and a master's degree to become a reading specialist, I accepted a job at Webster Groves High School. I was to design a course in civics for ninth graders experiencing reading problems. I welcomed the chance to work with older students and to use both certifications.

It was 1976 and Webster had already suffered the growing pains of merging—and therefore integrating three junior high schools into one. The high school students, both Black and White, were protesting for student rights and I sympathized. I have worked with students and teachers in Webster for sixteen years. I see Webster students as a representative sample of many cultural groups. I am comfortable in this arena. Although some see Webster as an isolated niche, I draw from my own web of isolations to see this instead as a place of assimilation.

The writing group provides an oasis. It's a center where we are supportive and of the same mind. When I extend my boundaries now, I know it is not in isolation and I know there is a ripple effect.

CHANGING
IMAGES

Changes in Student Writing

We did it!

Action research team in unison upon seeing holistic scores in June 1988

*Or did we? And what is **it**?*

Topic debated at 1991, 1992, and 1993 synthesis meetings

W e started our story with Daniel's writings about the qualities of a good teacher and his treasured fishing pole. Such improvement in actual student writing is the *real* proof of the pudding. You will see more pre and post writing samples in this chapter.

But the project started because of the differences between Black and White students' scores on the annual district assessment of writing. In our "fix the writing" phase, we designed our first grant proposal to show improvement in those scores. It seemed easy enough to plug the evaluation of our project into that existing assessment process. Little did we know! This is a story of our team becoming more sophisticated, research wise, and critical of our own work.

The holistic scoring process the district used (see Appendix Five) was modified in some way almost every year to better meet the needs of the classroom teachers. Our challenge was to achieve statistical validity for the project in a real-world setting where the rules kept changing.

The project required one change in the district's procedures: the project students had to write a "post" sample each year in the spring which we could compare with the "pre" sample from that fall. We knew that the typical growth for all students in one year's time (from fall to fall) on the district assessment was 1 point on the 16-point scale.[1] We also knew that the students to be targeted averaged 3 to 4 points below the mean for their grade level. We boldly set our goal in that first grant proposal: the target students' mean score in the spring would be 2 points greater than it had been in the fall. When the results came in that first year, we had accomplished our goal!

YEAR ONE SCORES
1987–88

GRADE	NUMBER OF TARGET STUDENTS	TARGET STUDENT MEAN FALL 1987	TARGET STUDENT MEAN SPRING 1988
7	6	4.2	8.0
8	6	7.8	8.5
10	6	8.3	9.6
11	1	7.0	11.0
19		6.8	8.8

Increase: 2.0

We were euphoric and held fast to those numbers as an "objective" validation of our work. But we harbored some doubts: we had worked with very few target students and we weren't statisticians. (We had designed the computer printouts and did our own interpretations.) We cautiously decided not to "go public" with our data unless the second year repeated the pattern.

The real significance of that first year's results was their effect on the research team. After nine months of nail biting—wondering whether we were accomplishing anything, fearful of what the post scores would show—we were elated when the numbers came in. As we created the bar graphs and interpreted the numbers, our commitment to the project grew. The anxiety and the success bonded us as a team and galvanized us for continued action into the second year. We didn't fully trust the numbers, we knew they had to be replicated, and yet those gains certainly looked impressive. We had our "proof" that our efforts had succeeded. The repetition of a growth pattern throughout the four years we did holistic scoring is strong evidence that the changes in scores were not any fluke.

The numbers are an important part of our story, but the significance we attach to them has changed over the years. Today we look at these numbers not so much as proof of our success as another "piece" of the descriptive data within our action research. In fact, our assessment of student writing was transformed through the process of action research. During the fifth year we tackled a new method of evaluation, portfolio assessment, in order to focus on the individual student.

This chapter presents the data for each year—pre and post writings of sample target students—and describes our move from holistic assessment to portfolio assessment.

STATISTICAL RESULTS: YEARS ONE THROUGH FOUR

Years One and Two: "The Beautiful Illusion"

Year One: 1987–88

We showed earlier that the nineteen target students in the first year increased their mean score from fall to spring by 2 points on a 16-point scale. The question is, How well did the rest of the students do?

This is such a simple question, but the answer is not easily given. The procedures already established for district assessment created some problems for our project.

The "rest of the students" were not identical for the pre and post writings. In 1987–88, all students enrolled in an English class in the fall produced a writing sample. In the spring, only those students in classes with target students were asked to write. Students of teachers not participating in the project had no post writings, nor did students in classes without any target students. In reporting the results for this chapter, we have tried to correct for it by using scores only for those students for whom we have both a pre score from the district assessment *and* a post score. But this means the number of total students shown on these tables is very small.

We know too that our data would have been much more reliable if the pre and post samples had been mixed together and scored at one time. Then the readers could not be accused of being more lenient with the papers written at the end of the year so that the scores would show improvement. But we needed those fall scores in order to identify target students—those students who were below the mean for their grade level. And the district wanted its scoring completed in the fall so teachers could use the results during the school year with the current students. We hoped to compensate for these limitations by comparing the target students' means with those of the "total students." At least the two problems would affect both groups. Doing anything close to quasi-experimental research in a real-world setting requires creative thinking and compromise!

The chart shows the mean scores of "total" students and the mean scores of target students. For example, looking at the first line, there were six target students in grade seven. In the fall district assessment, their six scores had a mean of 4.2 (on a scale of 16 points). In the spring, those six students' scores had a mean of 8.0. This dramatic jump of almost 4 points becomes more meaningful when compared with increase in the mean scores of "total students" in grade seven. Those ninety-eight students had a mean score of 7.3 in the fall, showing that the target students were clearly below average. In the spring, these ninety-eight seventh graders had a mean score of 9.8, an increase of 2.6 points. The seventh-grade target students had a mean increase of 3.8 points.

YEAR ONE SCORES
1987–88

GRADE	NUMBER OF TARGET STUDENTS	NUMBER OF TOTAL STUDENTS	ALL-STUDENT MEAN* FALL 1987	ALL-STUDENT MEAN SPRING 1988	TARGET STUDENT MEAN FALL 1987	TARGET STUDENT MEAN SPRING 1988
7	6	98	7.3	9.8	4.2	8.0
8	6	91	8.4	9.3	7.8	8.5
10	6	54	9.8†	10.4	8.3	9.6
11	1	5	7.2	11.8	7.0	11.0
	19	248	8.2	9.8	6.8	8.8

Increases: 1.6   2.0

_____

* *"All students" includes the target students.*

† *The five eleventh graders had an extremely low mean: they were all repeating the required sopho-more course, which they had failed the year before. In fact, they were in the same classes as the tenth graders on this chart. The district fall mean for all eleventh graders was 10.7; it was on the basis of that district mean that the one target student with a fall score of 7 was chosen.*

The district assessment includes standard deviations as well as means, but the point we want to make is muddied by so many figures. Since our purpose is to show a pattern, not to give data that is statistically significant, we are not including the standard deviations.

With this greater increase, the target students were well on their way to catching up with the rest of the students.

The means for all nineteen target students that first year showed an increase from fall to spring of 2 points compared with the total students' increase of 1.6 points.[2] Past assessments in our district had shown roughly a 1-point increase from grade to grade from fall to fall. We wanted our research results in the spring, and recognize that any one student writing in the spring is likely to produce better results than she will the following fall. The incentive to do one's best is greater when the teacher asking for the effort isn't a relative stranger and the summer has not intervened. Yet the target students still outpaced the total students, even though both groups benefited from the earlier post writing.

Definitely in Phase Two (Fix the Methods) at this point, we saw these results as validating our principles and strategies. We embarked on the second year, selecting target students who presented even greater risks—that is, who scored even lower initially and appeared to be more difficult to establish rapport with.

Year Two: 1988–89

The second year of the project, the district wanted to reduce the costs of the annual assessment and yet have a large enough sample to give valid data. Only half the students (last initials A through L and M through Z in alternating grades) were asked to write to the prompts. When we compiled our data for this second year, we once again used the scores only for students who participated in *both* pre and post writings. This careful pairing eliminated so many nonmatching pre and post scores that the number of total students is smaller for each grade than it was the first year.

This was just one problem we faced when we looked at the computer printouts that second year. The high school target students were in semester classes. We didn't realize the problem until too late: no post test had been given in January. It was pure coincidence that there were eight students in project teachers' classes both semesters; four of them were

Year Two Scores
1988–89

Grade	Number of Target Students	Number of Total Students Fall/Spring	All-Student Mean Fall 1988	All-Student Mean Spring 1989	Target Student Mean Fall 1988	Target Student Mean Spring 1989
7	11	46	6.8	9.3	4.0	5.9
8	12	76	8.0	9.6	4.8	8.5
	23	122	7.5	9.5	4.4	7.3

Increases: 2.0   2.9

identified by at least one of their teachers as target students. We seemed plagued by obstacles in our attempt to gather good data: half the alphabet, then no post scores for most of the high school students! Our real-world decision was to not include the high school data in our reports. From this point on, the high school data is reported separately from the middle school data. The charts for the four years for high school students are on page 371.

All students increased their mean score by 2 points, but the target students' mean score increased by 2.9 points—more than the increase shown in the first year. We can compare the increase of one year with the increase of another. We cannot compare mean scores of different years since the individual students are not identical nor are the prompts. (The prompts written to each year are in Appendix Five.)

Even better news was that nineteen of the twenty-three target students had improved scores in the spring. Only one target student had a lower score and three remained constant. For the second year, the increased mean score for the target students was not inflated by tremendous increases in a few individual scores.

This success gave us confidence to expand the project so that we could answer the obvious question: couldn't these results occur because of the individual attention the students are receiving? About this time, we were becoming research wise, learning about the statistical concept of "regression to the mean,"[3] which means these low-scoring students might have improved simply because their scores were so low they had no place to go but up. For these two reasons, and others already explained in Chapter 2, we decided to target all students, both Black and White, below their grade-level mean.

Years Three and Four: "More Numbers, Stronger Validation"

In the third year, we observed in our classrooms increased writing skills in most of our students. What would the pre and post assessment show?

YEAR THREE SCORES
1989–90

GRADE	NUMBER OF TARGET STUDENTS	NUMBER OF TOTAL STUDENTS FALL/SPRING	ALL-STUDENT MEAN FALL 1989	ALL-STUDENT MEAN SPRING 1990	TARGET STUDENT MEAN FALL 1989	TARGET STUDENT MEAN SPRING 1990
7	48	130	5.9	7.2	3.3	5.9
8	34	84	7.4	8.3	5.3	7.0
	82	214	6.5	7.7	4.1	6.4

Increases: 1.2   2.3

YEAR FOUR SCORES
1990–91

GRADE	NUMBER OF TARGET STUDENTS	NUMBER OF TOTAL STUDENTS FALL/SPRING	ALL-STUDENT MEAN FALL 1990	ALL-STUDENT MEAN SPRING 1991	TARGET STUDENT MEAN FALL 1990	TARGET STUDENT MEAN SPRING 1991
7	62	153	6.7	8.1	3.9	6.5
8	54	111	7.6	8.7	5.4	7.2
	116	264	7.1	8.4	4.6	6.8

Increases: 1.3   2.2

Hurrah! The pattern of increase continued through the third year even though the target students now represented over one-third of the total. Once again the pattern was created by the majority (82 percent) of the target students increasing their scores rather than a few showing great gains. Only seven of the eighty-two target students had a lower score in the spring.

The pattern was replicated one more time in the fourth year, again targeting roughly one-third of project teachers' students. And once more the increase was caused by the majority (76 percent) of the target students going up. Only 14 of the 115 target students had a lower score in the spring.

HIGH SCHOOL DATA
YEAR ONE
1987–88

GRADE	NUMBER OF TARGET STUDENTS	NUMBER OF TOTAL STUDENTS FALL/SPRING	ALL-STUDENT MEAN FALL 1987	ALL-STUDENT MEAN SPRING 1988	TARGET STUDENT MEAN FALL 1987	TARGET STUDENT MEAN SPRING 1988
10	6	54	9.8	10.4	8.3	9.6
11	1	5	7.2	11.8	7.0	11.0
	7	59	9.6	10.5	8.1	9.9

YEAR TWO
1988–89

GRADE	NUMBER OF TARGET STUDENTS	NUMBER OF TOTAL STUDENTS FALL/SPRING	ALL-STUDENT MEAN FALL 1988	ALL-STUDENT MEAN SPRING 1989	TARGET STUDENT MEAN FALL 1988	TARGET STUDENT MEAN SPRING 1989
9	1	2	5.0	6.0	6.0	4.0
10	3	6	7.0	7.8	7.0	6.3
	4	8	6.5	7.4	6.8	5.8

YEAR THREE
1989–90

GRADE	NUMBER OF TARGET STUDENTS	NUMBER OF TOTAL STUDENTS FALL/SPRING	ALL-STUDENT MEAN FALL 1989	ALL-STUDENT MEAN SPRING 1990	TARGET STUDENT MEAN FALL 1989	TARGET STUDENT MEAN SPRING 1990
9	12	67	8.6	10.8	5.8	9.1

YEAR FOUR
1990–91

GRADE	NUMBER OF TARGET STUDENTS	NUMBER OF TOTAL STUDENTS FALL/SPRING	ALL-STUDENT MEAN FALL 1990	ALL-STUDENT MEAN SPRING 1991	TARGET STUDENT MEAN FALL 1990	TARGET STUDENT MEAN SPRING 1991
9	47	80	7.2	8.2	5.5	7.0

Year three, our first year with so many target students, showed an unexpectedly high increase: over a full point's difference in favor of the target students. And again, year four repeated the success of year three, with about a 1-point difference in favor of the target students.

As data from more years accumulates, it is tempting to look for longitudinal growth, to see if the target students improve as they move from seventh to eighth grade. However, since the target students are not the same from year to year, it is impossible to look at the data in this way. Longitudinal growth can't be deduced for all students either, since the prompts are different modes for the two years and different parts of the alphabet participate in the district assessment each year.

Our conclusions? The pattern of growth over four years verifies the impact of the project. Target students (without that label) in the past were stagnating. Now they're learning just as *most* Webster Groves School District kids learn. In fact, they're learning faster and closing the gap.

All African American Target Students

In traditional research, variables are defined up front, tested, and remain constant. In action research, variables can evolve with the participants' questions and interpretations. As our definition of target students changed to include all students, Black and White, scoring below the mean, we changed our variables. But we didn't want to lose track of the progress of the African Americans in our classes. And so we added another step to our number crunching: we identified on the computer printouts all students who were both target and African American and showed those numbers on charts and bar graphs.

The scores in the following charts are for African American target students for whom we have both a fall and spring score. We have separated the high school grades from the middle school for the same reason we separated them in the earlier charts.

During the third year, the Black target students' mean score increased 1.5 points, just in between the 1.2 increase of all students and the 1.7 increase

372

AFRICAN AMERICAN TARGET STUDENTS
YEAR ONE
1987–88

GRADE	NUMBER	FALL 1988	SPRING 1989
7	6	4.2	8.0
8	6	7.8	8.5
	12	6.0	8.3

Increase: 2.3

GRADE	NUMBER	FALL 1988	SPRING 1989
10	6	8.3	9.6
11	1	7.0	11.0
	7	8.1	9.9

Increase: 1.7

YEAR TWO
1988–89

GRADE	NUMBER	FALL 1988	SPRING 1989
7	11	4.0	5.9
8	12	4.8	8.5
	23	4.4	7.3

Increase: 2.9

GRADE	NUMBER	FALL 1988	SPRING 1989
9	1	6.0	4.0
10	3	7.0	6.3
	4	6.8	5.8

Increase: −1.0

Year Three
1989–90

Grade	Number	Fall 1988	Spring 1989
7	16	3.0	4.9
8	15	5.4	6.7
	31	4.2	5.7

Increase: 1.5

Grade	Number	Fall 1988	Spring 1989
9	4	5.8	9.0

Increase: 1.7

Year Four
1990–91

Grade	Number	Fall 1988	Spring 1989
7	21	3.4	5.6
8	14	4.9	7.2
	35	4.0	6.3

Increase: 2.2

Grade	Number	Fall 1988	Spring 1989
9	18	4.8	6.1

Increase: 1.3

of all target students. We were encouraged that the Black target students still increased their mean score more than all students—but the difference was slight enough that we were concerned: Had the underachieving African Americans indeed gotten lost when we expanded the project?

The fourth year once again indicated that we got better as teachers when we did it twice. The Black target students' mean score increased 2.2

points from fall to spring, almost a full point more than all students' (1.3). The Black target students' increase was identical to the increase of all target students. Within both racial groups, the female target students were much stronger than the male target students. We did not lose our focus on the low-scoring African Americans when we targeted all students, Black and White, who scored below the mean in the fall.

The graphs in Figures 12-1 through 12-4 summarize the data, comparing the mean scores of all students, target students, and African American target students. The graphs show the means for only grades seven and eight.

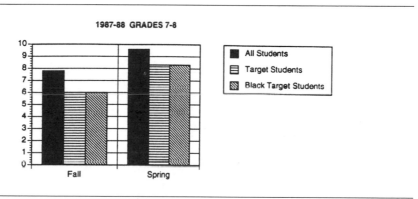

FIG. 12-1   *Pre and post mean scores, 1987–88.*

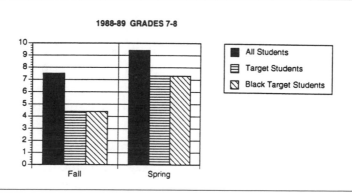

FIG. 12-2   *Pre and post mean scores, 1988–89.*

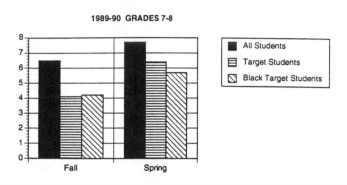

FIG. 12-3 *Pre and post mean scores, 1989–90.*

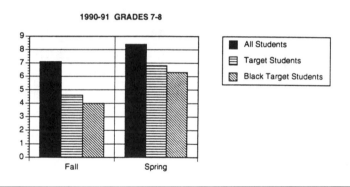

FIG. 12-4 *Pre and post mean scores, 1990–91.*

THE STORY BEHIND THE NUMBERS:
PRE AND POST WRITING SAMPLES

The consistent pattern of increased mean scores suggests that the eight principles and strategies developed through our classroom action research made a difference. But it's time for "show, don't tell." The students' papers illustrate what bare numbers cannot: the improvement in development, specific word choice, intros, and endings. We selected these pre and post comparisons because they were representative rather than the most dramatic. Herein lies the story behind the numbers.

These four samples, along with Daniel's, represent all four years of the project assessment by holistic scoring and show all three modes of writing. The first two samples were written by the same student, first in grade seven and then in grade nine. All four papers were written by African Americans, two males and one female, and they represent grades seven, eight, and nine.

William was a seventh grader the first year of our project. That fall, William wrote on the qualities of a good teacher and his paper received a score of four; in the spring, his writing scored an eight. In the ninth grade, William wrote in the fall on a change to be made at school and his paper was scored six. In the spring, his writing scored a nine. William's scores are not just representative. They are identical with the mean scores for target students at his grade level all four times.

All of William's writings are to his principal. It is interesting to see the consistency of his ideas over an eight-month time period. In the seventh grade, in both fall and spring, he considers a good teacher one who is intelligent, understanding, and smart. In the ninth grade, the desire to see longer lunch periods is the requested change in both pre and post writings. Most students changed topics, so William's writings afford us an opportunity to see how the same ideas are handled twice.

William's first assessment writing just jumps right in. He has no intro-duction—and no conclusion, either. Unfortunately, William still has not attempted a lead by the end of ninth grade. But a conclusion appears at the end of seventh grade with "So pick a smart teacher with intelligence, and understanding." Both pieces in ninth grade have conclusions (although his spring writing adds one final but tangential sentence). But William also reverted to writing a complete paper with no paragraphing.

William always did develop his ideas to some extent, and this improved over the years. In the first paper all the development occurs within a single sentence or run-on: "They should be real smart because all teachers would have to be smart are else the smartest student in the class would be smarter than her." This idea becomes a paragraph by the spring: "A good teacher should also be smart. If the teacher you hire is not smart, and she gets up in front of the class and start to teach and doesn't know what she's doing then you want learn nothing. You'll probly be smarter than the teacher. Dum teachers are not good teachers."

The seeming repetition of *smart* and *intelligent* in the fall writing is explained in the more developed, separate paragraphs of the spring paper. *Intelligence* appears to refer more to thinking ability and *smart* seems to refer to subject-matter knowledge. In the spring, William also combines the concepts of "kind and gentle" and even tempered into one characteristic: understanding. These changes, along with separate paragraphs for each characteristic, are evidence of the great improvement in William's sense of organization. By the end of the seventh grade, William has learned to develop his ideas with some details, some of which are anecdotal and others of which are explanatory.

The prewriting in the ninth grade is very disappointing but instructive to us, especially when we examine his rough drafts. (All prewriting and drafts are turned in with the final; only the final is read at the scoring session.) During the two assessment periods, William wrote four drafts. He makes three word changes, "go out to eat" becomes "go out to lunch," "I would think" becomes "I guarantee," and "lunch hour" becomes "lunch period." Most of William's time was spent checking on mechanics: the spelling of *guarantee, complaining, there,* and the writing out of numbers. Interestingly enough, William corrects a fragment in his very first draft but it reappears in the final draft.

He seems to have spent all his time on proofreading and recopying. He states only one developing reason ("Because when you go out for lunch you wouldn't have to rush there and back"); his concluding sentence suggests a second reason (people will stop complaining). This apparent regression illustrates a basic learning theory: when a student concentrates on a new skill, he temporarily loses some control over previously mastered skills. Focusing on mechanics in a limited time frame blocks the flow of ideas and the development of the paper.

But the post writing as a ninth grader shows a student well on his way to control over language in all aspects. William explains, convincingly, the difficulties of leaving campus for lunch and getting back in just thirty-four minutes. He expands the idea of being rushed by giving an example of going to McDonald's. He mentions the extra pressure on students staying after class that would be relieved. And he cites a neighboring high school as a precedent.

William has an idea not mentioned in his fall writing: to proceed democratically. He also shows awareness of the principal's point of view—a concern about shortening the class periods—but he does not address it. His rough draft suggests that William may not have been able to come up with a counterargument. He added and then crossed out "but just change them to 45 mins long."

The letter has an ending sentence, but William has reverted to writing a complete paper without paragraphing, and his first sentence is not really an introduction. However, this letter convinces a reader of William's sincerity and gives the reader some food for thought.

Overall, William has improved his development, organization, and conclusions, as well as his proofreading skills. The fact that this wasn't a gentle slope of improvement but, rather, a line with a big dip at one point, is typical of writing development.

———

William: Grade Seven, Fall, Year One
Score: 4
    Mean score of seventh-grade target students: 4
    Mean score of all seventh graders: 7
Prompt: Letter to principal telling what to look for in a new teacher

Dear _____,

    When you hire a teacher you should look first to see if she or he is well qualified. They should be real smart because all teachers would have to be smart are else the smartest student in the class would be smarter than her. The teacher should be kind and gentle to kids, when a kid has a problem he would need someone to understand are else his problem would be more worse. The teacher that you are looking for should be intelligent well skilled so that she would know what she's doing. And she shouldn't have a bad temper, because when someone askes a stupud question she shouldn't get mad and holler at him.

sincerly

———

William: Grade Seven, Spring, Year One
Score: 8
      Mean score of seventh-grade target students: 8
      Mean score of all seventh graders: 10
Prompt: Letter to principal telling what to look for in a new teacher

William
his address
St. Louis, Missouri
Dear _____,

      Intelligence for a teacher
      A good teacher should have intelligence. I think so, because if their intelligent they will know how to do things the right way. Intelligence inquires good thinking and hardworking. Intelligent teachers always get the job. How I know that intelligent teachers always gets the job, is because all my teachers are intelligent.
      A good teacher should be understanding to, because if you have a problem and the class is talking about something and she or he calls on you, and you are not listening, because you have a problem. Then you don't answer and she sends you out the room, and comes out their ands talk to you and tell her your problem she will understand. That's why you should look for a understanding teacher.
      A good teacher should also be smart. If the teacher you hire is not smart, and she gets up in front of the class and start to teach and doesn't know what she's doing then you want learn nothing. You'll probly be smarter than the teacher. Dum teachers are not good teachers. So pick a smart teacher with intelligence, and understanding.

William: Grade Nine, Fall, Year Three
Score: 6
     Mean score of ninth-grade target students: 6
     Mean score of all ninth graders: 9
Prompt: Letter to principal suggesting a change at school

Dear _____,

    You could make your school better by having a longer lunch period. Because when you go out for lunch you wouldn't have to rush there and back. Lunch should at least be forty or forty-five minutes long. If you change the lunch period and make it longer, I guarantee everyone would be happy and satisfyied and would stop complaining.

                          Sincerely,

William: Grade Nine, Spring, Year Three
Score: 9
     Mean score of ninth-grade target students: 9
     Mean score of all ninth graders: 11
Prompt: Letter to principal suggesting a change at school

Dear Principal,

    I think you should change and make the lunch period longer. Because our lunch is only about 34 mins long, and in that time there's nothing you can really do. For an example if you went out to eat at MacDonalds and you don't have a car by the time you get your food lunch will be over and you won't have no time to eat. The school will be improved if you made the lunch an hour long by, people wouldn't have to rush to go out to lunch. People who come to lunch late because they had to stay after class wouldn't have to rush and eat their food. Kirkwood High has an hour lunch that's not why I think we should have one but, we need one. A way to find out if our lunch should be changed to an hour long is to have a vote. Send letters to the students and have them sign the letter yes, no, or I don't no and out of all the letters the answer that gets picked the most should be choosen. If it's yes than lunch goes to an hour, if it's no than lunch stays the same, and if it's I don't no have one more finally vote. I think that's the fair way to do it. And if you have any concerns write back. I know one of your concerns will be about the class periods.

Sincerely,

———

Simone was an eighth grader the third year of the project. Her pre and post writings on the qualities of a good teacher were identical to the mean scores for eighth-grade target students: five and seven, respectively.

Simone begins the eighth grade with lots of ideas about a good teacher but not with too many ways of structuring a sentence. Her use of the singular *teacher* and *he/she* is remarkably consistent. Most of the characteristics are general ("nice," "good influence of kid"), although Simone develops her ideas about the value of homework, particularly on weekends.

Simone's primary improvement in the spring assessment is the use of complete sentences. Simone is still working on fluency. Her rough draft shows that her letter was half as long. She proofread it and then extended the letter. This kind of planning and editing was not obvious in the fall letter, which she wrote as a rough draft and then copied, adding some ideas as she went along.

But there's more happening here. At first the spring draft appears again just to list one characteristic after another, but this time in complete sentences. And while there's no suggestion that Simone has a planned organization for this letter, her thinking is more focused. Simone explores her desire for a lenient teacher, deciding "they should want you to learn, but not over work us."

———

Simone: Grade Eight, Fall, Year Three
Score: 5
    Mean score for eighth-grade target students: 5
    Mean score for all eighth graders: 7

Prompt: Letter to principal on what to look for in a new teacher

Dear Principal,

I think that good qualities of a teacher should be that: They're nice, enteligent, since of hummer, knows what he/she is doing, is good with kids of all ages, fun to be around, a good influence of kid, and has a good personality. Should never give home work on weekends, & never give lots of it if does. Should only give homework if he/she thinks we need to work on it more. He/she should also be remarkalby good in what he/she does.

———

Simone: Grade Eight, Spring, Year Three
Score: 7
     Mean score for eighth-grade target students: 7
     Mean score for all eighth graders: 8
Prompt: Letter to principal on what to look for in a new teacher

Dear Principal,

I think there should be a variety of qualities in a teacher. In my eyes a teacher should be good with kids of all races & ages. He/she should have good potentials. The person hired for the job should be leninte & yet on his/her P's & Q's. He/she shouldn't be so workitive. They should want you to learn, but not over work us. Teachers should be able to help you when you need it. Teachers should also, be good in more than more one subject. They should give you a break from your homework at least on Fridays.

Sincerely,
A Student

———

James, a seventh grader in the fourth year of the project, scored below the average target student in both the pre and post writings on a change to be made at school. Both his scores and the mean target student scores in seventh grade improved by three points over the year. James's scores went from a two to a five; the mean score went from a four to seven.

James's bitterness comes through loud and clear in the fall letter. He obviously has many complaints, feels strongly about all of them, and resents any infringements on his developing selfness. James advances the sense of fairness that is particularly strong for seventh and eighth graders.

The writing task asks students to focus on one change; our rubric assigns a low score for a list of changes. The fragments, misspellings, lack of development of any one change, and lack of organization doom this letter to the lowest possible score, a two.

When May rolls around, James hasn't lost his negative attitudes. But it's as if he gets those emotions expressed up front and then goes on to do the task. He focuses on one change, and develops it with reasons and explanations. The rough draft shows that James's first idea was to have a juice machine to supplement the water fountains. Overnight did the juice machine's money-making potential hit James and result in a new idea? Was he asked to pay for another field trip between rough and final drafts? At any rate, the final letter uses the beverage machine as a means to his real change: more accessible field trips. Eventually we see that his opening sentence was not just venting, but that his hate for spending his own money on school field trips is a direct lead into the body of the letter. James's letter has an ending (abrupt, but there) and ends on a civil note that is a pleasant juxtaposition to the opening sentence.

James has given attention to proofreading this final draft. Note the items found in the spring letter that were lacking in the fall letter: paragraphing, a comma *after* the salutation instead of in the middle, a salutation flush with the left margin, the correct spelling of *principal,* and James has used the spelling *or* instead of *are.* His handwritten original also shows concern for inserting missing words, making sure periods and capitals avoid run-ons, and a correction of *alot.*

James's letter may raise questions in the reader's mind: Do students pay for field trips? If they can't, are they left behind? Each team receives the same amount of money to be used for field trips (a pittance, as little as forty dollars). When that money is exhausted, students then pay the costs. A "scholarship" fund is used to cover costs for students unable to pay and this is handled very discreetly.

James: Grade Seven, Fall, Year Four
Score: 2
      Mean score for seventh-grade target students: 4
      Mean score for all seventh graders: 7
Prompt: Letter to principal on a change to make at school

Dear, Princial

    I think that we should wear what we want and who we want. If the high shool can chew gum we can to are they don't chew gum. And we shouldn't have teachers in the hall cause they saw we have to be responable but they threat us like kids. Our lunch should be 10 minutes longer. And we should have some made by the students. And the teachers should have the same rule cause they drink and eat things in our face.

Sincerely,
(wrote his student number)

James: Grade Seven, Spring, Year Four
Score: 5
      Mean score of seventh-grade target students: 7
      Mean score of all seventh graders: 8
Prompt: Letter to principal on a change to make at school

Dear Principal,

    I hate this school and some of the teachers and I hate spending my money.

    But I have a little idea to help out the school. First we can put in some beverage machines in the school. It can help us out a whole lot, because it would put some more money in the school budget. Or you

385

can use it to help the students for paying for the buses to go on a field trip.

    If the money we get from the beverage machine can go into buses, a lot of kids will be able to go on field trips. And the beverage machine can help both the students and the teachers cause of the sugar they won't be tired. And thats all I had to say. "THANKS".

Sincerely Yours,

BEYOND HOLISTIC SCORING

By the fourth year, the action research team was satisfied that the data we could collect had served our purpose: the same pattern of increased scores had been replicated for four years with varying numbers of target students. Meanwhile, as we moved into Phase Three, Fix the Relationships, we had questions that holistic scoring couldn't answer.

    The Webster Groves Writing Assessment Committee decided to drop the holistic scoring for one year to explore alternative methods, particularly portfolio assessment. We wanted information about individual writers, especially their developmental growth, that we couldn't get from a holistic score.

    Because we did not assess our students' writing that year, the state of Missouri required us to participate in its writing assessment. We were eager to see how our community of writers fared when compared with others outside our district.

Year Five: The Missouri Writing Assessment

In October 1991, our 321 eighth graders produced writing samples for the statewide assessment conducted by Missouri's Department of Elementary and Secondary Education. The state used a 6-point rubric and, as one might expect, 3.0 turned out to be the mean score of the fifty-seven thousand papers. The state assessment, like our own, was process oriented, with time provided for the development of the papers. We looked at the results as potentially validating our project. And in fact the data reaffirmed the power of the project's philosophy and practice.

> Sixty-seven percent of our eighth graders (215 students) scored above the state mean.
>
> Only 14 percent (45 students) scored below the state mean.
>
> Only 6 percent of the fifty-seven thousand writers in Missouri scored a 5, 5.5, or 6.
>
> Twenty percent of our eighth graders achieved these highest scores.

We received these results just as we were introducing portfolio assessment to our students.

Years Five and Six: Portfolio Assessment

For four years, we wanted it both ways: to do good qualitative research and to collect data that would be valid statistically. But once we entered the "fix the relationship" phase, we wanted more than one-shot writings and group data. For us, the ideal assessment would

- help to evaluate our curriculum and our teaching practices,
- involve the students' examining their own writings, and
- be authentic and rooted in classroom process.

We want an evaluation procedure, as does Jeff Howard (1990), that will assess "present capability (not innate ability) . . . [and be] a tool in the process of getting better, rather than the final judgment about how good one can become" (14).

Portfolios are a new direction in assessment, not only in writing but in other content areas as well. One beauty of portfolio assessment is that it can be designed by the teachers and students to meet their own purposes.

We wanted to involve our students in the assessment process so they would take responsibility for their learning and set goals for their improvement. What did *they* think good writing was? Could they identify their own strengths and weaknesses? Did they sense their own growth?

As we learned about portfolio assessment, we saw there were other advantages. It would better reflect classroom teaching. Our district holistic assessment was limited to one-shot writing (drafting and revising in two periods, no peer response except for the last year, and obviously only one mode). Portfolios could include writings in many modes and be done over time. The assessment could indeed reflect what was important to us philosophically.

The entire department read and listened while the research team experimented with portfolios during year five, exploring the latest question in our continuing action research: Would the writing samples in a student portfolio better reflect that student's actual writing achievement and the growth in writing skills?

During the synthesis week that summer, we shared our reactions to the process and the students' reflections on their own writing. Beth Ann wrote, "Portfolios are an unconditional success, enjoyable to read. This portfolio was a snapshot of their first semester. It is a sort of freeze frame of where they were at the time, on their way to being something else." Students saw themselves as writers. Quincy, an eighth grader, wrote, "I feel that this little exercise was very very helpful. It gave a chance to really look at my work and see what my week points and mistakes were so I would not make them in the future. . . . I've always felt that I was a good writer but until this portfolio I didn't know for sure." Students could also identify strengths and weaknesses in their own writings. Nicole, another eighth grader, wrote,

> I choose my first process paper "Without Warning" as my bad paper. The reason is was a bad paper is because there was notnough dialouge and it was to wordy. There were alot of misspelled words and incorrect punctuation. I know in my heart I could have done better. . . . My best

paper was "My Experience." . . . It had alot of dialouge and suspense, so to the reader it was an interesting paper. I saw improvement in my own writing; I was surprised.

It is important that students see their own growth. Nicole is not alone when she says she was surprised by her growth. All too often students think of themselves as a "B+ writer" or a "C- student." Most assessments insist on comparing a student with other students. The result is often the same "grade" over and over. A string of Cs on writings over the years doesn't spell "improvement" to a typical student. A portfolio shouts improvement. And what might the power of that be to the confidence of a young writer?

Sandra Murphy[4] conducted a portfolio assessment workshop the summer of 1992 for the entire English department. She helped us understand that our purposes for portfolios must be clear, that some purposes can be contradictory, and that portfolios cannot do all things.

The new portfolio categories—beauty and power, craft and care, thoughtful reflection, and variety and versatility (see Chapter 5)—that were used by all research team members and a few others in the department in year six can have important implications. The struggle to help students understand—and apply—and explain them in their own words implies real intellectual challenge. And the categories represent a very rich view of the writing curriculum. Jane finds it reassuring that "teenagers are being encouraged to consider anything so blatantly aesthetic and irrelevant to the job market as beauty and power!"

The students managed to select four pieces, but typically their reflective letters did not discuss the criteria! Instead, they spoke of their most and least satisfying pieces, just as they had the year before. While the selections in the portfolios embodied the criteria, the reflective letters shied away from analyzing how a particular piece of writing showed a particular criteria.

We are considering using just two categories, beauty and power and craft and care, which were more successful with the younger students in the seventh and eighth grades next year. We may also select some good reflective letters that do address the categories to use as models (see Bob's, which introduces Chapter 11). And we will watch for signs of burnout: "Not another portfolio!" That kind of complaint surfaced during the years of holistic assessment with "I've already written what a good teacher is!"

Sandra Murphy returned in January 1993 to help us examine our processes and product, and then she came again in May 1993 to help us determine our next steps. Some teachers expected that we would "score" several portfolios and develop standards for a district writing assessment. But we discovered through discussion that we no longer want an assessment that results in a number or score and want to move instead toward a curricular portfolio that demonstrates what is being taught and shows samples of work at different levels of proficiency. In this way, we can evaluate our curriculum. For example, are we in fact teaching a variety of modes? We already sense accomplishment toward our two goals of having authentic assessment that reflects classroom practice and involving students in self-evaluation. For now, our question is, What role will portfolios play in our department writing program and in our district writing assessment?

Action research evolves. Six years ago we set a goal of improving the writing of our African American students who scored below a grade-level mean. Three years ago we expanded our goal to improving the writing of all students scoring below the mean. As the project matured, we saw cooperative learning work its magic and we watched our classrooms become writing/reading workshops. Now we continue to search for a means of assessment that truly reflects and evaluates what goes on in our classrooms, that teaches students and teaches teachers. We look for better ways to help our students become good writers, yes, but *reflective* writers, able to assess their strengths and weaknesses, recognizing their own power.

NOTES

1. The district had assessed writing in grades seven through twelve since 1984.

2. The increased mean score of the target students was not caused by a few target students making outstanding jumps in their scores. Indeed, fourteen of the nineteen students showed improvement; five of the students showed a decrease.

3. Regression to the mean is a statistical concept that may be simplified as this: when there are very few scores and they are very low, they have no place to go but up. Hence on a second testing, those few individuals may go up, just as a few at the very top may come down, even though overall the mean of the entire group tested would remain fairly stable.

4. Sandra wrote with Mary Ann Smith *Writing Portfolios: A Bridge from Teaching to Assessment* (1991). Sandra is an associate professor at the University of California, Davis.

Changes in Student Attitudes

Andre's really beginning to think of himself as a writer.
NANCY CASON

Our students were changing. The evidence was in their writings, both for the assessment and for class. We sensed that the attitudes of all our students were changing, too, but we wanted evidence of that change. Individual conferences gave us some of this feedback, but we had questions that couldn't be answered by just a few students.

- Do target students have as much confidence as other students?
- Do they prefer sharing their writing with peers or getting teacher feedback?
- What topics do students prefer?
- Do they enjoy the journal writing?
- Do higher-skilled writers appreciate the value of revising more than lower-skilled writers?
- How do students perceive our efforts for improving their writing?

• What role do our students assign to the computer in their writing processes?

Knowing their perceptions—and how they differed if at all from other students'—could give us more clues about how to reach our target students. The more we hypothesized about the answers to these questions in our study sessions, the more important it became for us to find out just what our students thought.

We devised an attitude survey based on one developed by Janet Emig and Barbara King (1979). We came up with forty items that we piloted with 335 students that first spring (a list of these items is at the end of this chapter). The students had five response options: strongly agree, agree, disagree, strongly disagree, and don't know.

Codes on the computer data sheets allowed us to categorize the results according to race, gender, grade level, and writing ability, with writing ability a subjective evaluation by the teacher using a five-point scale.

As we analyzed the results the first spring, we formed some tentative hypotheses and revised a few statements that we feared had been ambiguous. We also wondered what changes had occurred, if any, over the course of the year. In other words, we wished we knew what the attitudes had been at the beginning of the year. The course was set: we would give the survey as pre and post the second year. Both pre and post surveys were given the third and fourth years, which means we are able to see definite patterns emerging.

Both pre and post surveys were tabulated at the end of each year. Unfortunately, we didn't know any of the results until the students had left our classrooms. Therefore, we've used the survey results to gauge attitudes of groups rather than to analyze individual students' responses, although each of us received a printout of the forty pre and post responses for each of our students.

This chapter describes the patterns that become clear—the generalizations we cautiously draw—by comparing post survey results over three years.

We also examine longitudinally the attitudes of the same students as they progressed through three years of the project. Each item's results are also reported in pre and post percentages within a given year. The survey has been given to large numbers:

1988–89	1989–90	1990–91
Year Two Pre and Post	Year Three Pre and Post	Year Four Pre and Post
453/453	617/628	682/690
357 in grades 7–8	476/483 in grades 7–8	459/463 in grades 7–8
96 in grades 9–11*	140/139 in grade 9	120/126 in grade 9
23 identified targets	195/188 target students	293/286 target students

grades 9–11 were low-skilled classes almost exclusively

We've eliminated the first year's results from our summary because we had no pretest, there were only 18 identified target students, and the wording of some of the questions was changed for the second year. As we look at patterns for the three later years, we have had to keep in mind that the number of target students changed from only 23 African American case study students in year two to approximately 190 low-achieving students, both Black and White, in year three to 290 students in year four.

The percentages for each item for all three years are at the end of the chapter. We will not discuss every item. Some of the results speak for themselves, showing consistently high percentages of the desired attitude (I almost always write a rough draft and then a final draft on an important piece of writing). Some were repetitious.[1] And some of the items are of more interest on an individual basis than in the aggregate (I think the grades I received on my writing were fair). We have not included such items in the discussion that follows. Instead we focus on those that invite interpretation and may speak to the readers. We have grouped the statements in categories of confidence and enjoyment, topics and journals, revising and proofreading, computers, peer response, teacher response, and time spent on writing. By and large, the responses each year were consistent regardless of race, gender, grade level, or writing ability. The exceptions will be noted, especially in the confidence and enjoyment and teacher response categories, where obvious racial differences appeared.

Confidence and Enjoyment

Although every item on the survey was of interest to us, we always looked first at those we classified as reflecting confidence.

28. I like to write. (agree responses)

	1988–89		1989–90		1990–91	
	Pre	Post	Pre	Post	Pre	Post
23 AA* targets	32%	68%				
200–300 targets			51%	58%	63%	66%
All students	64%	68%	64%	67%	70%	73%

AA= African American (all target students were Black the first year)

First, we should explain how to read these numbers. In the fall of 1988, 32 percent of the target students agreed or strongly agreed that they liked to write. At the end of the school year, 68 percent of the target students agreed or strongly agreed. Of all 453 students, 64 percent began the year agreeing with the statement; in the spring, 68 percent of the students agreed.[2]

We love the results on the short but significant item "I like to write." Every year, a positive change occurred. Over three years, the post percentages for all students have gone up, until almost three-fourths of our students say they enjoy writing. The most dramatic results with target students occurred the first year, when the percentage doubled—and these twenty-three were hard-to-reach kids. This increase was less impressive in 1989–90, when we expanded the number of students receiving intensive support. After we had a second year of experience working with larger numbers, the post percentages were up to the two-thirds mark again.

There is no doubt that it is easier to motivate two or three students within a classroom; however, the three-year results suggest strongly that it can be done with larger numbers with more attempts and more reflection to find what works. This general pattern of much larger differences in 1988–89 and smaller differences the following two years is found on item after item. It is easier to make an impact on twenty-three case study students than on three hundred students in a target pool. It is also true that the responses in the fall with the target pool students were often not so negative as with the twenty-three case study students.

As expected, each year the pre percentages do not match the previous year's post percentages. The same students do not take the post one spring and then a pre the following fall. Further, the target students are not the same from year to year.

For these reasons, we are interested in comparing the post results for all three years to identify patterns. The pre and post comparisons for any one year are of interest to us teachers in the project. We love seeing at-risk students double their percentage from pre to post in one year, but the comparisons aren't too meaningful for drawing tentative conclusions that others might find useful.

We predicted that providing students with a large repertoire of prewriting strategies would give them confidence in beginning a piece of writing.

36. Getting started on a writing assignment is difficult for me. (disagree responses)

	1988–89		1989–90		1990–91	
	Pre	Post	Pre	Post	Pre	Post
23 targets	40%	44%				
200–300 targets			42%	44%	43%	40%
All students	40%	46%	43%	46%	46%	42%

The post percentages throughout the three years are nearly constant, suggesting that most students will never find it easy to begin writing. As we reflected on our own writing experiences, we realized that we too put off that initial keystroke or penstroke, hoping for the serendipitous coincidence of time and mood to motivate us, particularly with assignments. We wonder if similar percentages would result if this question were put to students who are not in a writing workshop classroom or even to professional writers. There's much more to this statement than prewriting strategies: consideration of audience, the intimidating desire to have a strong lead, the mystery of what will actually emerge. The results we have seen, with 40 percent of our students reporting that getting started is *not* difficult, may in fact be quite high.

A third statement in the confidence category revealed how the kids perceived their improvement. Their responses were not influenced by the results of the assessment. Although their scores were never a secret, the scoring was in June each year, after they had responded to the attitude survey. So the percentages on this item reflect their impressions, influenced perhaps by our ongoing comments and grades during the year but not by a final grade or formal evaluative conference.

29. I think my writing improved during the last school year. (agree responses)

	1988–89		1989–90		1990–91	
	Pre	Post	Pre	Post	Pre	Post
23 targets	72%	88%				
200–300 targets			59%	73%	63%	76%
All students	68%	77%	65%	76%	71%	77%

Fantastic! Three-fourths of our kids, whether at risk or not, believe they improved their writing. This is as it should be, right? Of course we'd prefer 90 percent, but is that realistic? Nine months is not a large span of time in which to make perceptible differences in writing skill . . . especially when some studies suggest early adolescents experience plateaus in their learning curve. One might think that the 25 percent who disagreed or didn't know were skilled writers who perceived less room for improvement. This isn't the case, however. Generally, the higher the writing ability (as rated by teachers), the higher the percentage of students who agreed that their writing improved over the year.

Racial Differences

Some of the joys of writing are clarifying what you really think, discovering feelings you didn't know you had, surprising yourself with a well-turned phrase, and unearthing a relationship between ideas. Self-satisfaction during the process is the immediate reward; communicating clearly to others is a delayed fulfillment.

We wondered how many of our students had experienced these surprises and found the results were most interesting when we looked at the responses by race.[3]

17. Sometimes when I write I am surprised by what I say. (agree responses)

	1988–89		1989–90		1990–91	
	Pre	Post	Pre	Post	Pre	Post
23 targets	48%	80%				
200–300 targets			54%	54%	54%	54%
All students	54%	63%	55%	59%	58%	57%

9. Writing is a very important way for me to express my feelings. (agree responses)

	1988–89		1989–90		1990–91	
	Pre	Post	Pre	Post	Pre	Post
23 targets	44%	80%				
200–300 targets			47%	48%	54%	52%
All students	52%	59%	52%	56%	58%	57%

The results are very consistent with the exception of the target students in 1988–89. All twenty-three target students that year were African American and we find much more agreement with this statement among Black students of all ability levels all three years:

17. Sometimes when I write I am surprised by what I say. (agree responses)

	1988–89		1989–90		1990–91	
	Pre	Post	Pre	Post	Pre	Post
Black	63%	74%	70%	69%	68%	67%
White	50%	58%	50%	56%	55%	54%

9. *Writing is a very important way for me to express my feelings.* (agree responses)

	1988–89		1989–90		1990–91	
	Pre	Post	Pre	Post	Pre	Post
Black	60%	71%	62%	65%	71%	65%
White	50%	54%	50%	54%	53%	55%

In both items, two-thirds of the African American students agree whereas a little over half of the White students agree. Is it cultural stereotyping to hypothesize that African American writers value the expression of feelings more than White writers? Might there be a cultural difference that encourages African American writers to be freer in their writing, to pour out ideas without first "canning" their thoughts? Do White students tend to want to "get their thoughts straight" before putting pen to paper, and are they therefore less likely to be surprised by what they write? Or are White writers less likely to "admit" they find surprises, somehow assuming that good writers don't get surprised?

We held a small-group discussion in May 1990 to discuss some of the results of the survey. The students were all current eighth graders from several teachers. Some were target students in seventh or eighth grade, but others were not. Both races and genders were represented and the students ran the gamut of writing abilities. All of these students agreed that they had been surprised by what they wrote. Clarence, a White male with strong writing skills, said surprises were frequent: "Things pop into your head as you're writing and you just put it down. Sometimes you can make something really good just with this really crazy idea."

Two students who had been targeted in seventh grade were able to recall specific instances. Sadie, an African American female, revealed, "I was mostly surprised I could write some poetry that didn't have to rhyme but it made sense." And Robert, whom you met in Chapter 3, told us of "One time I just wrote down this sentence that was like something an author would write and then I just started [thinking] 'Hey, maybe I do know how to write.'" Robert started a sentence with "He was walking" and then "I used lots of details and description." He recalled segments of the final sentence: "Something about the sun, a background shadow, a reflection . . . creeping . . . crushing of leaves." He concluded, "It was really good. It really freaked me out."

Amy, a White target student as an eighth grader, surprised herself when writing an essay on how victims of Down's Syndrome were treated. She learned a great deal about her own attitudes by writing the essay.

Kinds of Writing: Topics and Journals

The vast majority of our kids have confidence and enjoy writing. What kind of writing and what topics do they prefer? We assumed students enjoyed journal writing and would prefer to write about topics they choose rather than those they are given. Item 8 reinforced our assumptions: close to three-fourths of the students prefer topics they choose as opposed to ones a teacher assigns. We were surprised, however, by the mixed response to journal writing. Since "journal writing" has as many interpretations as teachers who assign it, a description of our journal methods is in order. None of us has been able to maintain a set schedule of making journal entries. At least half of us have attempted a schedule—every Monday and Wednesday, for example, kids will write for ten minutes. When we do these ten-minute writes (or quick-writes), we typically give a few ideas for topics but students don't have to use any of them. Occasionally we require a particular topic, usually one that sets the stage for a concept in a piece of literature coming up. Some of us require journal writing outside of class, but again that is hit and miss rather than a routine.

We respond to journal entries; we do not evaluate them. If grades are involved, they are based on writing a full ten minutes (for example), not on the content or the mechanics. Journal entries are often used as springboards for more developed pieces of writing; they are frequently students' personal thoughts and feelings. More recently, journals are quite often responses to literature. The survey results apply more to the first two types of content.

16. *I enjoyed doing journal writing (freewriting, ten-minute writes, etc).* (agree responses)

	1988–89		1989–90		1990–91	
	Pre	Post	Pre	Post	Pre	Post
23 targets	76%	68%				
200–300 targets			54%	50%	60%	46%
All students	54%	53%	55%	52%	63%	47%

Learning that there's only a fifty-fifty chance that any given student enjoys such writing prompted us to cut back on the amount of open-ended journal writing in 1990–91. Yet the responses for that year showed even fewer students enjoying them! We assume the problem is not the frequency, the routine, or the few assigned topics since the journal experience is not identical from teacher to teacher. Students who do not enjoy journal writing have told us they are "tired of it." They've "done" journals before. The students don't appreciate all the distinctions we make among the kinds of journal entries; they assert "a journal is a journal is a journal."

The literature abounds with the advantages of journal writing: increasing fluency, clarifying thinking, gaining insights to kids' personal lives, creating writing that is free from evaluation, producing writing that provides seeds for further writing. Perhaps a clearer explanation of purpose for each journal writing would help students see its value. In fact, we don't do as much generic journal writing anymore, but middle school teachers do more literature-based entries in reading/writing workshop where students respond on a personal basis to literature, make connections, and take their first steps toward literary criticism.

Revising and Proofreading

We wanted a handle on how the students perceived various aspects of writing process. Do students recognize the central role of revising for all writers? Do they see the need for revising their own work? Do they feel more competent with some revision strategies over others?

Almost two-thirds of the students realize that revision is necessary for good writers as well as inexperienced writers (item 11). And generally 70 percent or more say they "almost always write a rough draft and then a final draft on an important piece of writing" (item 33).

When they revise, what do they do? We asked the students whether they were able to revise by adding details, rewording, combining sentences, and adding introductions and endings (items 37–40). Our students certainly have confidence! Anywhere from 61 percent to 78 percent claimed the ability to use these revising techniques in the last year of the survey.

The kids are less sure of the sentence-combining technique than of adding details and rewording. In fact, there is a drop from 1989–90 to 1990–91 on that item. This undoubtedly reflects our deemphasis on the strategy. We found that sentence expansion is much more effective, particularly with low-skilled writers, because their short sentences typically aren't related to each other. Each needs to have details added to it that will lengthen the sentence and increase the specificity.

Adding introductions and endings also lags behind adding details and changing words. One may question why we didn't qualify the statement so that *effective* introductions and endings are used. We found from our analysis of assessment samples that younger students were totally ignoring these two items. Thus, we were interested in whether they would check to see if these two elements were included. In our process approach, we often encourage the kids to just begin writing and not get hung up on a "good" introduction. We've found effective introductions that fit the body and appeal to the specific audience are easier to write after the first draft is completed. Worrying about a sparkling lead can cause writer's block faster than anything else—and all too often that "perfect" lead doesn't fit the finished draft!

In our teaching we make a strong distinction between revising and proofreading. We think we emphasize revising—adding details, substituting word choices, rearranging sentence structure and sentence order, and so on. So we would hope that our students spend more time on revision, "getting it right" in terms of their purpose and audience, than on correcting errors. Thus, the preferred response on the next statement is *disagree*.

1. *When I write more than one draft, the changes I make are mostly in spelling and proofreading.* (agree responses)

	1988–89		1989–90		1990–91	
	Pre	Post	Pre	Post	Pre	Post
23 targets	56%	80%				
200–300 targets			73%	74%	78%	69%
All students	66%	66%	67%	67%	71%	63%

These results are disappointing to us. More than two-thirds of our students equate revising with correcting mechanics. Concern over this item has led teachers to stress substantive revision even more. We hope students will balance their revisions between substantive changes in organization, adding details, improving their introductions, clarifying their ideas, and the necessary changes in proofreading that are also important for communicating to a reader.

Why, with our deemphasis on proofreading, do the target students say this is the kind of change they are likely to make? There are a couple of possibilities. Perhaps the students say they make changes mostly in spelling and proofreading because that's where they think their biggest weaknesses are. In other words, they see themselves as addressing the "critical injury." And they've identified spelling and proofreading as the critical injury only because teachers have consistently pointed out the proofreading problems.

As Robert pointed out in a discussion of this item in May 1990, "You put it [a word] down on a piece of paper and when you go back over it yourself you still don't see anything wrong with it." He went on to explain that the other kinds of revisions he can handle, but the proofreading errors are harder to find on his own paper.

Perhaps they are most comfortable with that kind of change; it is the one "revision" they know to do and do regularly. The other revision techniques—adding an introduction, or playing with sentence structure—have not become second nature to them. The other revision techniques are not used on every single paper, varying according to the writing task. Proofreading is always a requirement.

But perhaps the students are simply more pragmatic than we are. When they add details in two places and correct five run-ons, they perceive that most of the changes were in proofreading. We see the new details, which may have added four sentences, as having a greater impact on improving the paper than the five periods.

Perhaps when students write more than one draft on their own, their changes really are just proofreading. They may still need the assistance—or the impetus—from a teacher to make other revisions, and this occurs only in classroom-sponsored writing. They may feel most comfortable in finding surface errors. In fact, around two-thirds of our students express confidence in their proofreading abilities (item 30).

The Role of the Computer

Revisions and corrections are so much easier to do with the help of the computer. We wondered if the kids would agree, or if they would like the computer because of the neatness it provides? Do they prefer writing rough drafts by hand or on the computer? And finally, how many of them think their typing speed inhibits using the computer?

For two years, over 70 percent of the students on the spring survey appreciated the ease of revision as well as the neatness of the final product that the computer afforded (items 19–20). In the third year, the percentage remained high but dipped into the 60s. Is it possible that the kids who have had growing access to computers for most of their school careers are less impressed with its advantages? In other words, is this the beginning of a trend wherein computers will be viewed much as we view pencils now? Will students in the near future view these survey items much as we would view items such as "The main advantage of the pencil is the erasing it provides," or "The main advantage of the pen is the neatness it provides"? Since every major piece of writing uses the computer, perhaps the students don't fully appreciate the ease of revision. They seldom have to complete a final draft by hand and so have little basis for comparing the tools.

When we asked their preference for first-drafts tools, the results are erratic, but in general two-thirds of the students prefer writing the first draft by hand (item 31). This high percentage of students choosing to write the first draft manually reflects our routine at the time of the attitude survey before reading/writing workshop. There simply are not enough computers available for all our students to use them every time they write; having a written draft before going to the writing center saves computer time. Further, we know—and students recognize this, too, which may be influencing their responses—that the typing skill of kids in grades seven through nine is limited.

In fact, roughly half the students recognize that their slow typing cannot keep up with the speed of their thoughts, which makes composing at the keyboard a disadvantage for first drafts. As we would expect, the ninth graders are less likely to agree with this item. In 1990–91, only 35 percent of the ninth graders agreed, undoubtedly a reflection of their experience and keyboarding classes over the years. This percentage doesn't affect the totals as much as one might expect, because of the almost 700 responses to the survey that year, only between 120 and 126 were ninth graders.

Peer Response

24. *I learned most about improving my writing by sharing my writing with other students and reading theirs.* (agree responses)

	1988–89		1989-90		1990-91	
	Pre	Post	Pre	Post	Pre	Post
23 targets	44%	80%				
200–300 targets			42%	46%	44%	50%
All students	38%	49%	39%	41%	46%	43%

An interesting racial distinction showed on this item. Between one-half and two-thirds of the African American students agree, but only 40 percent or so of the White students report such agreement. These percentages and differences have been consistent for all three years. This difference might reflect the awareness of African American kids that they are, on the average, weaker writers.

If approximately one-half of the students (more than half of the African Americans and less than half of the Whites) think they learn from peer response, how helpful do they see themselves in giving peer response?

13. I can give helpful responses to other persons' writing. (agree responses)

| | 1988–89 | | 1989–90 | | 1990–91 | |
	Pre	Post	Pre	Post	Pre	Post
23 targets	32%	52%				
200–300 targets			48%	50%	50%	52%
All students	47%	61%	53%	58%	57%	58%

The post survey percentages are rather consistent for target students and all students and there is not a racial distinction. Just over one-half of the students think they contribute to others' writings. It is interesting that a few more students think they can give helpful feedback than think they learn from receiving such feedback.

Teacher Response

It's easy to assume that we grasp students' perceptions. When writing comments on a student's draft or responding spontaneously during a conversation, we have clear goals: to be specific in our feedback, whether positive or negative; to point the way for improvement rather than simply identifying the problem; to limit the suggestions and emphasize what is working; to maintain the author's ownership of the draft; to respond to the thinking and logic of the draft and help students clarify their thinking; and to motivate rather than judge. We also know these goals are difficult, particularly when reacting on the spot as we roam the room or when facing over a hundred drafts that need to be returned quickly.

We wondered first if students preferred written comments or oral feedback on their drafts (item 12). We wouldn't consider eliminating one or the other but thought we might learn something. Just over one-half of the students prefer talking over the draft; about one-third disagreed with the statement and preferred to get written comments. The rest of the students didn't know their preference—or, perhaps more accurately, didn't have a preference. These results aren't too surprising. The student plays a role only in the conversation, not in one-way written comments.

We included five more items on the survey, four with the stem "I learned most about improving my writing," to find out how students perceived our efforts.

25. *I learned most about improving my writing from what my teacher wrote on my drafts.* (agree responses)

	1988–89		1989–90		1990–91	
	Pre	Post	Pre	Post	Pre	Post
23 targets	44%	96%				
200–300 targets			41%	55%	49%	56%
All students	38%	50%	40%	48%	43%	49%

26. *I learned most about improving my writing during conversations with my English teacher.* (agree responses)

	1988–89		1989–90		1990–91	
	Pre	Post	Pre	Post	Pre	Post
23 targets	44%	72%				
200–300 targets			36%	45%	45%	52%
All students	42%	44%	36%	42%	46%	52%

We had hoped for a more clear-cut preference among students between conferences and written responses. We did not find it: not by race, gender, grade level, or writing ability. The other two methods completing the same stem were "writing and rewriting" and "sharing my writing with my peers." We had hoped the students would discriminate among the four methods, but we should have asked them to rank the four choices. Instead no item received a very strong agreement or disagreement and we didn't get much direction. The fifth survey item aimed at discovering how students perceived our efforts had a clear-cut response, but that response was less than we had hoped for.

14. *My English teacher almost always lets me know the strengths of my writing.*
   (agree responses)

	1988–89		1989–90		1990–91	
	Pre	Post	Pre	Post	Pre	Post
23 targets	44%	76%				
200–300 targets			38%	52%	46%	55%
All students	44%	50%	43%	53%	51%	56%

Even though the post percentages are increasing slightly (with the exception of three-fourths of those twenty-three case study students in 1988–89 who changed to a 76 percent agreement in just one year), we were disappointed that just over one-half of the students believe this occurs (and even more disturbed by the racial differences, which are discussed below). Perhaps it will be difficult to do better on this item. Negatives seem to make a stronger impact in human memory than positives. Further, we probably focus more on the strengths in the initial draft and don't repeat them in successive drafts.

It is good to see that the target students have very similar percentages on the post surveys the last two years even though they began each year much lower than all the students. But the 1988–89 results with the target students suggest that higher percentages are possible when the focus is on a very small number of students. There is an obvious logic to that. It's easier to double-check for positive written responses for two or three students than to all students. Yet if the response pattern becomes ingrained in us, we should find more student agreement with statements like this one.

The last item in this category was intended to find out how well we encourage students to maintain their "author-ity" over their own drafts (item 7). We do not want students to turn their writing over to us for revision, to give up authority over their own writing. We do not practice rewriting students' papers, crossing out their phrasing and substituting ours, or inserting new detail-filled sentences. Instead, we ask questions—even when reading a syntactically garbled sentence that we could easily "fix" ourselves. We may ask the student to read it aloud or read it aloud ourselves. Then we ask them, "Does that sound all right to you?" If the student says yes, and we are facing a situation not involving grammatically incorrect usage but definitely more than a matter of personal style, we will ask other students to read and respond to its flow. The student, to remain in control and to improve skill, must perceive a problem.

Of course, we recognize that inexperienced writers often have limited control of language and may at times have an intuitive sense that "something is wrong"; they may ask for our help in rephrasing such a sentence. Certainly at that time we will suggest one or, more likely, two options and encourage the student to come up with others and to select a solution that best fits the situation. This is very different from taking over a piece of writing and having the student revise by copying our "suggestions." For us, the second half of this item was the emphasis, and we did *not* want high percentages.

7. *I try to follow my teachers' suggestions even when I don't understand or agree with them.* (agree responses)

	1988–89		1989-90		1990-91	
	Pre	Post	Pre	Post	Pre	Post
23 targets	64%	80%				
200–300 targets			69%	68%	67%	64%
All students	65%	62%	65%	63%	68%	64%

Less-skilled writers have more reason to agree with this statement; our suggestions on their writings are likely to be pretty basic and necessary and we may in fact be more insistent in subtle ways when working with them. The surprise on this item was that the students rated by the teachers as having the weakest writing ability were the least likely to agree. What does this mean? Our weakest writers were the most independent in thought? We would hope all our students think independently. More likely the weakest writers simply didn't follow our suggestions—whether they understood them or not! The students rated strongest in writing ability were also less likely to agree with this statement, yet the survey found that over one-half of them agreed. Most puzzling of all, our African American students were much more likely to agree with this statement.

Racial Differences

7. *I try to follow my teachers' suggestions even when I don't understand or agree with them.* (agree responses)

	1988–89		1989–90		1990–91	
	Pre	Post	Pre	Post	Pre	Post
Black	68%	76%	74%	70%	78%	76%
White	63%	56%	62%	60%	65%	60%

Is there a cultural explanation for the higher percentages of African Americans that accept teacher suggestions they don't agree with? The literature suggests strongly that the teacher plays a different role in the lives of minority students than in the lives of middle-class majority students. Irvine (1988) reports on Coleman's 1966 research that found "Minority students are more teacher-dependent and more likely than middle-class students to hold teachers in high esteem" (507). Irvine also reviewed studies on Black students' academic self-concept and concluded that teachers are "significant others" to minority students and, further, that minority students' self-concepts are to a large extent determined by how they perceive that their teachers view them. This dependence on the "mirror image" as reflected in their teachers' eyes may well make minority students more susceptible to teacher suggestions.

The students themselves shed some light on this item in the small-group discussion with eighth graders from various teachers' classes held in May 1990. You will recall the students included both races and genders and ran the gamut of writing abilities. Some had been and/or were target students; other students had never been targeted. Amy was motivated to follow the teacher's suggestions primarily by the teacher's power to grade the final draft. "Most of them were really good comments. I would try to write them down so I would make my story better so I would get a better grade."

Sadie, who also followed the teacher suggestions she didn't understand or agree with, trusted the teacher's superior knowledge.

> [My teacher] used to tell us over and over how she wanted us to really show distinction in our writing and so I just . . . well, mostly she would put on our papers what *she* thought and what we should put in there. Sometimes I would just think it didn't have anything to do with it, the story, but I would go ahead and put it in since she suggested it.

Asked why she would go ahead, Sadie said, "So the paper could seem more to her approval than mine." Pushed for why the teacher's approval was more important than her own approval, she said, "She was the one who made the suggestions and she was the one who would give me the grade. I would impress her more by putting what she liked in it." Even though she had heard Amy's comment on grades, Sadie seemed more concerned with the teacher's approval than with the grade.

Robert also wanted the teacher's approval and trusted in the teacher's superior knowledge: "I wanted my writing to be better than before. I wanted my teacher to think I could write good—like, well, 'Maybe he is good.' Something like that."

Amy pointed out that the students would often be worn down by the same suggestions occurring on successive drafts: "If you don't put it in, she would keep putting it down in there and you get tired." Sadie agreed. "[My teacher] would just keep on writing the same comment over and over."

All eight students—Black and White, male and female, at all levels of writing skill—thought the preferred response was "agree" even though they readily responded to the question, "Whose paper is it?" with "The student's."

Students with stronger writing skills maintained more confidence in their own revisions and expressed more ownership of their writings—to the extent of giving what they thought was the nonpreferred response. Annette, an African American student whose teacher rated her writing as a four with five as the highest rating, disagreed with the statement with the simple explanation that "I didn't think she was right." When asked if she worried about the grade, Annette shrugged her shoulders. It would seem that the lower-skilled students perceived their weaknesses and relied on the teacher's experience and knowledge—even though we verbalize with students that the writer is the final decisionmaker on their work. The higher-skilled writers had more confidence in their writing and maintained their authority.

The survey results on this item still distress us. We do not want our students to be dependent on us. We continue our efforts to make suggestions while preserving the integrity of a writer's ownership. We continue to respond with questions rather than suggestions, to pull out the writer's evaluation of the paper's strengths and weaknesses before responding on the basis of our own assessment. We continue to stress with students that the author is the ultimate authority.

Another item produced obvious racial differences (item 14). Above we state that just over one-half the students, targeted or not, agreed with item 14. It is interesting to see that African American students were more likely to agree than White students.

412

14. *My English teacher almost always lets me know the strengths of my writing.*
(agree responses)

| | 1988–89 | | 1989–90 | | 1990–91 | |
	Pre	Post	Pre	Post	Pre	Post
Black	52%	68%	45%	57%	54%	67%
White	40%	42%	43%	51%	50%	53%

Have we made stronger efforts for African American students since the project focused solely on minority writers the first two years and maintained an emphasis on Black males the last two years? Are we guilty of subconscious racism by assuming that minority students need more encouragement? or that White students achieve more and don't need their strengths identified as much? Is there a cultural difference influencing the students' perceptions—do positive strokes from White teachers impact African American students more than White students? One step we could take is to examine a sample of our students' papers and compare the number of times strengths are identified in White students' papers and African American students' papers. This procedure is not as simple as it sounds, but it may be worthwhile.

Time Spent on Writing

Since we stress writing so much in our classrooms, we wondered if integrating writing with the study of literature and our language could be perceived by students as an overload. We included two items to find out what the students thought.

34. *I think we did too much writing this year.* (agree responses)

| | 1988–89 | | 1989–90 | | 1990–91 | |
	Pre	Post	Pre	Post	Pre	Post
23 targets	40%	28%				
200–300 targets			38%	33%	33%	29%
All students	36%	28%	30%	23%	26%	26%

5. *We need to spend more time on writing.* (agree responses)

	1988–89		1989–90		1990–91	
	Pre	Post	Pre	Post	Pre	Post
23 targets	36%	36%				
200–300 targets			37%	29%	31%	34%
All students	32%	36%	33%	34%	33%	35%

The juxtaposition of these two items is encouraging: typically one-third of the students see a need for more writing time and only one-fourth think we do too much writing. The results for 1989–90 (our first year with expanded target students) create a slight dip in the pattern, but we hypothesize there will always be some students who think any writing is "too much" and that for one-third to perceive a need for more is surprising when hardly a day goes by without writing in the classroom, when writing is the core of the English curriculum, and when writing folders are bulging at the end of the year. Is it possible that our kids realize that there is always a need for more writing—more revising, more practice with different modes, and more experience with different audiences? We think this is very sophisticated thinking for twelve- to fifteen-year-olds. Would students who write six papers a year and nothing else respond in higher percentages? Somehow we doubt it. The less writing one does, the less one sees the value of doing more.

Conclusion

We think the survey has been given enough years and to enough students to be informative to others. When we reflect, we see how much is lacking, but we keep feeding the results into our syntheses and study sessions. The students' voices have influenced what went on in the classroom. We have stopped the survey but not our interest in knowing how the students think. We are up-front about our efforts and occasionally have class discussions on how kids perceived an activity. We encourage journal entries on what's happening in the classroom. Portfolio reflections give voice to students' views of their written pieces and their processes.

We are now investigating the role that individual learning styles play in writing processes. We have become less focused on groups—Black and White, male and female, targeted and all students—and more interested in ways of identifying how each student learns best.

LOOKING IN THE MIRROR: THE RESEARCH TEAM CHANGES ATTITUDES

Our own attitudes have changed dramatically, too. In the beginning we identified the students' writing as the problem. How could we fix it? We looked closely at our methods. How could we modify them to help the students improve their writing? Only after two years (or more) did our attitudes focus on our teaching behaviors. We no longer believe that fixing the writing is our goal; improved writing is a result of deeper changes. We no longer believe that teaching methods—specific lessons—make *all* the difference.

Our interaction with, our concern for, and our immersion with our students as *persons* are the key. We individualize *and personalize*. Our definitions of the project's goals and of ourselves have changed. We began as teachers who wanted to learn how to help our students write better. Now we want to learn what our students have to teach us. We are still teachers of writing, but first we are teachers of students.

WHAT YOU CAN DO

Ask your students for their reactions to class activities, methods, and assignments. They can write and/or discuss their opinions.

Ask students to reflect on their own writing processes, habits, and strengths as a way of informing you about "what works" for each individual.

Try a minisurvey with your students. Scantron machines can save tabulating time. Students could enter their answers in a database that could manipulate the results in various ways.

Give assignment-specific items such as, "This paper was easy to get started," or "My biggest problem in revising this narrative was adding details that 'show, don't tell.' "

ATTITUDE SURVEY RESULTS
1988 Through 1991

1. *When I write more than one draft, the changes I make are mostly in spelling and proofreading.* (agree responses)

	1988–89		1989–90		1990–91	
	Pre	Post	Pre	Post	Pre	Post
23 targets	56%	80%				
200–300 targets			73%	74%	78%	69%
All students	66%	66%	67%	67%	71%	63%

2. *I like to write better now than at the beginning of last/this year.* (agree responses)

	1988–89		1989–90		1990–91	
	Pre	Post	Pre	Post	Pre	Post
23 targets	36%	96%				
200–300 targets			40%	53%	44%	62%
All students	44%	61%	45%	55%	48%	62%

3. *I think I write better than my English teacher thinks.* (disagree responses)

	1988–89		1989–90		1990–91	
	Pre	Post	Pre	Post	Pre	Post
23 targets	24%	32%				
200–300 targets			32%	35%	31%	35%
All students	38%	38%	40%	42%	36%	39%

4. *The biggest problem in using computers is that I don't type fast enough.* (agree responses)

	1988–89		1989–90		1990–91	
	Pre	Post	Pre	Post	Pre	Post
23 targets	56%	52%				
200–300 targets			56%	48%	54%	54%
All students	46%	50%	52%	48%	48%	47%

5. *We need to spend more time on writing.* (agree responses)

	1988–89		1989–90		1990–91	
	Pre	Post	Pre	Post	Pre	Post
23 targets	36%	36%				
200–300 targets			37%	29%	31%	34%
All Students	32%	36%	33%	34%	33%	35%

6. *I have a lot of confidence when it comes to writing.* (agree responses)

	1988–89		1989–90		1990–91	
	Pre	Post	Pre	Post	Pre	Post
23 targets	56%	72%				
200–300 targets			51%	50%	51%	51%
All students	56%	58%	56%	58%	57%	56%

7. *I try to follow my teachers' suggestions even when I don't understand or agree with them.* (agree responses)

	1988–89		1989–90		1990–91	
	Pre	Post	Pre	Post	Pre	Post
23 targets	64%	80%				
200–300 targets			69%	68%	67%	64%
All students	65%	62%	65%	63%	68%	64%

8. *I prefer topics I choose myself as opposed to ones the teacher gives.* (agree responses)

	1988–89		1989–90		1990–91	
	Pre	Post	Pre	Post	Pre	Post
23 targets	64%	60%				
200–300 targets			75%	72%	63%	69%
All students	74%	73%	72%	70%	66%	71%

9. *Writing is a very important way for me to express my feelings.* (agree responses)

	1988–89		1989–90		1990–91	
	Pre	Post	Pre	Post	Pre	Post
23 targets	44%	80%				
200–300 targets			47%	48%	54%	52%
All students	52%	59%	52%	56%	58%	57%

10. *I write better than I speak.* (agree responses)

	1988–89		1989–90		1990–91	
	Pre	Post	Pre	Post	Pre	Post
23 targets	24%	44%				
200–300 targets			19%	28%	32%	34%
All students	28%	34%	28%	34%	31%	35%

11. *Good writers are seldom satisfied with their first draft.* (agree responses)

	1988–89		1989–90		1990–91	
	Pre	Post	Pre	Post	Pre	Post
23 targets	48%	64%				
200–300 targets			55%	58%	54%	54%
All students	55%	66%	61%	65%	61%	64%

12. *I'd rather talk over my draft with my teacher instead of getting written suggestions from her.* (agree responses)

	1988–89		1989–90		1990–91	
	Pre	Post	Pre	Post	Pre	Post
23 targets	52%	52%				
200–300 targets			56%	55%	59%	58%
All students	55%	50%	58%	56%	61%	58%

13. *I can give helpful responses to other persons' writing.* (agree responses)

	1988–89		1989–90		1990–91	
	Pre	Post	Pre	Post	Pre	Post
23 targets	32%	52%				
200–300 targets			48%	50%	50%	52%
All students	47%	61%	53%	58%	57%	58%

14. *My English teacher almost always lets me know the strengths of my writing.* (agree responses)

	1988–89		1989–90		1990–91	
	Pre	Post	Pre	Post	Pre	Post
23 targets	44%	76%				
200–300 targets			38%	52%	46%	55%
All students	44%	50%	43%	53%	51%	56%

15. *My English teacher almost always gives me specific ways of improving my paper instead of marking what is wrong with it.* (agree responses)

	1988–89		1989–90		1990–91	
	Pre	Post	Pre	Post	Pre	Post
23 targets	64%	80%				
200–300 targets			49%	68%	64%	71%
All students	61%	67%	52%	70%	63%	71%

16. *I enjoyed doing journal writing (freewriting, ten-minute writes, etc.).* (agree responses)

	1988–89		1989–90		1990–91	
	Pre	Post	Pre	Post	Pre	Post
23 targets	76%	68%				
200–300 targets			54%	50%	60%	46%
All students	54%	53%	55%	52%	63%	47%

17. *Sometimes when I write I am surprised by what I say.* (agree responses)

| | 1988–89 | | 1989–90 | | 1990–91 | |
	Pre	Post	Pre	Post	Pre	Post
23 targets	48%	80%				
200–300 targets			54%	54%	54%	54%
All students	54%	63%	55%	59%	58%	57%

18. *I have written and revised writing that was not required this year.* (agree responses)

| | 1988–89 | | 1989–90 | | 1990–91 | |
	Pre	Post	Pre	Post	Pre	Post
23 targets	12%	44%				
200–300 targets			28%	35%	35%	38%
All students	34%	43%	34%	44%	40%	46%

19. *The main advantage of the computer is the neatness it provides.* (agree responses)

| | 1988–89 | | 1989–90 | | 1990–91 | |
	Pre	Post	Pre	Post	Pre	Post
23 targets	60%	76%				
200–300 targets			80%	76%	72%	70%
All students	69%	74%	71%	73%	73%	68%

20. *The main advantage of the computer is the time it saves in revising a piece of writing.* (agree responses)

| | 1988–89 | | 1989–90 | | 1990–91 | |
	Pre	Post	Pre	Post	Pre	Post
23 targets	60%	72%				
200–300 targets			72%	70%	62%	64%
All students	70%	73%	72%	71%	67%	66%

21. *My English teacher pays more attention to my mistakes in spelling and proofreading than to my ideas.* (disagree responses)

| | 1988–89 | | 1989–90 | | 1990–91 | |
	Pre	Post	Pre	Post	Pre	Post
23 targets	44%	44%				
200–300 targets			44%	52%	52%	59%
All students	37%	45%	44%	59%	54%	62%

22. *I did some writing this year that was not required or assigned.* (agree responses)

	1988–89		1989–90		1990–91	
	Pre	Post	Pre	Post	Pre	Post
23 targets	36%	56%				
200–300 targets			43%	44%	50%	46%
All students	47%	49%	50%	55%	55%	53%

23. *I think the grades I received on my writing were fair.* (agree responses)

	1988–89		1989–90		1990–91	
	Pre	Post	Pre	Post	Pre	Post
23 targets	56%	76%				
200–300 targets			55%	67%	60%	64%
All students	61%	68%	64%	72%	68%	70%

24. *I learned most about improving my writing by sharing my writing with other students and reading theirs.* (agree responses)

	1988–89		1989–90		1990–91	
	Pre	Post	Pre	Post	Pre	Post
23 targets	44%	80%				
200–300 targets			42%	46%	44%	50%
All students	38%	49%	39%	41%	46%	43%

25. *I learned most about improving my writing from what my teacher wrote on my drafts.* (agree responses)

	1988–89		1989–90		1990–91	
	Pre	Post	Pre	Post	Pre	Post
23 targets	44%	96%				
200–300 targets			41%	55%	49%	56%
All students	38%	50%	40%	48%	43%	49%

26. *I learned most about improving my writing during conversations with my English teacher.* (agree responses)

	1988–89		1989–90		1990–91	
	Pre	Post	Pre	Post	Pre	Post
23 targets	44%	72%				
200–300 targets			36%	45%	45%	52%
All students	42%	44%	36%	42%	46%	52%

27. *I learned most about improving my writing just by writing and rewriting.* (agree responses)

	1988–89		1989–90		1990–91	
	Pre	Post	Pre	Post	Pre	Post
23 targets	52%	68%				
200–300 targets			56%	58%	55%	48%
All students	56%	63%	56%	58%	55%	52%

28. *I like to write.* (agree responses)

	1988–89		1989–90		1990–91	
	Pre	Post	Pre	Post	Pre	Post
23 targets	32%	68%				
200–300 targets			51%	58%	63%	66%
All students	64%	68%	64%	67%	70%	73%

29. *I think my writing improved during the last school year.* (agree responses)

	1988–89		1989–90		1990–91	
	Pre	Post	Pre	Post	Pre	Post
23 targets	72%	88%				
200–300 targets			59%	73%	63%	76%
All students	68%	77%	65%	76%	71%	77%

30. *I am able to proofread.* (agree responses)

	1988–89		1989–90		1990–91	
	Pre	Post	Pre	Post	Pre	Post
23 targets	48%	56%				
200–300 targets			61%	67%	63%	61%
All students	62%	67%	65%	68%	66%	67%

31. *I prefer writing my first draft by hand rather than on the computer.* (agree responses)

	1988–89		1989–90		1990–91	
	Pre	Post	Pre	Post	Pre	Post
23 targets	40%	76%				
200–300 targets			55%	60%	65%	66%
All students	59%	66%	60%	60%	68%	63%

32. *What I learned in writing in English has helped me in writing for other classes.* (agree responses)

	1988–89		1989–90		1990–91	
	Pre	Post	Pre	Post	Pre	Post
23 targets	52%	76%				
200–300 targets			51%	64%	58%	64%
All students	50%	60%	53%	62%	61%	60%

33. *I almost always write a rough draft and then a final draft on an important piece of writing.* (agree responses)

	1988–89		1989–90		1990–91	
	Pre	Post	Pre	Post	Pre	Post
23 targets	52%	72%				
200–300 targets			62%	67%	69%	70%
All students	65%	77%	67%	73%	75%	73%

34. *I think we did too much writing this year.* (agree responses)

	1988–89		1989–90		1990–91	
	Pre	Post	Pre	Post	Pre	Post
23 targets	40%	28%				
200–300 targets			38%	33%	33%	29%
All students	36%	28%	30%	23%	26%	26%

35. Writing well is an important skill in our society. (agree responses)

	1988-89		1989-90		1990-91	
	Pre	Post	Pre	Post	Pre	Post
23 targets	68%	84%				
200–300 targets			63%	69%	68%	72%
All students	72%	80%	73%	78%	74%	78%

36. Getting started on a writing assignment is difficult for me. (disagree responses)

	1988-89		1989-90		1990-91	
	Pre	Post	Pre	Post	Pre	Post
23 targets	40%	44%				
200–300 targets			42%	44%	43%	40%
All students	40%	46%	43%	46%	46%	42%

37. I am able to revise a piece of writing so it has more details. (agree responses)

	1988-89		1989-90		1990-91	
	Pre	Post	Pre	Post	Pre	Post
23 targets	52%	76%				
200–300 targets			63%	71%	64%	69%
All students	68%	78%	73%	78%	73%	78%

38. I am able to revise a piece of my writing by making sure it has an introduction and an ending. (agree responses)

	1988-89		1989-90		1990-91	
	Pre	Post	Pre	Post	Pre	Post
23 targets	60%	92%				
200–300 targets			59%	65%	61%	66%
All students	61%	67%	63%	68%	65%	70%

39. *I am able to revise a piece of my writing by changing some words to more specific words.* (agree responses)

	1988–89		1989–90		1990–91	
	Pre	Post	Pre	Post	Pre	Post
23 targets	52%	76%				
200–300 targets			64%	71%	71%	70%
All students	72%	77%	74%	80%	74%	76%

40. *I am able to revise a piece of my writing by combining and/or rephrasing sentences.* (agree response)

	1988–89		1989–90		1990–91	
	Pre	Post	Pre	Post	Pre	Post
23 targets	44%	56%				
200–300 targets			61%	68%	56%	61%
All students	65%	72%	66%	73%	64%	68%

NOTES

1. We considered eliminating these after the second year but wanted the survey to be consistent.

2. For any item discussed, we show the same data. When there were interesting racial, gender, grade-level, or writing ability differences, we mention them as well—but do not routinely present that data.

3. Our racial data do not distinguish target students and nontarget students. In other words, the percentages by race in 1988–89 are for all students regardless of their role in the project. Here are the specific numbers of students:

	1988–89		1989–90		1990–91	
	Pre	Post	Pre	Post	Pre	Post
Black	130	133	146	150	166	158
White	311	322	471	475	515	531

Future Changes —
for Us and the Reader

Of teacher change, building bridges, and "sometimes going in the dark
where there ain't been no light"

MINNIE PHILLIPS

Hundreds of utility-hole covers erupt from the inner earth below as an overanxious little man runs in circles, feverishly trying to hammer the lids back level to the ground's surface. This is his quick fix. Soon, however, a new batch of eruptions spew forth, coming faster and in greater numbers. Our problem solver is compelled to run even faster and more furiously to stamp out the problems.

Our thought processes at the inception of the Webster Groves Writing Project were similar to those of this animated man in the video *Of Holes and Corks.* We began with the idea that we would fix the problems—with the students and with the teaching methods. Like the little man in *Of Holes and Corks,* we had to move out of our comfort zone, away from the solutions that we knew, stretching ourselves to brand-new, out-of-the-ordinary solutions. We did that through self-study, kid watching, and reflection.

That is when informed educational reform occurred. But we could make no headway solving our problems until we looked carefully at ourselves, studied what we saw, changed the vision, and realized a new solution—one out of the realm of what we already knew. Our collaborative growth and development became the permanent, ongoing solution to our dilemma.

But in spite of our growth, we still faced obstacles. Finding money to support the project had been a problem every year, requiring a continuous search for grant monies. At the end of the sixth year, the last grant supporting the project was about to expire—and the district was unable to provide funds for our study sessions and synthesis week as they had in earlier years when grant funding dried up.

On the first day of summer synthesis, all we could focus on was the future of the project. Naturally, the question arose, "Are we going to continue next year—unpaid?" Four new teachers were employed by the district, all hoping and expecting to be part of the Webster Groves Writing Project. But was the extra work of action research worth it? Jane recorded our sobering discussion:

> "Who would be hurt if we quit?"
>
> "If we stop, it will mainly hurt the new members who need support. *We'll* still teach the same way—the old project teachers will still use the strategies."
>
> "We would have to get together sometimes."
>
> "Yeah, we'd miss the across-building dialogue."
>
> "I'll probably still take field notes."
>
> "Maybe we could just give the two hours a month—keep doing the study sessions and skip the synthesis writing."
>
> "And skip all the presenting and disseminating to other districts, but we'd still meet."
>
> "You know, guys, we have to keep going."
>
> I [Jane] was very moved by this discussion. The fate of the whole project seemed to hang in the balance. But what emerged was that so much of the project had been internalized—not just principles, workshop, and portfolio, but the process of collaborative research and support—that

427

it would be unthinkable to walk away . . . I am proud to be associated with this team.

After much debate, we all realized that the work we were doing, the reform in our teaching, and the improvement in writing of our students was not for the district as much as it was for our professional integrity, interest, and personal growth. The real power of the action research was an inner power, what it did for us as teachers.

WHERE DO WE GO FROM HERE?

As is the nature of this beast called action research, when one question is resolved, it seems two more come forward. Each member of the project has found a subject to research—perhaps a little personal niche—in the form of an area of expertise like multicultural and multiethnic literature, reading/writing workshop, literature study sets, technology, interdisciplinary classes, and of course more study in action research.

The team reflects on new questions as they evolve. Can a group become too large for honest, forthright sharing and collaboration? How can we influence our more traditional colleagues to consider our approach to teaching? Can our model translate successfully to other disciplines? How do we use portfolios most effectively, respond to them, and study them and still have time to do anything else? And how do we continue to nurture and instruct our new teachers?

The Webster Groves Writing Project has already served as a successful model for two other school districts. Just last year, fifteen of our district teachers from kindergarten to sixth grade began their own action research in writing. The district, recognizing the power of the project, is eager to adapt its principles and action research methods to a new subject area: mathematics spanning kindergarten to ninth grade, beginning in the fall of 1994.

One of the seven elementary schools in the district has distressingly low achievement in mathematics. This school houses a larger percentage of African American students than any other school. Further, African American students represent only 10 percent of the advanced math classes at the high school, whereas they represent 20 percent of the advanced English classes. We believe the success of the Webster Groves Writing Project has contributed to the number of African American students enrolling in the more challenging English courses.

This new action research team will begin with the burning question, How do we improve achievement in mathematics of all students, but in particular our African American students? Writing project members will assist these mathematics teachers as they adapt our principles and strategies to their subject area.

WHAT YOU CAN DO TO START YOUR OWN ACTION RESEARCH

In many ways we've had the ideal team situation—a critical mass in two schools of teachers with the same question who wanted to investigate the same issues. We have had close support from the University of Missouri, St. Louis. Our own board of education and central office, from the three superintendents we have spanned to assistant superintendents to secretaries and on and on have supported us throughout these six years. Three principals at the middle school and two at the high school have, as middle school principal Don Morrison once put it, "moved out of the way and let us roll."

But what if you are isolated, with no administrative support or even other teachers who share your same burning question? What if you have no affiliation with or access to a university? We would like to leave the reader with suggestions for even the worst of situations.

Begin by learning how to organize and conduct action research, how to journal, and how to keep field notes. This book serves as a start. You can back up what you learn by reading some of the action research books mentioned in our bibliography. All of these books have aided us in our work.

Determine your "burning question." You will probably have hundreds of ideas from classroom management to student responses. Look for the umbrella that covers a multitude of smaller questions.

Identify the kids who need you most. You are one person in one classroom with a group of kids, and you are the professional. It is likely that you can instinctively spot the child who is at risk of being lost in today's educational system. You may know from prior history that a current student of yours was once considered lost by a previous teacher.

Vow that no child will get lost in your classroom, even if she tries her hardest to do so.

Next, kid-watch. Record what you see, feel, and learn about the child. Look for patterns, responses, changes, and motivators. Talk with your kids. But most of all, listen to what they say (see Chapter 2 for guidelines and examples of field-note material).

Journal as much as possible, even if at the time it is happening you can't figure out why it would ever become important to remember. Some things won't be important; yet many of the seemingly trivial events become meaningful when put into the whole picture of the child. If you can tape conferences with your target student, do it. If you learn something from a previous teacher, a friend, or a relative of the student, journal it and don't hestitate to pursue the answers to questions that might pop up.

If the child's cultural heritage is not your own, learn as much as you can about it. Read and talk to colleagues, friends, or neighbors who may share that heritage. Stretch your own cultural boundaries.

Network with other teachers if you can—either someone in your building or from another district, perhaps through telecommunications. Or contact one of us in the Webster Groves Writing Project. If you can't find another teacher, look for a friend, a student teacher, even a spouse. Often a person who does not know your target student can give insight to your reflections because she is not involved with the student.

Get proper, in-depth training in writing process. Contact your nearest National Writing Project site. There are over 150 affiliates nationwide, headquartered at the University of California, Berkeley. Most of these sites already have teachers involved in action research.

Explore the whole language philosophy. Teachers Applying Whole Language (TAWL) groups exist nationwide, and these groups support literacy learning. Contact your nearest site for information. Attend conferences sponsored by local TAWL groups and the Whole Language Umbrella.

Begin using literature sets and building your classroom library, reading the books yourself first. Appendix One tells more about how to use the sets and lists some helpful references.

Seek training in cooperative learning. Many staff development programs offer such training; we found the Johnson and Johnson inservice most helpful to us (see Chapter 7).

And, above all else, nurture the teacher-student relationship so you can open the doors of communication with all your students, especially your target students.

Even if you're just one person in a less-than-ideal setting, you have the power to reach the kids we all have been losing in the past. We were reminded of our potency as caring teachers at a study session one day when Minnie gave us a copy of some of her recent thoughts.

Of Teacher Change, Building Bridges and "Sometimes Going in the Dark Where There Ain't Been No Light" (Langston Hughes, "Mother to Son")

Remember how in childhood we sealed friendships by walking our best friends piece-a-way home? We'd stroll leisurely along, giggling, playing tag, or just walking in silence and thinking in unison until we reached the dreaded halfway point. We gauged good-byes by the sunset, lingering until the final seconds when we knew we'd have to part to reach our home by dark. The walk back became a solitary journey, filled with memories and longings and wonderings about what lurked out there in the near dark, and who'd get home first, and whether we'd both get home safely. That's how I feel now about my English 10 class—as if I walked them piece-a-way home.

That's how we feel about our students, our mirror images—at least we've made it piece-a-way home.

Sample Lesson:
Literature Study Groups

*Adapted from Ralph Peterson,
Arizona State University*

Developed by Cathy Beck

Principles

- Foster involvement with writing and reading
- Individualize and personalize
- Encourage cooperative learning
- Build on strengths
- Use process approaches to writing
- Build bridges, expand horizons
- Use computers

Why

- To allow students to become involved in their reading through student-selected books

- To deepen appreciation of literature by talking, writing, and thinking about it
- To allow students to share their insights and interpretations

Who

Eighth-grade students of all abilities; adaptable to all grade levels

How

Book Selection and Formation of Groups

1. Obtain financing for the purchase of multiple copies of paperback books that will be used during the literature study groups. To begin the project, I ordered five copies of fourteen different titles. (If money is not available through normal school sources, you might request money from PTOs or an outside grant.)

2. After obtaining your funds, begin selecting books that will be offered to students for literature study groups. Student reading interest, varying readability, quality, interdisciplinary units, and multicultural interests are some of the criteria I use in selecting books. This step may take a while, but it is *crucial* that the teacher read all of the books that finally are selected.

3. Give book talks to the class on each of the books being offered as possible selections. I tell the students only enough of the book to really hook them. You may also want to read a particularly exciting or interesting passage to the students. To allow for more student choice, you will want to give book talks on more books than you will ultimately have groups. To add variety to the presentation, invite the librarian in to assist with the book talks, or ask a student who has already read one of the selections to prepare a book talk.

4. At the end of the book talks, allow a time period (perhaps fifteen or twenty minutes) so that the students can look through the books that interest them most. Then ask students to fill out book request forms that will indicate their first, second, and third choice selections (see sample on p. 438).

5. Group students according to their first choice when at all possible. Student selection is a key element. When first choices are not possible (because groups would be too large or too small to be effective), ask students if they would mind joining the second-choice groups. I've never had a problem getting students to switch groups. Be sure, however, to give these students first choice next time.

Reading, Journaling, and Conferencing

1. Student groups set their own reading schedules based on the needs of individual group members. Because books are used in all class periods throughout the day, books cannot leave the room. All reading is done in class, and groups should design methods to keep students up with their own reading schedule. I let them know right away that they set the schedule and monitor progress. If someone falls behind, the group must plan how to get and keep that person current. Past groups have suggested and used the following methods: a reading buddy system in which a good reader reads with a less-proficient reader; a good reader reading into a tape recorder with the tape being used for absentees or for slower readers; securing personal copies of the book for slower readers so that they can read at home as well as in class; and reading the entire book aloud within the group.

2. After students read each day (I have them use the last ten to fifteen minutes of each class period), they record in a response journal their thoughts, feelings, reactions, questions, and other items of concern or interest about their books. This journal is used during group conferencing. Journaling must first be modeled if it is to be effective. I begin modeling this procedure at the start of the year by using student samples saved from the year before. I consider a journal entry effective when it shows a personal connection with a passage in the book. I model both effective and ineffective journal entries using both handouts and the overhead projector. By the time we participate in literature study groups, students have a very clear idea of what constitutes an effective response.

3. You can schedule conferencing with each group on a regular basis (such as every other day) or each group can schedule conferences on an as-needed basis. I prefer regularly scheduled conferences the first time literature study groups are used and then, after students become familiar with the procedure, I allow groups to schedule their own conference times. It is during conferencing that you will be able to gauge reader understanding of the text and that students will be able to share their interpretations and responses to the text. Posters or handouts showing several questions/comments that will keep group discussion going should be available to students during conferencing. Ideally, these questions/comments emerge from student brainstorming. For example, students may suggest "Had I been (a character) I would have done _____ instead of _____" and "My favorite part of the reading so far was _____." The teacher's role during conferencing is to participate as a functional group member, not solely as an evaluator, so you should be sharing your responses to the book along with the students.

Classroom Management

Much could be said about classroom management during literature study groups, but it really boils down to the individual teaching style of the teacher. I use literature study groups only after the class has developed a strong sense of cooperative learning as set forth by Johnson and Johnson and after students have become accustomed to response journals. Most importantly, I do not consider literature study groups until after the students and I have developed a level of familiarity, understanding, and trust that enhances classroom management. By this time I can allow students to sit on the floor or in the corner to read, and I can count on them to be reading or working on projects while I am conferencing. Certainly, students must not be allowed to disrupt conferencing time. In the beginning, it may seem that there is too much going on at once, but once you establish your own system, classroom management is really not as overwhelming as you may think. If you have doubts or concerns about classroom management, experiment with one class first. Then you can refine your approach before including all your classes in this activity.

Evaluation

Here are some approaches to grading that have worked for me. Try one or more, then develop your own system.

1. Students complete a self-evaluation that includes items like "I read my book on schedule," and "I participated in each conference session." Point values are assigned to each statement.

2. I outline conferences so that contributions of each group member are noted (sample form is included at the end of lesson plan). Point values are assigned to the students' contributions.

3. I give participation credit for keeping a response journal.

4. Students may complete individual and/or group projects that extend the literature as part of their grades. A list of possible group projects appears at the end of the lesson plan.

Suggested Reading

GILLES, CAROL. 1989. "Reading, Writing, and Talking: Using Literature Study Groups." *English Journal.* 78(1): 38–41.

PETERSON, RALPH, and MARYANN EEDS. 1990. *Grand Conversations: Literature Study Groups in Action.* New York: Scholastic.

```
┌─────────────────────────────────────────────────────────┐
│                                                         │
│       BOOK REQUEST— LITERATURE STUDY GROUPS             │
│                                                         │
│                                                         │
│   NAME: _____          │
│                                                         │
│                                                         │
│     1st Choice:  _____       │
│                                                         │
│     2nd Choice:  _____       │
│                                                         │
│     3rd Choice:  _____       │
│                                                         │
└─────────────────────────────────────────────────────────┘
```

Literature Study Groups—Possible Projects

1. Create a commercial to sell the book to adolescents. This requires designing and administering a survey that determines what adolescents like/dislike in books, scripting the commercial, creating scenery or back-drops, obtaining necessary props, and using video equipment.

2. Design two still advertisements to sell the book to adolescents. This requires designing and administering a survey that determines what adolescents like/dislike in books, drafting a proposal for the advertisements, and creating the polished artwork as it would appear in a magazine.

3. Create dioramas to represent major events in the book. In addition to the artwork required for a diorama, each diorama requires a written description of what has happened in the book to that point and an explanation of the scene's importance.

4. Create a mural depicting scenes from the book. A written description of the scenes and an explanation of their importance to the final outcome of the book are also required.

5. Design a series of posters showing the major events of the book. A written description of the scenes and an explanation of their importance in the work are required.

6. Create a puppet show using important parts of the plot. Scenery and backdrops would need to be created as well as the puppets themselves. The puppets should be designed to closely resemble the characters in the book. Scripts are required as well.

7. Create a new ending to the book. This requires rewriting the final chapter of the book and adding additional text that would bring the story to a different conclusion.

8. Create a newspaper based on the time period and the events in the book. Feel free to use any of the computer software that helps to format a newspaper. All of the elements of a newspaper should be included (weather, editorials, cartoons, entertainment news, society news).

9. Create diaries, journals, or letters written from the various characters' points of view. Entries should represent the entire time frame of the novel.

10. Develop a reader's theater from the literature. This involves scripting portions of the novel and rewriting descriptive passages as dialogue.

11. Create a board game or television game show. This project involves creating and administering student surveys to determine what games appeal to adolescents, writing rules, and creating game boards and pieces.

12. Design and create cooking experiences that would be typical of the book's setting. Recipes must be researched and adapted to modern kitchens, and four recipes are cooked and brought into the class for sampling. Additionally, a written piece that details the process to complete the above requirements is submitted.

13. Simulate an interview with the author of the book. Interview questions and answers are scripted, author background research is completed, other works by the same author are read, and the interview is taped on videotape.

14. Develop comparison charts or webs of related books or topics. This requires reading other books that have similar elements, presenting the similarities in chart format, and writing about the information contained in the charts.

15. I would be happy to discuss with your group any other ideas for group projects that you might like to do that I haven't included here.

CONFERENCING — LITERATURE STUDY GROUPS

Book Title: _____

Date: _____

[In these spaces I note comments and contributions of individual group members during conferencing. I also note students who are not keeping up with the reading or are having difficulty with comprehension.]

Sample Lesson:
Thumbprint Narratives

Developed by Joan Krater

This series of lessons begins with the oral, expressive, and personal. The first piece of writing, a personal narrative, becomes a bridge to the personal essay. Student samples of the narrative—the transitional activity—and the essay are included. The lesson as presented takes twelve days or so and along the way students read fiction, nonfiction, and review the mechanics of writing conversation.

Principles

- Foster involvement with writing and reading
- Encourage cooperative learning
- Build on strengths
- Use process approaches to writing
- Increase control of language
- Build bridges, expand horizons
- Use computers

Why

- To reflect on life to this point; to symbolize one's life with a shape
- To appreciate that what makes a piece of writing interesting is not the subject matter but the way the subject matter is handled
- To use oral rehearsal and art as prewriting
- To provide a natural introduction to peer groups; to model questioning within a peer group
- To allow time between the first draft and succeeding drafts
- To model "show, don't tell"
- To teach/review punctuation of dialogue
- To create a display for open house

Who

This is the first major writing project of the school year for eighth graders, but it could be adapted for grades four through twelve. The students have had experience in seventh grade with process writing, peer groups, and computers

Materials

- selected short story (I used "Mars Is Heaven" by Ray Bradbury)
- excerpts from writers such as Erma Bombeck, Andy Rooney, and Garrison Keillor
- *The Great Thumbprint Drawing Book* by Ed Emberley
- newsprint
- inked pads
- diaper wipes
- colored markers (thin pointed)

How

Prewriting/Drafting: Days One Through Five

Day One: *Life Shapes*

1. Students put the points of their pencils somewhere on a page in their notebook. "This represents the moment of your birth. Now draw a line representing your life up to this present moment. The line may show the shape of your life; for instance, it may have ups and downs or be circular or be chaotic." Students typically take a while to get started and may "copy" ideas from those who start early. As they struggle at first, I usually reinforce by saying, "the pencil shouldn't leave the page until you have reached this moment . . . unless you died and were reincarnated!" As they are drawing, I give each student a small piece of chalk.

2. All the students go to the chalkboard at the same time and draw their lifeshapes on the board. Many hold their hand-drawn lifeline in one hand, copying it on the chalkboard with the other hand. This is done so the drawings will be anonymous; those who finish early sit with their backs to the chalkboard until the last ones finish.

3. We take a few moments to look at the array of twenty-five or so shapes. Rhetorical questions and comments help the students focus. Some of you have lived strange lives! What impressions do you get from some of these shapes? Then we play psychiatrist, with the classroom becoming a conference of psychiatrists who are studying these shapes and sharing their interpretations. I ask if anyone can interpret a particular shape drawn on the board. Always some students have felt comfortable in this role playing and their comments serve as models for others who are not as sure of their role. As they respond, I refer to each student as "Dr. [student's last name]." After interpretations, "Does the person who drew this shape wish to identify himself or herself?" Following a few of these, I ask if any shapes perplex the group of doctors—and we learn their meanings from the artists if the artists so choose. Finally, I ask if anyone would like to explain his own shape.

4. The homework assignment is to explain the shape by writing a ten-minute journal entry. As always, students who prefer that no one read this journal, including me, simply fold it over in the notebook. If they are comfortable with me reading it but don't want others to read it, they write, "for your eyes only" at the bottom and I fold the entry after reading it. Students may draw new shapes if they like. (Always some students initially simply scribbled a "shape"; the discussion in 3 above gives them a better understanding of its purpose as well as giving everyone new ideas.)

Day Two

1. The ten-minute journal entry may be collected. I make mirror comments, ask sincere questions, and sometimes relate similar experiences in my life. These journals are returned the next day.

2. "Now think back to little, almost-forgotten events in your life. Skip over the big dramatic moments, the experiences we have all had, such as going to school for the first time or having a surprise birthday party. Search your memory for those events that were perhaps big at the time but have since faded in importance. For example, do you remember when you found out there was no Santa Claus? Have you ever been lost in a department store? Were you forced to eat spinach, or mushrooms, or liver? List each memory as it comes to you; order is not important."

The students push to get at least twenty memories as I prompt them with more possibilities: any episodes with a baby-sitter? your first haircut? a trip to the dentist? As students share memories that are triggered, I push for categories that will stimulate others' ideas. Our purpose now is to brainstorm a long list, not share detailed stories (that will come later). John will not tell us about suddenly missing his dog Taffy, searching, calling the police, making signs, and so on, but will mention "I couldn't find my dog," which we generalize and expand to losing a pet, getting a pet, naming a pet, a pet getting in trouble with a neighbor, you getting in trouble with a neighbor.

3. After most students have twenty phrases that represent memories, I ask them to place a given number of events on the shape of their life—their lifeline. They may match the event with a particular element in the shaped lifeline, such as the positive events with the ups of their lifeline. I suggest they use a shortcut at this stage by numbering their events in chronological order and placing the numbers on the lifeline. Some students decide to draw a new lifeline at this stage. They must have twelve events on the lifeline. (This number has varied; I recommend eight as a minimum for eighth graders with no maximum limit. The important thing is to have more on the original list than will be required on the lifeline.)

Day Three

1. I model making thumbprints on the overhead, show the Ed Emberley book (*The Great Thumbprint Drawing Book*), and have laminated thumbprint lifelines from last year's class as samples. The beauty of the thumbprints is that anyone can draw—even me!

2. Students form groups of four, pushing desks together, with each group getting one stamp pad. These first "official peer groups" of the year are randomly determined strictly by the easiest way to move desks together. They draw thumbprints to illustrate each of their events on the lifeline, getting ideas from each other as well as from Emberley and last year's students. I encourage students to share their life events as they draw. This first day of predrawing they thumbprint in their notebooks.

Suggestion: Students can make lots of thumbprints, use a diaper wipe, and then complete the illustrations with markers. This way the stamp pads can be collected relatively soon and some potential messes avoided. Students can, for example, finish the illustrations at home with pencils.

Day Four

Students begin the final thumbprint lifeline on newsprint in groups of four. I tell students they will be writing about one of the events and encourage them to get advice from others in the cooperative group as to which one would be most interesting.

Day Five

Students finish the final thumbprint lifeline. Today, as they work, each member of the group should tell in detail the story they will write about. Other students should ask questions to get more details. This exercise is oral rehearsal. This sharing of past events helps students in a culturally diverse class to begin the bonding process.

Important: During this day's work, I move from group to group listening to the oral rehearsals, particularly those of target students, and model the kinds of questions that can be asked to help development of details.

Students draft the story of one incident on their thumbprint lifeline—due in three or four days. Actual dialogue is to be included if at all possible.

Succeeding Days

Reading and Discussing Literature

We read "Mars Is Heaven" by Ray Bradbury, doing a number of activities relating more directly to literature. Then each student finds a favorite passage in Bradbury's story that demonstrates "show, don't tell" and several are read aloud. We discuss the kinds of details used in each passage and why they were effective. In all honesty, since this writing project takes place in September and/or October, I find myself modeling the kinds of comments that can be made rather than moderating a class discussion.

At some point we read excerpts from Erma Bombeck (*If Life is a Bowl of Cherries, How Come I Get All the Pits?* is an effective choice) and from Andy Rooney, noting that the topics written about are not earthshaking and dramatic, but rather very ordinary, even mundane. It's not the topic but the writing style that makes a story live for the reader.

Typically seven more school days are needed from this point until the finals are collected. Students continue drafting and revising, meeting on one scheduled day for peer response and conferring with each other and me as needed.

Revising

Their job is set: add details similar to Bombeck's, Bradbury's, and Rooney's to their draft. Their draft is now several days old, which may make it a little easier to switch from the writer's hat to the reader's hat. The class puts the revised draft on the computer; typically more revisions are made as students type.

Peer Response

Peer groups then meet to respond to each other's printouts. These are usually the same peer groups that did the thumbprints and oral rehearsal together, so they can remind the writer of details that are missing. The response sheet is on pages 456–57.

Revising

Students revise their drafts on a printout overnight using peer comments as a guide and putting the revisions on the computer the next day.

Lessons on Punctuating Dialogue

Because I believe there are too many punctuation rules to make memorizing feasible and because most adults do not have a grammar text or handbook handy, I suggest that students use a fiction book with dialogue as their model for correct punctuation. When they cannot find an example of the kind of conversation they are writing, they may want to revise their conversations. If published writers aren't using it, perhaps there is a reason. For instance, very few writers start a sentence with explanatory words such as "John said." Exceptions are found in books written for small children; apparently younger readers need to know who is talking before they know what is said.

I use examples of conversation from stories we have read to review correct punctuation and reinforce the idea of using published writing as a model rather than resorting to a handbook of rules. I have a different overhead transparency for each dialogue situation.

After a moment of identifying explanatory words, direct quotes, and noting where the commas and quotation marks are, the students are challenged to form a "living sentence."

Prior to class I have placed a small piece of posterboard on each desk. You will find a list of the items on these pieces on page 458. I color-code the items so that direct quotes might be green, explanatory words red, punctuation marks yellow, and indirect quotes beige. Some of the boards have words, and some have punctuation marks.

I dictate a sentence (whose structure is modeled on the current overhead) and the students with the appropriate boards line themselves in front of the class, creating the sentence with correct punctuation.

After the sentence group is satisfied with their sentence, we then open it up to the audience. Discussion reinforces the "rules" that are being followed. If the students don't make mistakes, I may force them: "John, switch with Mark. Now, isn't that okay to have the comma outside the quotation marks?"

We go through approximately seven living sentences; every student participates in at least one sentence. The dictated sentences I use are:

> "I heard you the first time," Bobby said.

Bobby said, "I heard you the first time."

"I heard you," Bobby said, "the first time."

Bobby asked, "Where have you been?"

"Where," Bobby asked, "have you been?"

"Have you been to the cafeteria?" Bobby asked.

Bobby said that he heard you the first time.

"I heard you the first time, Chuck," Bobby said.

Bobby asked, "Chuck, where have you been?"

The last two sentences include direct address, which is common in dialogue. Again, transparencies provide the model of how this is punctuated.

The only situation that we don't cover with living sentences is starting a new paragraph with each new speaker. The model on the overhead is chosen to show the importance of this. It is a conversation between Richard Wright and his mother in "The Kitten" (from *Black Boy*) wherein Richard is repeating the words of his mother. The explanatory words are omitted, but the students have no trouble recalling this portion, which they've already read. The importance of the paragraphing is highlighted as students envision this conversation without paragraphs.

The next day cooperative groups apply these rules, again using the transparencies as models when needed. It is important to break one of the "rules" of collaborative learning when doing this exercise. Usually we want students facing each other for better communication, but in this activity the three desks must be in a row.

Each trio receives an envelope with strips of paper inside—some with words and some with punctuation marks. (A master copy before being cut into strips is attached. These strips are also color-coded according to function.) As I dictate the sentences, the trio will arrange the corresponding written sentences, correctly punctuated. The dictated sentences are:

1. "I wish you'd hurry," said Tim.

2. "Will you please wait for me?" asked Jane.

3. Beth said, "Pass the sugar."

4. "No!" screamed Tim.

5. "I wish," Tim said, "you'd hurry."

6. Jane asked, "Will you please pass the sugar?"

   (After they have done this, I ask them to make it into two lines, starting the new line with "pass." After I check this, they add the next sentence to this one, keeping the same "margins.")

7. "No," said Beth, "we won't pass the sugar." *(Check for indentation for new speaker.)*

8. Tim said that you'd hurry.

9. "I will hurry," said Beth.

10. Beth said that she would hurry.

11. "Beth, I wish you'd hurry," said Tim.

12. Beth said, "Tim, pass the sugar."

The third day, students work individually, rewriting correctly a paragraph in their grammar text that has no punctuation of dialogue.

Proofreading

At this point, we return to the thumbprint narratives and students proofread their own drafts. They make the corrections on the computer, use the spelling checker, and turn in all drafts and response sheets. The prewriting list can be kept in a designated spot (such as the inside cover of a writing folder) to suggest other writing ideas when writer's block hits later in the year.

Evaluation

The evaluation guide sheet I will use is given to students just before they proofread (see page 459). This is the first paper of the year to go through the process and have formal evaluation, so some time is spent going over it.

I explain that each section will receive a letter grade and those section grades will be averaged for the final grade on the paper. The students can use it as a guide when making final revisions.

When the papers are returned, students must correct all proofreading errors, I check them, and they make corrections on the computer. Students may make revisions (triggered by the comments on evaluation), but this is not a requirement. For many students enough time has been spent on this, their first major paper of the year.

Publishing

The final beautiful printout is then displayed on the bulletin board next to the thumbprint lifeline. Lots of time had best be allowed for this final stage if there is a nonnegotiable deadline such as an open house. It can take days (not full class periods, but time squeezed in to take care of the few stragglers who have been absent, have been having trouble getting the errors fixed, or getting the necessary time to use the computer) to get almost-perfect papers from every student in the class.

We have also made printouts for a class book, in which case the thumbprint that relates to this particular experience is drawn on the final draft itself.

Sample Student Papers

The two sample papers show one female target student's work and one highly skilled writer's work. This was the second major piece of writing for the year for these students. Anikia's first final was almost unreadable; we had many one-on-one conferences—during class, during team time, after school—trying to get the dialogue punctuated correctly. Her second final— the thumbprint narrative—had only one error in dialogue punctuation: a forgotten comma. Whether it was the individual conferences, the personal attention and rapport established during these intense conferences, or the dialogue lessons that did the trick, I don't know. It was probably a combination of all three.

These papers evidence the philosophy that not every error is attacked. I ignored Anikia's lower-case *mom,* spelling of *brite,* and nonstandard phrasing along with her misuse of the past tense in "This was one of the most things that I have ever wanted." After the intense work on dialogue punctuation and the good results, it was time to let Anikia bask in her feelings of success. She was especially pleased with her added description of the bicycle, "rainbow brite," her ending sentence, and the fuzzy sentence "My rainbow brite bike was sitting there in the hallway reflecting sun light in my yellow blinds." When we ask students what they are pleased with, it seems to me that we have to respond accordingly unless there is a serious problem.

Ellen's paper also has a proofreading error (the double negative *didn't hardly*), which I normally would have caught and explained in conference. Her potential for sophisticated sentence structure is seen in the second-to-last paragraph, "She came flying down the driveway, eyes bulging out of her head, practically in tears, until she saw the three of us safely parked on the lawn and trying to get out of the car." Very few eighth graders use a noun absolute and not many will show the control of language Ellen evidenced in combining so many ideas into a single sentence. Ellen's potential was further developed later in the year when we worked specifically with sentence combining. Ellen was especially pleased with the metaphor "drown our fears in milk and cookies" and her ending sentence.

My Most Wanted Bike

Anikia

It was my 8th birthday! My mother had promised me a new rainbow brite bicycle. A week before my birthday mom came home from work and said, "Anikia, I am sorry, but I won't be able to get that new bike that you wanted." I was so enraged I started sobbing.

Mom said, "Anikia, you shouldn't act like that because I always get you want you want, no matter what it is."

I stopped crying. "Mom, I am sorry, but this was one of the most things that I have ever wanted for a long time." I started thinking to myself saying, "Well, I do get almost everything that I want. So maybe if I am good I will get it one day."

The next morning was March 4, my birthday. I woke up feeling dejected and looking out of the window saying this is going to be the worst most dreadful birthday that I have ever had. The next thing that I knew was that my mother came in and said, "Wake up, sleepy head. Happy Birthday."

My rainbow brite bike was sitting there in the hallway reflecting sun light in my yellow blinds. I ran to it and started pushing it out of the door. But something hit me. I remembered my mother so then I came back, and I kissed her on the cheek. "Thanks, mom." With the wind blowing in my hair I had the best ride of my life.

The Ride

by Ellen

When we climbed off the bus on that sunny afternoon, Elizabeth and I expected just to have some typical kindergarten fun playing outside. There was certainly no way we could've anticipated what would happen later that day.

After eating lunch outside, we ran, did cartwheels, jumped, slid, and swang, until about two, when Elizabeth's mom called us in. "I've got to run some errands, so get in the car. You can play when we get home."

With that, Elizabeth, her three year old brother Jacob, their mom, and I all got in the little car. Elizabeth and I giggled about school in the back, and Jake and his mom chatted aimlessly in front.

After going to a couple stores, we returned home. "Stay in the car," their mom warned. "I have to get some clothes that need to be dry cleaned, and I'll be right back out."

Elizabeth and I talked quietly, but Jake began to get wild. At first, we didn't hardly notice his jumping and laughing until his voice rose to a high pitched shriek of fright. The car jerked suddenly, and when we saw what was happening, Elizabeth and I joined in. Slowly, the car began to roll down the driveway, but it was gaining speed rapidly.

I looked ahead. A gate spanned the width of the driveway, and I let Elizabeth and Jacob know that I was sure it would stop us by changing my incredible scream into a decreasing whine. I was positive that this ride was almost over, but as we got closer, the gate almost seemed to jump out of our way. We continued down the driveway until we made a sharp turn right, almost tipping the car over. The tomatoes died a squishy death as we finally rolled to a stop.

That's when Elizabeth's mom came outside. She turned around to find the car missing, and her face turned sheet white in the terror that followed. She came flying down the driveway, eyes bulging out of her head, practically in tears, until she saw the three of us safely parked on the lawn and trying to get out of the car. She opened the door, and gasped in amazement when she saw that the emergency brake had been released.

After she helped us out of the car and into the house, she let us drown our fears in milk and cookies. Tears of relief glistened in our eyes in the comfort of the safe kitchen when we knew with that we were finally safe.

Thumbprint Drafts: Peer Response Form

Writer's Name: _____   Date: _____

Peer Responder: _____

The writer will read the draft aloud as you follow on your copy of
the printout. As you listen, feel free to mark on the printout.

After the writer finishes reading, each person should make one
honest, positive comment about the paper. Then the responders
fill in the following:

1. Underline phrases, star sections that appeal to you.

2. Put a question mark near any part that confuses you or isn't clear.
Write questions you will ask the writer in the space below.

3. Does the paper include dialogue?

If not, should it? Write "add dialogue" in margin where you
think conversation would be helpful.

If it does, is it realistic? Does it add to the paper? Write
your comments on the dialogue here:

4. Where could the writer add more details? On your copy of the
printout, write "add details" in the margin near those spots.

5. Circle any general words the writer could make more specific.
Also circle any words that are used over and over.

continued on page 457

continued from page 456

6. When all responders are finished with the five steps above, discuss the paper.

    A. Tell the writer what you underlined and starred and why you liked those parts. Be as specific as possible.

    B. Tell the writer what confused you (see your questions in #2 above and the question marks on the printout).

    C. Discuss the dialogue (see "add dialogue" or your comments on #3 above).

    D. Discuss the need for more details (where you wrote "add details").

    E. Discuss the need for changing some words (see your circles).

7. Give the writer your copy of the printout and this sheet.

8. The writer staples all response sheets and marked printouts behind the writer's draft.

LIST OF PHRASES AND MARKS FOR LIVING SENTENCES

On Green:

Where
where
have you been
Have you been
to the cafeteria
I heard you
the first time

On Red:

asked Bobby
Bobby said
Bobby asked

On Beige:

that
he heard you

On Yellow:

two commas
two beginning quotation marks
two ending quotation marks
one period
one question mark

Thumbprint Draft: Evaluation Sheet

Name: _____   Date: _____

_____1. Use of details

      _____Had good showing details   _____Needed more

      _____Had strong action verbs   _____Had well–chosen words

      _____Had mostly/some telling sentences

_____2. Use of dialogue _____

      _____Dialogue was appropriate, realistic

_____3. Mechanics (proofreading)

      _____run-ons/fragments   _____spelling

      _____dialogue: quotation marks, commas, capitals

      _____other: _____

_____4. Process

      _____prewriting

      _____first draft

      _____peer response forms and printouts

      _____considered peers' feedback

      _____obvious revisions (on hard copy)

      _____succeeding drafts

      _____obviously proofread

Comments:

Sample Lesson:
Thumbprint Essays

Bridging from Narrative to Essay Writing

Developed by Joan Krater

This personal essay picks up with the thumbprint narrative and continues the process. After students write an introduction and ending for a miniessay using the narrative as an extended anecdote, they work on a brand-new personal essay with a topic of their choosing.

Principles

• Build bridges, expand horizons

Why

• To make a transition from expressive to transactional writing
• To focus directly on aspects of transactional writing while unencumbered by other aspects of good writing
• To permit further revision of a previously "finished" piece of writing

Who

Used successfully with eighth graders, this activity could be adapted for grades four through twelve. The students have had experience in seventh grade and the first part of eighth grade with process writing, peer groups, and computers

Materials

- A previously completed draft that has gone through the entire process (in this case, the thumbprint final explained in the previous lesson)
- Sample essays from authors such as Lewis Grizzard, Ellen Goodman, Andy Rooney, Erma Bombeck, and Noel Perrin

How

1. Several months after the thumbprint writing (see previous lesson), we work on a nonfiction unit that focuses on personal essays. During the course of the unit, we do a variety of activities, some of which will lead to this bridging activity. As we read essays, we notice that many writers use anecdotes or short narratives to illustrate their points. We pull the thumbprint finals from the writing folders and consider what points our narratives may exemplify. Students work in pairs to come up with a list of possible points for their narratives.

2. They then select the point they think is most suitable and write it in a sentence. We again look at some of the essays we've read and notice that while some of the writers have a single sentence for an introduction, most develop it through explanation before leading into the illustrative examples.

3. Students write an introductory paragraph for their narratives. We then consider how tacking this paragraph on the top may force a change in the

461

narrative. For many students, a simple change of adding one transitional sentence may be all that is needed. Others may need to revise extensively, eliminating some details and emphasizing others with this new focus for the paper.

4. Students then write an ending sentence, typically rephrasing the introduction. I do not insist on a full paragraph of conclusion.

5. Students informally ask two to three other students to respond to their new drafts, using the response sheet on page 466 as a guide. They revise, proofread, and get new printouts on the computer. The evaluation guide I use is on page 466.

Sample Papers

Alleesha wrote her thumbprint narrative about her grandfather. This target student tries to draw a lesson from her experience—and then write directly to the reader with a rather didactic tone. (Reading this essay today is a poignant experience for me. Alleesha died two years after writing it.)

Mark's is fairly typical of what a target student will do with this bridging activity. He doesn't clearly show how his narrative relates to his point—how he had prepared for the first physical and still was surprised. But he does have an introduction and ending that keep the narrative from being strictly a story.

Chris has better writing skills in general. His introduction was particularly good, but his audience seemed to change in the ending.

The introductory paragraphs added to make the narrative into an essay are obvious, as are the endings. None of these three samples (nor any of the other student papers) is truly an essay using the narrative as an anecdote. They are instead improved narratives that have better leads and more focus. But the idea of having a point, an opinion, and an idea for a narrative is new to these students. That concept—of mixing opinion and narrative elements—is essential if they are to write interesting personal essays, which is the next step.

Lost Memories

Alleesha

Always show that you love people in your family and neighbors while they're around. Otherwise they'll think you don't care for them. After they're gone you won't be able to tell them how much you care about them. Even if it's a person that you're not too friendly with, let them know that they can be seen as a real person. This will make them feel the same way you do.

My long lost memories are when my grandfather used to come to my house all the time and talk with my mother, father, and me. We used to talk about when he was a little boy and all the changes he had to go through in life because he used to sing in night clubs when he was younger but when he got older he gave it up. He would tell me about all the old memories he used to have, like when he went to a party one time and he was put down by all the girls. He used to take me to the park all the time and chase me around to other special places like going to see my grandmother in her grave and giving her roses.

When I was with him he made me feel like a whole new person because I loved him so much. I was nine years old then. When he died I was eleven years old. I was so sad inside that it made me feel guilty. I thought that it was my fault that he died. because I always bothered him to take me places. I was so young I thought I was giving him a nervous breakdown. In a way I feel happy and sad, but I guess that's life.

So if you feel sorry or guilty for something that happens to a person you love, let them know now that you care.

My First Physical

By Mark

My parents told me to be prepared. I have always tried to be prepared. but one experience showed me that you can't be prepared for every thing.

To play football they have to give you a physical. One of the things they check in a physical, is if you have a hernia. As I was standing there the doctor said, "Drop your pants."

I said, "What for?"

He said, "So I can check for a hernia." It didn't seem right cause he was a stranger toe. I figured he was telling the truth so I dropped my pants.

Then he said, "Drop your underwear."

I asked him," Do I have to pull down my underwear?"

He said yes, so I did. It scared me when he pushed in the spot right next to my testicles. Besides his hand were cold. When he said I could pull up my underwear and pants and leave, I pulled them up and got out of there. After I got out, I was relieved it was over!

People try to be prepared for things. But some things you think you're prepared, you're not. Sometimes you can't be prepared for everything. So you will just have to be surprised.

" . . . You'll Break Your Arm!"

By, Chris

"Don't climb the fence of you'll break your arm!", said my dad in the summer of '79. Most of the time small children seem to want to do things their own way. Even though their parents tell them to do one thing, they think they know their idea is better. If and when they refuse to listen to their parents, something drastic could and may happen to them. I should know, I've been there.

I was five years old at that time and I was over at my two best friends' house. Our whole family went over there every weekend to eat dinner, talk and play. My friends Mikey, Shane and I wanted to play tag, but we had to go in the backyard to play. The back door was broken so we had to go out the front door all the way through the gate on the side of the house, and then we'd be in the backyard.

When we got to the gate it was locked. My dad was right by the gate so I asked him to unlock it for me. He said, "Hold on, I'm busy right now." I couldn't wait, so I started climbing the fence (it was a small, white, wooden picket fence, which seemed like it reached the sky, but you have to remember, I was only five). He saw me and said, "Don't climb the fence or you'll break your arm!" I got off the fence real fast! I waited until he wasn't looking and I started climbing over it. I was almost over when my foot slipped and I fell over, head first, and landed on my arm. My head didn't even hurt a bit, which nobody could believe, but my arm was hurting so bad that it felt like somebody was pounding at it with a forty-pound sledgehammer! The next thing I knew I was sitting in the car screaming all the way to the hospital, and you guessed it! I had my first broken arm!(or anything for that matter!).

There is nothing anybody can do about children who think they know it all except watch their every move. You might be dead by the time they start school, but it should be worth it!!

Response Sheet

Thumbprint Essay

1. Does the introduction have a point? Does the point fit the rest of the writing?

2. Is the point explained fully enough in the introduction? What else could the writer say to have a more developed lead-in to the example?

3. Does the introduction move smoothly into the rest of the paper?

4. Is there an ending? Does it match the introduction?

5. Is there anything in the narrative section that distracts from the point of the essay? If yes, tell the writer where you had the problem.

· ·

Evaluation Sheet

Thumbprint Essay

Introduction

____ has a point that is illustrated by the body of the paper
is a well-developed paragraph

Transition

____ the introduction moves smoothly into the rest of the paper

Body

____ the illustration focuses on the main idea of the essay

Ending

____ "matches" the introduction

____ gives a sense of closure to the paper

Bridging

The next piece of writing will be a personal essay. The students will have written four to eight short journal entries on topics that lend themselves to transactional writing. At least two of the entries were "free choice" topics. I always let students know a day in advance a free choice day is coming and in this case I encouraged them to write opinions rather than narratives. The other topics often came from the essays we were reading. For example, when reading Lewis Grizzard's "No Place for Soup Slurpers," the students wrote for ten minutes on a pet peeve they had. After reading other selections by authors such as Lewis Grizzard, Ellen Goodman, Noel Perrin, Andy Rooney, and Erma Bombeck, the students could write on any of three topics that could or could not relate to the readings: television and sports, superstitions, and whether or not the national anthem should be changed.

Other topics have included corporal punishment in school, snow days (our district traditionally provides for no snow days), and dealing with substitute teachers. The topics typically relate to events drawn from current news or school happenings.

When we get ready to write the personal essay, students may select one of these short-writes as a topic or may take a brand-new topic. By brainstorming potential audiences and purposes for each topic that interests them, they narrow the list to one.

Having done a transitional activity (thumbprint essay), they are more confident in beginning a piece of transactional writing that may or may not have narrative elements. The brainstorming session focusing on possible audiences and purposes is an essential element. Students become motivated as they move from wanting to write "about football" to deciding to write "to persuade a college coach that I deserve a football scholarship."

Sample Papers

These three papers are by the same students who wrote the samples of the thumbprint essays.

Alleesha's advice to substitute teachers does not include any narrative anecdotes, but she has wonderful specific advice. Her introduction is extremely informal and rather brief; the ending is better at summarizing this target student's point.

Mark really did want to write on the general topic of wrestling. He wanted to make several points, including that younger kids as well as girls would enjoy wrestling; that wrestling builds muscles, speed, and stamina; that wrestling requires more brain than brawn. Mark really didn't have an introduction or ending, nor did he use an anecdote. The essay definitely has an informative rather than narrative tone, but Mark was not really satisfied with it, as was discussed in Chapter 5 on process approaches to writing.

Chris, a skilled writer, uses rhetorical devices to persuade rather than researched facts. The tone is more oratorical, the arguments dependent upon irony, word play, and common sense. His concerns about the legality of cigarettes, alcohol, and snuff begin with a definite introduction and end with a brief but definite conclusion.

Substitute Teacher

by Alleesha

Hey, all you substitutes let me give some advice for subbing. I think that you should treat kids with respect like, giving everone the same privilages an be nice. Explain what you expect of them an their consequences, telling them the rules you exspect to let them know from the start that you are a good teacher.

But, if they act as if they don't want to abide by the rules you give them then you know it's time for disciplining before it's too late. You can put them in a place where they can work by themselves an think about what he/she is doing that is wrong. Or call their parents an have a conference with them to see if they can do something, which I think they can. But if that still don't work talk to the principle to see if he can talk to the student and tell him how important it is to be on his/her best behavior. If that don't work the only think left to do is to suspend that person and then maybe they will understand.

You should never look at subbing as a babysitting job because it's teaching. I know that some of you think that way. Look on the bright side of things. It also can be fun for you. I hope that all you subs of the world enjoy what you are doing an be proud of it.

Wrestling Has Many Benifits

By: Mark

I think kids, from ages 6 to 9 would enjoy wrestling. Even some girls might like wrestling too. A lot of people think it's a gay sport, because you grab all over the other wrestler. But if you wrestle you would see that it's not a gay sport, it's a rugged sport.

There are also benifits in wrestling. It builds muscles, and the way it builds muscles is by breaking holds, and by holding pins.

It also builds speed, by trying to escape from holds, and you also get quicker trying to get take downs.

It builds stamina, because you're constantly moving through the whole match.

You have to think, you have to think to know how to counter a hold. You also have to know when to go for a take down, or anything else.

The younger you start the better you will be, and you will win more matches. The reason I think you should wrestle at a young age is because if you start at a younger age, you will no a lot more moves, such as pinning combinations, reversals, and counters. You will also be a lot more smarter, in the area of wrestling, than your aponent, who's only been wrestling for maybe 1 year.

469

Legal Killers

By, Chris

Drugs are already a big problem in the U.S. and every other country in the world. Highly deadly drugs, cocaine, heroine, speed etc., are already are presently banned from use, but what about legal drugs? Cigarettes, alchohol, snuff and any other light drugs, drugs that aren't as damaging to the health, are still being used and sold. Of course legal drugs dont kill quite as easily as illegal drugs, but in the long run they're not the best thing to take unless you have some kind of death wish.

What about the people around the users? Are they too being affected by these bad habits? You bet they are! Why not just give a cigarette to every person who happens to choke on your smoke!? And snuff, you get sick just from smelling that junk! Why don't pregnant people give their premature baby a sip of booze every time they kick?

How do the drugs affect the users themselves? The people who use these drugs are hooked on death. Some of the substances in them are very addictive. Cigarettes and any other tobacco product contain nicotine which is highly addictive. Alchohol itself is addictive.

People say that they can't live without these drugs, but it is just the opposite. They can't live with them. Almost everybody who smokes knows that cigarettes cause lung cancer. They joke about it. Some people call them cancer sticks and yet they still smoke them. Chewing tobacco and snuff cause cancer too, except they don't cause lung cancer, they cause lip cancer. People have had to get their lip cut off because of it. Tobacco products aren't the only things that can be harmful. Alchohol makes the users do things that they usually wouldn't do if they were sober. They might beat somebody, drive recklessly, kill people or even kill themselves. All these drugs can be deadly.

Millions and millions of poeple abuse the use of legal killers in todays society. Is it really fun to kill yourself and others?

Sample Lesson: Dramatic Monologue

Developed by Minnie Phillips

Principles

- Individualize and personalize
- Build bridges to more challenging tasks
- Build on strengths
- Foster involvement with writing and reading
- Increase control of language

Why

- To draw on the showing-through-telling power of language to reveal nuance of character and meaning
- To extend writing experience by experimenting with an expressive oral style
- To engage readers intently as listeners

• To use the dramatic monologue as an indirect way of conveying personal experience, imparting information, or expressing a philosophical viewpoint

What and How

A dramatic monologue is a scene in a play, poem, or narrative in which the speaker addresses a listener or group of listeners who remain silent. I use monologues to introduce a drama unit in my basic-level tenth-grade English class. Yet I suspect they will work at any level where the emphasis is on audience, voice, or oral style.

Teachers might begin with classic models such as Robert Browning's poem "My Last Duchess" or more accessible works such as Langston Hughes' poem "Mother to Son." Laurence Holder's biographical play *Zora* (1989) uses a powerful monologue to introduce the author Zora Neale Hurston. John Murray's collection *Modern Monologues for Young People* offers twenty-five "humorous, royalty-free dramatic sketches for teenagers." I sometimes create my own model or have students start fresh once they understand what monologues are.

Monologues portray a persona or imaginary character during a "telling" moment or situation. The reader or audience discovers the kind of person the speaker is through what the character says, does not say, how the character says it, and the implied listener's response. The monologue will likely suggest through dialogue the speaker's values and social status as well as hopes, dreams, and fears.

Dialogue and delivery carry the monologue, so expect students to read their monologues aloud for full impact. They'll "hear" the rhythms of language and make discoveries about their narrators and about themselves. In this sense, the dramatic monologue becomes powerful psychodrama. It can be intense, riveting, solemn, worldly, breezy, zany, or wise—which makes it an excellent study of tone as well as character.

I spend about a week teaching and having students write monologues. I begin by reading my own model, although a student model might work as well. The important thing is for students to hear a dramatic monologue at work. Then they cull from their own experience, concerns, or from historical or contemporary issues an instance in which they "breathe life."

In the teacher sample that follows, I chose the persona of a poor, inner-city mother because I wanted to show the precariousness of rearing an African American male adolescent. Betsy, a White target student, chose to write her monologue about the possibility of AIDS spreading among females.

My students select topics based on personal interest. Although expected to revise their drafts, students write in standard English or dialect appropriate to the characters they create.

I give students a combined grade for the writing process, written product, and oral delivery. Like most writing assignments, however, evaluation of the dramatic monologue project depends on the teacher's goals.

Teacher Sample: Dramatic Monologue

Minnie Phillips

Okay, okay I'm comin'! Who is it? Yes, this is 725 Murray. Who is it? The police? Okay, I'll take the chain off. Lemme see your badge number. Just hold on, you can't just come in here any kinda way. . . .

Yes, Michael Hudgins is my son, but sometimes he don't come home nights. Why? Did something happen? Something happened, didn't it, I can tell. Lord, Lord what is it this time?

Shot! Did Michael shoot somebody? Michael was shot? You sure it was Michael Hudgins, Jr.? It wasn't Michael Hudgins, Sr., was it? It coulda been him. He's always doin' somethin' crazy. . . .

Yeah, Michael's seventeen, about five feet nine inches, weighs about 150 pounds, and has a birthmark 'bove his left eye. That sounds like Michael. I don't know what color shirt he had on. I told you, he's not here half the time! Yeah, he does have a gold tooth. . . . Oh Lord, Lord what done happened now?

Michael don' gone out there and got hisself mixed up with some kinda trouble. I tell Michael all the time, stay outta them streets. But he jus' laughs and says, "Aw Mama, I know how-ta take care of myself."

He used to be a good boy, made the honor roll in third grade, was some kinda math whiz. His teacher said he was the smartest kid she ever saw. But then, Big Mike, his daddy, left when he was in the fifth grade, and it seemed like Michael didn't care no more 'bout nothin'. He used to just sit over there in that big chair and look at cartoons on television. He wouldn't say nothin' to nobody. If Tasha, she two years older than Michael, said anything to him, he'd just stare at her real hard and walk outta the room.

Then his teachers started callin', sayin' he came to school late, didn't do his homework, just put him head down on his desk and said his stomach hurt. They acted like I didn't feed the boy nothin'. He might not of had the best food, 'specially on the check I get cleaning for the Fischers, but I show did try to keep some food on the table.

Well, things went on like that . . . . I mean with Michael. But seemed like he was gonna do okay in sixth grade. He went to that new middle school, and he had this one English teacher who took a interest in him. He said that was first time he heard 'bout William Shakespeare and Langston Hughes. So Michael, that boy show was somethin', used to come in here with them silly expressions, "To be, or not to be; that is the question." And I'd say, "To live and work till you die, that is the answer." He looked real puzzled and went off to his room.

Anyway, sixth grade went all right. Then came seventh and eighth, and he started running with the wrong crowd. The principal would call and say he thought Michael was with these boys who hot-wired one of the teacher's cars. Of course, I was upset and told them that that jus' didn't sound like Michael. But she kept callin' here, and each time it got worse and worse.

By high school, seemed like things was gon' change. Michael played basketball his freshman year, but at the end of the season his grades started droppin'. So they wouldn't let him play the first semester of his soph'more year.

He got a job at Popeye's the summer before school started though, and he started buyin' all these new clothes. He said he was growin' too fast to wear the ones I bought him last fall. He started takin' the bus out to that big new shopping center, said he liked to shop at Oak Tree, and he started wearin' some kinda cologne called Eternity. All these girls started callin' him. One wanted to know when Michael was gon' come see his baby. I said, "*Baby,* child, Michael only sixteen; he jus' a baby hisself!"

Well, I told Michael what she said, and he jus' gave me one of them sly little grins and said, "Aw Mama, you so old-fashioned. Every since Daddy left you been treatin' me like a baby. Look at me, Mama; I'm the man of the house now." Well, that show made me feel pretty good, but I still wondered where Michael was goin' all the time—leavin' first thing in the evenin' and comin' home way past midnight.

His high school principal started callin', said Michael was missin' school two and three days a week, said they took a beeper from him. . . thought he might be dealin'. I asked him was he crazy. Here I am slavin' everyday in some rich folks' house and my child out sellin' somebody dope. What kinda sense that make? I tried to put the whole thing outta my mind, but it kept gnawin' on me like a rat.

That's when Michael stopped comin' home nights, and when he did, he always wanted to know who called. I was a bundle of nerves, and Tasha, she was gettin' ready to graduate, so I didn't wanta worry her. Anyway, she used to always say Michael deep down was good hearted, and smart too, but the Big Mike in him was bound to come out. . .

One night, Michael came home about nine o'clock. He had sweat poppin' out on his forehead like he had a fever. He was pantin' like he been running. He said these men in a burgundy car tried to run over him when he crossed the street at Twelfth and Adams. Then they shot at him but missed. He said he knew who they was but wouldn't tell me.

After that, seemed like somethin' in him kinda snapped. He had this real icy stare and empty voice like he knew death was comin' for him. He wasn't scared no more, and I thought I saw him take a gun out from under his bed. I asked him 'bout it, and he said he needed a gun jus' in case somebody tried to break in. I was worried but jus' prayed. What could I do?

Now here you come tonight tellin' me Michael been shot. I guess I knew it was bound to happen sometimes. What hospital he in? Tasha, Tasha, get up and bring me that blue flowered dress I left hangin' over the doorpost; I got to go to the hospital. It's Michael, he hurt.

Oh Lord, let my baby be okay, don't let my baby die. What you lookin' at me like that for? Dead, Michael dead. Naw, naw, oh Lord, oh Lord, oh Lord . . . not Michael, not Michael, my baby!

Student Sample: Dramatic Monologue

by Betsy
English 10
16 December 1991

Hello, Sullivan residence. Yes, this is Kari Sullivan. What can I do for you? Well, yes, Dr. Mulligan, I know Tommy Ricsh. I used to date him. Ya, we did once. Why all the questions? What's wrong? Well, I can come to your office, but I can't make it until about three O'clock. Okay then, I'll see you at three.

Mom, I'm going to meet someone. I'll be back in about an hour. Hi, Can you tell me where I can find Dr. Mulligan's office, please. Thanks.

I'm here to see Dr. Mulligan. Yes, he's expecting me.

Dr. Mulligan, I'm Kari Sullivan. Oh, I'm fine. I think. Am I? What is it? Don't keep me in suspence.[pause] Tommy, Aids? Are you saying? No, not me.[as tears fall] How did Tommy get it? Drugs! He told me he was clean. He lied to me. No, I haven't been with anyone else. Tommy and I broke up only four months ago.

He was my first, ya know. We were together only about a month before it happened, but it felt right. I thought I loved him. He said he loved me too. Anyway, after that, things went down hill. I knew our relationship was coming to an end, but I tried holding on to what we had left cause I thought that it was special. Well, about two weeks later, we got into a horrible fight that ended with my heart broken.

Doc, I'm gonna die.[pause] I just keep babbling on hoping that the more I talk. Oh, I don't know. I don't want to believe it. Is there anything I can do, anything I can take?

Then what the hell are you doctors good for? You're suppose to make people better, not let them die. Oh, Dr. Mulligan, I'm sorry. I'm just scared. [silence hits the room for a moment]

How long do I have? What's "I'm not sure." You can't tell me that. What, am I just going to not wake up one morning? I don't know if I can except that, Doc. I'm so young.

What am I going to do? Well, I really don't think there's much I can do, is there? A support group; I'll call them tomorrow. I guess it's the best thing I can do at this point, huh? Well, I'll keep in touch, please do the same. Bye.

History of Holistic Assessment in Webster Groves School District

The district began its annual writing assessment in the spring of 1984. The early years reveal a spirit of action research (even though we had not heard the term) as the entire department, grades seven through twelve[1] reflected, read, discussed, and modified its procedures. This history provided our action research project with beneficial information, but the procedures also created some complications.

The district's first writing assessment for grades seven through twelve in the spring of 1984 was markedly different from our current assessment practices. But most substantive changes occurred during the first two years, so that the prompts and general procedures have remained consistent since the fall of 1986. Our project began in the fall of 1987, after the major changes had been made.

Assessment should reflect philosophical assumptions about writing. If students are asked to write only persuasive pieces when they are assessed, they quickly surmise that narrative and explanatory writings are of less importance. If they are taught that an audience and a purpose determine the selection of details and tone but are not given that information in an assessment, then the testing procedures contradict—and supersede—the teaching.

Prompts: Changes in Topic, Mode, Audience, Purpose, and Time

Writing assessment has developed its own terminology. The writing task given to students is commonly called the prompt. Our very first prompt was used only one year. Middle school students found it too difficult. In addition, senior high students had a problem becoming involved with the topic.

> Many people say that television is bad for us. They blame it for everything from the high crime rate to poor reading habits. Very few people take the time to say good things about television.
>
> What *good* things do *you* see in television? Discuss one or two of the ways in which you think television benefits the individual, the family, or society.
>
> Discuss your answers to this question by giving specific examples wherever you can.

Most important, this prompt did not identify an audience nor give a clear purpose. Although the implicit purpose was to persuade, the key word *discuss* was vague.

The scoring guide for holistic assessment is called a rubric. This list describes the criteria for each level of skill, typically represented by 4, 6, or 8 possible scores. We used a four-point rubric the first year, which we found did not sufficiently discriminate the varying skills of the students. Papers that had received the same score varied widely in their organization, development, style, and mechanics.

As we prepared for the second year's assessment, we read Myers (1980) and White (1985) and considered other prompts in other modes. We definitely did not want our students to receive a subtle message that persuasive writing was the only kind of writing that mattered.

This belief in the consistency between practice and assessment was tested most in the amount of time we allowed the students to produce the assess- ment draft. The first year students had only twenty minutes to comprehend the prompt and produce a final draft.[2] For us, the concern was that the assessment papers did not reflect the quality of writing we knew our students were doing in class. Essentially, the assessment was scoring first drafts and such procedures were negating everything we held dear about writing process.

So after much discussion and compromise within the department, we allowed students two days for the assessment beginning in the fall of 1986: one thirty-minute period of prewriting and one thirty-minute period for drafting.

It was also in the fall of 1986 that we changed from having the assessment in the spring. A spring assessment made sense at first: it is similar to a final examination and shows the cumulative effect of teaching up to that point. Papers written in the spring, however, are scored in the summer and the results aren't known until the fall—when we no longer have the same students. Many teachers wanted to have the results by midyear so they could work with their students on specific problems highlighted by the assessment.

To summarize, we made some key decisions during those first two years that have characterized the annual assessment ever since.

- The prompts should vary in their modes. We would assess the students in three modes: narrative, explanatory, and persuasive.
- The prompts must clearly identify an audience and purpose.
- We now use an eight-point rubric, which results in student scores ranging from 2 to 16 (after adding the two readers' scores).
- Students have one thirty-minute period for prewriting and one thirty-five minute period for drafting, which reflects at least minimally a concern for process. We enter the scoring session with the mindset that we are not reading final process papers.
- Assessment is held in the fall (usually late September) each year.

Descriptors

The real purpose of a district holistic assessment is to determine strengths and weaknesses of the curriculum. Yet while raw scores may suggest overall improvement or decline, they are inadequate in identifying specifics. For this reason, in the spring of 1985 we inaugurated a separate analysis, one we believe to be unique in district assessments. We called this analysis "descriptors," for we described the characteristics of the strongest papers and the average papers for each grade level, examining their method and depth of development, organization, sentence structure, tone, and mechanics. These descriptors also gave us a developmental approach to the teaching of writing. We knew what an average student was in fact able to do, and that gave us the goals for the below-average students. We knew what a skilled writer could accomplish at a given grade level, and that provided the objectives for the average students. In other words, we had clear evidence of what was developmentally possible and made those our objectives rather than basing our curriculum on a list or standards from a textbook based on *other* students, not knowing how similar or different our kids were.

At first glance, the descriptors may seem to be duplicating the rubric. However, the rubric gives comparative descriptions (a paper receiving a score of 8 has more development and fewer mechanical errors, for example, than a paper receiving a score of 6). The descriptors are more specific and lead to clear recommendations for improving the curriculum. For example, we discovered that seventh and eighth graders typically were omitting an introduction and an ending for their papers. After putting more emphasis on these aspects in our program, we found seventh and eighth graders improving in this aspect over the years. The descriptors also included sample student papers.

Schedule of Writing Samples

The biggest problem we faced was incorporating our philosophical beliefs while meeting certain practical needs. If we used at least three prompts, we couldn't compare results fairly until the fourth year when the first mode would be repeated. We devised a schedule whereby the even-numbered grades (eight, ten, and twelve) wrote to the explanatory prompt and the odd-numbered grades (seven, nine, and eleven) wrote to the persuasive prompt during the same assessment. The following year, all students wrote to the narrative prompt. This way we would have comparisons in the same mode every two years. Further, an individual student would write to each of the three prompts only two times in her secondary career. In order to make these comparisons as valid as possible, we decided not to change the prompts for each mode. With the same topic we could pull papers each year from the papers written two years earlier and feel more confident that scores were similar. Without this anchoring with the earlier year, we wouldn't know if our scores were higher or lower simply because of changed expectations.

The second practical need involved the number of papers to be read. Holistic scoring is labor intensive (read "time and dollars"), so the first two years (spring 1985 and spring 1986) we had only the even-numbered grades produce papers. This was not satisfactory, however. Although we could compare grade levels in the two years, we were not comparing the same students and had no longitudinal data. In the fall of 1986, we began testing all students. We used the same prompts again in the fall of 1987 as we were eager to have comparative data—using the same prompts, longitudinal and grade-level comparisons could be made. In the fall of 1988, we reduced the number of papers by having only half the students in each grade level produce drafts. Now the first half of the alphabet in alternating grades and the last half of the alphabet in other grades produce the samples each year. The master plan then went into effect: 50 percent of the students in grades seven through twelve would be assessed every year, writing to the narrative prompt in 1988 and then the explanatory and persuasive prompts the following two years. That three-year cycle would then be repeated.

Prompts and Procedures

Fall 1987 and Fall 1989: Explanatory and Persuasive Prompts

Explanatory Prompt

Imagine [name of school] is hiring a new teacher. Write a letter to [name of principal] explaining the qualities of a good teacher that you think he should look for when interviewing teachers.

Persuasive Prompt

[Name of principal] has asked for suggestions about how to make things better at [name of school]. Write a letter to your principal telling just *one* thing you think should be changed and how the school will be improved. Your job is to *convince* the principal to make the change.

Fall 1988: Narrative Prompt

Think about *one physical object* (not an animal or person) that has meaning for you. Visualize how you got it, how you felt about getting it, and the importance it has played in your life.

After you have decided upon an object, tell about its life with you. Do you keep it on display and out of sight, or is it always with you? Over the years, has your feeling for it changed?

Why is this object important to you? Have you had good times together? Does it remind you of an event or person? Does it remind you of how you have changed? Does it cheer you up?

Write about your object so your teacher (who has never seen the object) will know why it is important to you. Concentrate upon telling about the history you share with the object.

Students have thirty minutes allotted for prewriting. The prewritings are collected and distributed later in the same week for a thirty-five minute drafting period. All drafts are collected, with the final on top. The students identify their papers on the *back* and complete a computer data sheet with identifying information such as name, student number, grade, sex, teacher code number, and number of words in their final draft. The teachers add to this data sheet the race for each student.

All secondary English teachers (and on occasion a teacher or two from another department, typically trained in process writing) meet to score the papers. In recent years, we have found two weekday evenings more suitable for our staff than Saturdays. Teachers review the prompt and the essential procedures for holistic scoring.

Following procedures generally recommended for holistic scoring (Myers 1980; White 1985), the group reads a set of anchor papers chosen by the leaders from past scorings on the same prompt and ranks those papers until they reach consensus. The nine papers—all copies of the original handwritten papers—reflect one for each score (1 through 8) plus a 0 paper that is off topic. The scores given to each coded paper are recorded in a matrix on the overhead so that all participants can see how they fit into the group's consensus. Although we have a rubric devised from the earlier scoring sessions, we find that participants internalize the rubric rather easily and don't rely on the printed form.

This anchoring is repeated until the group is consistent—within one rubric point of each other. At that time, actual papers to be read are given to each table; readers record their score on the computerized data sheet, which is clipped *behind* the draft to preserve anonymity. The leaders of the session see to it that papers read by one table are given to a different table for a second reading and not always the same second table. The second reader records the score and notes whether it is within one point of the first reader's score. If it is not, the paper is given to a session leader for a third reading. The leaders keep track of how many papers require a third reading and attempt to identify any participant who is consistently scoring higher or lower than the group. If necessary, a leader confers with such a participant, emphasizing the importance of reliability.

After two hours of quiet scoring, the group takes a break and then anchors again. The number of anchor papers used depends on how reliable the scores have been (determined by the number of third readings needed).

The interreader reliability for district scoring sessions is typically 90 percent or better. In other words, fewer than 10 percent of the papers have required a third reading because of a disagreement of more than one point between the first two readers.

After the scoring sessions, a computer service determines the all-student grade-level means as well as the means for each grade level by gender and by race. We also receive a frequency distribution and a correlation between word count and score. Finally, we receive a printout for each teacher of that teacher's students and their individual scores so the students can be informed.

The individual student scores range from 2 through 16, since the two independent readers' scores are added together.

Adapting Assessment for Our Research Project

Since the district assessment was taking place in the fall each year, these scores become the pre scores for our project. The first year of our project every student produced a draft and received a score. Each teacher simply had to select her two or three target students for the case studies from the available pool. Things were not as simple the next two years, when only 50 percent of the students in each grade produced an assessment paper. The second year, each project participant chose her target students from the part of the alphabet that was assessed. The third year, however, was complicated by the fact that we wanted to select all students in our classes who scored below the grade-level mean, yet we had data for only half our students.

The middle school teachers resolved the problem by giving the fall assessment to *all* their students both years. This created concern within the English department for nonstandard procedures but allowed us to have pre scores for all the seventh and eighth graders in the project. All middle school English teachers were project participants whereas only a few teachers in the high school English department were project participants. The project participants, along with volunteer teachers who were not project participants, scored the fall writings for those students in the half of the alphabet not scored for the district's assessment.

The result was two sets of pre scores, one for the district assessment and one for the project assessment. We took great care to make the two sessions comparable, even though we can't prove they were identical. The project readers constituted 70 to 80 percent of the district readers. Both groups of readers used identical anchors, procedures, and rubric. Notwithstanding these efforts, we restrict the data in Chapter 12 to fall district assessments.

The post scoring for the project, held each spring, was always done by the project participants plus two to four other high school English teachers. It was essential that we have the scores in the spring for at least two reasons: the same students would be compared from fall to spring and our grants required results prior to July 1. If we waited until the next regular fall assessment, our project students (both target and others) would be scattered among various classes.

In the spring, all students in classes with target students wrote to the same prompt they had responded to in the fall. Again the readers used the same anchors, rubric, and scoring procedures.

These inherent difficulties with the assessment are of some concern, but even if they could be solved, we would still have descriptive data as opposed to experimental data. The significance of our charts and graphs is the repetition of the improved scores over four years—even when over 30 percent of all the students were target students. Moreover, we believe that the real proof of improved writing skill is found in the target students' pre and post writings, which follow the descriptive data in Chapter 12.

NOTES

1. Leadership in writing assessment involved many teachers; those particularly associated with planning and directing the assessment over the years were Jerry Solomon, Joan Krater, Agnes Gregg, Sandra Tabscott, and Bob Hutcheson.

2. This kind of time limit was in keeping with general practice across the country. Indeed, even today the National Assessment of Educational Progress (NAEP) permits students just fifteen minutes to respond to each of their three prompts, which may explain the low quality of the papers. Recently this fifteen minutes was doubled to thirty minutes for some subsets of writing samples, but NAEP maintains the increased time does not change the quality of writing.

Recommended Student Literature

Bell-Mathis, Sharon. 1972. *Teacup Full of Roses*. New York: Puffin Books.

Bernstein, Leonard, et al. 1958. *West Side Story*. New York: Random House.

Borland, Hal. 1964. *When the Legends Die*. New York: Bantam Books.

Bradbury, Ray. 1975. "Mars Is Heaven." In *Perception,* edited by G. Robert Carlsen and Ruth Christoffer Carlsen. New York: McGraw-Hill.

Chapman, Abraham, ed. 1968. *Black Voices: An Anthology of Afro-American Literature*. New York: NAL/Dutton.

Coe, Charles. 1990. *Young Man in Viet Nam*. New York: Scholastic.

Dasent, George W., trans. 1988. *East of the Sun and West of the Moon*. New York: Putnam Publishing Group.

Emberley, Ed. 1977. *The Great Thumbprint Drawing Book*. Boston: Little, Brown.

Ellison, Ralph. 1989. *Invisible Man*. New York: Random House.

Frank, Anne. [1947] 1989. *Diary of a Young Girl*. New York: Pocket Books.

Guy, Rosa. 1987. *And I Heard a Bird Sing*. New York: Laurel-Leaf Books.

Hamilton, Virginia. 1985. *The People Could Fly: American Black Folktales*. New York: Alfred A. Knopf.

Hansbury, Lorraine. 1989. *Raisin in the Sun*. New York: Penguin Books.

Harris, Eddie. 1989. *Mississippi Solo: A River Quest*. New York: HarperCollins.

———. 1992. *Native Stranger*. New York: HarperCollins.

Hayden, Robert. 1985. *Selected Poems by Robert Hayden,* edited by Frederick Glaysher. New York: Liveright Publishing.

Hesse, Hermann. 1982. *Siddhartha*. New York: Bantam Books.

Hughes, Langston. 1990. *Selected Poems of Langston Hughes*. New York: Random House.

Hurston, Zora Neale. 1990. *Their Eyes Were Watching God*. New York: HarperCollins.

Keyes, Daniel. 1966. *Flowers for Algernon*. New York: Bantam Books.

King, Stephen. 1988. *Misery*. New York: NAL/Dutton.

Lee, Harper. 1988. *To Kill a Mockingbird*. New York: Warner Books.

Lester, Julius. 1970. *Black Folktales*. New York: Grove Weidenfeld.

Morrison, Toni. 1984. *The Bluest Eye*. New York: Pocket Books.

———. 1988. *Beloved*. New York: NAL/Dutton.

Myers, Walter Dean. 1990. *Scorpions*. New York: Harper & Row.

———. 1991. *The Legend of Tarik*. New York: Scholastic.

Neufield, John. 1969. *Edgar Allen*. New York: Signet.

Noyes, Alfred. 1990. *The Highwayman*. San Diego, CA: Harcourt Brace.

O'Dell, Scott. 1976. *Sing Down the Moon*. New York: Dell Publishing.

Parks, Gordon. 1987. *The Learning Tree*. New York: Fawcett Book Group.

Richards, Arlene Kramer. 1991. *What to Do If You or Someone You Know Is Under 18 and Pregnant*. New York: Morrow, William & Co.

Scholl, Ralph. 1969. "The Golden Axe." In *Focus,* edited by Leo B. Kneer. New York: Scott, Foresman.

Shakespeare, William. 1988. *Romeo and Juliet*. New York: Bantam.

Smith, Lee. 1989. *Fair and Tender Ladies*. New York: Ballantine.

Speare, Elizabeth George. 1984. *Sign of the Beaver*. New York: Dell Publishing.

Steinbeck, John. 1983. *Of Mice and Men*. New York: Bantam Books.

Steptoe, John. 1987. *Mufaro's Beautiful Daughters*. New York: Scholastic.

Taylor, Mildred. 1981. *Let the Circle Be Unbroken*. New York: Bantam Books.

———. 1987. *The Friendship*. New York: Dial Books for Young Readers.

———. 1987. *The Gold Cadillac*. New York: Dial Books for Young Readers.

———. 1989. *Roll of Thunder, Hear My Cry*. New York: Bantam Books.

————. 1990. *The Road to Memphis.* New York: Puffin Books.

Updike, John. 1985. "August." In *The Oxford Book of Children's Verse in America,* edited by Donald Hall. New York: Oxford University Press.

Walker, Alice. 1983. *In Search of Our Mothers' Gardens: Womanist Prose.* San Diego, CA: Harcourt Brace Jovanovich.

Wright, Richard. 1989. *Black Boy.* New York: HarperCollins.

Young, Ed. 1989. *Egyptian Cinderella (Lon Po Po).* New York: Thomas Y. Crowell Junior Books.

Videotapes

Eyes on the Prize: America's Civil Rights Years. 1990. Produced, directed, and written by Paul Stekler and Jacqueline Shearer. 720 minutes. Blackside. Distributed by PBS Video. Six videocassettes.

The Last Emperor. 1987. Produced by Jeremy Thomas. Directed by Bernardo Bertolucci. 164 minutes. Hemdale Film Corporation. Videocassette.

West Side Story. [1961] 1984. Produced by Robert Wise. Directed by Robert Wise and Jerome Robbins. 152 minutes. CBS/Fox Video. Videocassette.

Team Member Biographies

Cathy Beck, who joined the district and the project in 1988, brought with her extensive knowledge and experience in applying whole language theory to seventh- and-eighth grade classes. She had taught fifteen years in two contrasting districts, one a very small town and the other a large and growing suburban district. The small town prided itself on being all-White, and although many parents commuted an hour to St. Louis County for work, they considered the county "too liberal." The anti-education attitude of the parents and students drove her from teaching to the business world; she was an editor for C. V. Mosby Publishing for two years. She loved working with the authors of college texts, learned a great deal about anthropology, forensic science, physical education, and a variety of other disciplines but was disillusioned by the way the business world treated its loyal employees.

She returned to teaching in a fast-growing district where parents were college educated and/or aspired to be and valued education for their children. The few rural students in this geographically large district lived in viable farming families. The enrollment was only $1\frac{1}{2}$ percent African American.

Around this time Cathy, who had a bachelor's degree in secondary education and a master's in English from Southeast Missouri State, took a class in whole language and became involved in a local Teachers Applying Whole Language (TAWL) group started by Shirley Crenshaw and Kathryn Pierce. She had used literature study groups before coming to Webster Groves and shared that practice along with her whole language knowledge with the other action research team members, who immediately saw the value of both approaches.

Cathy has made numerous presentations about our project to the National Council of Teachers of English, the Association for Supervision and

Curriculum Development, the National Staff Development Council, and the Writing Conference in Mobile, Alabama, as well as inservice workshops on whole language for teachers in the Archdiocese of St. Louis, the Alton School District, and Whole Language Umbrella conferences.

The Transescent, a publication of the Missouri Middle School Association, published Cathy's article "The Three Bears Prefer Pizza: Updating Fairy Tales Sparks Student Interest," in November 1989. Three of her lessons are found in *Hear You, Hear Me!* (Webster Groves Writing Project 1992).

Beth Ann Brady brought nine years of teaching to the writing project. She received her bachelor of journalism degree in 1976 from the well-respected journalism school at the University of Missouri, Columbia. After some years of teaching and raising children, she returned to classes at Webster University, receiving her master's in teaching in 1991.

Beth Ann taught English for grades nine through twelve at Webster Groves High School as well as journalism. The high school newspaper, *The Echo,* has received national recognition for its quality. She has helped in writing project presentations, notably at the National Council of Teachers of English fall convention in Louisville.

Her role in the project carried a slightly different twist since her teaching was with mostly junior and senior students specialized in journalism. She recognizes that all writers, from novice to advanced, can benefit from the principles and strategies of teaching. Beth Ann joined the project in its fourth year. She informed herself along the way, reading the syntheses and results of the four previous years, and remained a member of the team until the fall of 1993 when she began teaching journalism at Clayton High School in a neighboring district.

Nancy Cason earned her bachelor's degree in secondary education with majors in Spanish and English from the University of Missouri, Columbia. She received her master's in Teaching from Webster University.

Nancy began teaching in the Francis Howell School District in St. Charles, Missouri. She taught for three years, then "retired" to raise her son, Dan, and her daughter, Becca. During the eight years she did not teach, she remained extremely involved in education—the education of her children. She served on the executive board of the parent organization at Bristol Elementary School in the Webster Groves School District and worked on many volunteer committees

She returned to teaching in 1981 at Hixson Middle School and Webster Groves High School, teaching Spanish, journalism, and creative writing. Nancy teaches seventh and eighth graders and joined the project its first year. She has been the director of the writing project for the last four years. In this capacity, she has introduced our action research project to a number of audiences: the National Council of Teachers of English in Seattle and Louisville; the National Staff Development Council in Washington, D.C.; the Association of Supervision and Curriculum Development in Chicago and San Antonio; and to Missouri teachers in Washington, University City, Kirkwood, Valley Park, and at Webster University.

Nancy has coauthored several articles, including "Improving Writing of At-Risk Students with a Focus on African-American Males: A Collaborative Action Research Project," in the summer 1991 issue of *Breadloaf News* (Cason, Tabscott, and Krater-Thomas 1991). Two of her lessons are in *Hear You, Hear Me!* (Webster Groves Writing Project 1992).

As an original member of the project, she has seen it grow in the number of teachers involved and in scope. No longer do teachers just focus on target students. They have directed their study to encompass a wide range of topics—writers' workshop, portfolios, learning styles, multicultural literature, and writing across the curriculum. She believes that this working environment is indeed the best way for teachers and students alike to thrive and grow.

Stephanie Gavin came to Hixson Middle School in 1989 to teach eighth graders when the project was starting its third year. Fortunately, she had access to the synthesis reports and other materials from previous years. In the monthly study sessions, she could ask questions of her new colleagues as she tried to catch up. Making her first presentation at an Illinois state writing conference in February of 1990 was her initiation as a team member; she had to know and understand the project's history, principles, and current philosophy. She has continued to represent the team, most recently at the National Council of Teachers of English convention in Louisville in 1992.

A 1987 graduate from the University of Missouri, Columbia, in English Education, Stephanie was introduced to the secondary English curriculum in courses with Ben Nelms, current editor of *English Journal.* She was in one of the first classes to graduate with writing process courses on its transcripts. She taught briefly in Kansas City (a semester at Raytown High School and a year at Center Junior High), in middle-class integrated suburban schools much like Webster Groves.

Perhaps it was easier for Stephanie to adapt to the project because she had not yet formed more traditional teaching habits to break. In fact, her whole career path has evolved from writing project principles and the mentoring of veteran members. She completed her master's in English with a writing emphasis at the University of Missouri, St. Louis in 1993. The degree included credits for the Gateway Writing Project summer institute (1991) and a project in multicultural adolescent literature (based on the study groups we use at Hixson), which she field-tested with Jane Zeni's English methods course and will be teaching for the university. *Hear You, Hear Me!* (Webster Groves Writing Project 1992) includes two of Stephanie's lessons.

———

Agnes Gregg is a reading specialist who has spent her twenty-year career with classes labeled "basic," "at risk," or "remedial." She earned a bachelor's degree in sociology at the University of Missouri, St. Louis, and soon after graduation obtained her teaching certificates in social studies and English; her master's in reading followed.

After college, she served as a V.I.S.T.A. volunteer, followed by teaching middle school reading for three years at a Catholic school in St. Louis. She also volunteered for a while at a private school for teenagers with emotional problems.

Since 1976 she has taught in the Webster Groves School District, working with ninth and tenth graders in reading and English. Agnes has often been at the forefront of innovation. She led a grant-funded program for at-risk students combining English, reading, and social studies; she gave staff development workshops on reading in the content areas and contributed to a textbook. In 1979 she signed up for the Gateway Writing Project's summer institute, returning in 1984 to a GWP institute with a focus on computers and writing.

Agnes has brought to the team an understanding that reading, writing, and subject learning are inseparable. Her conviction that labeling and tracking do not support a democratic educational experience has energized the team to face these issues at the high school. Agnes has represented the team at the National Council of Teachers of English in Louisville.

———

Carolyn Henly came to Webster Groves High School as a second-year teacher in 1988, which was also the second year of the writing project. She had earned a bachelor's in linguistics from the University of California, Berkeley, in 1982 and a master's in secondary education from the University of Illinois in 1987. During her three years with the project, she contributed some of our most vivid and detailed field notes as well as some of our most complex and artful curriculum sequences. She brought to the team a focus on language—not only by using language carefully but also by reflecting on language and its implications for human beings.

Before coming to Webster Groves, Carrie had worked with two contrasting groups of students. As a teaching assistant at the University of Illinois in rhetoric and composition, she taught for two years in the Educational Opportunity Program, which served basic, mostly African American writers. As a first-year teacher at New Trier Township High School in Winnetka, Illinois, she worked in a privileged public school with affluent White students.

496

Carrie helped share our work at the Basic Writers' Conference in 1990 at Southern Illinois University, Edwardsville. She has made numerous presentations, including one on teaching how to revise at the National Council of Teachers of English (NCTE) convention in Seattle. Her presentation at NCTE in Baltimore on teaching fantasy and science fiction was later published in the *ALAN Review* (a publication of the Assembly on Literature for Adolescents of the National Council of Teachers of English).

Carrie writes consistently and in many modes. Her article on teaching Toni Morrisson's *Bluest Eye* appeared in the *English Journal* (Henly 1993). Two of her lessons are found in *Hear You, Hear Me!* (Webster Groves Writing Project 1992). Other articles by Carrie have been published in the *Illinois English Bulletin, Spectrum* (the journal of the Illinois Science Teachers Association), and the *English Journal.*

Carrie is a playwright as well. Her play, *My Sister's Marriage,* based on the short story of the same name, was produced in Chicago in 1991 and revived in 1992. Carrie has completed a novel, written poetry, and is currently writing her second play.

———

Mary Ann Kelly brings twenty-two years of teaching experience to her seventh-grade students. She grew up in Chicago, received her bachelor's degree from the College of St. Catherine in St. Paul, Minnesota, and started her family in Montana. Mary Ann received her master's in teaching from Webster University in Webster Groves, Missouri. Her undergraduate work led her to major in both theater and English while her graduate focuses were literature and the teaching of it.

Mary Ann joined the project in its second year, bringing to it her strong literature and drama background. She has introduced teachers and students alike to diverse literary selections.

A poet in her own right, Mary Ann has also authored a lesson, "Extended Family Interviews," in *Hear You, Hear Me!* a publication of the Webster Groves School District (1992).

A native St. Louisan, **Joan Krater** earned her bachelor's degree in elementary education from Webster University in 1963. She began teaching next door at a Webster Groves junior high school where "core" classes of English and social studies stayed together for both seventh and eighth grades. Thirteen years later, this school closed its doors as a junior high school and Joan moved to Hixson. By 1971 she had earned her master's in secondary education with a major in social studies at Indiana University and, of course, taught English ever after!

For three different years, Joan wrote and directed federal grant programs under Title VII, then Title VI, aimed at lessening the effects of segregation. Another grant she helped to write established the Gateway Writing Project, an affiliate of the National Writing Project. Participating in the project the summer of 1979, Joan was a consultant for the Shawnee Mission School District (in Kansas) during the summers of 1981 through 1983, teaching process writing to over a hundred teachers.

A leader in curriculum development and assessment, Joan spearheaded the district's holistic assessment of writing in 1985, helped Theresa Wojak write the initial grant for this project, and led the project until her sabbatical in 1989–90. During her sabbatical, Joan was an intern at the Regional Consortium for Educational Technology, learning about technology and leading workshops for teachers. Upon her return to the district, Joan took on a dual role of teaching gifted students and serving as the technology resource for Hixson. Joan has authored and coauthored several articles on the teaching of writing previously under the name Joan Krater Thomas. Joan retired from classroom teaching in the spring of 1993 but continues to work for the district in a variety of roles.

Chestra Peaslee grew up in an integrated neighborhood of Oak Park, outside of Chicago. She played on several athletic teams at her high school, which was 60 percent White and 40 percent Black.

Chestra majored in English Literature for her bachelor's degree, which she received from Washington University in St. Louis in 1987. She continued her studies to get teacher certification and her M.Ed. at the University of Missouri, St. Louis, with a major in secondary school curriculum. Chestra did her student teaching at Webster Groves High School and has been teaching ninth- and tenth-grade English courses for three years.

Chestra spoke at the induction ceremony for Kappa Delta Pi in the spring of 1993 on "Reaching Students Through Teaching," telling of the project and how it has helped her to reach those "floundering" students.

During the summer of 1993, Chestra moved to Detroit with her husband and child.

Minnie Phillips has spent almost all of her twenty-five year teaching career at Webster Groves High School. She came to the district shortly after graduating from the University of Missouri, Columbia in English education with minors in speech and drama. While at the high school she completed a master's degree in secondary education at the University of Missouri, St. Louis. She left Webster Groves for two years (1988–90) when she was recruited to teach at John Burroughs, a prestigious private secondary school. She returned to serve as coordinator of writing across the curriculum at Webster Groves High School while continuing to teach English at all grades (nine through twelve) and all levels (basic to honors).

Although Minnie grew up in a small African American community and started out in segregated public schools, she moved in predominantly White educational environments during college and graduate school as well as during her teaching career. She is working on a doctorate in administration with an emphasis on qualitative research (through seminars with Professor Lou Smith) and English (through the Gateway Writing Project summer institute in 1991).

As our only African American member, Minnie has been an invaluable resource to us, her colleagues, in the struggle to reach beyond our own racial and cultural experiences. Through her graduate work she has been immersed in issues of language, politics, and power; at team meetings, Minnie will listen to a set of classroom stories, then pull them together with questions or interpretations that move the discussion to a new level. She has copresented our research at the National Council of Teachers of English in Seattle in 1991 and in Louisville 1992.

Sandra Tabscott began her formal teaching career at the ripe old age of forty. She received her bachelor's degree from Concord College in Athens, West Virginia, and her master's in teaching from Webster University in St. Louis.

She has taught for sixteen years at Hixson Middle School. Besides teaching English classes, Sandra has worked in more specialized programs such as Title 1 classes, which is a language program for below-grade-level students in the days before the writing project. Since then, classes of this nature have been eliminated in favor of heterogeneous groupings of students.

Sandy joined the project the first year. In 1992, a National Endowment for the Humanities grant afforded her a summer study program in African American literature at Trinity College in Hartford, Connecticut, with the distinguished professor, James Miller.

She has represented the Webster Groves Writing Project in presentations at local, state, national, and international conferences such as the National Council Teachers of English in Seattle and Louisville; the National Staff Development Council in Washington D.C.; the Association for Supervision and Curriculum Development in Chicago; the Gulf Coast Conference on Writing in Mobile, Alabama; and Missouri's Write to Learn Conference.

Sandy was one of the authors of "Improving Writing of At-Risk Students with a Focus on African American Males: A Collaborative Action Research Project," which *Breadloaf News* published in the summer of 1991 (Cason, Tabscott, and Krater-Thomas 1991). Two of Sandy's lessons were published in *Hear You, Hear Me!* (Webster Groves Writing Project 1992).

Gail Taylor began her teaching career in Calhoun, Missouri, teaching speech and drama, which had been her minor at Southwest Baptist University in Bolivar, Missouri. The total high school enrollment in this rural town was approximately 120 students. Her husband was the pastor of a local church and her speech certification served the community well as they desired to improve the schools' rating from the state and one requirement was that they add speech courses to the high school curriculum. After two years the Taylors moved to a suburb of Chicago where Gail stayed home with her two preschoolers.

Six years later, Gail began substituting at Central Junior High in Steger, Illinois, where Hispanics were the sizable minority rather than African Americans. Gail taught Spanish and history as well as her major, English. After one year, they moved to St. Louis and Gail substituted almost every day, teaching almost every subject. After subbing for a year at Hixson and other schools, Webster Groves asked her to teach English full time.

Her only other teaching experience had been on the high school level, so her first year of teaching seventh-grade English was one of trial and error. The project began during her second year and she was eager to participate because she had a desire to understand the inequality of the district assessment scores and to learn teaching strategies that would help reverse this disparaging trend.

Gail earned her master's in teaching at Webster University in secondary language arts with an emphasis on communication. She copresented the project's work at the Missouri Middle School Association Conference in the spring of 1990. Two of her lessons are published in *Hear You, Hear Me!* (Webster Groves Writing Project 1992).

JoAnne Williams began her teaching career in the Missouri Ozarks with students from a variety of backgrounds: Amish, lake resort area people, and town residents. Generally middle class, the student enrollment was only 5 percent African American. After two years of teaching, JoAnne dabbled in retail work and the historical restoration of buildings and furnishings. During that time, she substituted in various classrooms. Six years later, JoAnne returned to teaching as an elementary reading specialist in a suburban district for one year and then joined the writing project at Webster Groves, where she has been for three years. All of her experience has been with seventh and eighth graders with the exception of her one year as reading specialist.

JoAnne's bachelor's degree in English was from Central Methodist College in Fayette, Missouri in 1976. After many years of part-time study, she earned her master's in teaching, majoring in communications with a speciality in reading from Webster University in 1989.

JoAnne has brought to the writing project her reading background, which has helped strengthen the reading/writing connection for all of us. Along with Gail Taylor and Stephanie Gavin, she copresented our work at the Missouri Middle School Association's Annual Conference in 1991.

———

Theresa Wojak began teaching in Webster Groves after receiving her bachelor's in English from the University of Missouri, St. Louis, in 1986. It was during her first year that Theresa provided the spark that led to the writing project. While teaching, she earned her master's in teaching in 1991 in the area of communications with an emphasis on secondary language arts from Webster University.

Theresa was in the project for three years, teaching primarily ninth-grade courses, although students from all four high school grades were often included. She presented our work at the University of Missouri, St. Louis, and at Southern Illinois University, Edwardsville, spreading the word about the project, its principles, and its strategies. Two of Theresa's lessons were published in *Hear You, Hear Me!* (Webster Groves Writing Project 1992).

No longer teaching, Theresa is pursuing a second career as a social worker and therapist. Her second master's degree, this one in social work with a mental health concentration and a family therapy specialization, was completed in December 1993 from Washington University in St. Louis. As a psychotherapist, Theresa provides outpatient therapy based on a biological-psychological-social-spiritual model. In addition, she provides inpatient care as a group facilitator for chemically dependent pregnant women and teaches a course in cognitive therapy.

———

During the twenty-four years since she began teaching, **Jane Zeni** has worked with every level—from preschool through doctoral students. Her home base since 1977 has been the University of Missouri, St. Louis, where she has taught preservice English education, composition (especially basic writing), and graduate writing courses. As director of Gateway Writing Project, she has led many summer institutes and inservice workshops and serves as consultant to action researchers.

Jane was born in New York City and earned a bachelor's at Harvard and a master's at the University of Pennsylvania in literature. In 1969 she joined six teachers planning an alternative school in Philadelphia; they sought diversity in race (Black and White students), class (with a sliding fee scale), and culture (meeting in the city and on a farm). After a year's immersion with ages nine through eighteen, she knew she had much to learn, so she earned her certification to teach English. She lived in Santa Fe, New Mexico, from 1970 to 1975 and taught kindergarten through sixth-grade classes at the Pueblo Indian day schools. Later she taught secondary English at St. Michael's High School in Santa Fe, where most students were Hispanic, bilingual, and college bound.

While Jane pursued her master's in curriculum at the Ontario Institute for Studies in Education, professors James Britton and Frank Smith introduced her to process-oriented teaching. Soon after arriving in St. Louis, she put this new knowledge to use by leading the first Gateway Writing Project summer institute. Working with teachers motivated her to enroll again in graduate school, completing her Ed.D. at the University of Missouri, St. Louis, in 1985. Her dissertation, an action research project involving computers, led to the book *WritingLands* (NCTE 1990). Jane has also published many articles on teaching English.

REFERENCES

American Tongues. 1986. Produced and directed by Louis Alvarez and Andrew Kolker, Center for Applied Linguistics. 56 minutes (40-minute version available). New York: New Day Films. Videocassette.

APPLEBEE, ARTHUR. 1981. *Writing in the Secondary School: English and the Content Areas*. NCTE Research Report no. 21. Urbana, IL: National Council of Teachers of English.

———. 1984. *Contexts for Learning to Write: Studies of Secondary School Instruction*. Norwood, NJ: Ablex.

———. 1986. "Problems in Process Approaches: Toward a Reconceptualization of Process Instruction." In *The Teaching of Writing, Eighty-fifth Yearbook of the National Society for the Study of Education*, Part 2, edited by A. Petrosky. Chicago: University of Chicago Press.

———. 1993. *Literature in the Secondary School: Studies of Curriculum and Instruction in the United States*. NCTE Research Report no. 25. Urbana, IL: National Council of Teachers of English.

ASCHER, CAROL. 1992. "School Programs for African American Males . . . and Females." *Phi Delta Kappan* 73(10): 777–81.

ATWELL, NANCIE. 1982. "Class-Based Writing Research." *English Journal* 71(3): 84–87.

———. 1987. *In the Middle: Writing, Reading, and Learning with Adolescents*. Portsmouth, NH: Boynton/Cook.

BAYER, ANN SHEA. 1990. *Collaborative Apprenticeship Learning: Language and Thinking Across the Curriculum, K–12*. Mountain View, CA: Mayfield.

BERNHARDT, STEPHEN, and BRUCE APPLEBY. 1985. "Collaboration in Professional Writing with the Computer: Results of a Survey." *Computers and Composition* 3(1): 29–42.

BISSEX, GLENDA, and RICHARD BULLOCK. 1987. *Seeing for Ourselves: Case Study Research by Teachers of Writing*. Portsmouth, NH: Heinemann.

BLEICH, DAVID. 1975. *Readings and Feelings: An Introduction to Subjective Criticism*. Urbana, IL: National Council of Teachers of English.

BOUTTE, GLORIA. 1992. "Frustrations of an African American Parent: A Personal and Professional Account." *Phi Delta Kappan* 73 (10): 786–88.

REFERENCES

BOYER, ERNEST. 1983. *The High School: A Report on Secondary Education in America*. New York: Harper & Row.

BRITTON, JAMES. 1970. *Language and Learning*. New York: Penguin.

BRITTON, JAMES, TONY BURGESS, NANCY MARTIN, ALEX MCLEOD, and HAROLD ROSEN. 1975. *The Development of Writing Abilities* (11–18). London: Macmillan.

BROOKS, CHARLOTTE, ed. 1985. *Tapping Potential: English and Language Arts for the Black Learner*. Urbana, IL: National Council of Teachers of English.

BRUFFEE, KENNETH. 1983. "Writing and Reading as Collaborative Acts." In *The Writer's Mind: Writing as a Mode of Thinking*, edited by J. N. Hays, P. A. Roth, J. R. Ramsey, and R. D. Foulke. Urbana, IL: National Council of Teachers of English.

BRUNER, JEROME. 1978. "The Role of Dialogue in Language Acquisition." In *The Child's Concept of Language*, edited by A. Sinclair et al. New York: Springer Verlag.

BURLING, ROBBINS. 1970. *English in Black and White*. New York: Holt, Rinehart, and Winston.

BUTLER, MELVIN, chair, and members of the Committee on CCCC Language Statement. 1974. *Students' Rights to Their Own Language. College Composition and Communication* 25(3): 1–32.

CALKINS, LUCY MCCORMICK. 1983. *Lessons from a Child: On the Teaching and Learning of Writing*. Portsmouth, NH: Heinemann.

———. 1986. *The Art of Teaching Writing*. Portsmouth, NH: Heinemann.

CARR, WILFRED, and STEPHEN KEMMIS. 1986. *Becoming Critical: Education, Knowledge and Action Research*. London: Falmer.

CASON, NANCY, SANDRA TABSCOTT, and JOAN KRATER-THOMAS. 1991. "Improving Writing of At-Risk Students with a Focus on African American Males: A Collaborative Action Research Project." *Breadloaf News* 5(1): 22–29, 37.

COCHRAN-SMITH, MARILYN, and SUSAN LYTLE. 1993. *Inside Outside: Teacher Research and Knowledge*. New York: Teachers College.

COLEMAN, JAMES S. et al. 1966. *Equality of Educational Opportunity*. Report #OE-38001. National Center for Educational Statistics. Washington, D.C.: U.S. Department of Health, Education, and Welfare.

CONCIATORE, JACQUELINE. 1990. "Shortage of Minority Teachers Leads Some to Look to Majority." *Black Issues in Higher Education* 7(10): 8–9.

CONNORS, ROBERT, and ANDREA LUNSFORD. 1988. "Frequency of Formal Errors in Current College Writing, or Ma and Pa Kettle Do Research." *College Composition and Communication* 39(4): 395–409.

CURETON, GEORGE. 1985. "Using a Black Learning Style." In *Tapping Potential*, edited by Charlotte Brooks. Urbana, IL: National Council of Teachers of English.

DANDY, EVELYN. 1991. *Black Communications: D* African American Images.

DAVIDOFF, SUE, and OWEN VAN DEN BERG. 1990. *C* *Challenge of the Classroom*. Teaching for Transfor South Africa: University of the Western Cape/Centaur

DELPIT, LISA. 1986. "Skills and Other Dilemmas of a Progress *Harvard Educational Review* 56(4): 379–85.

———. 1988. "The Silenced Dialogue: Power and Pedagogy in E People's Children." *Harvard Educational Review* 58(3): 280–98.

———. 1992. "Education in a Multicultural Society: Our Future's Greatest Cha *Journal of Negro Education* 61(3): 237–49.

DILLARD, J. L. 1972. *Black English*. New York: Random House.

DU BOIS, W. E. B. [1903] 1961. *The Souls of Black Folk*. Greenwich, CT: Fawcett.

ELLIOTT, JOHN. 1991. *Action Research for Educational Change*. Philadelphia: Open University Press.

ELLISON, RALPH. 1952. *The Invisible Man*. New York: HarperCollins.

EMIG, JANET. 1971. *The Composing Processes of Twelfth Graders*. Urbana, IL: National Council of Teachers of English.

EMIG, JANET, and BARBARA KING. 1979. "Emig/King Writing Attitude Scale." Unpublished test manuscript.

FARR, MARCIA, and HARVEY DANIELS. 1986. *Language Diversity and Writing Instruction*. Urbana, IL: National Council of Teachers of English.

FARRELL, THOMAS. 1987. "Literacy, the Basics, and All That Jazz." In *Sourcebook for Basic Writing Teachers*, edited by Theresa Enos. New York: Random House.

FARR-WHITEMAN, MARCIA. 1981. "Dialect Influence in Writing." In *Writing: The Nature, Development, and Teaching of Written Communication*. Vol 1, *Variation in Writing: Functional and Linguistic-Cultural Differences*, edited by M. Farr-Whiteman. Hillsdale, NJ: Erlbaum.

FITZGERALD, SALLYANNE. 1988. "Relationships Between Conferencing and Movement Between General and Specific in Basic Writers' Compositions." *Dissertation Abstracts International* 48 3040A.

FITZSIMMONS, ROBERT, and BRADLEY LOOMER. 1977. *Spelling: Learning and Instruction—Research and Practice*. Iowa City: University of Iowa.

FLORIO-RUANE, SUSAN. 1986. *Taking a Closer Look at Writing Conferences*. Presentation at the annual American Educational Research Association, San Francisco, April ERIC, ED 275–003.

ic Study of the Teaching

College." Unpublished

ck Student Writers." In

a, IL: National Council of

Literature, Writing, Word

Mendocino, CA: Creative

: Herder and Herder.

st as Author. Stanford, CA:

uccess in School of Poor

; Literature Study Groups."

nillan.

GLASER, BARNEY, and ANSLEM STRAUSS. 1967. *Discovery of Grounded Theory.* Chicago: Aldine.

GOMEZ, MARY LOUISE. 1991. "The Equitable Teaching of Composition with Computers: A Case for Change." In *Evolving Perspectives on Computers and Composition Studies: Questions for the 1990s,* edited by Gail Hawisher and Cynthia Selfe. Urbana, IL: National Council of Teachers of English.

GOSWAMI, DIXIE, and PETER STILLMAN. 1987. *Reclaiming the Classroom: Teacher Research as an Agency for Change.* Portsmouth, NH: Boynton/Cook.

GRAVES, DONALD. 1979. "What Children Show Us About Revision." *Language Arts* 56(3): 312–19.

———. 1983. *Writing: Children and Teachers at Work.* Portsmouth, NH: Heinemann.

GREENFIELD, ELOISE. 1986. *Honey, I Love.* New York: HarperCollins Children's Books.

GREENLEAF, CYNTHIA. 1992. *Technological Indeterminacy: The Role of Classroom Writing Practices in Shaping Computer Use.* Technical Report no. 57. Berkeley, CA: Center for the Study of Writing.

HALE-BENSON, JANICE. 1982. *Black Children: Their Roots, Culture and Learning Styles.* Provo, UT: Brigham Young University Press.

———. 1986. *Black Children: Their Roots, Culture, and Learning Styles.* Rev. ed. Baltimore: Johns Hopkins University Press.

————. 1988. "African Heritage Theory and Afro-American Cognitive Styles." *Educational Considerations* 15(1): 6–9.

HAMMERSLEY, MARTYN, and PAUL ATKINSON. 1983. *Ethnography: Principles in Practice.* London: Tavistock.

HANSON, BOB, HARVEY SILVER, and RICHARD STRONG. 1992. Series of workshops for the Webster Groves and Ladue School Districts on learning styles, August 1992–January 1993.

HARE, NATHAN, and JULIA HARE. 1985. *Bringing the Black Boy to Manhood.* San Francisco: Black Think Tank.

HARSTE, JEROME, KATHY SHORT, and CAROLYN BURKE. 1988. *Creating Classrooms for Authors: The Reading-Writing Connection.* Portsmouth, NH: Heinemann.

HEATH, SHIRLEY BRICE. 1983. *Ways with Words.* New York: Cambridge University Press.

HENLY, CAROLYN P. 1993. "Reader-Response Theory as Antidote to Controversy: Teaching *The Bluest Eye.*" *English Journal* 82(3): 14–19.

HILLOCKS, GEORGE. 1986. *Research on Written Composition.* Urbana, IL: National Council of Teachers of English.

HOOD, MARIAN WHITE. 1991. "African American Males in the Middle School: One School's Efforts at Empowerment." *The Clearing House* 65: 4–7.

HOWARD, JEFF. 1990. *Getting Smart: The Social Construction of Intelligence.* Detroit: The Efficacy Institute.

HOWARD, JEFF, and RAY HAMMOND. 1985. "Rumors of Inferiority." *The New Republic* (Sept. 9): 17–21.

HUGHES, LANGSTON. 1974. *Selected Poems.* New York: Random House.

HULL, GLYNDA. 1987. "Constructing Taxonomies for Error (Or Can Stray Dogs Be Mermaids?)." In *Sourcebook for Basic Writing Teachers,* edited by Theresa Enos. New York: Random House.

HUNT, KELLOGG. 1978. "Early Blooming and Late Blooming Syntactic Structures." In *Evaluating Writing: Describing, Measuring, Judging,* edited by Charles Cooper and Lee Odell. Urbana, IL: National Council of Teachers of English.

IRVINE, JACQUELINE. 1988. "An Analysis of the Problem of Disappearing Black Educators." *Elementary School Journal* 88(5): 503–13.

JENKINS, WILLIAM. 1990. *Essays on Education: The Most Definitive Word Yet on the Education of Black Children, Particularly the Black Male.* St. Louis: William Jenkins.

JOHNSON, DAVID, RICHARD JOHNSON, and EDYTHE JOHNSON HOLUBEC. 1988. *Cooperation in the Classroom.* Rev. ed. Edina, MN: Interaction Books.

KASH, M. M., and G. D. BORICH. 1978. *Teacher Behavior and Pupil Self-Concept.* Reading, MA: Addison-Wesley.

REFERENCES

KIRKLAND, JACK A. 1987. "Black Youth: A Sociological Perspective." *Connections* (Summer): 8–11.

KUNJUFU, JAWANZA. 1983. *Countering the Conspiracy to Destroy Black Boys.* Vol 1. Chicago: African American Images.

———. 1986. *Countering the Conspiracy to Destroy Black Boys.* Vol 2. Chicago: African American Images.

———. 1988. *To Be Popular or Smart: The Black Peer Group.* Chicago: African American Images.

LABOV, WILLIAM. 1970. *The Study of Nonstandard English.* Urbana, IL: National Council of Teachers of English.

LADSON-BILLINGS, GLORIA. 1990. "Culturally Relevant Teaching: Effective Instruction for Black Students." *The College Board Review* 155 (Spring): 20–25.

LANGER, JUDITH, and ARTHUR APPLEBEE. 1984. "Language, Learning, and Interaction: A Framework for Improving the Teaching of Writing." In *Contexts for Learning to Write: Studies of Secondary School Instruction,* edited by Arthur Applebee. Norwood, NJ: Ablex.

LEADERSHIP ACADEMY. 1989. "Satellite Academy Members Confront 'Rumors of Inferiority.'" *Missouri Leadership Letter* (April): 1.

LEAHE, DONALD, and BRENDA LEAHE. 1992. "African American Immersion Schools in Milwaukee: A View from the Inside." *Phi Delta Kappan* 73(10): 783–85.

LEBLANC, PAUL. 1994. "Politics of Literacy and Technology in Secondary School Classrooms." In *Literacy and Computers,* edited by Cynthia Selfe and Susan Hilligoss. New York: Modern Language Association.

LEE, CAROL. 1993. *Signifying as a Scaffold for Literary Interpretation.* Research Report no. 26. Urbana, IL: National Council of Teachers of English.

LEWIN, KURT. 1952. "Group Decision and Social Change." In *Readings in Social Psychology,* edited by G. E. Swanson, T. M. Newcombe, and F. E. Hartley. New York: Holt.

LYONS, BILL. 1981. "The P-Q-P Method of Responding to Writing." *English Journal* 70(3): 42–43.

MCCALL, GEORGE, and J. L. SIMMONS. 1969. *Issues in Participant Observation: A Text and Reader.* Reading, MA: Addison-Wesley.

MACRORIE, KEN. 1970. *Telling Writing.* Portsmouth, NH: Boynton/Cook.

———. 1988. *The I-Search Paper: Revised Edition of Searching Writing.* Portsmouth, NH: Boynton/Cook.

MALINOWSKI, BRONISLAW. [1922] 1961. *Argonauts of the Western Pacific.* London: Routledge.

510

MARCUS, STEPHEN. 1992. "Computers, Composing, and the Productivity Paradox." *Quarterly of the National Writing Project and the Center for the Study of Writing* 14(4): 13–28.

MOFFETT, JAMES. [1968] 1983. *Teaching the Universe of Discourse.* Portsmouth, NH: Boynton/Cook.

———. 1989. *Bridges: From Personal Writing to the Formal Essay.* Occasional paper no. 9. Berkeley, CA: Center for the Study of Writing. Reprint, *Active Voice.* Rev. ed. 1992. Portsmouth, NH: Boynton/Cook.

———. 1992. *Active Voice: A Writing Program Across the Curriculum.* Rev. ed. Portsmouth, NH: Boynton/Cook.

MOFFETT, JAMES, and B. J. WAGNER. 1992. *Student-Centered Language Arts, K–12.* 4th ed. Portsmouth, NH: Boynton/Cook.

MOHR, MARIAN. 1984. *Revision.* Portsmouth, NH: Boynton/Cook.

MOHR, MARIAN, and MARION MacLEAN. 1987. *Working Together: A Guide for Teacher-Researchers.* Urbana, IL: National Council of Teachers of English.

MORRIS, ANN, and HENRIETTA AMBROSE. 1993. *North Webster: A Photographic History of a Black Community.* Bloomington, IN: Indiana University Press.

MORRISON, TONI. 1970. *The Bluest Eye.* New York: Holt.

MURPHY, SANDRA, and MARY ANN SMITH. 1991. *Writing Portfolios: A Bridge from Teaching to Assessment.* Toronto: Pippin.

MURRAY, DONALD. 1968. *A Writer Teaches Writing.* Boston: Houghton Mifflin.

———. 1985. *A Writer Teaches Writing.* Rev. ed. Boston: Houghton Mifflin.

MURRAY, JOHN. 1972. *Modern Monologues for Young People.* Boston: Plays, Inc.

MYERS, MILES. 1980. *A Procedure for Writing Assessment and Holistic Scoring.* Urbana, IL: National Council of Teachers of English.

———. 1985. *The Teacher-Researcher: How to Study Writing in the Classroom.* Urbana, IL: National Council of Teachers of English.

NATIONAL ASSESSMENT OF EDUCATIONAL PROGRESS. 1980. *Writing Achievement, 1969–1979.* Vols. I–III, reports #10-W-01, 02, 03. Denver: Educational Commission of the States.

———. 1986. *The Writing Report Card: Results from the Fourth National Assessment,* edited by Arthur Applebee, Judith Langer, and Ina Mullis. Report #15-W-02. Princeton: Educational Testing Service.

———. 1990. *The Writing Report Card, 1984–88: Results from the Fifth National Assessment,* edited by Arthur Applebee, Judith Langer, and Ina Mullis. Report #19-W-01. Princeton: Educational Testing Service.

NELSON-BARBER, SHARON, and TERRY MEIER. 1990. "Multicultural Context a Key Factor in Teaching." *Academic Connections* (Spring): 1–5, 9–11.

Of Holes and Corks. 1967. Produced by Zagreb Films. Written, animated, and directed by Ante Zaninovic. 10 min. Chicago: International Film Bureau. Videocassette.

O'HARE, FRANK. 1975. *Sentencecraft*. New York: Ginn.

ONG, WALTER. 1983. *Orality and Literacy: The Technologizing of the Word*. New York: Rutledge.

Oxford English Dictionary. [1933] 1961. Edited by James A. H. Murray, Henry Bradley, W. A. Craigie, and C. T. Onions. 13 vols. London: Oxford University Press.

PAPROCKI, JOANNE. 1993. "Poet-Tees." *Notes Plus* 10(4): 7–8.

PETERSON, RALPH, and MARYANN EEDS. 1990. *Grand Conversations: Literature Groups in Action*. New York: Scholastic.

PETERSON, RALPH L. 1987. "Literature Groups: Intensive and Extensive Reading." In *Ideas and Insights: Language Arts in the Elementary School,* edited by Dorothy Watson. Urbana, IL: National Council of Teachers of English.

PERL, SONDRA. 1979. "The Composing Processes of Unskilled College Writers." *Research in the Teaching of English* 13: 317–36.

PERL, SONDRA, and NANCY WILSON. 1986. *Through Teachers' Eyes: Portraits of Writing Teachers at Work*. Portsmouth, NH: Boynton/Cook.

PIESTRUP, ANN MCCORMICK. 1973. *Black Dialect Interference and Accommodation of Reading Instruction in First Grade*. Monograph #4. Berkeley, CA: University of California/Language and Behavior Research Laboratory.

PILLER, CHARLES. 1992. "Separate Realities." *MacWorld* (Sept.): 218–30.

RICO, GABRIELLE. 1983. *Writing the Natural Way*. Los Angeles: Tarcher.

RIEF, LINDA. 1992. *Seeking Diversity: Language Arts with Adolescents*. Portsmouth, NH: Heinemann.

RODRIGUES, DAWN, and RAYMOND RODRIGUES. 1986. *Teaching Writing with a Word Processor, Grades 7–13*. Urbana, IL: National Council of Teachers of English.

ROSENBLATT, LOUISE. 1978. *The Reader, the Text, the Poem: The Transactional Theory of the Literary Work*. Carbondale: Southern Illinois University Press.

ROYSTER, JACQUELINE. 1985. "A New Lease on Writing." In *Tapping Potential,* edited by Charlotte Brooks. Urbana, IL: National Council of Teachers of English.

SELFE, CYNTHIA. 1989. "Redefining Literacy: The Multilayered Grammar of Computers." In *Critical Perspectives on Computers and Composition Instruction,* edited by Gail Hawisher and Cynthia Selfe. New York: Teachers College.

———. 1992. "Preparing English Teachers for the Virtual Age: The Case for Technology Critics." In *Re-imagining Computers and Composition,* edited by Gail Hawisher and Paul LeBlanc. Portsmouth, NH: Boynton/Cook.

SHAUGHNESSY, MINA. 1977. *Errors and Expectations: A Guide for the Teacher of Basic Writing.* New York: Oxford University Press.

SHOR, IRA. 1987. *Freire for the Classroom: A Sourcebook for Liberatory Teaching.* Portsmouth, NH: Boynton/Cook.

SIDDLE-WALKER, EMILIE V. 1992. "Falling Asleep and African-American Student Failure: Rethinking Assumptions About Process Teaching." *Theory into Practice* 31(4): 321–27.

———. 1993. "Interpersonal Caring in the 'Good' Segregated School of African American Children: Evidence from the Case of Caswell County Training School." *Urban Review* 25(1): 63–77.

SMITH, FRANK. 1982. *Writing and the Writer.* New York: Holt.

SMITH, LOU. 1979. "An Evolving Logic of Participant Observation, Educational Ethnography, and Other Case Studies." In *Review of Research in Education,* edited by Lee Shulman. Vol. 6. Chicago: Peacock.

———. 1988. *Innovations and Changes in Schooling: History, Politics, and Agency.* Explorations in Ethnography Series, vol. 3. New York: Taylor and Francis.

———. 1992. "Ethnography." In *Encyclopedia of Educational Research,* edited by M. Alkin. 6th ed. New York: Macmillan.

———. 1994. "Biographical Method." In *Handbook of Qualitative Research,* edited by N. Denzin and Y. Lincoln. Thousand Oaks, CA: Sage.

SMITHERMAN, GENEVA. 1977. *Talkin and Testifyin: The Language of Black America.* Detroit: Wayne State University.

———. 1985. "What Go Round Come Round: King in Perspective." In *Tapping Potential,* edited by Charlotte Brooks. Urbana, IL: National Council of Teachers of English.

———. 1994. "'The Blacker the Berry the Sweeter the Juice': African American Student Writers." In *The Need for Story: Cultural Diversity in Classroom and Community*, edited by Anne Haas Dyson and Celia Genishi. Urbana, IL: National Council of Teachers of English.

STEELE, CLAUDE. 1992. "Race and the Schooling of Black Americans." *Atlantic Monthly* (April): 68–78.

STEELE, SHELBY. 1990. *The Content of Our Character: A New Vision of Race in America.* New York: St. Martin's Press.

513

REFERENCES

STERNGLASS, MARILYN. 1974. "Close Similarities in Dialect Features of Black and White College Students in Remedial Composition Classes." *TESOL Quarterly* 8(3): 271–83.

STRONG, WILLIAM. 1973. *Sentence Combining: A Composing Book.* New York: Random House.

———. 1976. "Back to Basics and Beyond." *English Journal* 65 (Feb.): 56–68.

———. 1981. *Sentence Combining and Paragraph Building.* New York: Random House.

SUID, MURRAY. 1989. *Recipes for Writing.* New York: Addison-Wesley.

TAWL. 1983. *Strategies That Make Sense: Invitations to Literacy for Secondary Students,* edited by Mary Bixby, Shirley Crenshaw, Paul Crowley, Carol Gilles, Margaret Henrichs, Donelle Pyle, and Frances Waters. Mid-Missouri Teachers Applying Whole Language.

VYGOTSKY, LEV. 1962. *Thought and Language.* Cambridge: M.I.T. Press.

———. 1978. *Mind in Society: The Development of Higher Psychological Processes,* edited by M. Cole, V. John-Steiner, S. Scribner, and E. Souberman. Cambridge: Harvard University Press.

WARRINER, JOHN E. 1982. *English Grammar and Composition.* New York: Harcourt Brace Jovanovich.

WATSON, DOROTHY, ed. 1987. *Ideas and Insights: Language Arts in the Elementary School.* Urbana, IL: National Council of Teachers of English.

WEBSTER GROVES WRITING PROJECT. 1992. *Hear You, Hear Me: Lessons from the Webster Groves Writing Project.* Webster Groves, MO: Webster Groves School District.

WHITE, EDWARD. 1985. *Teaching and Assessing Writing.* New York: Jossey-Bass.

WILSON, DWAYNE EUGENE. 1990. "Challenge of Reversing the Black Male Crisis." *Black Issues in Higher Education* 7(10): 48.

WITTELS, HARRIET, and JOAN GREISMAN. 1973. *How to Spell It: A Handbook of Commonly Misspelled Words.* New York: Grosset and Dunlap.

WRIGHT, ANNE. 1988. "Teaching Writing While Jumping Through New Technological Hoops." *English Journal* 77(7): 33–88.

ZENI, JANE. 1990. *WritingLands: Composing with Old and New Writing Tools.* Urbana, IL: National Council of Teachers of English.

ZENI, JANE, and JOAN KRATER-THOMAS. 1990. "Suburban African American Basic Writers: A Text Analysis." *Journal of Basic Writing* 9(2): 15–39.

ZOELLNER, ROBERT. 1969. "Talk-Write: A Behavioral Approach to Writing." *College English* 30: 267–320.

The authors and publisher wish to thank those who have generously given permission to reprint borrowed material:

"Theme For English B" from *Montage of a Dream Deferred* by Langston Hughes. Copyright 1951 by Langston Hughes. Copyright renewed 1979 by George Houston Bass. Published by Harold Ober Associates. Reprinted by permission of Harold Ober Associates Inc.

Excerpt from *The Bluest Eye* by Toni Morrison. Copyright 1970 by Toni Morrison. Published by International Creative Management, Inc. Reprinted by permission.

Excerpts from *North Webster: A Photographic History of a Black Community* by Ann Morris and Henrietta Ambrose. Copyright 1993 by Ann Morris and Henrietta Ambrose. Published by Indiana University Press. Reprinted by permission.

Excerpts from *The Invisible Man* by Ralph Ellison. Copyright 1989 by Random House, Inc. Published by Random House, Inc. Reprinted by permission.

Excerpts from *Black Boy* by Richard Wright. Copyright 1989 by HarperCollins Publishers. Published by HarperCollins Publishers. Reprinted by permission.

Excerpt from *Black Communications: Breaking Down the Barriers* by Evelyn Dandy. Copyright 1991 by Evelyn Dandy. Published by African American Images, Inc. Reprinted by permission of African American Images, Inc.

Excerpts from "Reader-Response Theory as Antidote to Controversy" by Carrie Henly. From the *English Journal* (March, 1993). Copyright 1993 by the National Council of Teachers of English. Reprinted with permission.

Figure 11-1, "Bridges in the writing curriculum" by James Moffett. From *Active Voice*. Copyright 1992 by James Moffett. Published by Heinemann, A division of Reed Elsevier, Inc. Reprinted by permission of James Moffett.

Excerpts from *Getting Smart: The Social Construction of Intelligence* by Jeff Howard. Copyright 1990 by Jeff Howard. Published by The Efficacy Institute Inc. Reprinted by permission.

Excerpts from " 'The Blacker the Berry, the Sweeter the Juice': African American Student Writers" by Geneva Smitherman. From *The Need for Story: Cultural Diversity in Classrooms and Community,* edited by Anne Haas Dyson and Celia Genishi, NCTE 1994. Copyright 1994 by the National Council of Teachers of English. Reprinted with permission.